Aristotles Dialectic

Aristotle's Dialectic

Topics
Sophistical Refutations
&
Related Texts

Translated
With Introduction and Notes
By

C. D. C. Reeve

Hackett Publishing Company, Inc.
Indianapolis/Cambridge

For further information, please address
   Hackett Publishing Company, Inc.
   P.O. Box 44937
   Indianapolis, Indiana 46244-0937

   www.hackettpublishing.com

Cover design by Deborah Wilkes
Interior design by E. L. Wilson
Composition by Aptara, Inc.

Library of Congress Control Number: 2023947786

ISBN-13: 978-1-64792-167-5 (pbk.)
ISBN-13: 978-1-64792-168-2 (PDF ebook)
ISBN-13: 978-1-64792-169-9 (epub)

The paper used in this publication meets the minimum requirements of
American National Standard for Information Sciences—Permanence of Paper for
Printed Library Materials, ANSI Z39.48–1984.

∞

In memory of

Paul Woodruff

Contents

Topics

Book 1: Dialectic

Book 2: Coincidents

Contents

Book 6: Definitions

Book 7: Sameness and Distinctness

Book 8: The Practice of Dialectic

Contents

Sophistical Refutations

Related Texts

De Interpretatione

Prior Analytics

Posterior Analytics

Physics

De Caelo

On Coming to Be and Passing Away

De Anima

Contents

Generation of Animals

Metaphysics

Nicomachean Ethics

Eudemian Ethics

Politics

Rhetoric

Preface

In this volume are collected together for the first time the two quite technical treatises that Aristotle specifically devotes to dialectic, the *Topics* and *Sophistical Refutations*, along with all the significant passages from other treatises in which he discusses it. These writings, as will become clear, are of paramount importance for understanding his entire philosophy.

The translation aims to be as accurate and consistent as possible. It is traditional where the costs of innovation exceed the benefits, innovative where the benefits exceed the costs. In the case of *to ti ên einai, ousia*, and *epistêmê*, for example, the traditional and largely entrenched translations—"essence," "substance," and "scientific knowledge"—have been preserved here for these reasons, while those of *eidos* as "form," "kind," or "species," *genos* as "kind" or "genus," and *diaphora* as "difference" or "differentia," which are retained in many of the earlier New Hackett Aristotle Series editions, have been abandoned systematically in favor of the more accurate "form," "kind," and "difference," as they will be too in later editions. Readers can now generally determine for themselves how a given occurrence of any of these terms is best understood. Even a translation of this sort, however, needs to be accompanied by sufficient annotation to make it intelligible. Some of this can consist, as it does here, of passages selected from other works by Aristotle himself, but much must simply be explanatory, clarificatory, and interpretative.

To make the journey as convenient as possible, footnotes and glossary entries are replaced by sequentially numbered, cross-referenced endnotes, so that the information most needed at each juncture is available in a single place. The non-sequential reader, interested in a particular passage, will find in the detailed Index a guide to places where focused discussion of a term or notion occurs. The Introduction describes the book that lies ahead, explaining what it is about, what it is trying to do, and how it goes about doing it. It is not a comprehensive discussion of every aspect of the texts it includes, nor is it, I should add, an expression of scholarly consensus on the issues it does discuss—insofar as such a thing exists—but my own take on them. The same goes for many of the more interpretative notes. They are a place to start, not a place to finish—a first step in the rewarding enterprise of coming to understand Aristotle for oneself.

Some readers will, I have assumed, be new to these somewhat technical but essential texts, so I have tried to keep their needs in mind. But it is resolute readers that Aristotle most repays, and it is such readers, whatever their antecedent level of knowledge or sophistication, that all my editions of Aristotle's works are intended to serve.

I have benefited greatly from the work of previous translators and commentators, especially Jacques Brunschwig, Louis-André Dorion, Pieter Sjoerd Hasper, Myriam Hecquet, and Robin Smith, who also generously allowed me to include his translation of parts of the *Prior Analytics*. Anna Tigani read the translation of the *Topics* and *Sophistical Refutations* with great care, making many corrections and helpful suggestions. I am indebted to her for sharing her enviable knowledge with me. Sean Neagel assisted ably with the—to me, onerous—task of proofreading. I am grateful to him too. Finally, I thank Pavlos Kontos for combing carefully through everything, diligently suggesting improvements and making corrections. I am lucky to have him as a friend.

Equal devotion to Greek philosophical texts, albeit of a different sort, has again been demonstrated by Deborah Wilkes and her colleagues at Hackett Publishing Company, who have been my publishers, supporters, and friends for over thirty years.

I renew my thanks to ΔΚΕ, the first fraternity in the United States to endow a professorial chair, and to the University of North Carolina for awarding it to me. The generous research funds, among other things, that the endowment makes available each year have allowed me to travel to conferences and to acquire books, computers, and other research materials and assistance, without which my work would have been much more difficult. A research leave from my department in the fall of 2022 gave me the leisure needed to complete my work.

Abbreviations

ARISTOTLE

Citations of Aristotle's works are made to Immanuel Bekker, *Aristotelis Opera* (Berlin, 1831 [1970]), in the canonical form of abbreviated title and line number, or in some cases by book and chapter numbers. A † indicates a work whose authenticity has been seriously questioned, †† indicates a work attributed to Aristotle but generally agreed not to be by him (similarly, in the case of Plato). The abbreviations used are as follows:

APo.	*Posterior Analytics*
APr.	*Prior Analytics*
Cael.	*De Caelo* (Moraux)
Cat.	*Categories*
DA	*De Anima* (Corcilius)
Div. Somn.	*On Divination in Sleep* (Ross)
EE	*Eudemian Ethics*
Fr.	*Fragments* (Rose)
GA	*Generation of Animals*
GC	*On Coming to Be and Passing Away* (Rashed)
HA	*History of Animals* (Louis)
Insomn.	*On Dreams* (Ross)
Int.	*De Interpretatione*
Juv.	*On Youth and Old Age, Life and Death, and Respiration* (Ross)
MA	*Movement of Animals* (Primavesi and Corcilius)
Mem.	*On Memory* (Ross)
Met.	*Metaphysics* (Bk. 7 Frede-Patzig; Bk. 12 Alexandru)
Mete.	*Meteorology* (Fobes)

†*MM*	*Magna Moralia* (Susemihl)
NE	*Nicomachean Ethics*
PA	*Parts of Animals* (Louis)
Ph.	*Physics*
††*Phgn.*	*Physiognomics*
Po.	*Poetics*
Pol.	*Politics*
Protr.	*Protrepticus* (Düring)
Rh.	*Rhetoric* (Kassel)
††*Rh. Al.*	*Rhetoric to Alexander*
SE	*Sophistical Refutations* (Ross)
Sens.	*Sense and Sensibilia* (Ross)
Somn.	*On Sleep* (Ross)
Top.	*Topics* (Brunschwig)

I cite and translate the *Oxford Classical Texts* (OCT) editions of these works, where available, otherwise the editions noted:

Alexandru, S. *Aristotle's Metaphysics Lambda* (Leiden, 2014).

Brunschwig, J. *Aristote Topiques Livres I–IV, Livres V–VIII* (Paris, 1967, 2007).

Corcilius, K. *Aristoteles Über die Seele: De Anima* (Hamburg, 2017).

Düring, I. *Aristotle's Protrepticus: An Attempt at Reconstruction* (Göteborg, 1961).

Fobes, F. *Aristotelis Meteorologicorum Libri Quattor* (Cambridge, MA, 1919).

Frede, M., and Patzig, G. *Aristoteles Metaphysik Z: Text, Übersetzung und Kommentar* (Munich, 1988).

Kassel, R. *Aristotelis Ars Rhetorica* (Berlin, 1976).

Louis, P. *Les Parties des Animaux* (Paris, 1956).

———. *Histoire des Animaux* (Paris, 1964–1969).

Moraux, P. *Aristote: Du Ciel* (Paris, 1965).

Primavesi, O., and Corcilius, K. *Aristoteles: De Motu Animalium* (Hamburg, 2018).

Rashed, M. *Aristote: De la Génération et la Corruption* (Paris, 2005).

Rose, V. *Aristotelis Fragmenta*, 3rd ed. (Leipzig, 1886).

Ross, D. *Aristotle Parva Naturalia* (Oxford, 1955).

——. *Aristotelis Topica et Sophistici Elenchi* (Oxford, 1958; rev. ed. 1984).
Susemihl, F. *Aristotelis Magna Moralia* (Leipzig, 1883).
van Groningen, B., and Wartelle, A. *Aristote: Économique* (Paris, 2003).

PLATO

Ap.	*Apology*
Chrm.	*Charmides*
Crat.	*Cratylus*
Cri.	*Crito*
†Def.	*Definitions*
Euthd.	*Euthydemus*
Euthphr.	*Euthyphro*
Grg.	*Gorgias*
Hp. Ma.	*Hippias Major*
Hp. Mi.	*Hippias Minor*
Lg.	*Laws*
Men.	*Meno*
Phd.	*Phaedo*
Phdr.	*Phaedrus*
Phlb.	*Philebus*
Pol.	*Statesman*
Prm.	*Parmenides*
Prt.	*Protagoras*
Rep.	*Republic*
Sph.	*Sophist*
Tht.	*Theaetetus*
Ti.	*Timaeus*

Other Abbreviations and Symbols

Brunschwig = J. Brunschwig, *Aristote Topiques Livres I–IV, Livres V–VIII* (Paris, 1967, 2007).

DK = H. Diels and W. Kranz, eds., *Die Fragmente der Vorsokratiker*, 6th ed. (Berlin, 1951).

DL = T. Dorandi, ed., Diogenes Laertius, *Lives of Eminent Philosophers*, (Cambridge, 2013).

Dorion = L-A. Dorion, *Aristote Les Réfutations Sophistiques* (Laval, 1995).

Frede-Patzig = M. Frede and G. Patzig, *Aristoteles Metaphysik Z: Text, Übersetzung und Kommentar.* (München, 1988).

Hankinson = R. Hankinson, *Simplicius: On Aristotle's On the Heavens I.5–9* (Ithaca, 2004).

Heath = T. Heath, *Mathematics in Aristotle* (Oxford, 1949).

Hecquet = M. Hecquet, *Aristote: Refutations Sophistiques* in P. Pellegrin, ed., *Aristote: Topiques, Refutations Sophistiques: Organon V–VI* (Paris, 2015).

Isnardi = M. Isnardi Parente and T. Dorandi, *Senocrate e Ermodoro, Testimonianze e Frammenti* (Pisa, 2012).

Pacius = *In Porphyrii Isagogen, et Aristotelis Organum, Commentarius Analyticus* (Frankfurt, 1597; repr., Hildesheim, 1966).

Ps. Alex. *in SE* = M. Wallies, *Alexandri quod fertur in Aristotelis Sophisticos Elenchos commentarium* (Berlin, 1898).

Reinhardt = T. Reinhardt, *Das Buch E der Aristotelischen Topik: Untersuchungen zur Echtheitsfrage* (Göttingen, 2000).

Schiefsky = M. Schiefsky, *Hippocrates on Ancient Medicine: Translated with an Introduction and Commentary* (Leiden, 2005).

Simp. = Simplicius, *In Aristotelis De Caelo Commentaria* (Berlin, 1893).

Smith = R. Smith, *Aristotle Topics Book I and VIII* (Oxford, 1997).

Tarán = L. Tarán, *Speusippus of Athens* (Leiden, 1981).

TEGP = D. W. Graham, *The Texts of Early Greek Philosophy: The Complete Fragments and Selected Testimonies of the Major Presocratics* (Cambridge, 2010).

Van Ophuijsen = J. Van Ophuijsen, *Alexander of Aphrodisias: On Aristotle Topics I* (Ithaca, 2001).

A = B = A is identical to (equivalent to) B.

A ≈ B = A is roughly the same as or roughly equivalent or analogous to B.

A ⊃ B = If A then B, or A implies B.

Introduction

Life and Works

Aristotle was born in 384 BC to a well-off family living in the small town of Stagira in northern Greece. His father, Nicomachus, who died while Aristotle was still quite young, was allegedly doctor to King Amyntas of Macedon. His mother, Phaestis, was wealthy in her own right. When Aristotle was seventeen his guardian, Proxenus, sent him to study at Plato's Academy in Athens. He remained there for twenty years, initially as a student, eventually as a researcher and teacher.

When Plato died in 347, leaving the Academy in the hands of his nephew, Speusippus, Aristotle left Athens for Assos in Asia Minor, where the ruler, Hermias, was a patron of philosophy. He married Hermias' niece, Pythias, and had a daughter by her, also named Pythias. Three years later, in 345, after Hermias had been killed by the Persians, Aristotle moved to Mytilene on the island of Lesbos, where he met Theophrastus, who was to become his best student and closest colleague.

In 343, Aristotle seems to have been invited by Philip of Macedon to be tutor to the latter's thirteen-year-old son, Alexander, later called "the Great." In 335, Aristotle returned to Athens and founded his own institute, the Lyceum. While he was there his wife died and he established a relationship with Herpyllis, also a native of Stagira. Their son Nicomachus was named for Aristotle's father, and the *Nicomachean Ethics* may, in turn, have been named for him, as the *Eudemian Ethics*, in turn, may have been for Eudemus of Rhodes, a famous student of Aristotle's. In 323, Alexander the Great died, with the result that anti-Macedonian feeling in Athens grew stronger. Perhaps threatened with a formal charge of impiety, Aristotle left for Chalcis in Euboea, where he died twelve months later, in 322, at the age of sixty-two.

Legend has it that Aristotle had slender calves and small eyes, spoke with a lisp, and was "conspicuous by his attire, his rings, and the cut of his hair." His will reveals that he had a sizable estate, a domestic partner, two children, a considerable library, and a large circle of friends. In it Aristotle asks his executors to take special care of Herpyllis. He directs that his slaves be freed "when they come of age" and that the bones of his wife, Pythias, be mixed with his "as she instructed."

Although the surviving writings of Aristotle occupy almost 2,500 tightly printed pages in English, most of them are not works polished for publication but lecture notes and working papers. This accounts for some, though not all, of their legendary difficulty. It is unfair to complain, as a Platonist opponent did, that Aristotle "escapes refutation by clothing a perplexing subject in obscure language, using darkness like a squid to make himself hard to catch," but there is darkness and obscurity enough for anyone, even if none of it is intentional. There is also a staggering breadth and depth of intellect. Aristotle made fundamental contributions to a vast range of disciplines, including logic, metaphysics, epistemology, psychology, ethics, politics, rhetoric, aesthetics, zoology, biology, physics, and philosophical and political history. When Dante called him "the master of those who know," he was scarcely exaggerating.

What the Topics *and* Sophistical Refutations *Are*

One thing we might mean by the *Topics* and *Sophistical Refutations*, as with the Related Texts, is what we now find inscribed on the pages that make up the modern editions which are the basis of the present translations. These are the descendants of texts derived—via manuscripts copied in the Byzantine period (from the tenth to the fifteenth centuries AD)—from manuscripts that in turn derive from the edition of Aristotle's works produced by Andronicus of Rhodes in the first century BC. Like most other modern editions, they record in the textual apparatus at the bottom of the page various manuscript readings alternative to the ones printed in the body of his text. In some cases, I have preferred one of these readings and have, when important, indicated so in the notes. Divisions of the text into books and chapters are the work of editors, not of Aristotle himself. Also present are the page numbers of Bekker, *Aristotelis Opera*. These appear here in the margins of the printed version and enclosed in vertical lines (| |) in the electronic one at the end of the line to which they apply. Occasional material in square brackets in the text is my addition.

The second thing we might mean, and are perhaps more likely to mean, are the works themselves—those more abstract things that are embodied in the Greek texts and (ideally) in any translations of them. That they are works, or parts of works, dealing with dialectic no one will dispute, but what dialectic is, and what sort of work on it our two main treatises are, is a harder question.

Dialectic

A problem (*problêma*) is posed: Is pleasure choiceworthy, or not? The answerer claims that yes it is (or, alternatively, that no it is not). The questioner must refute him by asking questions—by offering him premises (*protaseis*) to accept or reject. The questioner succeeds if he forces the answerer to accept a proposition contrary to the one he undertook to defend (*SE* 165ᵇ3–4). The questioner fails if the answerer always accepts or rejects premises in a way consistent with that proposition. To a first approximation, dialectic is the art or craft (*technê*) that enables someone to play the role of questioner or answerer successfully (*Top.* 100ᵃ18–21, 164ᵇ2–4), and the *Topics* and *Sophistical Refutations* are handbooks of that craft.

At the heart of dialectic is the dialectical deduction (*dialektikos sullogismos*). This is the argument lying behind the questioner's questions, partly dictating their order and content, and partly determining the strategy of his attack. Understanding dialectic is primarily a matter of grasping the nature of dialectical deductions and the type of premises they employ.

In *Topics* 1.1, such deductions are contrasted with three other types of arguments: scientific, contentious, and fallacious. In *Sophistical Refutations* 2, they are distinguished from didactic, examinational, and contentious arguments. Our first task is to explore and coordinate these two sets of contrasts. When it is completed, we will first turn to a discussion of dialectical premises, acceptable beliefs, and puzzles, then to the uses of dialectic in training, encounters, and the philosophical sciences, and finally with its use in regard to scientific starting-points.

Dialectic, Contentious Argument, and Sophistry

Dialectical deductions differ from scientific ones only in their premises: the latter are deductions from scientific starting-points and hence are demonstrations; the former are deductions from acceptable beliefs (*endoxa*) (*Top.* 100ᵃ1–ᵇ23). In the case of contentious arguments, the differences are potentially twofold: they are either genuine deductions from apparently acceptable beliefs or apparent deductions from genuinely or apparently acceptable beliefs (100ᵇ23–25).

"In dialectic, a sophist is so called in virtue of his deliberate choice, and a dialectician is so called not in virtue of his deliberate choice, but in virtue of the capacity he has" (*Rh.* 1355ᵇ20–21). If dialectic is understood in this way, it is a neutral craft and a dialectician who deliberately decides to employ contentious arguments is a sophist (1355ᵃ24–ᵇ7). A contender also employs such arguments, but differs from a sophist in his purposes: "insofar as it is for apparent victory, it is contentious, while insofar as it is for apparent wisdom, it is sophistical" (*SE* 171^{b}32–33). In the *Topics* and *Sophistical Refutations*, however, the person who decides to use only genuine and never contentious arguments is a dialectician, since in both treatises dialectic differs from contentious argument precisely in employing genuine acceptable beliefs and genuine deductions rather than merely apparent ones (*Top.* 100^{a}29–30, 165^{b}3–8, 171^{b}34–172^{a}2). For clarity's sake, let us say that *plain dialectic* is the neutral craft that contenders, sophists, and honest dialecticians use for different purposes, imposing different restrictions on which of its resources may be legitimately employed.

Examinational Deductions and Sophistical Refutations

The examinational craft (*peirastikê*) is a sort of dialectic that "has in view not the person who knows, but the one who is ignorant and pretends to know" (*SE* 171^{b}4–6). It is the sort particularly useful in arguments with sophists, since they are the archetypal pretenders to knowledge and wisdom (165^{a}21). Though Aristotle usually uses the term *peirastikê* to refer to honest examination rather than to the plain craft (165^{b}4–6), he also uses it, as we will see, to refer to the plain craft too.

The best way to distinguish honest examination from honest dialectic pure and simple is by exploring sophistical refutations, which are the dishonest twins of honest examinational arguments: honest examinational arguments expose the genuine ignorance of a sophist answerer, who has only apparent knowledge and wisdom (*SE* 171^{b}3–6); sophistical refutations give the appearance of exposing the ignorance of someone who does have scientific knowledge (168^{b}4–10). Such refutations are of two sorts. An *a-type* sophistical refutation is "an apparent deduction and refutation that is not really one"; a *b-type* is "one that, though real, only appears to be proper to the thing at issue" (169^{b}20–23).

The fallacies proper to a craft or science are those based on the starting-points and theorems belonging to it (*SE* 171^{b}38–172^{a}1). Thus Hippocrates' argument for squaring the circle by means of lunes is a geometrical fallacy, because it is "directed against geometry only, because it is based on starting-points that are special to it" (172^{a}4–5). Someone who uses Zeno's argument that motion is impossible in order to refute a doctor's claim that it is better to take a walk after dinner, however, has produced a b-type sophistical refutation, since Zeno's arguments are not proper to geometry or medicine but "*koinos* (common)" (172^{a}9). Such an argument is fallacious, indeed, even when sound: "Bryson's way of squaring the circle, on the other hand, even if the circle is squared, is nonetheless sophistical, because it is not in accord with the thing at issue" (171ᵇ16–18). The difference between such fallacies and b-type sophistical refutations, then, is that the former have false premises proper to the answerer's science, while the latter have true premises that are not proper to it.

Because such fallacies do depend on premises proper to a science, it is the job of scientists themselves to diagnose and refute them. But it is not their job to deal with b-type sophistical refutations:

> As regards the refutation that is in accord with a particular science, it belongs to the corresponding scientist to get a theoretical grasp on whether it, not being a real one, only appears to be one, and if it is a real one, on why it is so. But to get one on a refutation based on what is common, and that falls under no craft, belongs to dialecticians. (*SE* 170ᵃ36–39)

Moreover, dialecticians must also deal with Antiphon's argument for squaring the circle, which is an a-type sophistical refutation, since by assuming that a circle is a polygon with a large but finite number of sides, it "does away with the starting-points of geometry" (*Ph.* 185ᵃ1–2)—in particular, with the principle that magnitudes are divisible without limit. Hence it cannot be discussed in a way that presupposes those starting-points (*Top.* 101ᵃ35–ᵇ4), and so must be discussed on the basis of "common things" (*APo.* 77ᵃ26–35).

What, then, are these common things? The only propositions that can figure as premises in dialectical arguments, as we saw, are acceptable beliefs. But common things too can figure as such premises: "it is evident that to the dialectician it belongs to be capable of getting hold of the things that a refutation, or apparent refutation, that comes about through what is common depends on, that is, a dialectical one or an apparently dialectical or examinational one" (*SE* 170ᵇ8–11). It seems to follow that common things are acceptable beliefs. The following two passages—the first referring to the second—settle the identification:

> Not even the possession of the most exact scientific knowledge would make it easy for us in speaking to persuade some listeners on the basis of it; for argument in accord with scientific knowledge is proper to teaching, but teaching is impossible [in their case]. Instead, it is necessary to produce our means of persuasion and arguments out of common things, as we said in the *Topics* about encounters with ordinary people. (*Rh.* 1355ᵃ24–29)

> [Dialectic] is useful in argumentative encounters, because, once we have cataloged the beliefs of ordinary people, we will engage in conversation with them, not by proceeding from the beliefs of others, but from their own, changing their minds about anything they appear to us to be stating incorrectly. (*Top.* 101ª30–34)

Common things are acceptable beliefs; acceptable beliefs are common things (see also *SE* 172ª36–38). Indeed, the "most stable (*bebaiotatê*) starting-point of all," the one it is "impossible to be deceived about" (*Met.* 1005ᵇ11–12), namely, the principle of non-contradiction (1011ᵇ13–14), is such a belief, and "all who are carrying out a demonstration lead it back to this as an ultimate belief; for this is by nature the starting-point of all the other axioms too" (1005ᵇ32–34). So logic, to call it that, is a common thing.

Honest examinational deductions deduce a contradiction "from things that seem so to the answerer and that it is necessary for the one who pretends to possess the relevant science to know" (*SE* 165ᵇ4–6). Premises of this sort are said to be based not on what the answerer knows, nor on things special to the subject matter of the relevant science, but "on their consequences, that is, on whichever things are of the sort that someone can know without knowing the craft in question, but which if he does not know, he is necessarily ignorant of the craft" (172ª23–27). Later in the same passage these consequences are identified as common things (acceptable beliefs):

> That is why everyone, even private individuals, makes a certain use of dialectic and the examinational craft; for everyone tries, up to a certain point, to test those who profess knowledge. And these are the common things; for they themselves know these no less [than the others do], even if they seem to speak from very far outside [the relevant sort of knowledge]. (*SE* 172ª30–34)

It follows that the premises of honest examinational deductions must be true, acceptable beliefs proper to the answerer's science—the one the person undergoing examination is pretending to know.

A person who in other respects does have scientific knowledge, however, may yet be the victim of a sophistical refutation, since he may find himself caught in contradiction when interrogated by a clever sophist. The mere fact that someone can be defeated in a dialectical argument is not enough to show that he lacks scientific knowledge. What is further required are the following: first, that this argument not be a sophistical refutation (its premises must be true and proper to the science in question); second, those premises must be such that anyone who knows the science would have to know them (otherwise, the answerer could reject them and still know the science); and finally, they must be propositions it is possible to know without knowing the science (otherwise, they could not figure in arguments available to non-scientists). Thus the various features that the premises of an honest examinational argument must have are entailed by the fact that their purpose is to enable non-scientists to unmask pretenders to scientific knowledge.

In *Topics* 8.5, Aristotle discusses "dialectical meetings . . . for those who produce arguments for the sake, not of competition, but of examining (*peiras*) and investigating" (159ª32–34). From the account he provides of these, it is clear that they do not fit our characterization of honest examination. For example, the questioner is not restricted to using true premises; he can and sometimes must use false ones:

> Since arguments of this sort are for the sake of training and examining, not of teaching, it is clear that not only true but also false conclusions must be deduced, and not always through truths but sometimes also through falsehoods; for often, when a truth has been posited, it is necessary for the dialectician to do away with it, so that he must use falsehoods as a premise. (*Top.* 161ª25–29)

Moreover, the answerer may defend a position he himself does not hold (*Top.* 159ᵇ27–35) and accept premises that are not proper to the topic of the argument (160ª1–2). Yet the very fact that Aristotle discusses how the answerer should deal with *improper* premises (8.6) in connection with dialectical explorations that examine and inquire suggests that such explorations are at least closely related to b-type sophistical refutations and honest examinational deductions. Indeed, it suggests that these dialectical explorations simply are exercises in *plain* examination.

When Aristotle tells us in *SE* 2 that he has already discussed examinational arguments, then, there is good reason to take him to be referring to the discussion of dialectical explorations that examine and investigate in *Topics* 8.5–11. But to secure that reference, in the face of the manifest differences between what the two treatises say about examination, we must recognize that *Sophistical Refutations* mostly deals with honest examination, *Topics* with plain examination.

Didactic Deductions

Didactic deductions (*didaskalikoi*) are "those that deduce from the starting-points proper to a given subject and not from the beliefs of the answerer (for the learner must take things on trust)" (*SE* 165^{b}1–3). This identifies them as scientific demonstrations of some sort, since teaching is "argument in accord with scientific knowledge" (*Rh.* 1355^{a}26). But if they are scientific demonstrations, why are they included with honest dialectical, examinational, and contentious arguments as one of the four types of argument used in dialectical discussions (*SE* 165^{a}38)? Didactic deductions, moreover, are not deductions "from the beliefs of the answerer" (*SE* 165^{b}2). Yet "a learner must always accept the things that seem true" (*Top.* 159^{a}28–29), suggesting that didactic arguments must indeed be deductions from the student's beliefs. Moreover, in *SE* 2, teaching sometimes takes the form of dialectical (or question-and-answer) discussions. Yet teaching is also contrasted with asking questions: "a person who is teaching must not ask questions but himself make things clear" (*SE* 171^{b}1–2).

To grasp the coherence of Aristotle's thought about didactic in the face of these apparent inconsistencies of doctrine, we need to appreciate the relevance to them of the distinction between an argument "intrinsically as an argument" and one "framed as questions" (*Top.* 161^{a}16–17). Suppose a student has acquired the starting-points of a science, and his teacher wants to test his knowledge of it. The natural thing for him to do is to examine the student by offering him premises (propositions) to accept or reject. And, of course, the student must, as we saw, "always accept the things that seem true" (159^{a}28–9), since otherwise the teacher will not be able to discover what he really knows. Here the teacher's didactic argument is "framed as questions." But the admissions made by the student are not premises in the didactic argument (the scientific demonstration treated intrinsically as such) that underlies these questions and partly dictates their order and content. *It* is not a deduction "from the beliefs of the answerer" (*SE* 165^{b}2).

Suppose, for example, that a phrase occurring in a scientific proposition is ambiguous, but that the student neither "knows nor supposes that the thing is said in another way" than the one he has in mind (*SE* 171^{a}32–34). Then "a person who is teaching must not ask questions but himself make things clear" (171^{b}1–2). For here, unlike in the previous case, the teacher is not trying to find out what the student knows by asking him questions. He already knows that the student is ignorant and is providing him with information. So he uses a didactic argument intrinsically as such to make things clear. Once we see that teaching may involve dialectical question-and-answer discussion as well as straightforward demonstration, so that didactic arguments can be understood in two different ways, we can see that these arguments do have a place in dialectic and that Aristotle's account of them is in fact consistent.

The Classification of Deductions

In *Top.* 1.1, deductions are divided into four classes:

(T1) scientific
(T2) fallacious
(T3) honest dialectic
(T4) contentious

In *SE* 2, they are also initially divided into four:

(S1) didactic
(S2) fallacious
(S3) honest dialectic
(S4) contentious

Then two more are added:

(S5) a-type sophistical refutations
(S6) b-type sophistical refutations

Though apparently discordant, the two classifications fit together to constitute a single systematic classification of dialectical deductions. For deductions are generally of two kinds:

(D1) genuine
(D2) apparent

And the premises of each may be

(P1) true and proper starting-points of a science
(P2) untrue but proper starting-points of a science
(P3) true acceptable beliefs proper to a science
(P4) true acceptable beliefs only apparently proper to a science
(P5) acceptable beliefs
(P6) apparent acceptable beliefs

(D1–2) and (P1–6) together determine the various kinds of dialectical deductions:

(D1)–(P1) scientific demonstrations (T1), presupposed in didactic arguments (S1)
(D1)–(P2) fallacies (T2)
(D1)–(P3) examinational deductions (S2)
(D1)–(P4) b-type sophistical refutations (S6)

(D1)–(P5) honest dialectic arguments (T3), (S3)

(D1)–(P6) contentious arguments or a-type sophistical refutations (T4), (S4), (S5)

(D2)–(P5) contentious arguments or a-type sophistical refutations (T4), (S4), (S5)

A striking feature of this classification is that it includes only one type of invalid deduction, namely, (D2)–(P5). This is so for a reason. The various kinds of formally valid and invalid deductions have already been studied in the *Prior Analytics*. *Topics* and *Sophistical Refutations* are primarily concerned not with them, therefore, but with sound or unsound ones—with the choice of premises rather than with the logical form of arguments: "We have pretty much said in universal terms, then, how one must select premises; we have gone through it in detail in our work on dialectic" (*APr.* 46ᵃ29–30). Hence the classification is both complete and systematic.

Dialectical Premises

> A dialectical premise is [1] a making of a question out of what is acceptable, either to everyone, to most people, or to the wise (and, among these, either to all, to most, or to the most notable), provided it is not unacceptable; for anyone would accept what seems to be so to the wise, provided it is not contrary to the beliefs of ordinary people. Dialectical premises also include [2] things that are like acceptable beliefs; [3] the contraries of what appear to be acceptable beliefs, when proposed by way of contradiction; and [4] all beliefs that are in accord with the established crafts. . . . ; for anyone would accept the things believed by those who have investigated these crafts—for example, a doctor about issues in medicine, or a geometer about those in geometry, and similarly in other cases. (*Top.* 104ᵃ8–37)

Later, in a reprise of this passage, Aristotle adds what seem to be two new cases to the account:

> [5] Further, whatever appears to be so in all or in most cases must be taken as a starting-point and seeming posit (for those who have not seen in which case it is not so accept it). [6] One must also select premises from written works and produce catalogs of them concerning each kind of subject, putting them

under separate headings—for example, concerned with goodness, concerned with life, and concerned with every sort of
goodness, starting with the what-it-is. (*Top.* 105^{b}10–15)

The fact that [2] describes propositions that are "like acceptable beliefs,"
that [3] speaks of the contraries of what "appear to be acceptable beliefs,"
and that [5] includes as acceptable beliefs things that merely appear to
be true to those "who have not seen in which case it is not so," strongly
suggests that these clauses refer to apparently acceptable beliefs. And
Aristotle's illustrative examples bear this out: (a) "if it is acceptable that
the science of contraries is the same, it would also appear to be acceptable
that the perception of contraries is the same" (*Top.* 104^{a}15–17); (b) "the
contraries of what appear to be acceptable beliefs, when proposed by way
of contradiction, will appear to be acceptable beliefs" (104^{a}20–23); (c) if
"the craft of grammar is one in number, then the craft of pipe playing is
one in number, while if there are several crafts of grammar, there are several of pipe playing" (104^{a}17–20). (a) and (b) explicitly refer to apparently
acceptable beliefs, while (c), though it does not explicitly mention them,
is described as "similar and akin to" (a). Since, then, both acceptable
beliefs and apparently acceptable beliefs can serve as premises in plain
dialectical deductions, we cannot identify genuine acceptable beliefs with
such premises or infer that everything said about the latter applies willy-
nilly to them.

The propositions referred to in [4] are in accord with the established
crafts, so they must be genuine. But because they only would be accepted
by anyone, they do not have to be already accepted to count as such. Since
written accounts are likely to have wise people or practitioners of the
established crafts as authors, [6] is probably a new source of something
already listed rather than a wholly new addition to the list. Aristotle himself suggests as much when he writes that we should note in the margins of
the lists we distil from these writings the identity of the thinkers, such as
Empedocles, who hold them, since "anyone might accept what was said by
a reputable (*endoxou*) person" (*Top.* 105^{b}17–18).

Because medicine is itself an acknowledged craft or established area
of expertise, the opinions of a doctor known to have studied medicine carry weight with everyone, whether or not the doctor himself has
already acquired a good reputation. Hence if a person can show that
he has been trained as a doctor, that is enough, everything else being
equal, to guarantee that the answerer would accept his opinion on medical matters. Of course, someone can be wise without being a practitioner of an established craft, but his epistemic authority cannot then
flow from his training. Nor is it enough that he *be* wise. If his opinions

are to have any standing, the answerer must recognize him as a wise person. In other words, like Solon or Thales, he must be *notable* for his wisdom or have a *reputation* as a wise man. Hence the reference to notability and reputation in the relevant clause of the definition of acceptable beliefs (*Top.* 100^b23).

[1] corresponds closely to the official definition of genuine acceptable beliefs as "things that seem so to everyone, to the majority, or to the wise—either to all of them, or to most, or to the best known and most reputable" (*Top.* 100^b21–23; repeated 101^a11–13). But it also adds something new, namely, that views held by all, most, or the most reputable wise people have to meet a negative condition if they are to count as acceptable beliefs—they cannot be unacceptable, that is, "contrary to the beliefs of ordinary people" (*Top.* 104^a11–12).

Some of the acceptable beliefs characterized in [1] are accepted by all or most answerers, because they are accepted by someone whose epistemic authority stems from his reputation for wisdom. Those characterized in [4] are accepted because they are accepted by someone whose epistemic authority stems not from his reputation, but from his having been trained in an acknowledged area of expertise. Some of the acceptable beliefs characterized in [1] and all of those characterized in [4] are thus *indirect*: they are (or would be) accepted by all or most answerers because they are accepted by someone whose authority they recognize. The other acceptable beliefs characterized in [1] are *direct*: they are accepted on other grounds.

Acceptable Beliefs and Things That Appear to Be So

Genuine acceptable beliefs, we saw, fall into three classes: (1) propositions that all or most ordinary people would accept; (2) propositions not contrary to what is already in (1), that all, or most, or the most notable of the wise accept; and (3) propositions in accord with (that follow from) the starting-points of the established crafts, since everyone, ordinary people included, would accept them. It seems, then, that (1) is acting as a sort of gatekeeper class. If a proposition p is in (2), it cannot be an acceptable belief unless it can be consistently added to (1). If p is a proposition in (3), it could, apparently, conflict with those in (1) while retaining its status as an acceptable belief, but only by joining (1) and depriving any conflicting propositions of membership in it.

The fact that all or most people believe something, Aristotle claims, leads us "to trust it as something in accord with experience" (*Div. Somn.* 462^b14–16). For they "are naturally adequate as regards the truth and in most cases hit upon it" (*Rh.* 1355ᵃ15–17), so that each person "has something of his own to contribute" to it (*EE* 1216ᵇ30–31). Thus experience—whether in the form of perception or correct habituation (*Top.* 105ᵃ3–7, *NE* 1095ᵇ4–8, 1214ᵇ28–1215ᵃ3)—must surely be what provides the evidence for direct acceptable beliefs in class (1). Directly acceptable beliefs are thus beliefs that seem true to us on the basis of experience. Presumably, that is why Aristotle occasionally refers to them as *phainomena*—as things that seem to be so (*Top.* 104ᵃ12, 105ᵃ37–ᵇ3).

Things that appear to be so include, in the first instance, basic perceptual observations: "Also bearing witness to these things is what is said by the mathematicians about astronomy; for the things that appear to be so, namely, the interchange of the configurations by which the order of the stars is determined, presuppose that the earth is situated at the center" (*Cael.* 297ᵃ2–6; also 297ᵇ23–25). But though things that appear to be so are for this reason typically contrasted with things that are supported by proof or evidence (*EE* 1216ᵇ26–28), there seems to be no a priori limit to the degree of conceptualization or theory-ladenness manifest in them. They need not be, and in Aristotle rarely are, devoid of interpretative content. It is something that appears to be so, for example, that "a person who lacks self-control, knowing that the actions he is doing are base, does them because of feeling, whereas one who has self-control, knowing that his appetites are base, does not follow them, because of his reason" (*NE* 1145ᵇ12–14).

Since all the crafts and sciences—indeed, all types of knowledge, however humble or exalted—rest ultimately on experience (*APr.* 46ᵃ17–18, *GC* 316ᵃ5–6), what is true of directly acceptable beliefs also seems true of indirect ones: they are propositions that seem true on the basis of experience, not to the untutored eyes of people in general, but to the relatively more trained ones of craftsmen and scientists, or the relatively more reflective ones of reputable philosophers. It follows, once we make proper allowance for the division of epistemic labor, that the entire class of acceptable beliefs—direct and indirect—is epistemically homogeneous: it consists of propositions that seem true on the basis of experience.

It is important to be clear, however, that Aristotle does not presuppose that acceptable beliefs are all guaranteed to be true. An acceptable belief has epistemic credentials that from the point of view of dialectic are *nonpareil*. But that is because dialectic deals with things only "in relation to belief" not, as philosophy does, "in accord with truth" (*Top.* 105ᵇ30–31). If a proposition is an acceptable belief, if it would be accepted by all or most people, it is everything an honest dialectician could ask for in a premise. But that does not mean that it will retain its credibility when the philosopher has done his *aporematic* or puzzle-related work on it.

Problems, Theses, and Puzzles

> A dialectical problem is a speculation, directed either to choice
> and avoidance or to truth and knowledge (either by itself or
> when working together with something else of this sort), about
> which [1] people believe nothing either way, or [2] ordinary
> people believe in a contrary way to the wise, or [3] the wise to
> ordinary people, or [4] each of them to themselves. . . . Problems
> also exist [5] where there are contrary deductions (for there is
> a puzzle as to whether it is so or not so, because there are per-
> suasive arguments concerning both sides), as well as [6] those
> we have no arguments about, because they are so large, thinking
> it difficult to give the why—for example, whether the cosmos is
> eternal or not; for one could also inquire into things of that sort.
> (*Top.* 104ᵇ1–17)

If there is disagreement over some proposition p, whether [2, 3] between
ordinary people and the wise or [4] within either party, p—or, more accur-
ately, the corresponding question, p?—is a problem. However, not all problems result from conflicts in belief or from the existence of unacceptable
beliefs, some exist [1] because we have no opinions about them or [6] no
arguments for or against them.

If p is unacceptable, however, but is held by even one notable philosopher, or if there is an argument for not-p, p (or p?) is a dialectical problem
of a distinctive sort:

> A thesis is: [a] an unacceptable supposition of someone well
> known for philosophy—for example, that contradiction is
> impossible (as Antisthenes used to say), or that everything
> moves (according to Heraclitus), or that what is, is one (as
> Melissus says); for to give thought to it when some random per-
> son declares things contrary to our beliefs is simpleminded. Or:
> [b] something contrary to our beliefs for which we have an argu-
> ment—for example, that not everything that is either has come
> to be or is eternally, as the sophists say; for a musician who is
> grammatical is so without having become so or being so eter-
> nally; for even if someone does not believe this, he might believe
> it because of having an argument. (*Top.* 104ᵇ19–28)

Whenever there is some reason, however slight, in favor of an unacceptable
proposition, a problem exists. But this means that the acceptable beliefs to
which such a proposition is contrary become problematic—especially as

dialectical premises. The class of acceptable beliefs, as we might put it, has a built-in tendency toward consistency—a tendency that dialectical practice itself helps further.

A puzzle, [5] suggests, is a problem of a second particular sort, namely, where there are strong arguments for a proposition p and strong arguments against it:

> A certain sophistical argument constitutes a puzzle; for because [sophists] wish to refute people in unacceptable ways, in order to be clever when they engage in argumentative encounters, the resulting deduction turns into a puzzle; for thought is tied up when it does not wish to stand still, because what has been concluded is not pleasing, but cannot move forward, because of its inability to resolve the argument. (*NE* 1146ª21–27)

Philosophy, as we will see, is particularly concerned with problems of this sort.

Uses of Dialectic

Dialectic has four apparently distinct uses, three of which are the focus of the present section: (1) training, (2) argumentative encounters, and (3) in the philosophical sciences (*Top.* 101ª26–27). Dialectic's usefulness for (1) training is "immediately evident," because "if we have a methodical inquiry we will more easily be able to argue dialectically about whatever is proposed" (101ª28–30). Since all other uses provide training too, just as all sports provide physical training, this use is presumably the broadest one. If we are *dialektikos*—if we are "skilled at dialectic" (164ᵇ3)—we will be better able to deal with any question put to us by any sort of questioner. Contrariwise, dealing with all sorts of questioners will tend to make or keep us skilled in dialectic.

Dialectic is useful in (2) argumentative encounters because, as we saw, "once we have cataloged the beliefs of ordinary people, we will engage in conversation with them, not by proceeding from the beliefs of others, but from their own, changing their minds about anything they appear to us to be stating incorrectly" (*Top.* 101ª31–34). Here, it is dialectic's systematic collecting and cataloging of acceptable beliefs (105ᵇ12–18) that proves particularly helpful. For by knowing what people will accept as premises, we will be better able to argue effectively and persuasively against them when they seem to be mistaken—even if, due to their lack of dialectical training, arguments with them "necessarily become bad" (164ᵇ9–10).

Aristotle sometimes applies the term *philosophia* (or sometimes *sophia* alone) to any science aiming at truth rather than action: "It is also correct for philosophy to be called 'scientific knowledge of the truth'; or of theoretical science the end is truth, whereas of practical science it is work" (*Met.* 993ᵇ19–21). In this sense of the term, all the broadly theoretical sciences count as branches of philosophy, and *philosophia* is more or less equivalent in meaning to *epistêmê* in its most exact sense. *Philosophia* also has a narrower sense, however, in which it applies exclusively to sciences providing knowledge of starting-points: "*Sophia* is a sort of science concerned with starting-points" (1059ᵃ18; also *NE* 1141ᵃ16–18). It is in this sense that there are just "three theoretical philosophies—mathematical, natural, and theological" (*Met.* 1026ᵃ18–19). In addition to these, Aristotle occasionally mentions practical philosophies, such as "the philosophy of human affairs" (*NE* 1181ᵇ15). It is among these that his own ethical writings belong (*Pol.* 1282ᵇ18–23).

It is hard to know which sense of "philosophical sciences" is pertinent in [3]. Fortunately, not much hangs on settling the matter. For what makes dialectic useful to these sciences, however we identify them, is that "the capacity to go through the puzzles on both sides of a question will make it easier to judge what is true and what is false in each" (*Top.* 101ᵃ34–36), and that seems like a capacity that any scientist might need. What it involves is explained more fully as follows:

> In relation to knowledge and philosophical wisdom, being able to get a comprehensive view, or to have gotten a comprehensive view, of the consequences of either hypothesis is no small instrument; for it remains [only] to choose one or the other of them correctly. In relation to this sort of thing, one must be naturally well-disposed. And this is what it is to be naturally well-disposed as regards truth: to be able to correctly choose the true and avoid the false. And this is just what the naturally well-endowed are able to do; for it is by loving and hating in the correct way what is put before them that they judge well what is best. (*Top.* 163ᵇ9–16)

Suppose that the puzzle a philosopher faces is, as before, to determine whether or not pleasure is always choiceworthy. If he is a competent dialectician, he will be able to follow out the consequences of supposing that it is, as well as those of supposing that it is not. He will be able to see what puzzles these consequences in turn face, and he will be able to go through these and determine which can be solved and which cannot. For this is just what a dialectician has to be able to do in order successfully to play the role of questioner or answerer in a dialectical argument about the choice-worthiness of pleasure. But this ability alone will not tell the philosopher where the truth lies. For that he also needs to be naturally well disposed. A requirement to which we will return.

In the end, the philosopher will have concluded, we may suppose, that some sorts of pleasure are sometimes choiceworthy, while others are never choiceworthy. But in the process of reaching that conclusion, some of the acceptable beliefs on both sides will almost certainly have been modified or clarified, partly accepted and partly rejected: "objecting is making one thing into many (for one either divides or does away with, grants or does not grant, the things that are proposed)" (*Top.* 164^{b}6–7). Others will have been decisively rejected as false. But these the philosopher will need to explain away:

> One must not only state the true view, but also the cause of the false one (for that contributes to our conviction; for when a reasonable explanation is given of why an untrue view appears true, this makes us more convinced of the true view). (*NE* 1154^{a}24–25)

In other words, some beliefs that seemed to be genuinely acceptable will have been revealed to be merely apparently so. But if "most of them, and the most authoritative ones" have been left in place, that would be an "adequate proof" of the philosopher's conclusion (*NE* 1145^{b}5–7).

It might seem that philosophy, at least in its aporematic, or puzzle-related, role, has now simply collapsed into honest dialectic; but this is not so. In an honest dialectical argument, the answerer may refuse to accept a proposition that a philosopher would accept:

> The philosopher, who is investigating by himself, does not care whether, though the things through which his deduction proceeds are true and known, the answerer does not grant them (because they are close to what was initially at issue, and he foresees what is going to result), but rather the philosopher is presumably eager for his claims to be as known and as close to what is at issue as possible; for it is from things of this sort that scientific deductions proceed. (*Top.* 155^{b}10–16)

Since the truth may well hinge on propositions whose status is just like the premises referred to here, there is no guarantee that honest dialectic and aporematic philosophy will reach the same conclusion on a given problem.

Perhaps enough has been said about this particular philosophical use of dialectic to show that it is relatively uncontroversial from the methodological and epistemological points of view. Dialectical ability helps an aporematic philosopher reach the truth in a way that is readily intelligible, but does not guarantee that he will reach it. For that he needs to be naturally well disposed as well. The philosopher employs acceptable beliefs as premises of his arguments, but he does not employ all and only those available to a dialectician. And he does not simply accept them. They are presumptively true, but this presumption can be cancelled.

Philosophy and Dialectic

> Dialecticians and sophists in fact cut the same figure as the philosopher; for sophistic is only apparently wisdom, and dialecticians discuss all [these] things, and being is common to all [these], but clearly they discuss them because they properly belong to philosophy. Sophistic and dialectic, then, are indeed concerned with the same kind as philosophy, but philosophy differs from dialectic in the way its capacity is employed, and from sophistic in the life it deliberately chooses; for dialectic is examinational about the issues philosophy seeks to know about, while sophistic appears to be but is not. (*Met.* 1004^{b}17–26)

Because it can draw out the consequences of each of the hypotheses (p, not-p) in a problem and go through the puzzles they face, dialectic can examine those hypotheses. But it cannot achieve knowledge, because it lacks a type of power that philosophy possesses. The question is, What is this power?

When dialectic has done its testing of p and of not-p, as we saw, it "remains [only] to choose one or the other of them correctly" (*Top.* 163^{b}11–12). And a good natural disposition, which involves "loving and hating in the correct way what is put before them," is what enables someone to "judge well what is best" (163^{b}15–16). The reference to "what is best" suggests too that the natural disposition in question may be the sort referred to in the following passage:

> A person's seeking of the end . . . is not self-chosen, rather, we must be born possessed of a sort of sight by which to judge correctly and choose what is truly good, and a person in whom this by nature operates correctly is naturally well disposed; for this is what is greatest and noblest . . . and, when it is naturally such as

> to be in a good and noble condition, will be the naturally good
> disposition in its complete and true form. (*NE* 1114^{b}5–12)

And that in fact is what the distinction between philosophy and sophistry, which uses all of plain dialectic's resources, might lead us to expect, since "philosophy differs from . . . sophistic in the life it deliberately chooses" (*Met.* 1004^{b}23–25).

A deliberate choice of how to live is *au fond* a choice of an ultimate end or target for one's life: "anyone capable of living in accord with his own deliberate choice posits some target for living nobly, whether honor, reputation, wealth, or education, looking toward which he will do all his actions" (*EE* 1214^{b}6–9). And what "teaches correct belief" about this end or target, thereby ensuring that the deliberate choice of it is itself correct, is "virtue, whether natural or habituated" (*NE* 1151^{a}18–19). It is this, we may infer, in which a good natural disposition consists. Hence if we possess it, when we hear from political science that the starting-point it posits as the correct target for a human life is "activity of the soul in accord with virtue, and, if there are more virtues than one, in accord with the best and most complete" (1098^{a}16–18), we will accept it as true, and so strive to clear away the puzzles that block our road to it. If, on the other hand, we do not possess it, we will reject this starting-point and strive to sustain the puzzles, so that in our choice between p and not-p, we will go for the wrong one. For "the truth in practical matters must be judged from the works and the life; for these are what have the controlling vote. When we examine what has been previously said, then, it must be judged by bringing it to bear on the works and the life, and if it is in harmony with them, one must accept it, but if it clashes, one must suppose it mere words" (1179^{a}17–22).

In the *Rhetoric*, however, we learn of an apparently different sort of good natural disposition, which seems from the company it keeps to be an exclusively intellectual trait: "a good natural disposition, memory, ease at learning, readiness of wit, and all such things" (1362^{b}24–25). When it comes to solving dialectical problems bearing on "truth and knowledge," we might conclude, such an apparently intellectual good disposition is all a philosopher needs, even if, when it comes to those bearing on "pursuit and avoidance" (*Top.* 104^{b}1–2), he also needs its apparently more ethical namesake. Whatever we decide about this, our account of this intellectual good disposition can nonetheless take the account of an ethical good disposition as a useful guide.

In various places, Aristotle refers to what he calls a well-educated person (*pepaideumenos*). This is someone who studies practically all subjects, not to acquire expert scientific knowledge in all of them (which would be impossible) but in order to become a good judge (*PA* 639^{a}1–6, *Met.* 995^{a}6–14,

NE 1094ᵇ28–1095ᵃ2, *EE* 1216ᵇ40–1217ᵃ10, *Pol.* 1282ᵃ3–7). Generally educated in medicine, for example, he is as capable of judging whether or not someone has treated a disease correctly as a doctor is (1282ᵃ3–7). Acquainted with many subjects, methodologies, and areas of study, he knows "what we should and should not seek to have demonstrated" (*Met.* 1106ᵃ5–11) and looks for "the degree of exactness in each kind of investigation that the nature of the subject itself allows" (*NE* 1094ᵇ23–27). And because he is able to judge the works and advice of experts, he is free from the sort of intellectual enslavement to them that would otherwise be his lot. He knows who is and who is not worth listening to on any matter and so can get good expert advice when he needs it. But he is also free from the inner enslavement that is all too often the lot of the narrow expert, whose imagination is straightjacketed by the one thing he knows too well. For, while he has indeed studied all the "free sciences," he has done so only "up to a point," and not so assiduously or pedantically as "to debase the mind and deprive it of leisure" (*Pol.* 1337ᵇ14–17). Whether identical to our intellectual good disposition, or a state developed from it by intellectual training in the way that habituated virtue is developed from natural virtue by adequate upbringing, it is surely this sort of educatedness that the aporematic philosopher needs in order to perform the task Aristotle assigns to his intellectual good disposition. For if he is well educated he will be a discerning judge in the realm of knowledge, able to distinguish genuine sciences from specious or sophistic look-alikes, and so be able to determine which starting-points he should be trying to find a puzzle-free way toward.

Aporematic philosophy is not the only sort of philosophy Aristotle recognizes, of course. As we saw, he also recognizes a number of philosophies or philosophical sciences, some theoretical (mathematical, natural, theological) and some practical (ethics, politics). The way to the starting-points of these, as to those of all sciences, is aporematic. But the philosophies themselves—at any rate, insofar as they are or are like genuine Aristotelian sciences—are presumably structures of demonstrations from starting-points. But that means that their methodology, when it is not dialectical, is simply that of such sciences. Dialectic, in other words, is not just the method of *aporematic* philosophy, but has a claim to being regarded as the distinctive method of Aristotelian philosophy generally.

What a Topic Is

The word *topos*, which has given the *Topics* its title, does not occur in it until the final line of Book 1, and just what a *topos* (a "place" in ordinary Greek) is, it never tells us. The *Rhetoric*, however, is more forthcoming. There we learn that "dialectical and rhetorical deductions are those concerned with what we call 'topics,' which are common when they concern what is just, what is natural, what is political, and many things that differ in form—for example, the topic of the more and the less" (*Rh.* 1358ᵃ10–14). These topics, moreover, are the elements of enthymemes (the rhetorical equivalent of dialectical deductions): "By 'element (*stoicheion*)' and 'topic,' I mean the same thing" (1396ᵇ20–21). Now, a deduction has two sorts of things in it that we might intuitively call "elements," namely, premises and a logical form determinative of the deduction's syllogistic mood, which is something like a rule of inference. And, as we saw in the case of the principle of non-contradiction, common things include such rules or premises that express them:

> By the "starting-points of demonstration" I mean the com-mon beliefs (*koinas doxas*) on the basis of which we all prove things, such as that in every case it is necessary either to affirm or deny, and that it is impossible for something at the same time to both be and not be, and any other premises like that. (*Met.* 996ᵇ27–29)

And in keeping with this idea is the association of topics with acceptable beliefs: "It is clear that it is possible to produce a counter-deduction on the basis of the same topics [as a deduction]; for the deductions are based on acceptable beliefs, and many things that seem to be so are contrary to one another" (*Rh.* 1402ᵃ32–34).

Apparently somewhat at odds with this picture of topics, however, is their characterization as something "into the province of which many enthymemes fall (*eis . . . empiptei*)" (*Rh.* 1403ᵃ17–18). But here the *Topics* comes to our aid:

> One must also try to get possession of the [headings] into the province of which other arguments most often fall (*eis . . . empi-ptousin*). . . . For just as in mnemonics, the mere mention of their places (*topoi*) immediately makes the things themselves be remembered, so these [headings] will make one more capable at deducing, because one sees these items defined and numbered. And it is a common premise, rather than an argument, that should be committed to memory; for to be well equipped with a starting-point—that is, a hypothesis—is [only] moderately dif-ficult. (*Top.* 163ᵇ22–33)

A common premise (or premise for a dialectical deduction), it shows us, is also something that can serve as a mnemonic device—a *topos*—for arguments, and as such is an item into the province of which these arguments fall. It is this that allows Aristotle to speak of topics in the two ways that seemed to be in conflict. In one way they are common premises; in another they are common premises serving as reminders of correlative arguments. They are thus at once headings in those catalogs of evidence that are all important in any science and items falling under them.

What Dialectic Is

Aristotle usually classifies sciences (*epistêmai*) into the theoretical, the practical, and the productive (*Met.* 1025ᵇ25), as he does in the *Topics* as well (145ᵃ15–16, 157ᵃ10–11). Moreover, he is quite catholic in what he counts as a science: even boxing and wrestling are classed as *epistêmai* (*Cat.* 10ᵇ3–4). The question naturally arises, then, as to where, if anywhere, dialectic fits in this classification. Is it a science? If so, what sort? If it is not a science, what exactly is it?

In speaking about the examination craft, Aristotle writes:

> All, then, practice refutation; for they share in an un-craftlike way in what dialectic does in a craftlike one, and the one who by means of the craft of deduction is examinational is a dialectician. Since there are many of these [common things] and they apply with respect to everything, and are not such as to constitute a certain nature and kind, but instead are like negations, while others are not of this sort but special, it is possible, on the basis of them, to undertake an examination about anything, and for this to constitute a certain craft, though one that is not like the sorts that prove things. (*SE* 172ᵃ34–ᵇ1)

And what a craft is, is precisely a productive science: "there is no craft that is not a productive state involving reason and no such state that is not a craft, a craft is the same as a productive state involving true reason" (*NE* 1140ᵃ8–10).

When science receives its focused discussion in the *Ethics*, Aristotle is explicit that if we are "to speak in an exact way and not be guided by mere similarities" (1139ᵇ19), we should not call anything a "science" unless it deals with eternal, entirely exceptionless facts about universals that are wholly necessary and do not at all admit of being otherwise:

> What admits of being known scientifically is by necessity. Hence it is eternal; for the things that are unconditionally necessary are all eternal, and eternal things cannot come to be or pass away. (*NE* 1139ᵇ22–24)

Since he is here explicitly epitomizing his more detailed discussion of science in the *Posterior Analytics* (1139^{b}27), we should take the latter too as primarily a discussion of science in the exact sense, which it calls *epistêmê haplôs*—unconditional scientific knowledge. It follows—and we should acknowledge this—that only the strictly theoretical sciences are sciences in the exact sense. Hence dialectic, if it is a science at all, is clearly not an unconditional one.

Having made the acknowledgment, though, we must also register the fact that Aristotle himself mostly does not speak in the exact way but instead persistently refers to bodies of knowledge other than the strictly theoretical sciences as *epistêmai*. His division of the *epistêmai* into theoretical, practical, and productive is a dramatic case in point. But so too is his use of the term *epistêmê* within the *Topics*, which we encounter being applied to rhetoric itself at 101^{b}10 (compare *Rh.* 1355^{b}19–20: "one person is an orator in virtue of his scientific knowledge, another in virtue of his deliberate choice").

So the interesting question is not whether dialectic is a science, since the answer to that is obvious: it is not a science if we are being absolutely exact about the matter, but it is a science if we allow ourselves to be guided by Aristotle's own general use of the terms *epistêmê* and *technê*, on the assumption that it was itself guided by the similarities between the things he applies it to and the strictly theoretical sciences. The interesting questions are: What are these similarities? Just how like a canonical or theoretical science is dialectic?

An Aristotelian science of any sort is a state of the soul, not a body of propositions in a textbook—although the state does involve having an affirmational grasp on a set of true propositions:

> Let the states in which the soul grasps the truth by way of affirmation and denial be five in number: craft knowledge, scientific knowledge, practical wisdom, theoretical wisdom, and understanding. (*NE* 1139^{b}14–16)

Some of these propositions are indemonstrable starting-points, which are or are indicated in definitions, and others are theorems demonstrable from them. We can have scientific knowledge only of the theorems, since—exactly speaking—"what is scientifically known is demonstrable" (*NE* 1140^{b}35). Yet—in what is clearly another lapse from exact speaking—Aristotle characterizes "the most exact of the sciences," which is theoretical wisdom (*sophia*) or primary philosophy, as also involving a grasp by understanding (*nous*) of the truth where the starting-points themselves are concerned:

> A theoretically-wise person not only must know what follows from the starting-points but also must grasp the truth where the starting-points are concerned. So theoretical wisdom would be understanding plus scientific knowledge. (*NE* 1141ᵃ16–20)

He does the same thing in the *Metaphysics,* where theoretical wisdom is the *epistêmê* that provides "a theoretical grasp on the primary starting-points and causes"—among which are included "the good or the for-the-sake-of-which" (982ᵇ7–10). Indeed, the grasp we have of such starting-points must result in their being "better known" than the theorems we demonstrate from them if we are to have any scientific knowledge of the exact sort at all: "if they are not better known than the conclusion, it is in a coincidental sense that he will have scientific knowledge" (1139ᵇ34–35).

How like that is dialectic? Are there starting-points there too and things demonstrable from them? We might think this is an easy question to answer. After all, the methodical inquiry the *Topics* and *Sophistical Refutations* themselves exemplify does not seem to include any demonstrations whatever, and neither does "the craft of deduction" (*SE* 172ᵃ35), developed in the *Prior Analytics,* on which it draws. For a demonstration is, among other things, a deductively valid argument that is syllogistic in form, and deductions of any sort are scarcely to be found in the *Topics* and *Sophistical Refutations,* though many are examined or discussed.

If we think of a science in the exact sense as consisting exclusively of what is demonstrable, as we have seen that Aristotle himself sometimes does, we will be right to conclude that a treatise without demonstrations in it cannot be scientific. But if, as he also does, we include knowledge of starting-points as parts of science, we will not be right: a treatise could contribute to a science not by demonstrating anything but by arguing to the starting-points themselves—an enterprise that could not possibly consist of demonstrations from those starting-points, since these would be circular. We might reasonably infer, therefore, that dialectic is a sort of science—a craft—just because it contributes to the correct definition and secure grasp on starting-points without which no science can exist. The same idea might be employed in the case of many of Aristotle's other treatises. They too, we might suppose, are scientific in just this sense.

Topics

1: DIALECTIC

1.1

Aim of the work

100ᵃ18 The proposed aim of this work is to find a methodical inquiry by which we will be capable of constructing deductions on any problem that is proposed, proceeding from acceptable beliefs, and, when submitting to argu-

20 ment ourselves, of avoiding saying anything contradictory.[1] First, then, we must say what a deduction is, and what its different varieties are, in order to grasp what a dialectical deduction is; for this is what we are inquiring about in the proposed work.

A deduction, then, is an argument in which, certain things being pos-
25 ited, something distinct from the things proposed follows of necessity because of the things proposed. It is a demonstration when the deduction proceeds from things that are true and primary, or are such that our know-ledge of them has a starting-point in things that are primary and true, and
30 a deduction is dialectical when it deduces from acceptable beliefs.[2]

The things that are true and primary are those that are persuasive not because of other things but because of themselves (for in the case of sci-
100ᵇ18 entific starting-points we must not further inquire about why they are
20 so, instead each of the starting-points must be intrinsically persuasive).[3] Acceptable beliefs, by contrast, are things that seem so to everyone, to the majority, or to the wise—either to all of them, or to most, or to the best known and most reputable.

A contentious deduction is one that proceeds from what appear to be, but are not, acceptable beliefs, and a deduction from what are, or what
25 appear to be, acceptable beliefs is an apparent one; for not everything that appears to be an acceptable belief actually is one.[4] For none of the things said to be acceptable beliefs wears this appearance entirely on its face, which is what actually occurs in the case of the starting-points of conten-tious arguments; for in their case the nature of their falsity is for the most
30 part immediately clear to those capable of seeing even small things.[5] Let us
101ᵃ1 say, then, that the first sort we mentioned is a contentious deduction and a [genuine] deduction, while the other sort is a contentious deduction, but not a [genuine] deduction, since it appears to deduce, but does not deduce.
5 Further, beyond all the sorts of deductions just mentioned, there are the fallacies that proceed from things proper to a given science, as happens

2

in the case of geometry and other sciences akin to it.[6] For this mode of
argument would seem to be different from the sorts of deductions we mentioned; for someone who draws false diagrams does not deduce from true
and primary things, nor from acceptable beliefs either.[7] For they do not fall   10
within the definition; for he does not take [as his starting-points] things
that seem so to all, to the majority, or to the wise (whether all of them,
or most, or the most reputable), rather he produces his deduction from
premises proper to the science but not true—for example, he produces his
fallacy either by defining the semicircles in a way that he should not, or by   15
drawing certain lines in a way in which they should not be drawn.[8]

The foregoing, then, may be taken as an outline of the forms of deductions there are.[9] And as a universal remark both about all the things mentioned and about those we will discuss later, we may say that this will be the
extent of our determinations. This is because of our deliberately choosing   20
not to give an exact account of any of these things, rather our wish is to give
an outline of them, since we consider it fully adequate, for the purposes of
the proposed methodical inquiry, to be able to know each of them in some
way or other.

1.2

Usefulness of the work

Our next task, after what we have said, is to say how many areas, and also   25
of what sorts, our work is useful in. It is useful, then, in three: in training,
in argumentative encounters, and in the philosophical sciences.[10]

That it is useful in training is immediately evident; for if we have a methodical inquiry we will more easily be able to argue dialectically about whatever is proposed.[11] It is useful in argumentative encounters because, once   30
we have cataloged the beliefs of ordinary people, we will engage in conversation with them, not by proceeding from the beliefs of others, but from
their own, changing their minds about anything they appear to us to be
stating incorrectly.[12] And it is useful in the philosophical sciences because
the capacity to go through the puzzles on both sides of a question will
make it easier to judge what is true and what is false in each.[13]   35

Further, dialectic is useful as regards the primary [starting-points] in
each science. For it is impossible to say anything about these based on the
starting-points proper to the science in question, since these starting-points
are prior to everything else; instead, these must be discussed through the
acceptable beliefs about each of them. And this is a task that is special to,   101^b1
or, at any rate, characteristic of, dialectic, which, because of its capacity to

stand outside and examine, provides a route toward the starting-points of all methodical inquiries.[14]

1.3

What it is to possess the methodical inquiry

5   We will possess the methodical inquiry completely when we possess it as we do in the case of rhetoric, medicine, or other capacities of this sort.[15] For the rhetorically competent person will not try to persuade, nor will the doctor try to cure, on the basis of every mode [of persuasion or of treatment], but if he omits none of the possible ones, we say that he possesses
10 the science adequately.[16]

1.4

What the methodical inquiry is based on

First, then, we must get a theoretical grasp on the things on which the methodical inquiry is based.[17] If, then, we could grasp how many and what sorts of things arguments are related to, and on what they are based, and how to become well equipped with these, we would have an adequate grasp on what we proposed.[18]

The things arguments are based on are equal in number to, and the same as, the things that the deductions are concerned with. For arguments are
15 from premises, while the things that the deductions are concerned with are problems.[19] And every premise, as well as every problem, indicates either a kind, a special thing, or a coincident; for in fact the difference, since it is of the kind, must actually be classified together with the kind.[20] But since of what is special one part signifies the essence and another part does not
20 signify it, let us divide what is special into both of the parts just stated, and let us call the part that signifies the essence a "definition," while the remaining part, in keeping with the name commonly assigned to them, may be called a "special affection."[21] It is clear, then, from what has been said that, according to the present division, it turns out that there are four in all: spe-
25 cial affection, definition, kind, and coincident. But let no one suppose us to be saying that each of these stated by itself is a premise or a problem, but rather it is from these that problems and premises are generated.[22]

A problem is different from a premise in its mode. For said in this way, "Is
30 'two-footed terrestrial animal' the definition of human?" or "Is animal the kind of human?" it is a premise; but said in this way, "Whether 'two-footed

4

terrestrial animal' is the definition of human or not," it becomes a problem.[23] And similarly in the case of the others. So it makes perfect sense that
problems and premises are equal in number; for one makes a problem out   35
of any premise by exchanging its mode.

1.5

What a definition, a special affection, a kind, and a coincident are

We must say, then, what a definition, a special affection, a kind, and a
coincident are. A definition is an account that signifies the essence. It is
assigned either as an account in place of a name or as an account in place
of an account; for it is also possible to define some of the things that are   102^{a}1
[already] signified by an account.[24] Those who merely assign a name, whatever it is, clearly do not assign the definition of the thing, since every definition is an account.

   Nonetheless, this sort of thing—for example, that the noble is the   5
appropriate—must also be posited as akin to definition. Similarly, whether
perception and scientific knowledge are the same or distinct; for in fact,
where definitions are concerned, most of our time is taken up with whether
things are the same or distinct. Putting it simply, let us call all things "akin
to definitions" that fall to the same methodical inquiry as definitions. And
it is immediately clear that all the cases just mentioned are of this sort. For   10
if we are able to argue dialectically that things are the same or that they
are distinct, we will also be well equipped to attack definitions in the same
way; for by proving that the two things are not the same, we will have done
away with the definition. The converse of what we have just said, however,
does not hold; for to establish a definition it is not enough to prove that   15
two things are the same, although to disestablish one it is sufficient to prove
that they are not the same.

   A special affection is one that does not indicate the essence of a thing,
belongs to that thing alone, and is counterpredicated of it.[25] Thus it is a
special affection of humans to be receptive of grammar; for if someone is
human, he is receptive of grammar, and if he is receptive of grammar, he   20
is human. For no one would say that something is a special affection if it
admits of belonging to something else—for example, no one would say
that sleeping is a special affection of humans, even if at some time it happened to belong only to them. Therefore, if something of this sort were said
to be a special affection, it would be said to be such not unconditionally,
but rather a special affection at a time, or in relation to something.[26] Being   25
on the right, for example, is said to be a special affection of something

at a time, and two-footed is said to be a special affection in relation to
something—for example, a special affection of humans in relation to horses
or dogs. It is clear that nothing that admits of belonging to something else
is counterpredicated of a thing—for example, if something is asleep, it is
30   not necessary for it to be human.

A kind is what is predicated in the what-it-is of many things that differ
in form.[27] And let us say that what are predicated in the what-it-is are the
sorts of things that it would be fitting to mention if we were asked what the
proposed thing is—just as it is fitting in the case of a human, when asked
35   what it is, to say that it is an animal. The problem of whether one thing is in
the same kind as another, or in a distinct one, is also akin to the kind; for
this sort of problem also falls to the same methodical inquiry as the kind.
For if we argue dialectically that animal is the kind of human, and similarly
of ox, we will have argued dialectically that they are in the same kind, while
102^b1   if we prove that it is the kind of one and that it is not the kind of the other,
we will have argued dialectically that they are not in the same kind.[28]

A coincident is something that is none of these (whether a definition,
5   a special affection, or a kind), yet does belong to the thing. Also, it is what
can belong or not belong to one and the same thing—for example, being
seated can belong or not belong to the same thing, and so similarly can
being pale; for nothing prevents the same thing from being at one time
pale, at another time not pale. The second of these two definitions of a
10   coincident is better; for if the first is stated, anyone who is going to comprehend it must already know what a definition, a kind, and a special affection
are; while the second definition is complete in itself for knowing what the
thing meant is intrinsically.

We may also add to what is coincident the comparisons between one
15   thing and another that are stated in some way that derives from what is
coincident—for example, whether the noble or the advantageous is more
choiceworthy, or whether the life in accordance with virtue or the life of
indulgence is more pleasant, or anything else that might be stated in a way
that is close to these; for in all such cases, the inquiry arises as to whether
the coincident that is predicated belongs to a higher degree to one or to
20   the other.

It is clear from these things that nothing prevents a coincident from
becoming a special affection of something at a time or in relation to something—for example, sitting down, which is a coincident, will be a special
affection at a time when only one person is sitting down, and when he is
not the only one sitting down it will be a special affection of his in relation
to those who are not sitting down. So nothing prevents a coincident from
becoming a special affection either in relation to something or at a time.
25   Unconditionally, however, it will not be a special affection.

1.6

No universal methodical inquiry

One must not overlook the fact that the things said with regard to a special affection and a kind will all fit a definition too. For when we have proved that what is given as a definition does not belong solely to what is under definition (as we also do in the case of a special affection), or that it is not the [correct] kind that is assigned in the definition, or that one of the things stated in the account does not belong to the thing (which is just what might also be said in the case of a coincident), then we will have done away with the definition.²⁹ So, in accord with the account given previously, all the things we have enumerated would be in a way akin to definitions.³⁰ But one must not, because of this, seek a single universal methodical inquiry applicable to all cases; for this is not an easy thing to find, and if it were found, it would be entirely lacking in perspicuousness and difficult to use for the proposed work.³¹ On the other hand, if we were to assign a special methodical inquiry to each of the kinds we have distinguished, on the basis of what is proper to each, a methodical route through the proposed thing could easily be produced.³² So we must, as was said previously, make an outline division, and as for the rest, we must attach whichever is most proper to each, and call them, "akin to definitions," or "akin to kinds." The ones we mentioned have pretty much been assigned to each.³³

1.7

The number of ways in which things are said to be the same

First of all we must determine the number of ways in which things are said to be the same.³⁴ And sameness, taken in outline, would seem to be divided into three parts. For we usually call things the same in number, in form, or in kind: in number, when the names are several but the thing is one—for example, cape and cloak; in form, when, though the things are several, they are undifferentiated with respect to form—for example, one human and another human, or one horse and another horse (for things of this sort, which fall under the same form, are said to be the same in form); in kind, similarly, those things are the same that fall under the same kind—for example, horse and human.

It might seem that water from the same spring is said to be the same in a way that has some difference from those mentioned. Nonetheless, this too, at any rate, must be placed in the same part as things said to be the same in some way or other with respect to form; for all such things seem to be akin

20   and quite similar to each other. For all water is said to be the same in form
as all other water because it possesses a certain similarity, and water from
the same spring is different in no other way than that the similarity is much
more pronounced. That is why we do not separate this case from those that
are said to be the same in some way or other with respect to a single form.

What is one in number seems to be most of all agreed to be said by
everyone to be the same. But even this is usually assigned in several ways.
25   The strictest and primary way is when sameness is assigned by a name
or a definition—for example, "cloak" assigned to cape, or "two-footed terrestrial animal" to human.³⁵ Second, when sameness is assigned by a special affection—for example, "receptive of scientific knowledge" assigned to
human, "what by nature spatially moves upward" to fire. Third, when it is
assigned from a coincident—for example, "the one seated" or "the musical
30   one" to "Socrates"; for all these mean to signify oneness in number.

That what has just now been said is true may most of all be learned
from cases in which we change the ways we call people; for often when we
give an order to call someone who is seated, using his name, we change
35   it, when the person to whom we give it happens not to understand us, on
the supposition that he will understand us better from a coincident of the
person, and so we tell him to call over to us, "the one seated," or "the one
talking," clearly taking the same thing to be signified by the name as by
the coincident.

1.8

Basis for the proposed division of predicates

103^b1   Let sameness, then, as was said, be divided into three parts.³⁶

Of the fact that arguments are based on the things mentioned previously, are through these and for these, one means of persuasion is by
induction; for if one were to look at each premise or problem, it would be
5   evident that it has stemmed either from definition, special affection, kind,
or coincident.³⁷

Another means of persuasion is by deduction. For it is necessary for
everything that is predicated of something either to be or not to be counterpredicated of the thing. And if it is counterpredicated, it must be either a definition or a special affection (a definition, if it signifies the essence; a special
10   affection if it does not signify it; for we saw that this is what a special affection
is, what is counterpredicated but does not signify the essence).³⁸ On the other
hand, if it is not counterpredicated of the thing, it either is or is not among
the things mentioned in the definition of the underlying subject.³⁹ And if it

8

is among the things mentioned in the definition, it must be either a kind or a difference, since a definition is composed of a kind and differences.[40] But if it is not among the things mentioned in the definition, it is clear that it must be a coincident; for a coincident was said to be what is neither a definition, nor a kind, nor a special affection, but still belongs to the thing at issue.[41]

1.9

The categories of predicates

After this, therefore, we must determine the kinds of predication in which the four we mentioned are found. These are ten in number: what-it-is, quantity, quality, relative, where, when, position, having, doing, and being affected.[42] For the coincidents, the kind, the special affections, and the definition will always be in one of these categories; for all premises [produced] through these signify either a what-it-is, a quantity, a quality, or some other category.

It is clear from the nature of the things themselves that what signifies the what-it-is will sometimes signify substance, sometimes quality, and sometimes some other category.[43] For when human is set forth as an example and it says that what is set forth is human or animal, it says what it is and signifies substance. But when white color is set forth and he says that what is set forth is white or color, he says what it is and signifies quality. Similarly, if what is set forth is yard-long length, if he says that what is set forth is yard-long length, he says what it is and signifies quantity. And similarly in the case of the other categories; for each of these sorts of predicate, both when it itself is said of itself and when its kind is said of it, signifies what it is. But when it is said about another thing, it does not signify what it is, but its quantity, quality, or one of the other categories.

So, what arguments are about and based on are these and this many things. How we can get hold of them, and through what means we can be well equipped with them, must be stated next.

1.10

Dialectical premises

First, therefore, it must be determined what a dialectical premise is and what a dialectical problem is.[44] For not every premise or every problem must be counted as dialectical; for no one with any understanding would propose as a premise what no one believes, or as a problem what is evident to everyone; for the latter involves no puzzle, and the former no one would accept.

A dialectical premise is a making of a question out of what is acceptable, either to everyone, to most people, or to the wise (and, among these,
either to all, to most, or to the best known), provided it is not unacceptable
for anyone would accept what seems to be so to the wise, provided it is
not contrary to the beliefs of ordinary people.[45] Dialectical premises also
include things that are like acceptable beliefs; the contraries of what appear
to be acceptable beliefs, when proposed by way of contradiction; and all
beliefs that are in accord with the established crafts.[46]

For if it is acceptable that the science of contraries is the same, it would
also appear to be acceptable that the perception of contraries is the same.[47]
And if it is acceptable that the craft of grammar is one in number, then the
craft of pipe playing is also one in number, while if there are several crafts
of grammar, then there are also several of pipe playing; for all these seem
to be similar and akin.

Similarly, the contraries of what appear to be acceptable beliefs, when
proposed by way of contradiction, will appear to be acceptable beliefs; for
if it is acceptable that one must do good to one's friends, it is also acceptable that one must not do them evil. It is contrary that one must do one's
friends evil, but by way of contradiction it is that one must not do them
evil. Similarly, if one must do good to one's friends, to one's enemies one
must not do it. And this is so too by way of contradiction of the contraries;
for the contrary is that one must do one's enemies good. It is also the same
way in other cases.

And, in juxtaposition, the contrary about the contrary will also appear to
be acceptable. For example, if one must do good to one's friends, one must
do evil to one's enemies. (To do good to one's friends might also appear to
be contrary to doing evil to one's enemies, but whether this is truly so or
not will be stated in our discussion of contraries.[48])

It is also clear that whatever beliefs are in accord with crafts are dialectical premises; for anyone would accept the things believed by those who
have investigated these crafts—for example, a doctor about issues in medicine, or a geometer about those in geometry, and similarly in other cases.

1.11

Dialectical problems

104^{b}1   A dialectical problem is a speculation, directed either to choice and avoidance or to truth and knowledge (either by itself or when working together

with something else of this sort), about which people believe nothing either way, or ordinary people believe in a contrary way to the wise, or the wise to ordinary people, or each of them to themselves.[49] For it is use- ⁵ ful to know some problems only in relation to choice and avoidance (for example, whether pleasure is choiceworthy or not), while it is useful to know others only in relation to knowledge (for example, whether the cos- mos is eternal or not). But others are intrinsically of no use in relation to either of these but work together with some things of this sort; for there are many things that we do not wish to know intrinsically, but rather for ¹⁰ the sake of other things, in order that, through them, we come to know something else.

Problems also exist where there are contrary deductions (for there is a puzzle as to whether it is so or not so, because there are persuasive argu- ments concerning both sides), as well as those we have no arguments about, because they are so large, thinking that it is difficult to give the why—for ¹⁵ example, whether the cosmos is eternal or not; for one could also inquire about things of that sort.[50]

Let problems and premises, then, be determined as has been stated.

A thesis is: an unacceptable supposition of someone well known for philosophy—for example, that contradiction is impossible (as Antisthenes ²⁰ used to say), or that everything moves (according to Heraclitus), or that what is, is one (as Melissus says); for to give thought to it when some ran- dom person declares things contrary to our beliefs is simpleminded.[51] Or: something contrary to our beliefs for which we have an argument—for example, that not everything that is either has come to be or is eternally, as ²⁵ the sophists say; for a musician who is grammatical is so without having become so or being so eternally; for even if someone does not believe this, he might believe it because of having an argument.[52]

A thesis, then, is also a problem, but not every problem is a thesis, since some problems are such that we have no belief about them either way. That ³⁰ a thesis is also a problem is clear; for it is necessary from what has been said either that ordinary people disagree with the wise about a thesis, or that one or the other lot disagrees among themselves, since a thesis is a cer- tain unacceptable supposition. As things stand, pretty much all dialectical problems are called "theses." But let it make no difference whatever they are ³⁵ called; for it is not because we wish to make up names that we have distin- guished them in this way, but in order that we not fail to consider whatever differences there actually are of them.   **105ᵃ1**

We must not, however, look at every problem or every thesis, but rather those that someone might puzzle over who is in need of arguments, not punishment or perception; for those who puzzle over "whether one must ⁵ honor the gods and love one's parents or not" need punishment, while those who puzzle over "whether snow is white or not" need perception.[53] Nor, indeed, must one look at those whose demonstration is near at hand, or those whose demonstration is too remote; for the former involve no puzzle, while the latter involve more of one than is in accord with [dialectical] training.

1.12

Deduction and induction

10 Having determined these things, then, we must distinguish how many forms of dialectical argument there are. One is induction, another deduction.[54] And what deduction is was stated previously.[55] Induction is the route from particulars to the universal—for example, if a ship's captain with scientific knowledge is the most excellent one, and so with a charioteer, then, in gen-
15 eral, the person who has scientific knowledge about anything is best. Induction is more persuasive, more perspicuous, better known by perception, and common to ordinary people, but deduction has greater force and is more effective against those skilled in logico-linguistic disputation.[56]

1.13

The four instruments

Let the kinds, then, of the things arguments are about and on which
20 they are based be determined as was stated previously.[57] The instruments through which we will become well equipped with deductions are four: one is getting hold of premises; the second is being able to distinguish in how many ways something is said of things; the third is finding the differences; and the fourth is the investigation of likeness.[58] There is a way in
25 which the last three of these are also premises, since it is possible to make a premise of each of them—for example, that either the noble, the pleasant, or the advantageous is choiceworthy; or that perception differs from scientific knowledge in that it is possible to get the latter back again after
30 losing it but not the former; or what conduces to health is related to health as what conduces to the good state is to the good state. The first is a premise from what is said to be something in many ways; the second is one from differences; the third is one from like things.

1.14

(1) Getting hold of premises

Premises must be selected in as many ways as were determined in connection with premises, by having ready to hand the beliefs either of everyone, of most, or of the wise (and of these, the beliefs of all, most, or the best known), provided they are not contrary to the apparent ones, and whatever beliefs are in accord with the crafts (but one must propose even the contraries of apparently acceptable premises by way of contradiction, as was stated previously).[59]

It is also useful in selecting these to produce not only the ones that are acceptable but the ones that are like them—for example, that the perception of contraries is the same (for the science of them is too), or that we see by taking something in, not sending something out (for it is this way too in the case of the other perceptual capacities, since we hear by taking something in, not sending something out, taste in the same way, and it is the same way too in the case of the others). Further, whatever appears to be so in all or in most cases must be taken as a starting-point and seeming posit (for those who have not seen in which case it is not so accept it).

One must also select premises from written works and produce catalogs of them concerning each kind of subject, putting them under separate headings—for example, concerned with goodness, concerned with life, and concerned with every sort of goodness—starting with the what-it-is. And one must also take note of the beliefs of particular people—for example, that it was Empedocles who said that there are four elements of bodies (for anyone might accept what was said by a reputable person).[60]

In outline, there is a three-part division of premises and problems; for some premises are ethical, some are natural scientific, and some are logico-linguistic. Premises such as the following are ethical—for example, whether one must obey one's parents rather than the laws, if they disagree; logico-linguistic—for example, whether the science of contraries is the same or not; natural scientific—for example, whether the cosmos is eternal or not.[61] And similarly for the problems. What each of the ones mentioned is like, though, is not easily given in definitions concerning them, and one must try to come to know each of them by the intimacy that comes through induction, examining them by reference to the paradigms that were mentioned.[62]

In relation to philosophy, premises and problems must be treated in accord with truth, but dialectically, in relation to belief.

All premises must be selected in the most universal version possible, and one premise made into many—for example, "the science of opposites

is the same" must be made into "the science of contraries is the same, and
the science of relatives is."⁶³ Then these premises must in turn be divided
35   up in the same way, as far as is possible to divide them up—for example,
"the science of good and bad is the same, and that of white and black, and
that of cold and hot." And similarly in the case of the others.

1.15

(2) Distinguishing in how many ways something is said of things

106ᵃ1   About premises, then, the foregoing remarks are sufficient. As regards the
number of ways [something is said to be something], we must not only
treat those that are said to be something in distinct ways but also try to give
accounts of them—for example, not only that justice and courage are said
to be good in one way, while what conduces to a good state and what con-
5   duces to health are said to be so in a distinct one, but also that the former
are said to be such by being themselves of a certain sort, while the latter are
said to be such by being productive of something, and not by being themselves of a certain sort. And in like manner in the other cases.

  Whether the ways in which something is said to be something are many
or one in form is something one must get a theoretical grasp on by means
of the following:

  First, look at the contrary to see whether it is said of things in many ways
10   and if they disagree either in form or in name. For sometimes their distinctness is immediately visible in their very names—for example, to sharp
in sound dull is contrary, while in a body blunt is. It is clear, then, that what
is contrary to sharp is said of things in many ways. But if that is so, sharp is
15   too; for in each of these cases a distinct thing will be what is contrary. For
the same sharp will not be contrary to blunt and dull; yet sharp is contrary
to each. Again, to dull in sound sharp is contrary, but in a body round is,
so that dull is said of things in many ways, since its contrary is too. And
similarly to noble in the case of an animal ugly is the contrary, while in the
20   case of a house ramshackle is, so that noble is homonymous.⁶⁴

  In some cases there is no disagreement whatever in the names, but in
the form, the difference in them is immediately clear—for example, in the
25   case of bright and dark. For a voiced sound is said to be bright or dark, and
similarly a color.⁶⁵ In names, these do not disagree at all, but in the form the
difference in them is immediately clear; for a color and a voiced sound are
not said to be bright in the same way. This is also clear through perception;
for the same perceptual capacity perceives things that are the same in form,
30   but we do not discern bright in the case of a voiced sound and of a color by

the same perceptual capacity, rather we perceive the latter by sight and the former by hearing. It is the same way with sharp and dull in tastes and in bodies: we discern the latter by touch, the former by taste. For these too do not disagree in name, neither in the case of themselves nor in the case of their contraries; for in fact dull is what is contrary to each.   35

Further, see whether there is something that is contrary to one, while to the other there is simply nothing—for example, to the pleasure that derives from drinking the pain that derives from being thirsty is contrary, while to the pleasure that derives from getting a theoretical grasp on the fact that the diagonal is incommensurable with the side nothing is contrary. So things are said to be a pleasure in many ways. And hating is contrary to   106^{b}1 loving in thought, while to loving as bodily activity nothing is.[66] It is clear, then, that loving is homonymous.

Further, in the case of intermediates, see whether there is something intermediate to one [pair of contraries] but nothing to the other, or if there is something in both cases, but not the same thing—for example, between   5 bright and dark in color, there is gray, but in sound there is none, unless it is husky, as some people say that the husky voice is intermediate. So bright is homonymous, and similarly dark.

Further, see whether there are several intermediates for one pair but one for the other, as in the case of bright and dark; for in the case of colors   10 the intermediates are many, while in the case of voiced sounds there is one, husky.

Further, look at the contradictory opposite to see whether it is said of things in many ways; for if it is said of things in many ways, what is opposite to it will also be said of things in many ways. For example, not   15 seeing is said of things in many ways, one of which is not having sight and the other not activating sight. But if not seeing is said of things in many ways, then seeing must be too; for to each not seeing something is opposed: having sight to not having it, and activating sight to not activating it.   20

Further, look at things said by way of privation and having; for if one of these is said of things in many ways, the remaining one is too.[67] For example, if having perception is said of things in many ways, as soul and also as body, lacking perception will also be said in many ways, as soul and also as body. And that it is by way of privation and having that the things   25 just mentioned are opposed is clear, since it is natural for animals to have each of the two sorts of perception both as soul and as body.

Further, one must look at the inflections. For if justly is said of things in many ways, just will be said of things in many ways too; for there is a just   30 corresponding to each justly. For example, if justly is said of both judging in accord with one's own consideration and judging as one should, it is

similar too with just.[68] In like manner, if conduces to health is said of things
in many ways, then conducively to health will be said in many ways too.
For example, if what conduces to health is productive of, protects, or is a
35   sign of health, then conducively to health will be productively, protectively,
or by way of being a sign of it. And similarly in other cases, when something is itself said of things in many ways, an inflection derived from it will
107^a1   also be said of things in many ways, and if the inflection is, so is it itself.

Look too at the kinds of predication of the name to see whether these
are the same in all cases; for if they are not the same, it is clear that the
5   name mentioned is homonymous. For example, the good in foods is what
is productive of pleasure, in medicine, what is productive of health, while
in the case of the soul, it is being of a certain sort (for example, temperate,
courageous, or just), and similarly in the case of a human being. Sometimes it is a time—for example, what is opportune (for what is opportune
10   is said to be good). Often, it is a quantity—for example, in the case of the
moderate amount (for the moderate amount is also said to be good), so
that good is homonymous.

In like manner, bright is a color in the case of a body, but in the case of
a voiced sound it is what is easy to hear. Sharp is quite similar; for in like
manner, it is not said in the same way of things in all cases; for it is the rapid
15   sound that is sharp (as those who do arithmetical harmonics say), but it is
the angle less than a right one that is sharp [acute], or a knife with a sharp-
angled edge.[69]

Look too at the kinds of things that fall under the same name to see
whether they are distinct and not one subordinate to another. For example,
donkey: both the animal and the implement; for the account that corres-
20   ponds to the name is distinct for these; for the one will be said of things as
animal of a certain sort, the other as implement of a certain sort.[70] But if the
kinds are one subordinate to another, it is not necessary for the accounts
to be distinct. For example, of raven both animal and bird are kinds. When
we say that a raven is a bird, then, we also say that it is a certain sort of
25   animal, so that both kinds are predicated of it. Similarly, when we say that
a raven is a flying two-footed animal, we say that it is a bird. In this way
too, then, both kinds are predicated of the raven. But in the case of kinds
not subordinate one to another, this does not happen; for when we say that
something is an implement, we do not say that it is an animal; nor, when
30   we say that it is an animal, do we say that it is an implement.

Look not only at the proposed thing to see whether the kinds are distinct
and not one subordinate to another, but also its contrary; for if its contrary
35   is said of things in many ways, it is clear that the proposed thing is too.

It is also useful in the case of a definition to look to see what comes
about when it is of a composite—for example, of bright body or bright

16

sound; for if what is special is subtracted, the same account must remain. But this does not happen in the case of homonyms—for example, in the case of the ones just mentioned; for the one is body having such-and-such color, and the other is sound that is easy to hear. When we sub-   107^{b}1
tract body and sound, then, what remains in each is not the same. But it certainly should have been, if indeed the white said in each case was synonymous.[71]   5

But often something homonymous follows along unnoticed in the accounts themselves. That is why one must in fact look at the accounts too. For example, if someone says that what is a sign of and productive of health is what is in moderation, one must not give up but rather must look to see what in each case he has meant by "what is in moderation"—for example, if the one is of such a quantity as to produce health and the other is such as   10
to signify of what sort the state is.

Further, one must look to see whether they are not comparable with respect to more or equally—for example, a bright sound and a bright cloak, or a sharp taste and a sharp sound; for these are not said to be equally bright or equally sharp, nor is one said to be more so than the other, so that   15
bright and sharp are homonymous. For all synonymous things are comparable; for either they will be said to be equally such, or one more so than the other.

Since the differences of kinds that are distinct and not one subordinate to another are also distinct in form, for example, of animal and of scientific knowledge (for the differences of these are distinct), look to see whether   20
the things falling under the same name are differences of kinds that are distinct and not one subordinate to another—for example, sharp [said] of a voiced sound and of a body; for one voiced sound is differentiated from another by sharpness, and similarly one body from another. So sharp is homonymous; for these sharpnesses are differences of kinds that are distinct and not one subordinate to another.   25

Again, see whether the things falling under the same name have themselves distinct differences—for example, those of color in the case of bodies and in pieces of music; for the differences of color in the case of bodies are dilating and contracting of sight, while in the case of pieces of music, the difference are not the same.[72] So color is homonymous; for the same things   30
have the same differences.

Further, since the form is not a difference of anything, look at the things falling under the same name to see whether one is a form and the other a difference—for example, bright in the case of bodies is a form of color,   35
while in the case of sounds it is a difference; for one sound is differentiated from another by being bright.

17

1.16

(3) Finding differences

One must investigate the many ways [in which one thing may be said of another], then, by means of these and the like [procedures].

108ᵃ1   As for differences, one must look at those within the same kinds in relation to each other, for example, in what respect justice differs from courage, or practical wisdom from temperance (for all these are in the same kind), and in those from one kind in relation to another, if they are not too very far apart (for example, in what respect perception differs from scientific knowledge); for in the case of things that are very far apart, the differences
5   are immediately clear.⁷³

1.17

(4) Seeing similarities

As for similarity, one must first look at it in the case of things in distinct kinds, on the supposition that as one is to one, so the other is to the other (for example, as scientific knowledge is to the scientifically knowable, so perception is to the perceptible), and that as one thing is in one, so another
10   is in another (for example, as sight is in the eye, so understanding is in the soul, or as calm is in the sea, so stillness is in the air).⁷⁴ We must train ourselves above all on things that are very far apart; for in the case of the rest, we will more easily be able to see the points of similarity. And one must also look at things in the same kind to judge whether anything that is the
15   same belongs to all of them—for example, to human, horse, and dog; for to the extent that the same something belongs to all of them, to that extent they are alike.

1.18

Usefulness of the last three instruments

It is useful, on the one hand, to have looked at how many ways something is said of things with an eye to perspicuousness (for someone would better know what he is positing, if it had been made evident in how many
20   ways it is said of things) and to making deductions that are related to the thing at issue itself and not to a name; for when it is unclear in how many ways something is said of things, it is possible that the answerer and the

questioner are not directing their thought to the same thing. But when it has been made evident in how many ways it is said of things, and to which of them the answerer is directing his thought in positing it, the questioner would appear ridiculous, if he did not make his argument about this. It is also useful with an eye to not getting trapped by a fallacy and to trapping others by a fallacy. For if we know in how many ways something is said of things, we will not be trapped by a fallacy ourselves, but rather will know if the questioner did not produce his argument in relation to the same thing [as we answered about]. And when we ourselves are questioning, we will be able to trap others by a fallacy, if the answerer should happen not to know in how many ways something is said of things. This is not possible in every case, but only when some of the things said in many ways are true and others false. This mode [of argument], however, is not proper to dialectic, which is why dialecticians must altogether avoid this sort of thing, arguing dialectically regarding a name, unless one is otherwise wholly unable to argue dialectically about the proposed thing.

Finding differences, on the other hand, is useful both with an eye to deductions about same and distinct and to knowing what each given thing is. That it is useful with an eye to deductions about same and distinct is clear (for when we have found any difference whatever between the things proposed, we will already have proved that they are not the same); and it is useful in relation to knowing what something is, because we usually separate the special account of the substance of each thing by the differences that are proper to it.[75]

Getting a theoretical grasp on similarity is useful in relation to inductive arguments, deductions from a hypothesis, and giving definitions:

It is useful in relation to inductive arguments, because it is by induction from particulars, in the case of their similarity, that we claim we have a right to bring in the universal; for it is not easy to do an induction if we do not know the points of similarity.

It is useful in relation to deductions from a hypothesis, because it is an acceptable belief that as it is in the case of one of a number of like things, so it is in the case of the rest. So, whichever of these we may be well equipped to argue dialectically about, we will obtain an agreement beforehand that however things stand in their case, so they also stand with the proposed thing. And when we have proved the former, we will also have proved what was proposed on the basis of a hypothesis; for it was by hypothesizing that however things stand in the case of these, so they also stand with the proposed thing, that we produced our demonstration.

It is useful in relation to giving definitions, because if we can see what is the same in each case, we will not be puzzled as to what kind the proposed thing falls into when we are defining it; for of what is common, what is predicated in the what-it-is would most likely be the kind.[76] In the same way, getting a theoretical grasp on the similarity in things that are very far apart is also useful in relation to definitions—for example, that a calm in the sea and a stillness in the air are the same (for each is a quietness), or a point in a line and a unit in a number (for each is a starting-point).[77] So, if we assign what is common to all of them as the kind, we will not seem to be defining in an irrelevant way. And, in fact, those who define things are pretty much accustomed to giving definitions in this way; for they say that the unit is the starting-point of number and that the point is the starting-point of line.[78] It is clear, then, that they place them in the kind that is common to both.

These, then, are the instruments through which deductions are made. The topics in relation to which the ones mentioned are useful are as follows.[79]

2: COINCIDENTS

2.1

Issues concerning problems

Among problems, some are universal, others particular.[80] Examples of universal ones: every pleasure is good, no pleasure is good. Examples of particular ones: some pleasure is good, some pleasure is not good. And the procedures for universally establishing and disestablishing are common to both kinds of problems; for when we have proved that F belongs to all, we will also have proved that it belongs to a particular one; and similarly, if we prove that F does not belong to any, we will also have proved that it does not belong to all.[81] First, then, we must speak about the procedures for universally disestablishing, because such procedures are common both to universal and to particular problems, and because people more often introduce theses consisting in F belonging than in F not belonging, while those who are arguing dialectically with them seek to disestablish this.[82]

It is very difficult, however, to convert a name deriving from a coincident that is proper to something; for belonging in some way but not universally is possible only in the case of coincidents.[83] For when it derives from a definition, a special affection, or a kind, it is necessarily convertible. For example, if it belongs to something to be a two-footed terrestrial animal, it will be true by conversion to say that it is a two-footed terrestrial animal.[84] Similarly, if the name derives from a kind; for if being animal belongs to something, then it is an animal. And the same things are so in the case of a special affection; for if being receptive of grammar belongs to something, it will be receptive of grammar. For none of these admits of partly belonging or not belonging, but must unconditionally belong or not belong. In the case of coincidents, however, there is nothing to prevent one—for example, whiteness or justice—from partly belonging, and so it is not enough to prove that whiteness or justice belongs to someone in order to prove that he is white or just; for it is open to dispute whether he is [only] partly white or partly just. So in the case of coincidents, conversion is not necessarily valid.

We must also determine the errors that occur in problems, because these are twofold, caused either by false statement or by violation of the established style of speech; for those who make false statements, and say that F belongs to something it does not belong to, commit error; while those who call things by the names of other things—for example, calling a plane-tree "human"—violate the established use of names.

2.2

Various topics

One topic is looking to see whether one's opponent has assigned as a coincident something that belongs in some other way.[85] This error is most often
committed in regard to kinds—for example, if someone were to say that
to be a color is a coincident of white; for being a color is not a coincident
of white, but rather the kind of it is color. It is possible, of course, for an
opponent in fact to determine his use of the name in what he posits—for
example, saying that being a virtue is a coincident of justice. But often, and
without such a determination, it is immediately clear that he has assigned
the kind as a coincident—for example, if someone were to say that whiteness is colored or that walking is in movement. For a predicate of the kind
is never said paronymously of the form, but always the kinds are predicated
synonymously of the forms; for the forms take on both the name and the
account of their kinds.[86] A person, then, who says that white is colored has
not assigned colored as its kind, since he has spoken paronymously, nor as
a special affection, nor as a definition; for the definition and special affection of a thing belong to nothing else, while many other things are also
colored—for example, a piece of wood, a human, a horse. It is clear, then,
that he assigns colored as a coincident.

Another topic is to examine cases where F has been said to belong to all
or to none. Look at them form by form and not in their unlimited number;
for then the inquiry will proceed in a more methodical way and in fewer
steps. And one must look at, and start with, the primary ones, and then
proceed step by step toward the indivisible ones.[87] For example, if a person has said that of opposites the science is the same, one must look to see
whether of relatives, of contraries, of privation and having, and of things
said by way of contradiction the science is the same. And if the situation is
not yet evident at this level, one must again divide these until one comes to
the indivisible ones, and see, for example, whether it be so of just and unjust
things, the double and the half, blindness and sight, or being and not being.
For if in any case it is proved that the science is not the same, we will have
done away with the problem. One proceeds in the same way if a predicate
belongs in no case. This topic is convertible for purposes of establishing
and disestablishing. For if, when we have introduced a division, F appears
to belong in all or in many cases, one must demand that the opponent posit
the universal, or else bring an objection and show in what case it is not so;
for if he does neither of these, not positing it will make him appear absurd.[88]

Another topic is to produce accounts both of a coincident and what it is
a coincident of, either of both, each taken singly, or else of one of them, and

then look to see whether anything untrue in these accounts has been assumed as true. For example, if the problem is whether it is possible to do injustice to a god, ask: "What is doing injustice?" For if it is to harm voluntarily, it is clear that it is not possible for a god to suffer injustice; for it is not possible for a god to be harmed. And if it is whether the excellent person is envious, ask: "What is the envious person and what is envy?" And if envy is pain at the apparent doing well of some decent person, it is clear that the excellent person is not envious; for then he would be base.[89] And if it is whether the indignant person is envious, ask: "What is each of them?" For thus it will be immediately evident whether what was stated is true or false. For example, if the envious person is the one who is pained at good people's doing well, and the indignant person is the one who is pained at bad people's doing well, it is clear that the indignant person would not be envious. One must also replace the names in the accounts with their accounts, and not stop until one comes to one that is known; for often, though the whole account has been assigned, what is being inquired about is not yet clear, while if an account is stated of one of the names in the account, it becomes clear immediately.

Further, one must make the problem into a premise for oneself and then bring an objection; for an objection will serve as an attack against the thesis.[90] This topic is pretty much the same as the topic that one must look into cases where F is said to belong in all or in none of something, but it differs in its mode.[91]

Further, one must determine what sorts of things must be called what ordinary people call them and what sorts must not; for this is useful both for establishing and for disestablishing something. For example, one must say that the things at issue must be named using the names as ordinary people do, but that when we ask which of the things at issue are of such-and-such a sort or not of such-and-such a sort, one must no longer turn one's attention to ordinary people. For example, one must say that to conduce to health is to be productive of health, as ordinary people do, but when it comes to whether the proposed thing is productive of health or not, one must no longer name it as ordinary people do, but as the doctor does.

2.3

Topics relating to things said in many ways

Further, if F is said of things in many ways, and it has been proposed that it belongs or that it does not belong to something, one must prove it to do so or not to do so in one of the ways, if one cannot prove it in both.[92] This [topic] must be used in cases that escape notice; for if it does not escape

23

notice that F is said of things in many ways, the opponent will object that the very one he raised a puzzle about has not been dialectically argued against but rather the other one. This topic is convertible both for purposes of establishing and for purposes of disestablishing. For if we wish to establish, we will prove that in one way F belongs, if we cannot prove it belongs in both; while if we are disestablishing, we will prove that in one way F does not belong, if we cannot prove it does not belong in both.

Except, in disestablishing there is no need to argue dialectically from something that is agreed to, either when F is said to belong to all or to none; for if we prove that F does not belong to something (whatever it is), we will have done away with its belonging to all. Similarly, if we prove that F belongs to one thing, we will do away with its belonging to none. If, however, we are establishing, we must obtain an agreement beforehand that if F belongs to something (whatever it is), it belongs to all, provided this claim is a persuasive one.[93] For it is not enough for purposes of proving that it belongs to all to argue dialectically that it belongs to one—for example, if the human soul is immortal, all soul is immortal. So an agreement must be obtained beforehand that if some soul (whatever it is) is immortal, all soul is immortal. This is not to be done in every case, but only when we are not well equipped to state a single argument that applies to all cases in common, as the geometer can that the triangle has its angles equal to two right angles.

But were it not to escape notice that F is said of things in many ways, distinguish in how many ways it is said, both when disestablishing and when establishing.[94] For example, if what must be done is what is advantageous or what is noble, one must try to establish or to disestablish both concerning the proposed thing—for example, proving that it is both noble and advantageous, or that it is neither noble nor advantageous. But if it is not possible to prove both, one must prove one, and add a sign that while in one way it is so, in the other it is not so. The same argument also applies when the number of ways distinguished is more than two.

Again, there are those F's that are said of things in many ways, not homonymously, but in some other way. For example, the science of many things is one, in the way one thing is the end, another what furthers the end—for example, medicine is the science both of producing health and of dieting; or in the way that both are ends, as the science of contraries is said to be the same (for one is no more an end than the other); or intrinsically and coincidentally—for example, the triangle has its angles equal to two right angles intrinsically, but the equilateral has them so coincidentally: for it is coincidental to the equilateral to be a triangle, and it is by this that we know that it has angles equal to two right angles.[95] If, then, it is not possible in any of these ways for the science of many things to be the same, it is clear that this is wholly impossible; or, if it is possible in some way, it is clear that it is possible. One must distinguish as many ways as are useful. For example, if we wish to establish something, we must put forward the sorts in which it is possible, and distinguish only those that are useful for establishing some- thing. But if we wish to disestablish it, we must do so with those in which it is impossible, and leave the rest aside. One must also do this when the number of ways in which F is said of things escapes notice. 30

Also, that this is, or is not, of [or for] that must be established on the basis of the same topics—for example, that this science is of that, either as an end or as what furthers the end, as what is coincidental, or, again, as 35 what is not of something in any of these ways. And the same argument also applies concerning appetites and whatever else is said to be of [or for] sev- eral things; for an appetite that is for a certain thing may be for it as an end (for example, for health), or as what furthers the end (for example, for tak- **111ᵃ1** ing medicine), or as what is coincidental, as in the case of wine, the lover of sweet things has an appetite for it not because it is wine but because it is sweet. For he has an appetite intrinsically for the sweet, but coincidentally for the wine; for if it is dry, he no longer has an appetite for it. Hence his 5 appetite for it is coincidental.

This topic is useful in the case of relatives; for cases of this sort are pretty much cases of relatives.

2.4

Additional topics

Further, there is substituting for a name one that is better known—for example, substituting "perspicuous" in a supposition for "exact," and "med- dlesome person" for "busybody"; for the thesis becomes easier to attack 10 when what is stated is better known. This topic is also common both to establishing and to disestablishing.

In order to prove that contraries belong to the same thing, look at its kind. For example, if one wishes to prove that there is correctness and error 15 with regard to perception, and to perceive is to discern, and discerning can be done correctly or incorrectly, then there would be correctness and error with regard to perception too. In the present instance, the demonstration proceeds from the kind and is with regard to the form; for discerning is the kind of perceiving; for the one who perceives discerns in a way. But it may proceed in the contrary direction, from form to kind; for whatever belongs 20 to the form belongs also to the kind—for example, if there is a base and an excellent scientific knowledge, there is also a base and an excellent dispos- ition; for disposition is the kind of scientific knowledge.[96]

The first topic is false for purposes of establishing something, but the
second is true. For it is not necessary for whatever belongs to the kind to
belong also to the form; for animal is winged and two-footed, but human
is not. But whatever belongs to the form does necessarily belong also to the
kind; for if human is excellent, animal is excellent too. On the other hand,
for purposes of disestablishing something, the first topic is true, but the
second is false; for all that do not belong to the kind do not belong to the
form either, but those that do not belong to the form do not necessarily not
belong to the kind.

It is necessary for those things of which the kind is predicated to have
one of its forms predicated of them too, and those things that are possessed of the kind or are paronymously said to be what they are from the
kind must also be possessed of one of its forms or be paronymously said
to be what they are from one of its forms (for example, if scientific knowledge is predicated of something, then grammatical or musical knowledge,
or knowledge of one of the other sciences, will also be predicated of it;
and if anyone possesses scientific knowledge or is paronymously said to
be what he is from scientific knowledge, he will also possess grammatical
or musical knowledge or knowledge of one of the other sciences, or will
be paronymously said to be what he is from one of them—for example,
a grammarian or a musician).⁹⁷ And since that is so, if a thesis is stated
that derives something in any way from a kind (for example, that soul is
moved), look to see whether it is possible for soul to be moved with any of
the forms of movement—for example, whether it can grow, pass away, or
come to be, or move with any of the other forms of movement; for if it is
moved with none of them, it is clear that it is not moved at all.⁹⁸ This topic
is common for the purposes of both uses—for those of establishing and
for those of disestablishing; for if the soul moves with one of the forms of
movement, it is clear that it does move, but if it moves with none of these
forms, it is clear that it does not move.

If one is not well equipped to attack a thesis, look at it on the basis of the
definitions, whether really of the thing proposed or seeming to be so, and,
if one is not enough, draw on several. For it will be easier to attack once
definitions have been given; for against defined things attack is easier.⁹⁹

In the case of the thing proposed, look to see what if it is so, then the
one proposed is so, or what thing is of necessity so, if the thing proposed
is so. If one wishes to establish it, look to see what if it is so, then the one
proposed will be so (for if the former is proved to be so, the one proposed
will also have been proved to be so).¹⁰⁰ On the other hand, if one wishes
to disestablish it, look to see what is so if the thing proposed is so; for if
we prove that what follows from the thing proposed is not so, we will have
done away with the one proposed.¹⁰¹

Further, look at time to see whether there is any discordance anywhere— for example, if the opponent has said that what is nourished of necessity grows; for animals are nourished all the time, but are not growing all the time. Similarly, if he has said that scientifically knowing is remembering; for the latter is of time past, but the former is also of the present and the future. For we are said to scientifically know present things and future ones (for example, that there will be an eclipse), but it is impossible to remember anything other than what is past.

2.5

A sophistical topic and others

Further there is the sophistical topic, which consists in leading the discussion into the sort of thing against which we are well equipped with lines of attack.[102] Sometimes it will be a necessity, sometimes an apparent necessity, sometimes neither an apparent necessity nor a necessity.[103]

It is a necessity when the answerer has refused to grant one of the things made use of in relation to the thesis, and the questioner makes his arguments against it, and it happens to be of the sort against which he is well equipped with lines of attack.[104] Similarly, it is also a necessity when the questioner, producing an abduction against something due to what is proposed, tries to do away with it; for when it has been done away with, what is proposed is done away with too.[105] It is an apparent necessity, when what the arguments come to proceed against appears to be useful and proper to the thesis, without being so, either when the one who is standing up to the argument has refused to grant it, or when the questioner, from an acceptable abduction based on the thesis, has proceeded with refuting it. The remaining case is when what the arguments come to proceed against is neither a necessity nor an apparent necessity, but, contrary to what should be so, the answerer happens to be refuted on a side issue. One must watch out for the last mode of those stated; for it seems to be wholly far away from and foreign to the craft of dialectic.[106] That is why too the answerer must not lose his temper, but grant things that are not useful against his thesis, but adding a sign when he does not believe one, though he grants it. For questioners for the most part find themselves more puzzled if, when all premises of this sort have been granted to them, they do not reach a conclusion.

Further, each time a person says anything whatever he in a way says many things, since each thing he says has many necessary consequences—for example, the person who has said that something is a human has also said that it is an animal, animate, two-footed, and receptive of understanding and scientific knowledge, so that by doing away with any one of these consequences whatever, the thing said initially is also done away with. But one must watch out for making a substitution of a more difficult premise; for sometimes a consequence is easier to do away with, but sometimes the thing proposed itself is.

2.6

Additional topics

As for things to which of necessity only either F or G belongs (for example, to a human either disease or health), if we are well equipped to argue dialectically against one of the two belonging or not belonging, we will be well equipped against the remaining one as well. And this is convertible for both establishing and disestablishing; for if we have proved that one belongs, we will have proved that the remaining one does not belong; but if we prove that the one does not belong, we will have proved that the remaining one does belong. It is clear, then, that this topic is useful for both.

Further, there is attacking by translating a name in accord with its [literal] account, as more fitting to take than the established [equivalent] name—for example, taking "good souled" (*eupsuchos*) not as "courageous" (*andreios*), as now established, but as "having good in one's soul" (*ton eu tên psuchên echonta*), just as "optimistic" (*euelpis*) too is "the one hoping for good things" (*ton agatha elpizonta*).[107] Similarly, *eudaimôn* ("happy") may be taken as "the one whose *daimôn* is excellent"— as Xenocrates calls "happy" the one who has an excellent soul; for the soul is each person's *daimôn*.[108]

Since some things at issue are so of necessity, some for the most part, and some however luck may have it, if what is so of necessity is posited as being so for the most part, or what is so for the most part as being so of necessity (either it itself or what is its contrary for the most part), it always provides a topic for the purposes of attack. For if what is so of necessity is posited as being so for the most part, it is clear that the answerer says that F does not belong to all, when it does belong to all, so that he was in error. As he is too if he has stated that what is said to be so for the most part is so of necessity; for then he has stated that it belongs to all, when it does not belong to all. Similarly, if he has stated that the contrary of what is so for the most part is so of necessity; for the contrary of what is so for the most part is always said of things comparatively rarely—for example, if human beings are for the most part base, they are good comparatively rarely. So he was in still greater error, if he has stated that they are of necessity good.

It is the same way too if he has stated that what is however luck may have it is so of necessity or for the most part; for what is however luck may have it is so neither of necessity nor for the most part. And even if the opponent has made his statement without distinguishing whether something holds for the most part or of necessity, if in fact the thing at issue is so for the most part, it is possible to argue dialectically as if he had stated it to be so of necessity. For example, if he has stated, without drawing a distinction, that disinherited people are bad, one may argue dialectically as if he had stated it to be so of necessity.

Further, also look to see whether the opponent has posited something as a coincident of itself, on the supposition that it is a distinct thing because it has a distinct name, as Prodicus used to divide pleasures into joy, delight, and merriment; for all these are names of the same thing: pleasure.[109] If, then, someone says that enjoying is a coincident of being merry, he would be saying that it is a coincident of itself.

2.7

Contraries

Since contraries can be combined with each other in six ways, and four of these combinations produce contrariety, one must get hold of contraries in such a way as would be useful both for doing away with things and for establishing them. In any case, it is clear that there are six ways of combining them. For each of the contrary predicates will be combined with each of the contrary subjects, and this in two ways—for example, doing good to friends and doing evil to enemies, or conversely doing evil to friends and doing good to enemies.[110] Or both predicates with one subject, and this also in two ways—for example, doing good to friends and doing evil to friends, or doing good to enemies and doing evil to enemies. Or one predicate with both subjects, and this also in two ways—for example, doing good to friends and doing good to enemies, or doing evil to friends and doing evil to enemies.

The first two, then, of the stated combinations do not produce contrariety. For doing good to friends is not contrary to doing evil to enemies; for both are worthy of choice and belong to the same character. Nor is doing evil to friends contrary to doing good to enemies; for in fact both are worthy of avoidance and belong to the same character. And one thing worthy of avoidance does not seem to be contrary to another, unless the one is said to be so with respect to an excess and the other with respect to a deficiency; for excess seems to be among the things worthy of avoidance as, likewise, does deficiency. The remaining four, however, all produce contrariety. For doing good to friends is contrary to doing evil to friends; for it stems from the contrary character, and the one is worthy of choice, the other of avoidance. It is the same way too in the case of the others; for in each pair, one is worthy of choice, the other of avoidance, and the one belongs to a decent character, the other to a base one.

It is clear, then, from what has been said that the same thing has more than one contrary; for to doing good to friends both doing good to enemies and doing evil to friends are contraries. Similarly, if we look at the others in the same way, it will be evident that each has two contraries. Hence we must take whichever of the two contraries would be useful against the thesis proposed.

Further, if a coincident of a thing has a contrary, look to see whether it belongs to the precise thing to which the coincident has been said to belong; for if the former belongs, the latter could not belong; for it is impossible for two contraries to belong to the same thing at the same time.

Or, if something has been said of something, look to see whether it is such that, if true, contraries must belong to the same thing—for example, if the opponent has said that the Forms are in us; for then it will follow that they are both moving and resting, and further, both perceptible and intelligible.[111] For those who posit the Forms believe that those Forms are at rest and intelligible.[112] But if they are in us, it is impossible for them to be unmoved; for when we move, necessarily everything that is in us moves along with us. And it is clear that they are also perceptible, if indeed they are in us; for it is by means of the perceptual capacity of sight that we know the shape present in each thing.[113]

Again, if a coincident is proposed that has a contrary, look to see whether what is receptive of the contrary is precisely the thing that is also receptive of the coincident; for it is the same thing that is receptive of contraries.[114] For example, if the opponent has said that hatred follows anger, then hatred would be in the spirited part; for that is where anger is.[115] Look to see, then, if its contrary—loving—is also in the spirited part; for if it is not, but is in the appetitive part, hatred could not follow anger. Similarly, if he has said that the appetitive part is ignorant; for it would be receptive of scientific knowledge as well, if indeed it were also receptive of ignorance. But this is precisely what he does not believe, that the appetitive part is receptive of scientific knowledge.

When disestablishing, then, as was said, this must be used.[116] But when establishing that the coincident belongs this topic is not useful—although it is useful for establishing that it is possible for something to belong. For having proved that the thing is not receptive of the contrary, we will have proved that the coincident neither belongs nor can possibly belong. On the other hand, if we prove that the contrary belongs, or that the thing is receptive of the contrary, we will not yet have proved that the coincident also belongs, but rather our proof will have gone only this far: that it is possible that it belongs.

2.8

The four sorts of opposition

Since opposites are of four sorts, in the case of contradictory ones, look to   15
see whether [arguments can be] based on reversing their sequence, both
when doing away with things and when establishing them, obtaining it by
induction.[117] For example, if what is human is animal, what is not animal is
not human. It is the same way in the other cases too. For there their sequence
is reversed; for animal follows from human, but not-animal does not follow   20
from not-human, but rather the reverse, not-human from not-animal. One
must claim this, then, to be so in all cases—for example, if the noble is pleasant, the not pleasant is also not noble, and if the latter is not so, the former
is not so either. Similarly, if the not pleasant is not noble, then the noble is
pleasant. Clearly, then, reversing the sequence in the case of contradictories   25
is convertible with an eye to both [establishing and disestablishing].

In the case of contraries, look to see whether contrary follows from contrary, either in the same sequence or in reverse, both when doing away
with things and when establishing them, obtaining these too by induction,
so far as is useful.[118] The sequence is the same in the case, for example, of   30
courage and cowardice; for virtue follows along with the one and vice the
other, and being worthy of choice follows the one and being worthy of
avoidance the other. In the latter case again, the sequence is the same; for to
being worthy of choice being worthy of avoidance is the contrary. It is the
same too in the other cases. On the other hand, the sequence is reversed
in such cases as this: health follows the good state, but disease does not   35
follow the bad one, but rather the bad one follows disease. It is clear, then,
that in these cases the sequence is reversed. Reversal is rare in the case of   114^{a}1
contraries; in most of them, the sequence is the same. If, then, the sequence
of one contrary and that of the other is neither the same nor reversed, it is
clear that neither, in the case of the things stated, does the sequence of one
follow along with that of the other. But if in the case of the contraries they
do so, then in the case of the things stated as well, it is necessary for that of   5
one to follow along with that of the other.

One must look at cases of privation and having in the same way as contraries, except that in the case of privations there is no reverse. Instead, the

sequences are of necessity always in the same direction, just as perception
10   follows along with sight, but non-perception follows along with blindness.
For perception is opposed to non-perception as having is to privation; for
one of them is a having, and the other a privation.

One must treat cases of relatives in the same way as cases of having
and privation[119]; for the sequence of these is in the same direction too.
For example, if triple is a multiple, one third is a fraction; for something
15   is said to be a triple relative to a third, and a multiple relative to a fraction.
Again, if scientific knowledge is supposition, the scientifically knowable
is also supposable; and if sight is a perceptual capacity, what is visible is
also perceptible. (Objection: There is no necessity, in the case of rela-
20   tives, for the sequence to occur in the way stated; for the perceptible is
scientifically knowable, but perception is not scientific knowledge. And
yet the objection does not seem to be true; for many people deny that
there is scientific knowledge of perceptible things.[120]) Further, the [topic]
mentioned is no less useful for the contrary—for example, that the perceptible is not scientifically knowable; for perception is not scientific
25   knowledge either.

2.9

Coordinates and inflections

Again, look at the case of the coordinates and the inflections, both when
doing away with things and when establishing them. Things such as the
following, for example, are said to be coordinates: just things and the just
person are coordinates of justice, and courageous things and the courageous person are coordinates of courage. Similarly, the things that produce
something or that protect it are coordinates of what they produce or pro-
30   tect—for example, things conducive to health are coordinates of health,
and things conducive to the good state are coordinates of the good state.
And the same way in the case of the others. Things of this sort, then, are
usually said to be coordinates, while things said to be inflections are, for
example, justly, courageously, and healthily, and such as are said of things
35   in that way. But inflections also seem to be coordinates—for example,
justly seems to be a coordinate of justice, and courageously of courage.
Indeed, all things said in the same column are coordinates—for example,
justice, just person, just thing, justly.[121] Hence it is clear that when any one
member, whatever sort it is, that belongs in the same column, is proved
to be good or praiseworthy, then all the rest also come to be proved so—
114^b1   for example, if justice is something praiseworthy, then a just person, a just

thing, and justly done are praiseworthy things. And things done justly will also be said to be done praiseworthily, by the same inflection deriving from praiseworthy as they are said to be justly done by the one deriving from justice. 5

Look at the contrary not only in the case of the very thing mentioned, but also in the case of its contrary. For example, argue that the good is not necessarily pleasant; for the bad is not necessarily painful either; or that if the latter is the case, so is the former. Also, if justice is scientific knowledge, injustice is also ignorance; and if doing something justly is doing it scientifically and experiencedly, doing it unjustly is doing it ignorantly and inexperiencedly. On the other hand, if the latter are not the case, neither are the former, as in the case of the one stated just now; for doing some- 10 thing unjustly would appear closer to doing it experiencedly than inexperi- encedly. This topic was stated previously in connection with the sequences of contraries; for all we are claiming now is that contrary follows along with contrary.¹²² 15

Further, both when doing away with things and when establishing, look at comings to be and passings away, and at what produces things and what destroys them. For those things whose comings to be are good are themselves good, and if they themselves are good, their comings to be are also, but if their comings to be are bad, they themselves are also bad. In the case of passings away, however, it is the reverse; for if the passings away are good, the things themselves are bad, but if the passings away are 20 bad, the things themselves are good. And the same argument applies to what produces things and what destroys them; for things produced by good things are themselves good, but things destroyed by good things are themselves bad.

2.10

Similarity

Again, look at similar things to see whether they hold in a similar way—for example, if one science is of several things, so is one belief; and if to have 25 sight is to see, to have hearing is also to hear. It is the same way in the case of other things too, both in the case of those that are similar and of those that seem so. This topic is useful for both [establishing and disestablish- ing]; for if something holds in the case of one of the similar things, it also holds of the other similar ones, while if it does not hold in the case of one, it does not hold in the case of the others either. Look to see too whether 30 the thing holds in a similar way in one case as it does in many, since in some cases there is a discordance. For example, if to scientifically know something is to be thinking of it, to scientifically know many things is also to be thinking of many things. But this is not true; for it is possible to scientifically know many things, but not to be thinking of them. If, then, this is not true, neither is the former, which says that in the case of one thing to scientifically know it is to be thinking of it.

Further, [argue] based on the more and less.[123] There are four topics of the more and less.[124] The first consists in looking to see whether more follows along with more—for example, if pleasure is a good, whether more pleasure is also more good, and if doing injustice is bad, whether doing more injustice is more bad. This topic is useful for both [establishing and disestablishing]; for if an increase in the coincident follows along with an increase in the underlying subject, as in the examples stated, it is clear that it coincides with it, while if it does not follow along, it does not coincide.[125] Get hold of this by induction. Another is when one F is said of two things. If F does not belong to the thing to which it is more likely to belong, it does not belong either to the thing to which it is less likely to belong; and if F belongs to the thing to which it is less likely to belong, it also belongs to the thing to which it is more likely to belong. Conversely, when two things (F and G) are said of one thing. If the one (F) that seems to belong to it more does not belong, neither does the one (G) that seems to belong to it less, and if G does belong, F does too. Further, when two things (F and G) are said of two things. If the one (F) that seems to belong more to the one thing does not belong, nor does the remaining one (G) belong to the remaining thing; and if the one that seems to belong less (G) to the one thing does belong, the remaining one (F) also belongs to the remaining thing.

Further, on the basis of F belonging or seeming to belong in a similar degree, [argue] in three ways, as in the case of the more, in the case of the last three topics mentioned. For if F belongs, or seems to belong, in a similar degree to two things, if it does not belong to the one thing, neither does it belong to the remaining thing. Or, if two things (F and G) belong in a similar degree to the same thing, if F does not belong neither does the remaining one (G), while if F does belong, the remaining one (G) does too. It is the same way too if two things (F and G) are said in a similar degree of two things; for if F does not belong to the one, neither does the remaining one (G) belong to the remaining one, while if F does belong to the one, the remaining one (G) does belong to the remaining one.

2.11

Addition and unconditional versus conditional predications

On the basis of the more and less and of similarity, then, it is possible to   25
argue dialectically in these many ways.

Further, it is possible to do so on the basis of addition. If one thing added
to another makes it good or white, while the latter was not good or white
before, then what was added will be good or white—which is also precisely
the quality it makes the whole possess. Further, if a thing added to what
already possesses a quality makes it be possessed of more of that quality,   30
then the thing itself will also possess it. It is the same way in other cases too.
This topic is not useful in all cases, however, but rather in those in which
exceeding with respect to more is found to occur.[126] And this topic is not
convertible for the purposes of disestablishing. For if what is added does
not make the thing good, it is not yet clear whether it itself is not good; for   35
the addition of good to bad does not of necessity make the whole good, nor   115^b1
that of white to black.

Again, if F is said of things more and less, it also unconditionally belongs
to them; for things that are not good or white will not be said to be more or
less good or white; for a bad thing will never be said be more or less good   5
but rather more or less bad. This topic too is not convertible for the purposes of disestablishing; for many things that are not said of things more
and less do unconditionally belong to them; for someone is not said to be
more or less human, but he is not, because of this, not human at all.[127]   10

In the same way, also look at: in some respect, when, and where; for if
a thing is possible in some respect, it is also unconditionally possible. It is
the same way with when and where; for what is unconditionally impossible
is not possible either in some respect or at some place or time. (Objection:
There are people who are in some respect excellent by nature, for example,   15
generous or temperate, who are not unconditionally excellent by nature.
Similarly, it is possible for something that admits of passing away not to
pass away at a given time, but it is not possible for it unconditionally not to
pass away. In the same way too, it is advantageous in some places to follow
such-and-such a diet, for example, in pestilential places, but not unconditionally advantageous to follow it. Further, in certain places it is possible   20
for there to be one person, but it is not unconditionally possible for there
to be only one person. In the same way too, it is noble in some places to
sacrifice one's father, for example, among the Triballi, but it is not unconditionally noble.[128] Or this may signify a relation not to place but to persons;
for it makes no difference where they may be; for wherever they are it will
be noble for them, since they are Triballi.[129] Again, at certain times it is   25

advantageous to take medicine, for example, when one is sick, but it is not unconditionally so. Or this may signify a relation not to a certain time, but to being in a certain condition; for it makes no difference when he takes it, provided he is in that condition.) What is unconditionally so, however, is what, without any addition, one will say is noble or the contrary—for example, one will not say that it is noble to sacrifice one's father, but rather that for some people it is noble, but not therefore unconditionally noble, while, one will say, with no addition, that to honor the gods is noble; therefore, it is unconditionally noble. So whatever, with no addition whatever, seems to be noble or shameful of anything else of that sort, will be said to be unconditionally so.

3: COINCIDENTS AGAIN

3.1¹³⁰

Relative choiceworthiness (1)

As for which of two or more things is more choiceworthy or better, look at it on the basis of the following. First, determine that the investigation being made is not into things that are very far apart from each other, or exhibit great difference from each other (for no one raises any puzzles about whether happiness or wealth is more choiceworthy), but into things that are quite close, and about which we dispute as to which we must side with more, because we see no point of superiority of one relative to the other. Clearly, then, in cases of this sort, if one point of superiority can be proved, or more than one, our thought will entirely agree that this is the more choiceworthy, whichever of the two is superior.

First, then, what is longer lasting or more stable is more choiceworthy than what is less so. Also, what the practically wise person or the good man would choose more than other things; or what the correct law would; or people excellent in particular areas, when they make their choice insofar as they are such; or those with scientific knowledge in a given kind, either all of them or most of them—for example, in medicine, or in building, most or all doctors [or builders]; or, in general, what most people, or all of them, or all things would choose—for example, the good; for all things aim at the good.¹³¹ And one must lead the discussion toward whichever of these would be useful. And what is unconditionally better or more choice-worthy is what is in accord with the better science, but what is better or more choiceworthy for a certain thing is what is in accord with the science proper to it.¹³²

Next, what is precisely a this something is better or more choiceworthy than what is not in the kind—for example, justice than a just person; for the one is in the kind of the good, while the other is not, and the one is precisely good and the other is not.¹³³ For nothing is said to be precisely the kind that is not in the kind—for example, pale human is not precisely color. It is the same way in the other cases too.

Also, what is choiceworthy because of itself is more choiceworthy than what is choiceworthy because of something else—for example, being healthy than athletic training; for the former is choiceworthy because of itself, the latter because of something else. Also, what is intrinsically choiceworthy is more choiceworthy than what is coincidentally so—for example, that one's friends be just than that one's enemies be just. For the former is intrinsically choiceworthy, the latter coincidentally so; for we coincidentally choose our enemies to be just, in order that they do us no harm. This [topic] is the same as the one before it, with a difference in mode; for we choose that our friends be just because of itself, even if nothing will come to us at all, and even if they may be in India, while we choose that our enemies be so because of something else, that is, in order that they do us no harm.[134]

Also, the intrinsic cause of a good thing is more choiceworthy than its coincidental cause—for example, virtue than luck (for the former is intrinsically, and the latter coincidentally, a cause of good things), and so with anything else of this sort.[135] Similarly, in the case of the contrary; for what is intrinsically the cause of a bad thing is more to be avoided than what is so coincidentally—for example, vice than luck; for the former is intrinsically the cause, while luck is coincidentally so.[136]

Also, what is unconditionally good is more choiceworthy than what is good for a certain thing or person—for example, becoming healthy than having surgery; for the former is unconditionally good, the latter only for a certain person, the one who needs surgery. Also, what is good by nature is more choiceworthy than what is not good by nature—for example, justice than the just person; for the one is good by nature, while the other's good is something acquired. Also, what belongs to what is better and more estimable is more choiceworthy—for example, to a god than to a human, and to a soul than to a body.[137]

Also, what is special to the better is better than what is special to the worse—for example, to the god than to the human; for with respect to the common ones in both they do not differ at all from each other, but it is in what is special that the one is superior to the other.[138] Also, what resides in better things, prior ones, or more estimable ones is better—for example, health than strength or beauty; for health resides in moist things and dry ones, hot ones and cold ones, and (simply speaking) in all the primary constituents from which a living being is composed, while the others reside in posterior ones.[139] For strength resides in the sinews and bones, while beauty seems to be a sort of symmetry of the limbs.

Also, the end seems to be more choiceworthy than what furthers the end, and of two things that do so, the one that is closer to the end. Also, in general, what furthers the end of life is more choiceworthy that what furthers some other end—for example, what tends to further happiness than what tends to further practical wisdom. Also, what is possible is more choiceworthy than what is impossible.

Further, of two productive factors, the one whose end is better is more choiceworthy, while of a productive factor and an end, it is based on a proportion: when the superiority of one end over the other is greater than that of the latter over its own productive factor (for example, if happiness is more superior to health than health is to what conduces to health), then what is productive of happiness is superior to health. For what is produc- 30 tive of happiness is as superior to what conduces to health as happiness is to health. But it is assumed that health is less superior to what conduces to health; so what is productive of happiness is more superior to what con- duces to health than health is to what conduces to health. It is clear, then, that what is productive of happiness is more choiceworthy than health, 35 since its superiority to the same thing is greater.

Further, what is intrinsically more beautiful, more estimable, and more praiseworthy is more choiceworthy—for example, friendship than wealth, justice than strength; for the former are intrinsically estimable and praise- worthy, while the latter are not intrinsically so, but rather because of some- thing else. For no one honors wealth because of itself, but rather because of 117ᵃ1 something else, but friendship is honored intrinsically, even if nothing else will come to us from it.

3.2

Relative choiceworthiness (2)

Further, when two things are very similar to each other and we cannot see 5 any point of superiority in the one over the other, one must look at them from their consequences. For the one that is followed by the greater good is more choiceworthy; or, if the consequences are bad, the one that is fol- lowed by less evil is more choiceworthy; for, though both are choiceworthy, there is nothing to prevent some disagreeable consequence from following. 10 The investigation stemming from things that follow, however, is twofold; for what follows can be either prior or posterior—for example, for the per- son who learns, being ignorant is prior, being scientifically knowledgeable posterior. For the most part, the posterior consequence is better.[140] One must take, then, whichever of the consequences is useful [dialectically]. 15

Further, a greater number of goods is more choiceworthy than a smaller, either unconditionally or when the one is included in the other, that is, the smaller number in the greater.[141] (Objection: Unless perhaps one is for the sake of the other; for then the two together are not more choiceworthy than the one—for example, becoming healthy plus health than health, since we choose to become healthy for the sake of health. And there is nothing to 20 prevent things that are not [all] good from being more choiceworthy than things that are [all] good—for example, happiness plus another thing that is not good than justice plus courage.[142]) Also, the same things with pleasure are more choiceworthy than without pleasure. Also, the same things with absence of pain than with pain.

Also, each thing, when its capacity is greater, is at the same time more choiceworthy— for example, absence of pain in old age more than in youth; for its capacity is greater in old age. In line with the same reasoning, practical wisdom is more choiceworthy in old age; for no one chooses young people as leaders, because they do not expect them to be practically wise. With courage, it is the reverse; for it is in youth that activity in accord with courage is most necessary. It is the same way with temperance; for young people are more troubled by their appetites than older ones.

Also, what is more useful at all, or at most, times is more choiceworthy— for example, justice and temperance than courage; for they are always useful, while courage is useful [only] at times.[143] Also, of two things, the one whose possession by all implies that we do not need the other is more choiceworthy than the one whose possession implies that we still need the remaining one in addition, as in the case of justice and courage; for if all were just, courage would be of no use, but if all were courageous, justice would still be useful.[144]

Further, [argue] on the basis of the passings away and losses, the comings to be and acquisitions, and the contraries of things; for things whose passings away are more to be avoided are themselves more choiceworthy. It is the same way in the case of the losses and contraries of things; for a thing whose loss or contrary is more to be avoided is itself more choiceworthy. On the other hand, in the case of comings to be and acquisitions, it is the reverse; for things whose acquisition or coming to be is more choiceworthy are themselves more choiceworthy.

Another topic: What is closer to the good is better and more choiceworthy. Also, what is more similar to the good—for example, justice is better and more choiceworthy than a just person. Also, of two things compared, what is more similar to a better [third one], as Ajax is better than Odysseus, because he is more like Achilles. (Objection that this is not true: For nothing prevents the respects in which Achilles is best from not being the ones in which Ajax is more similar to him, while Odysseus is good though not similar to Achilles. Look to see too whether the similarity is more in the direction of caricature, like the similarity of a monkey to a human being, while a horse is not similar; for the monkey is not more nobly beautiful, though it is more similar to a human.)

Again, of two things, if one is more similar to the better and the other more similar to the worse, the one that is more similar to the better is better. (But this admits of objection too: For nothing prevents one thing from being slightly similar to the better, while the other is strongly similar to the worse—for example, if the similarity of Ajax to Achilles is slight, while that of Odysseus to Nestor is strong.[145] It also admits of objection, if what resembles the better were to resemble it in the direction of the worse, while what resembles the worse does so in the direction of the better, as in the similarity of a horse to a donkey and of a monkey to a human.)

Another [topic]: What is more remarkable is more choiceworthy than what is less so, as is what is more difficult; for we like better having things that are not easy to get. Also, what is more special than what is more commonly shared. Also, what is less commonly shared with bad people.

Further, if this is unconditionally better than that, then the best in this is better than the best in the other—for example, if human is better than horse, the best human is also better than the best horse. Also, if the best in the one is better than the best in the other, then the one is also unconditionally better than the other—for example, if the best human is better than the best horse, then human is unconditionally better than horse.

Further, things that our friends can share are more choiceworthy than those they cannot. Also, things that we would choose to do to a friend more than to a random person are more choiceworthy—for example, doing justice and doing good more than seeming to do them; for we choose to do good to friends more than to seem to do them, while to random people it is the reverse.

Also, what depends on abundance is better than what is necessary, and sometimes also more choiceworthy; for living well is better than living, and living well depends on abundance, while life itself is a necessity. But sometimes what is better is not also more choiceworthy; for it is not the case that if something is better, it is necessarily more choiceworthy; at any rate, to do philosophy is more choiceworthy than to make money, but it is not more choiceworthy for one in need of the necessities.[146] But what depends on abundance is so when, having the necessities, one procures other things that are noble in addition. Roughly speaking, what is necessary is perhaps more choiceworthy, but what depends on abundance is better.

Also, what cannot be procured from another is more choiceworthy than what can also be procured from another, as is the case with justice as compared to courage.[147] Also, if this is choiceworthy without that, but not that without this, [the former is more choiceworthy]—for example, capacity is not choiceworthy without practical wisdom, but practical wisdom is choiceworthy without capacity.[148] Also, if we renounce one of two things in order that the remaining one seems to belong to us, then the one we wish to seem to belong to us is more choiceworthy—for example, we renounce the love of hard work in order that we seem to be naturally clever.

Further, what it is less criticizable for people to be annoyed at the absence of is more choiceworthy; also what it is more criticizable for people not to be annoyed at the absence of is more choiceworthy.

3.3

Relative choiceworthiness (3)

Further, of things that fall under the same form, the one that has the virtue proper to the form is more choiceworthy than the one that does not have it, and if both have it, the one that has it to a higher degree.

Further, if one thing makes good what it is present in, while another does not, the one that makes it good is more choiceworthy, as too what warms is warmer than what does not. And if both make it good, the one that makes it good to a higher degree, or that makes the better and more controlling thing good, is more choiceworthy—for example, if the one makes the soul good, the other the body.¹⁴⁹

Further, [determine their relative choiceworthiness] from their inflections, uses, actions, and works, and the latter from the former; for they follow along with each other. For example, if justly done is more choiceworthy than courageously done, justice is more choiceworthy than courage; and if justice is more choiceworthy than courage, justly done is more so than courageously done. And in a quite similar way in the other cases too.

Further, if one is a greater and the other a lesser good than the same [third] thing, or if one is greater than a greater good, the greater is more choiceworthy. But, again, if there are two things that are both more choiceworthy than something, the one that is so to a higher degree would be more choiceworthy than the one that is so to a lesser degree. Further, if the excess of one thing is more choiceworthy than the excess of another, the one is more choiceworthy than the other— for example, friendship than wealth; for an excess of friendship is more choiceworthy than an excess of wealth. Also, what a person would wish to be himself the cause of for himself more than that for which [he would wish] someone else [to be the cause] is more choiceworthy—for example, friends than wealth.

Further, [argue] on the basis of an addition, looking to see whether [of two things] added to the same [third] thing, one makes the whole more choiceworthy [than the other]. But one must watch out for proposing a case in which the common thing uses, or in some other way works together with, one of the things added to it, but does not use or work together with the remaining one—for example, a saw or a sickle together with the craft of carpentry; for in their combination the saw is more choiceworthy, but

it is not unconditionally more choiceworthy. Again, [one thing is more   15
choiceworthy than another] if, when added to the lesser of two [other]
things, it makes the whole greater [than the addition of the other to the
greater of them]. Similarly, [one may argue] on the basis of subtraction;
for a thing whose subtraction from the same thing makes the remainder
a lesser [good than the subtraction of the other], would be greater, whichever one it is whose subtraction makes the remainder a lesser one.

Also, [look to see] whether one thing is choiceworthy because of itself
and the other because of the reputation it brings[, since the former is more
choiceworthy]—for example, health than beauty. And the defining mark   20
of reputation is that if no one else knew about it, one would not be eager
to have it. Also, it is more choiceworthy if it is so both because of itself
and because of its reputation, while the other is so because of only one of
the two. Also, whichever is more estimable because of itself is also better
and more choiceworthy. A thing would be more estimable because of itself
[than another thing] if we would choose it more for its intrinsic self [than
that other thing], when we are going to have nothing else because of it.   25

Further, determine in how many ways things are said to be choiceworthy and for the sake of what—for example, the advantageous, the noble, or
the pleasant; for what is useful in furthering all or furthering most of them
would be more choiceworthy, provided they are so to a similar degree. And
if the same things belong to both, look to see which they belong to more,   30
that is, which is more pleasant, more noble, or more advantageous. Again,
what is for the sake of a better thing is more choiceworthy—for example,
for the sake of virtue than of pleasure. It is the same way too in the case of
things to be avoided; for what more impedes what is choiceworthy is more
to be avoided—for example, illness than ugliness; for both to pleasure and
to excellence disease is a greater hindrance.   35

Further, [argue] on the basis of proving that the thing proposed is
equally worthy of avoidance and choice. For the sort of thing that one
would equally both choose and avoid is less choiceworthy than another
that is choiceworthy only.

3.4

Unconditional choiceworthiness

Comparisons of things with each other must be made, then, in the way
stated. But the same topics are also useful for proving that something is   119ᵃ1
[unconditionally] worthy of choice or avoidance; for we need only subtract
the excess of one thing over another. For if what is more estimable is more

desirable, what is estimable is desirable, and if what is more useful is more
choiceworthy, what is useful is choiceworthy, and it is the same way too in
the case of other things of the sort that admit of comparison. For in some
cases, while comparing one thing with another, we from the outset state
too that each of the two things is choiceworthy, or that one of the two is—
for example, when we state that the one is good by nature and the other not
by nature; for it is clear that what is good by nature is choiceworthy.

3.5

More and greater

The topics concerned with the more and the greater must be taken in their
most universal version; for, when so taken, they would be useful for a larger
number of cases. It is possible to make some of the ones mentioned more
universal by a slight alteration in their formulation. For example: what is
by nature F is more F than what is F not by nature. Also, if one thing makes
something that has it, or that it belongs to, F, and another does not, the one
that makes it F is more F than the one that does not make it F; and if both
make it F, the one that makes it more F.

Further, if one thing is more F and another less F than the same [third]
thing, and also, if one thing is more F than a [third] thing that is F, and
another is more F than a [fourth] thing that is not F, it is clear that the first
is more F. Further, [argue] on the basis of addition, looking to see whether
the addition of one to the same thing makes the whole more F [than the
addition of the other], or if when added to what is less F, it makes the whole
more F. Similarly, [argue] on the basis of subtraction; for a thing whose
subtraction makes the remainder less F, is itself more F. Also, things that
have less of an admixture of the contrary of F are more F—for example, a
thing is whiter that has less of an admixture of black.

Further, beyond what was said previously, something that more admits
of the account proper to the F proposed [is more F]—for example, if the
account of white is "color that dilates sight," what is more of a color that
dilates sight is whiter.[150]

3.6

Particular predications

If a problem is posed in a particular and not in a universal version, the
first universal topics mentioned for establishing or disestablishing are all

useful.[151] For when doing away with or establishing something universally, we also prove it in particular; for if it belongs to all, it also belongs to some, and if to none, it does not belong to one either. The topics that are most handy and common are those based on opposites, coordinates, and inflections.[152]

For the claim that if all pleasure is good, all pain is also bad, and the claim that if some pleasure is good, some pain is also bad, are similarly acceptable beliefs.[153] Further, if some perception is not a capacity, some non-perception is not a lack of capacity.[154] And if something supposable is scientifically knowable, some supposition is scientific knowledge.[155] Again, if some unjustly done thing is good, some unjust thing is good. Also, if something pleasantly done is to be avoided, some pleasure is to be avoided. In line with the same reasoning, if something pleasant is beneficial, some pleasure is good.

Also, in the case of what destroys, and of comings to be and passings away, it is the same way. For if something that destroys pleasure or scientific knowledge is good, some pleasure or some scientific knowledge would be bad. Similarly, if some passing away of scientific knowledge is good or some coming to be of it is bad, some scientific knowledge will be bad—for example, if someone's forgetting the shameful things he has done is something good, or remembering them something bad, to know scientifically the bad things he has done would be something bad. It is the same too in the other cases; for what is an acceptable belief is similarly so in all of them.

Further, [argue] on the basis of the more and the less and the similar. For if something in another kind is more F [than the thing mentioned in the problem], and nothing in its kind is F at all, the thing mentioned could not be F either—for example, if some science is more of a good than pleasure, while no science is a good at all, pleasure would not be a good either. Also, on the basis of the similar or the less [argue] in the same way; for it will be possible both to do away with things and to establish them, except that, while both are possible on the basis of similarity, on the basis of the less it is possible only to establish things, not to disestablish them. For if some capacity and some science are similarly good, and some capacity is good, some science is good too, and if no capacity is good, no science is either. On the other hand, if some capacity is less good than a science, and some capacity is good, a science is also good. But if no capacity is good, it is not necessary that no science be good either. It is clear, then, that only establishing is possible on the basis of the less.

It is possible to disestablish things not only on the basis of another kind, but also on the basis of the same one, by taking a case that is most of all F—for example, if it is proposed that some science is good, and if it were to be proved that practical wisdom is not good, no other science will be

good either, since not even the one that is most of all believed to be good is good. Further, [argue] on the basis of a hypothesis, claiming similarly that
³⁵ if F belongs (or does not belong) to one, it belongs (or does not belong) to all—for example, if the soul of a human is immortal, the other souls are too, but if it is not, neither are the others. If, then, it is proposed that F belongs to some [members of a kind], it must be proved that it does not belong to some; for it will follow because of the hypothesis that it belongs to none at all. But if it is proposed that F does not belong to any, it must
^{120ᵃ1} be proved that it belongs to some; for it will also follow in this way that it belongs to all. It is clear that the one responsible for the hypothesis makes the problem universal, though it was proposed in a particular version; for he claims that one who agrees to it in a particular version must also agree to it in a universal one, since if F belongs to one case, he claims that it
⁵ belongs to all alike.

When the problem is indeterminate, it is possible to do away with things in only one way—for example, if the opponent has said that some pleasure is good or is not good, and has not made it further determinate in any other way.¹⁵⁶ For if he said that some pleasure is good, it must be proved universally that none is, if the thing proposed is going to be done away
¹⁰ with. Similarly, if he said that some pleasure is not good, it must be proved universally that all are. It is not possible to do away with it in any other way; for if we prove that some pleasure is not good or is good, we will not yet have done away with the thing proposed. It is clear, then, that it is possible to do away with a premise of this sort in only one way, but possible to
¹⁵ establish it in two ways; for whether we prove universally that all pleasure is good or prove that some pleasure is good, the thing proposed will have been proved. Similarly, when we must argue dialectically that some pleasure is not good, if we prove that no pleasure is good or that some pleasure is not good, we will have argued dialectically in two ways, both universally
²⁰ and in particular, that some pleasure is not good.

If, on the other hand, the thesis is determinate, it will be possible to do away with it in two ways—for example, if it consists in positing that it belongs to some pleasure to be good and does not belong to some pleasure to be good; for whether it is proved that all pleasure is good or that none is good, the thing proposed is done away with. And if what the opponent has posited is that only one single pleasure is good, it is possible to do away
²⁵ with it in three ways; for by proving that all, no, or more than one pleasure is good, we will have done away with the thing proposed. And if the thesis is made still more determinate (for example, if it consists in positing that practical wisdom alone of the virtues is scientific knowledge), it is possible to do away with it in four ways; for if it has been proved that all virtue is scientific knowledge, that none is, that some other virtue (for example,

46

justice) is too, or that practical wisdom itself is not scientific knowledge,   30
the thing proposed will have been done away with.

It is also useful to look at the particular instances, in cases where F has
been said to belong or not to belong, just as in the cases of universal problems. Further, one must look among the kinds, dividing them by their
forms until one reaches the indivisible ones, as was said previously; for   35
whether F were to appear to belong in all cases or in none, after introduc-
ing many instances, one must claim that the opponent must either agree
to the universal or bring an objection showing in what case it does not
hold.[157] Further, in cases in which it is possible to determine the coincident
either by form or by number, look to see whether none of them belongs—
arguing, for example, that time is not moved and that it is not a movement
either, by enumerating how many forms of movement there are; for if none   **120ᵇ1**
of these belongs to time, it is clear that it is not moved, nor is it a movement.[158] Similarly, [argue] that the soul is not a number by determining
that all number is either odd or even; for if the soul is neither odd nor even,
it is clear that it is not a number.   5

As regards the coincident, then, one must argue dialectically by means
of these and in such a way.

4: KINDS

4.1

Kinds, forms, and special affections

Next we must investigate the [topics] related to kind and special affection. These are elements of the topics related to definitions, but the investigations of those practicing dialectic are seldom concerned with these by themselves.[159]

15   If, then, some kind is proposed for some of the beings, first look at all the beings akin to the one mentioned, to see whether the kind is not predicated of some of them, just as in the case of a coincident.[160] For example, if good is proposed as the kind of pleasure, see whether some pleasure is not good; for if this is so, it is clear that good is not the kind of pleasure; for the kind

20   is predicated of everything falling under the same form. Next, look to see whether it is predicated not in the what-it-is but as a coincident, as white is predicated of snow or self-moved of soul. For snow is not precisely white, which is why white is not the kind of snow, nor is soul precisely what is moving, rather its being moved is coincidental to it, just as it often is of

25   the animal to walk or to be walking.[161] Further, "moving" does not seem to signify what a thing is but something it does or has done to it. It is the same way with "white"; for it does not indicate what snow is, but rather some quality of it. So neither of them is predicated in the what-it-is, while the kind is predicated in the what-it-is.[162]

30   Most of all, look at the definition of coincident to see whether it fits the stated kind, as is also the case in the ones just mentioned; for it is possible for a thing to move itself and not to do so, and possible, similarly, for it to be white and not to be white.[163] So neither of these is a kind but rather a coincident, since we said that a coincident is what admits of belonging to a

35   subject and of not belonging to it.[164]

Further, look to see whether the kind and form are not in the same division, but rather that the one is substance and the other quality, or the one relative and the other quality.[165] For example, snow and swan are each substance, while white is not substance but quality, so that white is not the kind either of snow or of swan. Again, scientific knowledge is among the

relatives, while good and noble are each a quality, so that good, or noble, is not the kind of scientific knowledge; for the kinds of relatives must themselves also be relatives, as in the case of double; for in fact multiple,

which is the kind of double, is itself also a relative.¹⁶⁶ To speak in universal   5
terms, the kind must fall under the same division as its form; for if the form
is substance, the kind is also, and if the form is quality, the kind is also
quality—for example, if white is quality, color is too. It is the same way in
the other cases too.

Again, look to see whether it is necessary or possible for the kind to par-   10
ticipate in what has been put in the kind. And the definition of participate
is "admit of the account of what is participated in." It is clear, then, that the
forms participate in the kinds, but not the kinds in the forms; for the form
admits of the account of the kind, but not the kind of the account of the
form. One must look to see, then, whether the assigned kind participates,
or admits of participating, in the form—for example, if someone were to   15
assign something as the kind of being (*to on*) or of one; for it will follow
that the kind participates in the form; for being and one are predicated of
all beings, so that their account is as well.

Further, look to see whether there is something of which the assigned
form is truly predicated although the kind is not—for example, whether   20
what is (*to on*) or what is scientifically knowable is posited as the kind of
the believable. For believable will be predicated of what is not (*to mê on*)
(for many things that are not are believable), but it is clear that what is and
what is scientifically knowable is not predicated of what is not. So neither
what is nor what is scientifically knowable is the kind of the believable; for
what the form is predicated of, the kind is predicated of as well.   25

Again, look to see whether what is put in the kind admits of participating in none of its forms; for it is impossible for it to participate in the kind if
it participates in none of its forms, unless it just is one of the forms reached
at the first division, which do participate in the kind alone.¹⁶⁷ If, then,   30
movement is posited as the kind of pleasure, one must look to see whether
pleasure is neither spatial movement nor alteration nor any of the rest of
the sorts of movement assigned to things.¹⁶⁸ For then it would be clear that
it participated in none of the forms, and so not in the kind either, since it
is necessary for what participates in the kind also to participate in some of
the forms. So pleasure could not be a form of movement, nor could it be   35
any of the individuals that fall under the form of movement for the beings;
for the individuals also participate in the kind and the form—for example,
the individual human participates both in human and in animal.

Further, look to see whether the extension of what is put in the kind is
wider than that of the kind—for example, as that of what is believable is   121ᵇ1
wider than that of what is; for both what is and what is not are believable,
so that what is believable could not be a form of what is; for the extension of the kind is always wider than that of the form. Again, look to see
whether the form and the kind have the same extension—for example, if of

what follows along with everything, as being and one do, one were posited as form, another as kind; for everything is a being and one, so that neither is the kind of the other, since they have the same extension.¹⁶⁹ It is the same way too if first and starting-point were subordinate one to the other; for the starting-point is first and the first is starting-point, so that either both of the things mentioned are the same or neither is the kind of the other. An element [or topic] relevant to all cases of this sort is that the extension of the kind is wider than that of the form and its difference; for the extension of the difference is also narrower than that of the kind.

See also whether of something, among the things that do not differ in form, the stated kind is not the kind, or does not seem to be the kind—or, if establishing, whether it is the kind of one of them. For the kind of all things that do not differ in form is the same. If, then, it is proved to be the kind of one, it is clear that it is the kind of all, and if not of one, it is clear that it is the kind of none. For example, if someone positing indivisible lines were to say that the indivisible is their kind; for of lines that admit of division, the one mentioned is not the kind, and these do not differ in form from indivisible ones; for all straight lines are no different in form from each other.¹⁷⁰

4.2

Kinds, forms, and differences

Look to see too whether there is any other kind of the assigned form which neither encompasses the assigned kind nor falls under it. For example, if someone were to posit that scientific knowledge is the kind of justice; for virtue is also its kind, and neither of the kinds encompasses the remaining one. So scientific knowledge could not be the kind of justice; for it seems that when one form falls under two kinds, one encompasses the other.¹⁷¹ But some cases of this sort involve a puzzle; for it seems to some people that practical wisdom is a virtue and also a science, and neither of these kinds is encompassed by the other. Of course, not everyone would concede that practical wisdom is scientific knowledge. If, however, someone were to concede the truth of the affirmation, still for one to fall under the other, or else for both to fall under the same kind, would seem necessary, just as actually happens in the case of virtue and scientific knowledge; for they both fall under the same kind; for each of them is a state and a disposition.¹⁷² Look to see, then, whether neither of these belongs to the assigned kind.¹⁷³ For if it is neither the case that one of the kinds falls under the other, or the other under the one, nor that both fall under the same kind, then the assigned one could not be the kind.

Look too at the kind of the assigned kind, and in this way always at the kind above, to see whether they are all predicated of the form, and predicated in the what-it-is; for all the higher kinds must be predicated of the form in the what-it-is.[174] If, then, there is a discordance anywhere, it is clear that what was assigned is not the kind. Again, look to see whether the kind, either itself or one of the higher kinds, participates in the form; for the higher kind participates in none of the lower ones. For disestablishing, then, it must be used in the way stated.

For establishing, on the other hand, if the stated kind is agreed to belong to the form, but that it belongs as kind is disputed, it is enough to prove that one of the higher kinds is predicated of the form in the what-it-is. For if one is predicated in the what-it-is, all of them, both higher and lower ones (if indeed they are predicated), will be predicated in the what-it-is. So the assigned kind too will be predicated in the what-it-is. But the fact that if one kind is predicated in the what-it-is, all the rest as well (if indeed they are predicated) will be predicated in the what-it-is, must be got hold of by induction. But if it is disputed whether the assigned kind belongs at all, it is not enough to prove that one of the higher kinds is predicated in the what-it-is. For example, if someone has assigned spatial movement as the kind of walking, in order to have proved that walking is spatial movement, it is not enough to have proved that it is movement, since there are also other forms of movement. Instead, it must be further proved that walking participates in no other forms in the same division as spatial movement; for what participates in the kind must of necessity also participate in one of the forms in the first division of it. If, then, walking participates neither in increase nor decrease, nor in any of the other forms of movement, it is clear that it would participate in spatial movement, so that spatial movement would be the kind of walking.

Again, in cases in which the posited form is predicated as kind, look to see whether the assigned kind too is predicated in the what-it-is of precisely the things of which the form is predicated, and similarly whether all the kinds higher than this kind are so predicated as well. For if there is a discordance anywhere, it is clear that what is assigned is not the kind; for if it were the kind, all the higher kinds, and it itself, would have been predicated in the what-it-is of precisely the things of which the form too is predicated in the what-it-is. For disestablishing, then, it is useful to see whether the kind is not predicated in the what-it-is of just the things of which the form too is predicated.

For establishing, on the other hand, it is useful to see whether the kind is predicated in the what-it-is. For then it will follow that the kind and the form are predicated in the what-it-is of the same thing, so that the same thing falls under two kinds. It is necessary, then, for one of the kinds to fall under the other. If, then, it were proved that the one we wish to establish as kind does not fall under the form, it is clear that the form would fall under it, so that it would have been proved that ours is the kind.

Look also at the accounts of the kinds to see whether they apply both to the assigned form and to the participants in the form; for it is necessary for the accounts of the kinds to be predicated of the form and also of the participants in the form. If, then, there is a discordance anywhere, it is clear that what is assigned is not the kind.

Again, look to see whether the opponent has assigned a difference as kind—for example, immortal as kind of god; for immortal is a difference of living things, since of the living things, some are mortal, others immortal. It is clear, then, that an error has been made; for a difference is not a kind of anything. And that this is true is clear; for no difference signifies a what-it-is but rather a quality, as do "terrestrial" and "two-footed."

Also, look to see whether the opponent has put the difference in the kind—for example, saying that odd is precisely number; for odd is a difference of number, not a form.[175] Neither, it seems, does the difference participate in the kind; for everything that participates in the kind is either a form or an individual, but the difference is neither form nor individual. It is clear, then, that the difference does not participate in the kind. So neither could odd be a form, since it does not participate in the kind.

Further, look to see whether the opponent has put the kind into the form—for example, saying that contact is just continuity, or that mixture is just fusion, or—in accord with Plato's definition—that spatial movement is just movement with respect to place.[176] For contact is not necessarily continuity, but rather the reverse: continuity is necessarily contact; for what is making contact with something is not always conjoined with it, while what is conjoined with something is always making contact with it. It is the same way in the case of the rest as well; for not all mixture is fusion (for a mixture of dry things is not a fusion), nor is all movement with respect to place spatial movement; for walking does not seem to be spatial movement; for pretty much [only] things that change one place for another non-voluntarily—as happens in the case of inanimate things—are said to be in spatial movement.[177] It is clear too that the extension of the form is wider than that of the kind in the given cases, but it must be the reverse.

Again, look to see whether the opponent has put the difference into the form—for example, saying that what is immortal is precisely god. For it will follow that the form has the same extension or a wider one. But the difference always has the same extension as the form, or a wider one.[178] Further, look to see whether he has put the kind into the difference—for example, saying that color is precisely contracting or number precisely

odd.[179] Also, look to see whether he has stated the kind as difference; for it
is also possible for someone to introduce a thesis of this sort—for example,
making mixture the difference of fusion or change of place that of spatial
movement. All such cases must be looked at by means of the same proced-   5
ures; for their topics are interrelated; for the extension of the kind must be
wider than that of the difference and must not participate in its difference.
But if the kind is assigned as difference, neither of these things can follow;
for the extension of the kind will be narrower and the kind will participate
in the difference.   10

Again, if none of the differences belonging to the kind are predicated of
the assigned form, the kind will not be predicated of it either—for example,
neither odd nor even is predicated of soul, so that number is not predicated
of it either. Further, look to see whether the form is prior in nature, and
does away with the kind along with itself; for it seems that the contrary is
so.[180] Further, look to see whether it is possible for the stated kind, or for its   15
difference, to be absent from the form—for example, for movement to be
absent from soul or true and false from belief—for then neither can be its
kind or its difference; for the kind and difference seem to follow along with
the form, as long as it exists.

4.3

Contraries, inflections, and coordinates

Look to see too whether what is put in the kind participates in something   20
contrary to the kind, or could possibly participate in it; for then the same
thing will participate in contraries at the same time, since the kind is never
absent from it, while the thing at issue also participates in what is contrary
to the kind, or could possibly participate in it. Further, look to see whether
the form shares in something that cannot at all belong to what is in the
kind—for example, if the soul shares in life, while no number can possibly   25
be alive, the soul could not be a form of number.

Look also to see whether the form is homonymous with regard to the
kind, using the elements [or topics] already stated for dealing with the
homonymous; for the kind and the form are synonymous.[181]

Since of every kind there are several forms, look to see whether it is
not possible for there to be another form of the stated kind [besides the   30
assigned one]; for if there is none, it is clear that what is stated could not
be a kind at all.

Also, look to see whether the opponent has assigned as the kind what
is said of things by means of a metaphor—for example, temperance is

harmony; for it is in its literal sense that every kind is predicated of the
35   [several] forms, but harmony is predicated of temperance not in its strict
sense but by means of a metaphor; for every harmony consists of notes.[182]

123^{b}1   Further, if the form has a contrary, one must look at it. This investigation
takes place in various ways. First of all, look to see whether the contrary is
also in the same kind, when the kind has no contrary; for contraries must
be in the same kind, if there is no contrary to the kind. On the other hand,
if the kind has a contrary, look to see whether the contrary of the form is
5   in the contrary kind; for the contrary form is of necessity in the contrary
kind, if indeed the kind has a certain contrary. Each of these points is evident by induction. Again, look to see whether the contrary of the form is
not in any kind at all, but is itself a kind—for example, the good; for if this
is not in any kind, the contrary of it will not be in any kind either, but will
10   itself be a kind, as happens in the case of the good and the bad; for neither
of them is in a kind, but each is itself a kind.[183]

Further, look to see whether both kind and form each has a contrary,
and whether there is an intermediate between one pair of contraries but
not the other. For if there is an intermediate between the kinds, there is also
one between the forms, and if there is one between the forms, there is also
15   one between the kinds, as in the case of virtue and vice, justice and injustice; for each pair has an intermediate. (An objection to this: There is no
intermediate between health and disease, though there is one between bad
and good.) Or look to see whether, though there is a middle term between
both pairs (that is, between the forms and between the kinds), there is not
20   one in the same way, but rather in one case it is by way of negation, while
in the other it is as underlying subject.[184] For it is an acceptable belief that
it is the same way in both, as in the cases of virtue and vice and justice and
injustice; for in both cases the middle terms are by way of negation.

Further, when there is no contrary to the kind, look to see not only
whether the contrary is in the same kind, but whether the middle term
is too; for it is the kind the extremes are in that the middle terms are also
25   in—as, for example, in the case of white and black; for color is the kind of
these and also of all the middle colors. (Objection: Deficiency and excess
are in the same kind—for both are in the kind of bad; but the moderate
amount, which is intermediate between them, is not in the kind of bad,
30   but in that of good.) Also, look to see whether, while the kind is contrary
to something, the form is not contrary to anything. For if the kind is contrary to something, the form is too, as virtue is the contrary of vice, and
justice of injustice.[185] Similarly, if one were to look at the other cases, this
would seem evident. (Objection in the case of health and disease: Health is
35   unconditionally the contrary of disease, yet certain disease—for example,
fever, eye disease, and each of the others—has no contrary.)

When doing away with things, then, investigate in this many ways; for if   124ᵃ1
the stated things do not belong to it, it is clear that what has been assigned
is not the kind.

When establishing, on the other hand, one must look in three ways.
First of all, look to see whether the contrary [of the form] is in the stated
kind, when the kind has no contrary; for if the contrary is in it, it is clear
that the one proposed is too. Further, look to see whether the intermediate   5
is in the stated kind; for what the intermediate is in, the extremes are also
in. Again, if the kind has a contrary, look to see whether the contrary form
is also in the contrary kind; for if it is, clearly the form proposed is in the
kind proposed.

Again, in the case of the inflections and coordinates [of form and kind],
look to see whether they follow along in a similar way, both when doing   10
away with things and when establishing them; for whatever belongs or does
not belong to one, at the same time belongs or does not belong to all—for
example, if justice is a sort of scientific knowledge, what is done justly is
done in a scientifically knowledgeable way and a just person is a scientific
knower. But if any of these is not so, none of the rest is either.

4.4

Additional topics (1)

Again, look at things that bear a similar relation to each other. For example,   15
pleasant bears a similar relation to pleasure as beneficial does to good; for
in each case, the one is productive of the other. If, then, pleasure is precisely
good, pleasant will also be precisely beneficial; for it is clear that it would
be productive of good, since pleasure is good. It is the same way too in the
case of comings to be and passings away—for example, if to build is to be   20
active, then to have built is to have been active, and if to learn is to remember, to have learned is to have remembered, and if to be dissolved is to pass
away, to have been dissolved is to have passed away, and dissolution is a
sort of passing away. And look in the same way at what causes coming to
be and what causes passing away, at the capacities and uses of things, and,   25
in general, both when doing away with things and establishing them, look
at them in the light of any similarity whatever, as we just stated in the case
of coming to be and passing away. For if what causes things to pass away
causes them to dissolve, to pass away is to be dissolved; and if what causes
things to come to be causes them to be produced, to come to be is to be
produced, and coming to be is production. It is the same way too in the   30
case of capacities and uses; for if a capacity is a disposition, to be capable of

something is to be disposed to do it, and if the use of something is an activity, to use is to be active and to have used is to have been active.

If the opposite of a form is a privation, there are two ways to do away with [a claim]. First, look to see whether the opposite is in the assigned kind; for either the privation is unconditionally not anywhere at all in the same kind or not in the ultimate kind—for example, if sight is in perception as its ultimate kind, blindness will not be perception.[186] Second, if a privation is opposed both to the kind and to the form, but the opposite form is not in the opposite kind, neither would the assigned form be in the assigned kind. When doing away with things, then, use the ways as stated. When establishing, on the other hand, there is only one way; for if the opposite form is in the opposite kind, the form would be in the kind proposed—for example, if blindness is a certain sort of non-perception, sight is a certain sort of perception.[187]

Again, look at the denials in reverse order, as was stated in the case of the coincident—for example, if pleasant is precisely good, what is not good is not pleasant; for it is impossible, if indeed good is the kind of pleasant, for anything not good to be pleasant; for what the kind is not predicated of, the form is not predicated of either.[188] Also, when establishing, look in the same way; for if what is not good is not pleasant, what is pleasant is good, so that good is the kind of pleasant.

If the form is a relative, look to see whether the kind is also a relative; for if the form is a relative, the kind is too—for example, double and multiple; for each is a relative. If, on the other hand, the kind is a relative, it is not necessary for the form also to be one; for scientific knowledge is among the relatives, but the craft of grammar is not.[189] (Alternatively, perhaps not even the first thing stated would be believed to be so; for virtue is precisely noble and precisely good, and virtue is among the relatives, but good and noble are not among the relatives, but are qualities.)

Again, look to see whether the form is not said relative to the same thing both intrinsically and with respect to the kind—for example, if double is said of things as double of half, then multiple must be said of things as multiple of half. If it is not, multiple would not be the kind of double.

Further, look to see whether the form is not said relative to the same thing both with respect to the kind and with respect to all of the kinds of the kind. For if double is multiple of half, it will also be said to be "in excess" of the half, and, with respect to all the higher kinds, will unconditionally be said relative to half. (Objection: Something is not necessarily said of things intrinsically and with respect to the kind relative to the same thing; for scientific knowledge is said to be of the scientifically knowable, but a state or disposition is not of the scientifically knowable, but of the soul.)

Further, look to see whether the kind and form are said in the same way with respect to the inflections—for example, whether to something, of something, or in as many other ways as there are. For as the kind is said of things, so too is the form, as in the case of double and its higher kinds; for both double and multiple are of something. It is the same way too in the case of scientific knowledge; for both scientific knowledge itself and its kinds—for example, disposition and state—are of something. (Objection: In some cases it is not so. For different and contrary are from or to something, but other, which is their kind, is not from or to, but than something; for something is said to be other than something.)

Again, look to see whether the relatives said in accord with the inflections are similar or not similar when converted, as in the case of double and multiple. For each of these is said to be of something, both it itself and in accord with its conversion; for both a half and a fraction are of something. It is the same way too in the case of scientific knowledge and supposition; for these themselves are of something and, when converted, are similar; for both the scientifically knowable and the supposable are so *to* something.[190] If, then, in some cases the conversions are not similar, it is clear that one is not the kind of the other.

Again, look to see whether the form and kind are not said relative to the same number of things. For it seems that both are said in the same way and of the same number of things, as in the case of gift and giving; for a giving is said to be of something to someone, and a gift is of something to someone. And giving is the kind of gift; for a gift is a giving without a giving in return. In some cases, however, the thing is not said relative to the same number of things; for double is double of something, while excess and greater is of something in something; for everything that is in excess (or greater) is always in excess in something and in excess of something. So the things mentioned are not the kinds of double, since they are not said relative to the same number of things. (Alternatively, perhaps it is not universally true that the form and kind are not said relative to the same number of things.)

See too whether the opposite of the kind is the kind of the opposite form—for example, whether, if multiple is the kind of double, fraction is the kind of half; for the opposite of the kind must be the kind of the opposite form. If, then, someone posits that scientific knowledge is precisely perception, the scientifically knowable must also be precisely the perceptible. But it is not; for not everything that is scientifically knowable is perceptible; for in fact some scientifically knowable things are intelligible. So the perceptible is not the kind of the scientifically knowable. And, if this is so, perception is not the kind of scientific knowledge either.

Since of things said as relatives: Some are of necessity in, or have to do with, those things relative to which they happen at any time to be said (for example, disposition, state, and commensurability; for the things just mentioned cannot possibly belong in anything other than the things relative to which they are said). Others, by contrast, do not necessarily belong in those things relative to which they happen at any time to be said, although it is possible (for example, if the soul is said to be scientifically knowable; for there is nothing to prevent the soul from having scientific knowledge of itself, although it is not necessary; for it is possible for this same scientific knowledge to belong in something else).[191] Others cannot possibly belong unconditionally in those things relative to which they happen at any time to be said (for example, the contrary in the contrary, or scientific knowledge in the scientifically knowable, unless the scientifically knowable happens to be a soul or a human). Look, then, to see whether the opponent has put something of one sort into a kind that is not of that sort—for example, if he has said that memory is the persistence of scientific knowledge; for all persistence is in what persists and has to do with that, so that the persistence of scientific knowledge too is in the scientific knowledge. Memory, therefore, is in the scientific knowledge, since it is the persistence of scientific knowledge. But this is impossible; for all memory is in the soul.

The topic just stated is common also to the coincident; for it makes no difference whether we say that persistence is the kind of memory or that it is a coincident of it; for if memory is in any way whatever the persistence of scientific knowledge, the same argument will apply to it.

4.5

Additional topics (2)

Again, look to see whether the opponent has put a state in an activity or an activity in a state—for example, by saying that perception is a movement through the body; for perception is a state, while movement is an activity.[192] Similarly, if he has said that memory is a state that retains a supposition; for no memory is a state, but rather an activity.[193]

People also err who place a state in the capacity that follows along with it—for example, saying that mild-manneredness is the self-control of anger, courage of fears, and justice of profits; for courageous and mild-mannered are said of someone who feels no [anger or fear that needs controlling], while the self-controlled person is the one who feels but is not led by [these].[194] Perhaps each of these states is indeed followed along with by a capacity of such a sort that, if the person were to feel these feelings, he

would not be led by them but rather would control them. But yet this is not   25
what the being for courage is or the being for mild-manneredness, which
is rather not to feel such feelings at all.[195]

Sometimes too people posit as kind whatever follows along with [the
form]—for example, positing pain as kind of anger and supposition as that
of conviction; for while both of the things just mentioned follow along in
a way with the assigned forms, neither of them is their kind. For when   30
the person who is feeling anger is pained, the pain has come about in him
beforehand; for the anger is not the cause of the pain, but rather the pain of
the anger, so that anger is not pain unconditionally.[196] In line with the same
reasoning, conviction is not supposition either; for it is possible to have the
same supposition without actually being persuaded of it, while this is not   35
possible if indeed conviction is a form of supposition; for it is not possible
for a thing to persist as still the same if it is wholly changed in form, just as
it is not possible either for the same animal to be at one time a human and
at another not. But if someone said that a person who has a supposition is
of necessity also persuaded of it, supposition and conviction will have the   40
same extension, so that not even in this way could the one be kind of the   **126ᵃ1**
other; for the kind must have a wider extension.

See too whether both naturally occur in the same thing; for what the form
occurs in, the kind also occurs in—for example, what white occurs in, color
also occurs in, and what the craft of grammar occurs in, scientific knowledge also occurs in. If, then, someone said that shame is fear, or anger pain,   5
it will follow that kind and form do not belong in the same thing; for shame
is in the rationally calculative part, while fear is in the spirited one, and pain
in the appetitive one (for pleasure is also in it), while anger is in the spirited
one.[197] So that what are assigned are not the kinds, since they do not natur-   10
ally occur in the same thing as the form. Similarly, if love is in the appetitive
part, it is not a sort of wish; for all wish is in the rationally calculative part.[198]

This topic too is useful in relation to the coincident; for the coincident
and what it is coincident with are in the same thing, so that if they do not
appear in the same thing, it is clear that it is not a coincident.[199]   15

Again, look to see whether the form participates in the proposed kind
only in a certain respect; for the kind seems not to be participated in only
in a certain respect. For human is not only in a certain respect animal, nor
the craft of grammar only in a certain respect science. It is the same way
in the other cases too. Look to see, then, whether in some cases the kind is   20
participated in only in a certain respect—for example, if animal is said to
be precisely what is perceptible or precisely what is visible.[200] For it is only
in a certain respect that animal is perceptible or visible; for in respect of its
body it is perceptible and visible, but in respect of its soul it is not. So visible and perceptible could not be the kind of animal.   25

Without noticing it, people also sometimes put the whole in the part—for example, saying that animal is animate body. But the part is not predicable of the whole at all, so that body cannot be the kind of animal, since it is a part.

30 See too whether the opponent has put anything that is blameworthy or to be avoided in [the kind of] capacity or the capable—for example, saying that a sophist, slanderer, or thief is one who is capable of stealing in secret what is another's; for none of those just mentioned is said to be of the sort that he is because he is capable of one of these things.[201] For both the god and the excellent person are capable of doing base things, but are not of 35 that sort; for the base are all said to be such with respect to their deliberate choice.[202] Further, every capacity is choiceworthy; for even the capacities for base things are worthy of choice, which is why we say that a god and an excellent person have them; for we say that they are capable of doing 126^b1 base things. So capacity cannot be the kind of anything blameworthy; for otherwise it will follow that something blameworthy is worthy of choice; for there will be a certain capacity that is blameworthy.

Also, look to see whether he has put anything that is estimable or choiceworthy because of itself in [the kind of] capacity, the capable, or 5 the productive; for every capacity and everything capable or productive is choiceworthy [only] because of something else.[203]

Or look to see whether he has put anything that is in two or more kinds in only one of them; for there are some things that cannot be put in only one kind—for example, the cheat and the slanderer; for neither the one with the deliberate choice to do it but without the capacity, nor the one 10 with the capacity but not the deliberate choice, is a slanderer or a cheat, but rather the one with both. So he must be placed not in one kind, but in both of the kinds just mentioned.

Further, sometimes, reversing the order, people assign the kind as difference or the difference as kind—for example, saying that amazement is 15 the excess of wonder, and conviction is intensity of supposition. For neither excess nor intensity is kind but difference; for amazement seems to be excessive wonder and conviction intense supposition, so that wonder and conviction are kind, while excess and intensity are difference.[204]

20 Further if excess and intensity are assigned as kind, inanimate things will be persuaded and amazed; for the intensity and excess of a given thing are present in what they are the intensity and excess of.[205] If, then, amazement is the excess of wonder, amazement will be present in wonder, so 25 that the wonder will be amazed. Similarly, conviction will be present in supposition, if indeed it is intensity of supposition, so that the supposition will be persuaded. Further, assigning things in this way will result in saying that intensity is intense and excess excessive. For there is intense

conviction. If, then, conviction is intensity, intensity would be intense. It
is the same way there is also excessive amazement. If, then, amazement is   30
excess, excess would be excessive. But neither of these seems to be so, any
more than scientific knowledge is a scientifically knowable thing or movement a moving thing.

Sometimes people also err in putting an affection in what has been
affected, as its kind—for example, those who say that immortality is eternal   35
life; for immortality seems to be an affection or coincident of life.[206] And
that what is said is true would be clear were one to concede that someone
could become immortal from having been mortal; for no one will say that
he gets a distinct life, but rather that a coincident or affection is added to   40
this same life. So life is not the kind of immortality.   127ᵃ1

Again, look to see whether they say that an affection is what it is an
affection of—for example, saying that wind is moving air. For the same
air persists both when moving and when at rest. So wind is not air at all;   5
for otherwise there would be wind even when the air was not moving, if
indeed the same air that was wind still persists. It is the same way in other
cases of this sort too. Even, then, if one must in this case concede that
wind is moving air, nonetheless one must not concede the sort of thing   10
that is assigned with regard to everything of which the kind is not true, but
only where the assigned kind is truly predicated. For in some cases—for
example, mud and snow—it does not seem to be true. For people say that
snow is frozen water and that mud is earth mixed with moisture. But snow
is not water, nor is mud earth. So neither of the assigned things could be   15
the kind; for the kind must always be true of every form. Similarly, wine is
not fermented water either, in the way that Empedocles speaks of "water
fermented in wood"; for, unconditionally, wine is not water at all.[207]

4.6

Additional topics (3)

Further, look to see whether what is assigned is not kind of anything at
all; for clearly it is not then the kind of the form mentioned. Look on the   20
basis of there being no difference in form between the participants of the
assigned kind—for example, white things; for these do not differ at all in
form from each other, but the forms of all the kinds are different from each
other. So white could not be the kind of anything.   25

Again, look to see whether the opponent has stated as kind or difference something that follows along with everything; for there are several
things that follow everything—for example, being and one follow along

with everything. If, then, he has assigned being as kind, it is clear that it
would be the kind of everything, since it is predicated of them. The kind in
30   fact is not predicated of anything except its forms. So *one* would also be a
form of being. It follows, then, that the form too is predicated of everything
that the kind is predicated of, since being and one are predicated unconditionally of everything, but the form must be predicated of fewer things. If
he has said that what follows everything is a difference, it is clear that the
35   difference will have the same extension as the kind or a wider one; for if the
kind too is one of the things that follow everything, the difference will have
the same extension, but if the kind does not follow everything, the difference will have a wider extension than the kind.

Further, look to see whether the assigned kind is said to be in the form
127^b1   as in an underlying subject, as, in the case of snow, white is, so that it is
clear that it could not be the kind; for the kind is only said of the form as
underlying subject.²⁰⁸

5   Look to see too whether the kind is not synonymous with the form; for
the kind is always predicated synonymously of all the forms.

Further, there is the case where both the kind and the form have a contrary, and your opponent puts the better of the contrary [forms] in the
worse kind; for it will follow that the remaining forms will be in the remain-
10   ing kind, since the contraries are in contrary kinds, so that the better form
will be in the worse kind, and the worse in the better; but it seems that the
kind of the better is also better. Also, look to see whether, if the same thing
is similarly related to both, the opponent has put it in the worse and not
in the better kind—for example, saying that the soul is just movement or
15   a thing in movement. For the same soul seems to be similarly capable of
rest and capable of movement; so, if rest is better, he should have put soul
in this kind.²⁰⁹

Further, look on the basis of the more and the less, when disestablishing, to see whether the kind admits of the more, while the form does not
do so, neither itself, nor anything said to be what it is in accord with it. For
20   example, if virtue admits of the more, justice and the just person do too;
for one person is said to be more just than another. If, then, the assigned
kind admits of the more, but the form itself does not do so, and neither
does anything said to be what it is in accord with it, the assigned one could
25   not be the kind.

Again, if what seems more to be the kind [than what is assigned], or
seems equally to be so, is not the kind, it is clear that what is assigned is not
the kind either. This topic is useful especially in the sorts of cases where
several things appear to be predicable of the form in the what-it-is, no distinction having been drawn between them, nor can we say which of them
30   is kind. For example, both pain and supposition seem to be predicated of

anger in the what-it-is, for the angry person both feels pain and supposes he is being treated with contempt. The same investigation is also applicable in the case of the form, by comparing it to another form; for if what seems more or equally to be in the assigned kind is not in the kind, it is clear that   35
the assigned form could not be in the kind either.

When doing away with things, then, use what was just stated. When establishing, on the other hand, the topic of looking to see whether both the assigned kind and the assigned form admit of the more is not useful; for even though both admit of it, there is nothing to prevent one from   128^{a}1
not being the kind of the other; for both noble and white admit of it, and neither is kind of the other. By contrast, the comparison of the kinds and the forms with each other is useful—for example, if this kind and that one   5
equally seem to be kinds, if one is a kind, the other is too. Similarly too, if the one that less seems to be so is a kind, the one that more seems to be so is also—for example, if capacity more seems to be the kind of self-control than virtue does, and virtue is a kind, so is capacity. The same things will be fitting to say also in the case of the form; for if this and that equally seem to be a form of the kind proposed, if one of them is a form of it, the remaining   10
one is as well. And if what less seems to be a form is one, what more seems to be a form is one too.

Further, for the purposes of establishing, look to see whether, of the things of which something has been assigned as kind, it has been predicated in the what-it-is, in the case where not one but several different forms are assigned; for then it is clear that it will be a kind. If, on the other hand,   15
a single form is assigned, look to see whether the kind is predicated of the other forms as well; for then again it will follow that it is predicated of several different ones.

Since it seems to some people that the difference too is predicated of the   20
form in the what-it-is, the kind must be separated from the difference by the use of the elements [or topics] mentioned: first, the kind has a wider extension than the form; further, in assigning the what-it-is it is more fitting to state the kind than the difference (for someone who says that what is human is animal makes the what-it-is more clear than someone who says   25
that it is what is terrestrial); the difference always signifies a quality of the kind, while the kind does not signify a quality of the differences (for someone who says "terrestrial" says "animal of a certain quality," while someone who says "animal" does not say "terrestrial of a certain quality").

This, then, is how the difference must be separated from the kind. Since   30
it seems that if what is musical is, insofar as it is musical, scientifically knowledgeable, music is a sort of scientific knowledge, and if what walks is in movement by walking, walking is a sort of movement—look, in the way just mentioned, at any kind in which one wishes to establish the presence

of something. For example, if one wishes to establish that scientific knowledge is precisely conviction, see whether the person who is scientifically
35   knowledgeable, insofar as he knows scientifically, is persuaded; for then it is clear that scientific knowledge would be a sort of conviction. And look in the same way at other cases of this sort too.

Further, since it is difficult to separate what always follows along with a thing and is not convertible with it from what [make it] not be of its kind, if this always follows along with that, but not that with this (as, for example,
128^b1   calm always follows along with absence of wind and divisible with number, but not conversely—for what is divisible is not always a number, nor a calm an absence of wind), one may oneself use as kind of a thing what always accompanies it, when the other is not convertible with it. If, on the other
5   hand, the other person proposes it, one must not grant it in every case. Objection to this: What is not always does follow along with what is coming to be (for what is coming to be is not) and is not convertible with it (for what is not is not always coming to be); nonetheless, what is not is not the kind of coming to be; for, unconditionally, what is not has no forms.
10   Concerning the kind, then, inquire in the ways stated.

5: SPECIAL AFFECTIONS[210]

5.1

Sorts of special affections

To see whether what is stated is a special affection or not, look in the following ways.

A special affection is assigned either intrinsically and always so or in relation to something else and at a time.[211] An example of an intrinsic special affection: a human is "by nature a tame animal"; of one in relation to something else: soul in relation to body (that the one is suited for prescribing and the other for serving); of one that is always so: a god is an "immortal animal"; of one that is so at a time—for example, for a certain human, "walking about in the gymnasium."[212]

What is assigned as a special affection in relation to something else is either two or four problems. For if one assigns this same special affection in relation to one thing and refuses it to another, only two problems arise, as when one assigns "two-footed" as a special affection of the human in relation to the horse. For someone might attack it both by arguing that the human is not two-footed and by arguing that the horse is two-footed. And in both ways the special affection would be undermined.[213] But if, of two affections, one assigns one and refuses the other to each of two things, there will be four problems, as when one assigns to the one "two-footed" and to the other "four-footed" as a special affection of the human in relation to the horse. For it is possible to attack this both by arguing that the human is not two-footed and by arguing that it is naturally four-footed, and also possible to attack it by arguing that the horse is two-footed and by arguing that it is not four-footed. In whatever way it is proved, then, what has been proposed is done away with.

An intrinsic special affection of something is one assigned in relation to everything, and separates it from everything, as, in the case of a human, does "mortal living being receptive of scientific knowledge." One in relation to something else is one that distinguishes a thing not from everything else but from a certain specified thing, as, in the case of virtue in relation to scientific knowledge, does the fact that virtue by nature comes about in more than one place, while scientific knowledge does so only in the rationally calculative part and in those naturally possessing a rationally calculative part.[214] One that is always so is one that is true of its subject at all times

15

20

25

30

35

129ᵃ1   and is never absent from it, as, in the case of a living thing, is "composed of
soul and body."²¹⁵ One that is so at a time is one that is true of its subject at
a certain time and does not of necessity always accompany it, as, in the case
5   of a certain human, is "walking about in the marketplace."

To assign a special affection in relation to something else is to state a difference that holds either in all cases and always, or for the most part and in
most cases. For example, in all cases and always: in the way that it is a special affection of the human in relation to horse that it is "two-footed"; for
human is always and in every case two-footed, while no horse at any time
10   is two-footed.²¹⁶ For the most part and in most cases: in the way that it is a
special affection of the rationally calculative part in relation to the appetitive part and to the spirited part that it prescribes and the other serves;
for the rationally calculative part does not always prescribe, sometimes it
is also prescribed to, and the appetitive part and the spirited part are not
15   always prescribed to either, but sometimes—when the soul of a human
being is depraved—also prescribe.²¹⁷

Among the special affections, the most logico-linguistic are the ones
that are so intrinsically and always and the ones that are so in relation to
something else. For a special affection that is so in relation to something
else is several problems, as we also said previously; for the problems that
20   arise are of necessity either two or four.²¹⁸ Hence the arguments that
arise in regard to these are several. The one that is intrinsically so and
the one that is always so may be attacked in relation to many things or
looked out for in relation to several times. The one that is intrinsically
so can be attacked in relation to many things (for it is in relation to each
of the beings that the special affection of a particular being must belong
to it, so that if this being is not separated by it in relation to all of them,
25   the special affection could not have been correctly assigned); the one
that is so always can be looked out for in relation to many times; for if
it does not belong, did not belong, or is not going to belong, it will not
be a special affection.²¹⁹ On the other hand, the one that is so at a time
we look at in relation to the now-said time.²²⁰ There are not, then, many
arguments with regard to it. But a logico-linguistic problem is one with
30   regard to which it is possible for arguments that are both many and
good to arise.

What has been said to be a special affection in relation to something
else, then, must be looked at on the basis of the topics dealing with the
coincident, to see whether it is coincident with one thing and not coincident with another. But on those that are so always and on those that are
35   intrinsic, one must look at by means of the following [topics].

5.2

The correct assignment of a special affection (1)

First, look to see whether the special affection has been incorrectly or correctly assigned. To see whether it is incorrectly or correctly assigned, one [topic] is to see whether the special affection is proposed through things that are not better known or through things that are better known—when disestablishing, see whether they are not proposed through things that are better known; when establishing, whether they are proposed through things that are better known.[221]   129^b1

To prove that it is assigned through things that are not better known, one way is to look to see whether the special affection one assigns is wholly more unknown than the subject whose special affection one has stated it to be; for then the special affection will not have been correctly proposed. For it is for the sake of knowledge that we render the special affection.[222] The subject must, then, be separated by means of things that are better known; for this way it will be possible to understand it more adequately. For example, since a person who has posited "most similar to soul" as a special affection of fire makes use of soul, which is more unknown than fire (for we know more what fire is than soul), "most similar to soul" would not be correctly proposed as a special affection of fire.   10

Another way is to look to see whether this special affection is not better known as belonging to this subject. For not only must this special affection be better known than the thing in question, but also it must be better known as belonging to this subject; for a person who does not know whether this one belongs to this thing will also not know whether it belongs to it alone, so that, whichever of the two situations occurs, the special affection comes to lack perspicuousness. For example, since a person who has posited "what soul is naturally found primarily in" as a special affection of fire has made use of something more unknown than fire, namely, whether soul is found in fire and whether it is found primarily in it, "what soul is naturally found primarily in" would not be correctly proposed as a special affection of fire.   20

When establishing, on the other hand, look to see whether the special affection is proposed through things that are better known, and whether the "better known" holds in each of the two ways.[223] For then the special affection will in this respect have been correctly proposed; for of the topics useful for establishing that a special affection is correctly proposed, some will prove that in this respect only it is correctly proposed, others that it is unconditionally correctly assigned. For example, since a person who has stated "possessing perception" as a special affection of animal has assigned   25 it through things that are better known, in accord with each of the two ways, "possessing perception" would in this respect have been correctly assigned as a special affection of animal.

Next, when disestablishing, look to see whether any of the names assigned in [the account of] the special affection is said of things in many ways, or whether too the account as a whole signifies several things; for then the special affection will not have been correctly proposed. For example, since "to perceive" signifies several things, to have perception and to be using perception, "to naturally perceive" would not be correctly proposed as a special affection of animal. Because of this, neither a name nor an account said of things in several ways must be used in signifying a special affection, because what is said of things in many ways makes what is said lack perspicuousness, puzzling the person about to attack it as to which of the several things being said one means; for a special affection is assigned for the sake of learning. Further, in addition to this, it is necessary for those who assign a special affection in this way to submit to a sort of refutation, when someone produces a deduction in the case of one of the many ways in which the thing is said where there is a discordance.²²⁴

When establishing, on the other hand, look to see whether all the names and also the account as a whole do not signify several things; for the special affection will then in this respect be correctly proposed. For example, since "body" does not indicate many things and neither does "what is most easily moved upward" or the whole composed by putting these together, "the body that is most easily moved upward" would be correctly proposed in this respect as a special affection of fire.

Next, when disestablishing, look to see whether what the special affection is assigned to is said of things in many ways, but it is not made determinate in which of them one is positing it as a special affection; for then the special affection will not have been correctly assigned. The cause due to which this is so is not unclear from what was said previously; for the same things necessarily follow.²²⁵ For example, since "the scientific knowledge of this" signifies many things (for it signifies its having scientific knowledge, its using scientific knowledge, having scientific knowledge of it, and using the scientific knowledge of it), a special affection of "the scientific knowledge of this" would not be correctly assigned, without its having been made determinate of which of them one is positing it as a special affection.

When establishing, on the other hand, look to see whether the thing one posits the special affection of is not said of things in many ways, but is rather one and simple; for then the special affection will in this respect be correctly proposed.²²⁶ For example, since human is said of things in one way, "animal tame by nature" would be correctly proposed in this respect as a special affection in the case of human.

Next, when disestablishing, look to see whether the same thing has been said several times in the special affection; for often, without its being noticed, people do this in special affections too, just as they also do in definitions. And a special affection to which this has happened will not be correctly proposed; for what is said many times confuses the listener. Thus it necessarily becomes non-perspicuous, and in addition the proposers seem to babble.[227] Saying the same thing several times will happen in two ways: one is when someone has used the same name several times—as would happen if someone were to assign "the body that is the lightest of bodies" as a special affection of fire (for he has said body several times); second, if he were to assign accounts in place of names—as would happen if he were to assign "the substance that of all bodies is, in accord with nature, most spatially moved downward" as a special affection of earth, and were then to put "substances of such-and-such sort" in place of "bodies," since body and substance of such-and-such sort are one and the same; for in this way "substance" will be said several times. So neither of these special affections would have been correctly proposed.

When establishing, on the other hand, look to see whether one is not using the same name several times; for then the special affection would in this respect have been correctly assigned. For example, since a person who has stated "animal receptive of scientific knowledge" as a special affection of human has not used the same name several times, the special affection of human would in this respect have been correctly assigned.

Next, when disestablishing, look to see whether the opponent has assigned in the special affection anything of the sort that belongs to every-thing. For what does not separate the subject from certain things will be useless, while what is said in special affections must separate it, just as what is said in definitions also must. Hence the special affection will not be correctly proposed. For example, since a person who has posited as a special affection of scientific knowledge, "supposition that is incap-able of being persuaded to change by argument, since it is one," has used something in the special affection—the "one"—that belongs to everything, the special affection of scientific knowledge would not have been correctly proposed.[228]

When establishing, on the other hand, look to see whether one has used not something common, but something that separates the subject from something; for then the special affection will in this respect be correctly proposed. For example, since a person who has stated "possessing a soul" as a special affection of living thing has used nothing common, "possess-ing a soul" would in this respect have been correctly proposed as a special affection of living thing.

Next, when disestablishing, look to see whether the opponent has assigned several special affections to the same thing, without determining that he is positing several; for then the special affection will not be correctly proposed. For just as in definitions nothing more must be proposed beyond the account that indicates the substance, so too in special affections nothing must be assigned beyond the account that makes what is stated the special affection; for something of that sort is useless. For example, since a person who has stated "the most fine-grained and lightest body" as a special affection of fire has assigned several special affections (for each of the two is truly stated of fire alone), "the most fine-grained and lightest body" would not have been correctly proposed as a special affection of fire.

When establishing, on the other hand, look to see whether one has not assigned several special affections to the same thing, but rather only one; for then the special affection will be in this respect correctly proposed. For example, since a person who has stated "body that is brought to assume any shape" as a special affection of liquid has assigned one thing and not several as its special affection, the special affection of liquid would in this respect have been correctly proposed.

5.3

The correct assignment of a special affection (2)

Next, when disestablishing, look to see whether the opponent has made additional use either of the subject itself whose special affection one is assigning, or something belonging to it; for then the special affection will not be correctly proposed. For a special affection is assigned for the sake of learning.²²⁹ The subject, on the other hand, is as unknowable as itself, while anything belonging to it is posterior to it, and hence no better known than it is, so that through these we cannot learn anything more.²³⁰ For example, since a person who has stated "substance of which human being is a form" as a special affection of living thing has made additional use of something belonging to it, the special affection would not have been correctly proposed.

When establishing, on the other hand, look to see whether one is not using either the subject itself or anything belonging to it; for then the special affection will in this respect be correctly proposed. For example, since a person who has posited "composed of soul and body" as a special affection of living thing has not made use of the thing itself or anything belonging to it, the special affection of living thing would in this respect have been correctly assigned.

In the same way, look in the case of other things that do not make the subject better known. When disestablishing, look to see whether the opponent has made additional use of anything that is either opposite to the subject or, in general, anything simultaneous in nature with it or posterior to it; for then the special affection will not be correctly proposed.[231] For the opposite of a thing is simultaneous by nature with it, and what is simultaneous by nature with a thing and what is posterior to it do not make it better known.[232] For example, since a person who has stated "most opposed to bad" as a special affection of good has made additional use of the opposite of good, the special affection would not have been correctly assigned.

When establishing, on the other hand, look to see whether one has not made additional use of anything that is either opposite to the subject or, in general, simultaneous in nature with it, or posterior to it; for then the special affection will in this respect have been correctly assigned. For example, since a person who has posited "most persuasive supposition" as a special affection of scientific knowledge has not made additional use of anything either opposite to, simultaneous in nature with, or posterior to the subject, the special affection of scientific knowledge would in this respect have been correctly proposed.

Next, when disestablishing, look to see whether the opponent has not assigned as a special affection something that does not always accompany the subject but rather something that sometimes ceases to be a special affection; for then the special affection will not be correctly stated. For the name of the subject is not of necessity true of what we find the special affection to belong to, nor is the name of the subject of necessity not applied to what we find the special affection does not to belong to, so that the special affection would not have been in this respect correctly proposed. Further, in addition to this, even when he has assigned the special affection, it will not be evident that it belongs, if indeed it is the sort of thing that may be absent.[233] The special affection, then, will not be perspicuous. For example, since a person who has posited "moving" as a special affection of living thing has assigned the sort of special affection that is sometimes not a special affection, the special affection would not have been correctly proposed.

When establishing, on the other hand, look to see whether one has assigned what of necessity is always a special affection; for then the special affection will in this respect be correctly proposed. For example, since a person who has posited "what makes its possessor excellent" as a special affection of virtue has assigned as a special affection what always accompanies its subject, the special affection of virtue would have been in this respect correctly assigned.

Next, when disestablishing, look to see whether in assigning a now-
special affection, the opponent has not made it determinate that it is a
now-special affection that he is assigning; for then the special affection
will not be correctly proposed. For, first, anything beyond what is customary always needs to be made additionally determinate, and people are for
the most part accustomed to assigning as a special affection what always
accompanies the subject. Second, a person is unclear who has not made it
determinate whether it is a now-special affection that he wished to posit,
and one must not give any pretext for critical investigation. For example,
since a person who has posited "sitting with a certain someone" as a special
affection of a certain human being posits a now-special affection, the special affection would not have been correctly assigned, if indeed he stated it
without making this determinate.

When establishing, on the other hand, look to see whether in assigning
a now-special affection one has posited it making it determinate that one
is positing a now-special affection; for then the special affection will in this
respect be correctly proposed. For example, since a person who has stated
"walking about now" as a special affection of a certain human being has
made this determinate in his statement, the special affection would be correctly proposed.

Next, when disestablishing, look to see whether the special affection
the opponent has assigned is of the sort whose belonging is not evident
except to perception; for then the special affection will not be correctly
proposed.²³⁴ For every perceptible thing becomes unclear when outside the
range of perception; for it is not evident whether it still belongs, because
this is known only by perception.²³⁵ And this will be true in the case of any
affections that do not always and of necessity follow along with the subject.
For example, since a person who has posited "the brightest star spatially
moving above the earth" as a special affection of the sun has used in the
special affection "spatially moving above the earth" a sort of thing that is
known only by perception, the special affection of the sun would not have
been correctly assigned; for it will be unclear, when the sun sets, whether it
is spatially moving above the earth, because the perception is then absent
from us.

When establishing, on the other hand, look to see whether the special
affection one has assigned is of the sort that is not evident to perception,
or, if it is perceptible, clearly belongs of necessity to the subject; for then
the special affection will in this respect be correctly proposed. For example,
since a person who has posited "the primary thing that is colored" as a special affection of surface has made use of something perceptible ("colored"),
but this is of a sort that evidently always belongs to it, the special affection
of surface would in this respect have been correctly assigned.

Next, when disestablishing, look to see whether the opponent has assigned the definition as special affection; for then the special affection will not be correctly proposed; for a special affection must not indicate the essence.²³⁶ For example, since a person who has stated "terrestrial two-footed animal" as a special affection of human has assigned what signifies its essence as a special affection of human, the special affection of human would not have been correctly assigned.

When establishing, on the other hand, look to see whether the special affection one has assigned is counterpredicated with the subject but does not indicate the essence; for then the special affection will in this respect have been correctly assigned. For example, since a person who has posited "by nature a tame animal" as a special affection of human has assigned as special affection something that is counterpredicated of the subject but does not indicate its essence, the special affection of human would in this respect have been correctly assigned.

Next, when disestablishing, look to see whether the opponent has assigned the special affection but has not put [the subject] in its what-it-is.²³⁷ For in special affections, just as in definitions, the first thing to be assigned must be the kind, and then the rest must be attached immediately afterward and must make the separation.²³⁸ So a special affection that is not proposed in this way would not have been correctly assigned. For example, since a person who has stated "having a soul" as a special affection of living thing has not put the living thing in its what-it-is, the special affection of living thing would not have been correctly proposed.²³⁹

When establishing, on the other hand, look to see whether one has put the subject, whose special affection one is assigning, in its what-it-is, and then attaches the rest; for then the special affection will in this respect have been correctly assigned. For example, since a person who has posited "animal receptive of scientific knowledge" as a special affection of human has put the subject kind in its what-it-is and then assigned the special affection, the special affection of human would, in this respect, have been correctly proposed.

5.4

Whether an affection assigned as special is in fact special (1)

To see whether the special affection has been correctly assigned, then, look by means of these [topics]. But one must look at whether what is stated is a special affection, or not a special affection at all, on the basis of the following ones. For the topics that simply establish that the special affection is

25   correctly proposed will be the same as those that make it a special affection at all, and thus will be stated in connection with these.

First, then, when disestablishing, take a look at each subject of which the opponent has assigned the special affection, to see, that is, whether it belongs to none of them, or whether it is not true of them in the relevant
30   respect; for then what is proposed as being a special affection will not be a special affection. For example, since "not being deceivable by argument" is not true of the geometer (for he could be deceived when a false diagram is drawn), "not being deceivable by argument" would not be a special affection of the scientific knower.[240]

When establishing, on the other hand, look to see whether the special
35   affection is true of every case and true in the relevant respect; for then what is proposed as not being a special affection will be a special affection. For example, since "animal receptive of scientific knowledge" is true
132^b1   of every human, and true of him insofar as he is human, "animal receptive of scientific knowledge" would be a special affection of human. {This topic, when disestablishing, goes this way: look to see whether the account is not true of what the name is true of, and whether the name is not true of what the account is true of; when establishing, on the other hand: look to
5   see whether the account too is predicated of what the name is predicated of, and whether the name too is predicated of what the account is predicated of.}[241]

Next, when disestablishing, look to see whether the account is not said of what the name is said of, and whether the name is not said of what the
10   account is said of; for then what was proposed as being a special affection will not be a special affection. For example, since "living thing that shares in scientific knowledge" is true of the god, but "human" is not predicated of the god, "living thing that shares in scientific knowledge" would not be a special affection of human.

When establishing, on the other hand, look to see whether the name too is predicated of what the account is predicated of, and whether the account too is predicated of what the name is predicated of; for then what
15   is proposed as not being a special affection will be a special affection. For example, since "living thing" is true of "what has a soul" is true of, and "having a soul" is true of what "living thing" is true of, "having a soul" would be a special affection of living thing.[242]

Next, when disestablishing, look to see whether the opponent has assigned the underlying subject as a special affection of what is said to be
20   in the underlying subject; for then what is proposed as a special affection will not be a special affection.[243] For example, since a person who proposes "fire" as a special affection of the body having the finest-grained particles has assigned the underlying subject as a special affection of

what is predicated of it, "fire" would not be a special affection of the body having the finest-grained particles.[244] That is why the underlying subject will not be a special affection of what is in the underlying subject, because the same thing will then be a special affection of several things that differ in form. For several things that differ in form belong to the same thing, which are said of it alone, and of all of these the underlying subject will be a special affection, if one posits the special affection in this way.

When establishing, on the other hand, look to see whether one has assigned what is in the underlying subject as a special affection of the subject; for then what is proposed as not a special affection will be a special affection, if indeed it is predicated only of it in the way that a special affection is said. For example, since a person who has stated as a special affection of earth "body heaviest in form" has assigned as a special affection of the underlying subject what is said of that thing alone and in the way that a special affection is predicated, the special affection of earth would have been correctly proposed.

Next, when disestablishing, look to see whether the opponent has assigned the special affection by virtue of participation; for then what is proposed as a special affection will not be a special affection. For what belongs by virtue of participation contributes to the essence, and, as such, would be a difference said of some one form.[245] For example, since a person who has stated "two-footed terrestrial" as a special affection of human has assigned the special affection as something by virtue of participation, "two-footed terrestrial" would not be a special affection of human.

When establishing, on the other hand, look to see whether one has not assigned the special affection as something by virtue of participation, nor as indicating the essence, though the thing is counterpredicated of it; for then what is proposed as not being a special affection will be a special affection. For example, since a person who has posited "naturally having perception" as a special affection of animal has assigned the special affection neither by virtue of participation nor as indicating the being, though the thing is counterpredicated of it, "naturally having perception" would be a special affection of animal.

Next, when disestablishing, look to see whether the special affection admits of not belonging at the same time as the name, but rather admits of belonging posterior or prior to it; for then what is proposed as a special affection will not be a special affection—either not ever, or not always. For example, since "walking through the marketplace" admits of belonging to someone both prior and posterior to "human," "walking through the marketplace" would not be a special affection of the human—either not ever, or not always.[246]

When establishing, on the other hand, look to see whether the special affection of necessity always belongs at the same time, without being either a definition or a difference; for then what is proposed as not being a special affection will be a special affection. For example, since of necessity "animal receptive of scientific knowledge" always belongs at the same time as "human" does, and is neither a difference nor a definition, "animal receptive of scientific knowledge" would be a special affection of human.

Next, when disestablishing, look to see whether the same thing is not a special affection of the same things, insofar as they are the same; for then what is proposed as being a special affection will not be a special affection. For example, since "appearing good to certain people" is not a special affection of the worthy of pursuit, neither would "appearing good to certain people" be a special affection of the choiceworthy; for the worthy of pursuit and the worthy of choice are the same.

When establishing, on the other hand, look to see whether the same thing is a special affection of something that is the same thing [as the subject], insofar as it is the same; for then what is proposed as not a special affection will be a special affection. For example, since "having a tripartite soul" is said to be a special affection of human, insofar as it is human, it would also be a special affection of mortal, insofar as it is mortal, to have a tripartite soul.[247] This topic is also useful in the case of the coincident; for to the same things, insofar as they are the same, the same ones must belong, or not belong.

Next, when disestablishing, look to see whether the special affection of things that are the same in form is not always the same in form; for then the proposed special affection will not be a special affection of the stated subject either. For example, since horse and human are the same in form, and it is not always a special affection of a horse "to stand still of its own accord," it would not always be a special affection of a human "to move of its own accord"; for moving of its own accord and standing still of its own accord are the same in form, each of them occurring to an animal insofar as it is animal.[248]

When establishing, on the other hand, look to see whether the special affection of things that are the same in form are always the same in form; for then what is proposed as not being a special affection will be a special affection. For example, since it is a special affection of human to be "two-footed terrestrial," it would also be a special affection of bird to be "two-footed flyer"; for each of these is the same in form, the one lot, insofar as they are forms falling under the same kind, since they fall under animal, and the other lot, insofar as they are differences of the kind "animal." This topic is false when one of the special affections mentioned belongs to one certain form only, while the other belongs to many—for example, "four-footed terrestrial."

Since same and distinct are said of things in many ways, it is hard work, faced with someone who takes things in a sophistical way, to assign a special affection of some one thing and of it alone; for what belongs to something that has something as a coincident will also belong to the coincident taken together with the thing it is a coincident of. For example, what belongs to human will also belong to pale human, if human is pale, and what then belongs to pale human will also belong to human. One might, then, attack many special affections by making the underlying subject one thing when taken intrinsically and a distinct thing when taken together with a coincident of it—for example, saying that human is one thing and pale human a distinct thing.[249] And further, by making the state and what is said in accord with the state distinct. For what belongs to the state also belongs to what is said with respect to the state, and what belongs to what is said with respect to the state belongs to the state too. For example, since a scientific knower is said to be in a certain state with respect to scientific knowledge, "incapable of being persuaded to change by argument" would not be a special affection of scientific knowledge; for then the scientific knower too will be incapable of being persuaded to change by argument.

When establishing, on the other hand, one must say that the thing a coincident belongs to is not unconditionally distinct from the coincident taken together with the thing it is a coincident of, but is said to be distinct from it because the being for each of them is distinct; for the being for human is not for a human the same thing as being for pale human is for a pale human. Further, one should look at the inflections and say that the scientific knower will not be *what* is incapable of being persuaded to change by argument, but *who* is incapable of being persuaded to change by argument, and that scientific knowledge is not *what* is incapable of being persuaded to change by argument but *which* is incapable of being persuaded to change by argument; for against the person who offers every sort of objection, one must put up every sort of resistance.[250]

5.5

Whether an affection assigned as special is in fact special (2)

Next, when disestablishing, look to see whether, while wishing to assign [as a special affection] what belongs by nature, the opponent posits it by his speech in such a way as to signify what always belongs; for then the proposed special affection would seem to be undermined.[251] For example, since a person who has stated two-footed as a special affection of human wishes to assign what belongs by nature, but signifies by his speech one that

10   belongs always, two-footed would not be a special affection of human; for not every human has two feet.

When establishing, on the other hand, look to see whether one wishes to assign as a special affection what belongs by nature, and by one's speech signifies it this way; for then the special affection will not in this respect be undermined. For example, since a person who assigns "animal receptive of scientific knowledge" as a special affection of human both wishes

15   and by his speech signifies, the [sort of] special affection that belongs by nature, "animal receptive of scientific knowledge" would not in this respect be undermined as not being a special affection of human.

Further, it is hard work to assign the special affection of whatever sorts of things are said to be so primarily with respect to something else or as themselves primarily so; for if one has assigned a special affection as belonging to what is so with respect to something else, it will also be true

20   of what is primarily so; but if you have posited it as belonging to what is primarily so, it will also be predicated of what is so with respect to something else. For example, if one has assigned "colored" as a special affection of surface, "colored" will also be true with respect to body, while if one has assigned it as a special affection of body, it will also be predicated of surface. So it will not hold that what the account is true of, the name will

25   also be true of.²⁵²

In the case of some special affections, it for the most part happens that a certain error occurs from not determining how and of which things the special affection is posited. For everyone tries to assign as the special affection what belongs by nature (as to human, "two-footed" does); what

30   actually belongs (as to a certain human, "having four fingers" does); what belongs to the form (as to fire, "having the finest-grained particles" does); what belongs unconditionally (as to animal, "living" does); what belongs with respect to something else (as to soul, "practically wise" does); what belongs primarily (as to the rationally calculative part, "practically wise" does); what belongs because of the subject having a certain thing (as to the scientific knower, "incapable of being persuaded to change by argu-

35   ment" does—for it will be because of nothing other than having a certain thing that he is incapable of being persuaded to change by argument); what belongs because the subject is had by a certain thing (as to scientific knowledge, "incapable of being persuaded to change by argument"

134^b1   does); what belongs because the subject is participated in by something (as to animal, "perception" does—for something else, such as human, also perceives, but because animal already participated [in it]); or what belongs because the subject participates in something (as to a certain animal, "living" does).

Someone errs, then, if he does not add "by nature," because what belongs   5
by nature admits of not actually belonging to what it belongs to by nature
(as to human, "having two feet" does). —Also if he does not determine
that he is assigning what actually belongs, because it will not be such as to
belong to that subject, like "having four fingers" to human. —Also if he has
not made clear that he is positing it as primarily so or as so with respect
to something else, because then it will not hold that what the account is   10
true of, the name will also be true of (as is the case with "colored," whether
assigned as a special affection of surface or of body). —Also, if he has not
stated beforehand that he has assigned the special affection either because
of the subject having a thing, or because of a certain thing having the subject, because then it will not be a special affection; for if he assigns it because
of a certain thing having the subject, it will belong to what has the thing,   15
while if he assigns it because of what has the thing, it will belong to the
thing that is had (as "incapable of being persuaded to change by argument"
belongs when posited as a special affection of scientific knowledge and of
the scientific knower). —Also if he has not, in addition, signified that he
assigns it because of the subject participating in something or because of
it being participated in by something, because then the special affection
will belong to certain other things as well; for if he assigns it because of the
subject being participated in by something, it will belong to the partici-   20
pants, and if he assigns it because of its participating in something, it will
belong to the things participated in (as is the case if one has posited "living"
as a special affection of a certain animal and of animal). —Also if he has
not explicitly distinguished the special affection as belonging to the form,
because then it will belong to only one of the things that fall under what
he is positing the special affection of; for the superlative degree belongs
to only one of them (as to fire, "lightest" does). Sometimes, though, one
has erred even if one has added "to the form." For the things mentioned   25
will have to be of one form when "to the form" is added. But in some cases
this does not happen (as it does not in the case of fire; for there is not only
one form of fire; for glowing ember, flame, and light are distinct in form,
though each of them is fire).²⁵³

It is because of this that, when "in form" is added, there must not be a
form other than the one mentioned: because the special affection stated   30
will belong to some things more and to others less (as in the case of fire
"having the finest-grained particles" does; for light consists of finer-grained
particles than ember-glow or flame does). And this should not happen
unless the name too is predicated more of what the account is more true of   35
(otherwise it will not be the case that what the account applies to more, the
name also applies to more). Further, in addition to this, the same thing will

135ᵃ1 be the special affection both of the unconditionally so and of the most so in respect of what is this unconditionally (as "having the finest-grained particles" is in the case of fire; for this same thing will also be a special affection of light; for it is light that has the finest-grained particles). If, therefore, someone else assigns the special affection in this way, one must attack it. But for oneself, one must not give an opening for this objection, but in positing the special affection one must immediately determine in what way one is positing the special affection.

Next, when disestablishing, look to see whether the opponent has posited a thing as a special affection of itself; for then what is proposed as being a special affection will not be a special affection. For a thing itself always indicates the being of it; and what indicates the being is not a special affection but a definition.²⁵⁴ For example, since a person who has stated "appropriate" as a special affection of noble has assigned the thing as a special affection of itself (for the noble and the appropriate are the same thing), appropriate would not be a special affection of noble.²⁵⁵

When establishing, on the other hand, look to see whether, though one has not assigned the thing itself as a special affection of itself, one has posited as a special affection something counterpredicated; for then what has been proposed as not being a special affection will be a special affection. For example, since a person who has posited "animate substance" as a special affection of animal has not posited the thing itself as a special affection of itself, but has assigned something counterpredicated, "animate substance" would be a special affection of animal.

Next, in the case of uniform things, look to see, when disestablishing, whether the special affection of the whole is not true of the parts, or if that of a part is not said of the whole; for then what is proposed as being a special affection will not be a special affection.²⁵⁶ In some cases it happens that this occurs; for in the case of uniform things, someone might assign a special affection, sometimes looking to the whole, and sometimes giving his attention to what is said of the parts. And in neither case will the special affection be assigned correctly. For example, in the case of the whole, since a person who has stated "the greatest quantity of salt water" as a special affection of sea has posited the special affection of something uniform, but has assigned one of such a sort as is not true of the part (for a certain sea is not the greatest quantity of salt water), "the greatest quantity of salt water" would not be a special affection of sea.²⁵⁷ In the case of the parts, for example, since a person who has posited "breathable" as a special affection of air has stated the special affection of something uniform, but has assigned one of such a sort as is true of certain air, but is not said of the whole (for the whole air is not breathable), "breathable" would not be a special affection of air.²⁵⁸

When establishing, on the other hand, look to see whether, while it is true of each part of the uniform things, it is a special affection of them as a whole; for then what is proposed as not being a special affection will be a special affection. For example, since "by nature spatially moved downward" is true of all earth, but this is a special affection of a certain [piece of earth] by virtue of earth, "by nature spatially moved downward" would be a special affection of earth.

5

5.6

Opposites

Next, one must look on the basis of opposites.

First, look on the basis of contraries. When disestablishing, do so to see whether the contrary of what is proposed is not a special affection of the contrary [subject]; for then neither will the contrary be a special affection of the contrary [subject]. For example, since injustice is contrary to justice, and the worst evil to the best good, but it is not a special affection of justice to be "the best good," it would not be a special affection of injustice to be "the worst evil."

When establishing, on the other hand, look to see whether the contrary is a special affection of the contrary; for then the contrary to the first will also be a special affection of the contrary to the second. For example, since bad is contrary to good, and the worthy of avoidance to the worthy of choice, and "worthy of choice" is a special affection of good, "worthy of avoidance" would be a special affection of bad.

Second, look on the basis of relatives. When disestablishing, do so to see whether the relative [to what is proposed] is not a special affection of the relative [to the subject]; for then neither will the relative [to the subject] be a special affection of the relative [to what is proposed]. For example, since double is said of things relative to half, and exceeding to being exceeded, and "exceeding" is not a special affection of double, "being exceeded" would not be a special affection of half.

When establishing, on the other hand, look to see whether the relative [to what is proposed] is a special affection of the relative [to the subject]; for then the relative [to the subject] will also be a special affection of the relative to [what is proposed]. For example, since double is said of things relative to half, and two-to-one relative to one-to-two, and it is a special affection of two to be "as two-to-one," it would be a special affection of half to be "as one-to-two."

Third, when disestablishing, look to see whether what is said as a having is not a special affection of the having; for then neither will what is said as a privation be a special affection of the privation. Also, if what is said as

10

15

20

25

a privation is not a special affection of the privation; for then neither will what is said as a having be a special affection of the having. For example, since being "the absence of perception" is not said to be a special affection of deafness, neither would being "the presence of perception" be a special affection of hearing.

When establishing, on the other hand, look to see whether what is said as a having is a special affection of the having. For then what is said as a privation will be a special affection of the privation. Also, if what is said as a privation is a special affection of the privation, what is said as a having will also be a special affection of the having. For example, since "to see" is a special affection of sight, in as much as we have sight, it would be a special affection of blindness "not to see," in as much as we do not have the sight it is natural for us to have.

Next, look on the basis of positive and negative terms.

First, on the basis of the predicates themselves. This topic is useful only when disestablishing. For example, see whether the positive predicate or what is said in terms of the positive predicate is a special affection of the subject; for then neither the negative one nor what is said in terms of the negative one will be a special affection of the subject. Also, if the negative one or what is said in terms of the negative one is a special affection of the subject, neither the positive one nor what is said in terms of the positive one will be a special affection of the subject. For example, since "animate" is a special affection of living thing, "not-animate" would not be a special affection of living thing.

Second, look on the basis of the predicates, positive or negative, and on the basis of the subjects they are affirmed or denied of. When disestablishing, do so to see whether the positive predicate is not a special affection of the positive subject; for then neither will the negative be a special affection of the negative. Also, if the negative predicate is not a special affection of the negative subject, neither will the positive be one of the positive. For example, since "animal" is not a special affection of human, neither would "non-animal" be a special affection of non-human. Also, if "non-animal" appears not to be a special affection of non-human, neither will "animal" [appear to] be a special affection of human.[259]

When establishing, on the other hand, look to see whether the positive predicate is a special affection of the positive subject; for then the negative will also be a special affection of the negative. Also, if the negative predicate is a special affection of the negative subject, the positive will also be a special affection of the positive. For example, since "not-living" is a special affection of non-animal, "living" would be a special affection of animal. Also, if "living" appears to be a special affection of animal, "not-living" will appear to be a special affection of non-animal.

82

Third, look on the basis of the underlying subjects themselves. When dis-establishing, do so to see whether the special affection assigned is a special affection of the positive subject; for then the same thing will not also be a special affection of the negative subject. Also, if the special affection assigned is a special affection of the negative subject, it will not be a special affection of the positive subject. For example, since "animate" is a special affection of living thing, "animate" would not be a special affection of not-living thing.

When establishing, on the other hand, look to see whether the special affection assigned is not a special affection of the positive subject; for then it would be one of the negative subject. But this topic is false; for a positive predicate is not a special affection of a negative subject, nor a negative one of a positive one. For a positive predicate does not belong to a negative sub-ject at all, whereas a negative predicate, while it does belong to a positive subject, does not belong as a special affection.

Next, look on the basis of the coordinate members of a division. When disestablishing, do so to see whether none of the coordinate members in the division is a special affection of any of the remaining members; for then neither will what is proposed be a special affection of what it is proposed as a special affection of. For example, since "perceptible living thing" is not a special affection of any of the other living things, "intelligible living thing" could not be a special affection of a god.

When establishing, on the other hand, look to see whether any of the remaining coordinate members of the division whatever is a special affec-tion of each of these coordinate members; for then the remaining one will also be a special affection of what it has been proposed as not being a spe-cial affection of. For example, since it is a special affection of practical wis-dom to be "intrinsically and naturally a virtue of the rationally calculative part," then, if each of the other virtues is taken in this way, it would be a special affection of temperance to be "intrinsically and naturally a virtue of the appetitive part."

5.7

Inflections and similarity of relations

Next, look on the basis of the inflections. When disestablishing, do so by seeing whether one inflection [of the predicate] is not a special affection of the corresponding inflection [of the subject]; for then neither will another inflection of it be a special affection of the corresponding inflection. For example, since "nobly" is not a special affection of justly, neither would "noble" be a special affection of just.

When establishing, on the other hand, look to see whether one inflection [of the predicate] is a special affection of the corresponding inflection [of the subject]; for then another inflection of it will also be a special affection of the corresponding inflection. For example, since "two-footed terrestrial" is a special affection of human, it would be a special affection of the *by* a human to be said to be "*by* a two-footed terrestrial."[260]

Look at the inflections not only of the actual thing mentioned but also of its opposites, as was said in the case of the earlier topics as well.[261] When disestablishing, do so by seeing whether one inflection of one opposite is not a special affection of the corresponding inflection of the other opposite; for then neither will another inflection of the one be a special affection of the corresponding inflection of the other. For example, since "well" is not a special affection of justly, neither would "badly" be a special affection of unjustly.

When establishing, on the other hand, look to see whether one inflection of one opposite is a special affection of the corresponding inflection of the other opposite; for then another inflection of the one opposite will also be a special affection of the corresponding inflection of the other opposite. For example, since "best" is a special affection of the good, "worst" will also be a special affection of the bad.[262]

Next, look on the basis of similarity relations. When disestablishing, do so by seeing whether one thing that has a similarity relation to one thing is not a special affection of a second thing that has a corresponding similarity relation to a second thing; for then neither will it be a special affection of the first thing to have the relevant similarity relation to the first thing. For example, since the builder has a relation to producing a house that is similar to the one the doctor has to producing health, and it is not a special affection of the doctor to "produce health," it would not be a special affection of the builder to "produce a house."

When establishing, on the other hand, look to see whether one thing that has a similarity relation to one thing is a special affection of a second thing that has a corresponding similarity relation to a second thing; for then it will also be a special affection of the first thing to have the relevant similarity relation to the first thing. For example, since a doctor has a relation to being productive of health that is similar to the one the athletic trainer has to being productive of a good condition, and it is a special affection of the athletic trainer to be "productive of a good condition," it would be a special affection of the doctor to be "productive of health."[263]

Next, look on the basis of things that have the same relations. When disestablishing, do so to see whether what has the same relation [to something] is not a special affection of it when it has the same relation [to something else]; for then neither will it be a special affection [of the first thing]

to have the same relation [to the first thing]. If, on the other hand, it is a   10
special affection [of the second thing], it will not be a special affection of
what it is proposed as being a special affection of.[264] For example, since
practical wisdom has the same relation to the noble and to the shameful
(for it is the scientific knowledge of each of them), and it is not a special
affection of practical wisdom to be "the scientific knowledge of the noble,"
it would not be a special affection of practical wisdom to be "the scientific
knowledge of the shameful." But if it is a special affection of practical wis-   15
dom to be "the scientific knowledge of the noble," it would not be a special
affection of it to be "the scientific knowledge of the shameful"; for it is
impossible for the same thing be a special affection of several things.[265]

When establishing something, on the other hand, this topic is of no use;
for what has the same relation is one thing brought into combination with
several things.   20

Next, when disestablishing, look to see whether the predicate that is
said with respect to being is not a special affection of the subject that is said
with respect to being; for then neither will the predicate that is said with
respect to ceasing to be, be a special affection of the subject that is said with
respect to ceasing to be, nor will the predicate that is said with respect to be
coming to be, be a special affection of the subject that is said with respect
to coming to be. For example, since "animal" is not a special affection of
human, neither would "coming to be animal" be a special affection of com-   25
ing to be human, nor would "ceasing to be animal" be a special affection
of ceasing to be human. In the same way, precisely as it now has been said
from being to coming to be and to ceasing to be, one must also get from
coming to be to being and ceasing to be, and from ceasing to be to being
and coming to be.

When establishing, on the other hand, look to see whether the predicate   30
assigned with respect to being is a special affection of the subject assigned
with respect to being; for then the predicate that is said with respect to
coming to be will also be a special affection of the subject said with respect
to coming to be, and the predicate with respect to ceasing to be will be a
special affection of the subject that is said with respect to ceasing to be. For
example, since "mortal" is a special affection of human, "coming to be mortal" would be a special affection of the coming to be human, and "ceasing   35
to be mortal" of the ceasing to be human. In the same way, one must also
get from coming to be and ceasing to be to being, and to these from these,   137[b]1
as one was told to do when disestablishing.

Next, take a look at the [Platonic] Form of what is proposed. When disestablishing, do so to see whether the special affection does not belong to
the Form, or not with respect to that which it was said to be by the person
who proposed it as the special affection; for then what was proposed as

being a special affection will not be a special affection. For example, since "at rest" does not belong to human-itself, insofar as it is human, but rather insofar as it is a Form, "at rest" would not be a special affection of human.[266]

When establishing, on the other hand, look to see whether the special affection belongs to the Form, and belongs to it with respect to that which it was said to be insofar as what was proposed is not a special affection of it. For then what was proposed as not being a special affection will be a special affection. For example, since it belongs to animal-itself to be "composed of soul and body," and belongs to it insofar as it is animal, "composed of soul and body" would be a special affection of animal.

5.8

The more and the less and similarity of degree

Next, look on the basis of the more and the less.

First, when disestablishing, do so to see whether the more so is not a special affection of the more so; for then neither will the less so be a special affection of the less so, nor the least so of the least so, nor the most so of the most so, nor the unconditionally so of the unconditionally so.[267] For example, since "more colored" is not a special affection of what is more a body, neither would "less colored" be a special affection of what is less a body, nor would "colored" be one of body at all.[268]

When establishing, on the other hand, look to see whether the more so is a special affection of the more so; for then the less so will also be a special affection of the less so, the least so of the least so, the most so of the most so, and the unconditionally so of the unconditionally so. For example, since "more perceiving" is a special affection of the more living, and "less perceiving" would be a special affection of the less living, and "most so," then, of the most so, and "least so" of the least so, and "unconditionally so" of the unconditionally so.[269]

Also, look on the basis of the unconditionally so toward those same things. When disestablishing, do so to see whether "unconditionally so" is not a special affection of the unconditionally so; for then neither will "more so" be a special affection of the more so, nor "less so" of the less so, nor "most so" of the most so, nor "least so" of the least so. For example, since "excellent" is not a special affection of human, neither is "more excellent" a special affection of the more human.

When establishing, on the other hand, look to see whether "unconditionally so" is a special affection of the unconditionally so; for then "more so" will be a special affection of the more so, "less so" of the less so, "least

so" of the least so, and "most so" of the most so. For example, since "mov-   35
ing spatially upward in accord with nature" is a special affection of fire,
"moving more spatially upward in accord with nature" would be a special
affection of what is more fire.²⁷⁰ In the same way, look at all these on the   138ᵃ1
basis of the others.

Second, when disestablishing, look to see whether the "more" is not a
special affection; for then neither will the "less" be a special affection. For   5
example, since "perceiving" is more a special affection of living thing than
"scientifically knowing" is of human, and "perceiving" is not a special affection of living thing, "scientifically knowing" would not be a special affection of human.²⁷¹

When establishing, on the other hand, look to see whether the "less" is
a special affection; for then the "more" will also be a special affection. For
example, since to be by nature "tame" is less a special affection of human   10
than "living" is of animal, and it is a special affection of human to be "tame
by nature," "living" would be a special affection of animal.

Third, when disestablishing, look to see whether the special affection
[proposed] is not a special affection of what it is more a special affection of;
for then neither will it be a special affection of what it is less a special affection of; but if it is a special affection of the first, it will not be a special affection of the second. For example, since "colored" is more a special affection   15
of surface than of body, and it is not a special affection of surface, "colored"
would not be a special affection of body, while if it is a special affection of
surface, it would not be a special affection of body.

When establishing, on the other hand, this topic is not useful; for it is
not possible for the same thing to be a special affection of several things.   20

Fourth, when disestablishing, look to see whether what is more a special
affection of a given subject is not a special affection of it; for then neither will what is less a special affection of it be a special affection of it.
For example, since "perceptible" is more a special affection of animal than
"divisible" is, and "perceptible" is not a special affection of animal, neither
would "divisible" be a special affection of animal.²⁷²

When establishing, on the other hand, look to see whether what is less a   25
special affection of a given subject is a special affection of it; for then what
is more a special affection of it will be a special affection. For example,
since "perceiving" is less a special affection of animal than "living" is, and
"perceiving" is a special affection of animal, "living" would be a special
affection of animal.²⁷³

Next, look on the basis of special affections that belong in a similar way.
First, when disestablishing, to see whether what is a special affection in a   30
similar degree is not a special affection of that of which it is a special affection in a similar degree; for then neither will what is a special affection

in a similar degree be a special affection of that of which it is a special affection in a similar degree. For example, since "appetitive desiring" is a special affection of the appetitive part in a degree similar to that in which "rational calculating" is a special affection of the rationally calculative part, and "appetitive desiring" is not a special affection of the appetitive part, neither would "rationally calculating" be a special affection of the rationally calculating part.[274]

When establishing, on the other hand, look to see whether what is a special affection in a similar degree is a special affection of that of which it is a special affection in a similar degree; for then what is a special affection in a similar degree will also be a special affection of that of which it is a special affection in a similar degree. For example, since "the primary locus of practical wisdom" is a special affection of the rationally calculative part in a degree similar to that in which "the primary locus of temperance" is a special affection of the appetitive part, and "the primary locus of practical wisdom" is a special affection of the rationally calculative part, "the primary locus of temperance" would be a special affection of the appetitive part.

Second, when disestablishing, look to see whether what is in a similar degree a special affection of a given subject is not a special affection of it; for then neither will what is in a similar degree a special affection be a special affection of it. For example, since it is in a similar degree that "seeing" and "hearing" are special affections of human, and "seeing" is not a special affection of human, neither would "hearing" be a special affection of human.

When establishing, on the other hand, look to see whether what is in a similar degree a special affection of it is a special affection of it; for then what is in a similar degree a special affection of it will be a special affection of it. For example, since "appetitive due to a part of itself being primarily so" is in a similar degree a special affection of soul as "rationally calculative due to a part of itself being primarily so," and it is a special affection of soul to be "appetitive due to a part of itself being primarily so," it would be a special affection of soul to be "rationally calculative due to a part of itself being primarily so."

Third, when disestablishing, look to see whether it is not a special affection of what it is in a similar degree a special affection of; for then neither will it be a special affection of what it is in a similar degree a special affection of; while if it is a special affection of the first, it will not be a special affection of the second. For example, since "to burn" is to a similar degree a special affection of flame and glowing ember, and "to burn" is not a special affection of flame, "to burn" would not be a special affection of glowing ember, while if it is a special affection of flame, it would not be a special affection of glowing ember.

When establishing, on the other hand, this topic is not at all useful.

The topic based on similarity relations differs from the one based on special affections that belong in a similar degree, because the former is got hold of by analogy not by looking at the belonging of some affection, while the latter is based on what belongs being brought into combination with other things.[275]

25

5.9

Capacities and superlatives

Next, when disestablishing, look to see whether, in assigning the special affection as a capacity, the opponent has not assigned the special affection also as a capacity in relation to what is not, when the capacity does not admit of belonging to what is not; for then what is proposed as being a special affection will not be a special affection.[276] For example, since a person who has stated "breathable" as a special affection of air has, on the one hand, assigned the special affection as a capacity (for the breathable is the sort of thing that can be breathed), and, on the other hand, has assigned the special affection also in relation to what is not (for air in fact admits of being even though no animal is of a sort to naturally breath the air; yet if no animal is, nothing can breathe; so neither will it be a special affection of air to be "the sort of thing that can be breathed at a time when there is no animal of the sort that can breathe it")—[since all that is so,] it would not be a special affection of air to be "breathable."

30
35

When establishing, on the other hand, look to see whether in assigning the special affection as a capacity, one assigns the special affection either as a capacity in relation to what is or—when the capacity admits of belonging to what is not—in relation to what is not; for then what is proposed as not being a special affection will be a special affection. For example, since a person who assigns "capable of being affected or of affecting" as a special affection of what is assigns the special affection as a capacity, and has assigned the special affection in relation to what is (for when what is, is, it will be capable of being affected or of affecting in some way), so that "capable of being affected or of affecting" would be a special affection of what is.[277]

139ᵃ1
5

Next, when disestablishing, look to see whether the opponent has posited the special affection as a superlative; for then what is proposed as being a special affection will not be a special affection. For the result for those who assign the special affection in this way is that what the name is true of, the account is not true of; for when the thing has passed away, nonetheless

10

the account will be [true of something]; for it will belong most of all to things that are.[278] For example, if someone were to assign "the lightest body" as a special affection of fire; for if fire has passed away, there will still be some body that is the lightest. So "the lightest body" would not be a special affection of fire.

When establishing, on the other hand, look to see whether one has not posited the special affection as a superlative; for then the special affection will in this respect be correctly proposed. For example, since a person who has posited "by nature a tame animal" as a special affection of human has not assigned the special affection as a superlative, the special affection would in this respect be correctly proposed.

6: Definitions

6.1

Definitions

Where definitions are concerned, the work has five parts; for one must prove that it is not true at all to apply the account also to what the name applies to (for the definition of human must be true of every human); that though the subject to be defined has a kind, the opponent has not put it in the kind, or has not put it in its proper kind (for the definer must put the subject in the kind and then attach the differences; for of the things in the definition the kind seems most of all to signify the substance of the thing defined); that the account is not special (for the definition must be special, as was said previously); that, though having done all the things mentioned, he has not given a definition, that is, not stated the essence of the thing defined.[279] And beyond the things mentioned it remains to see whether, though he has given a definition, he has not given it correctly.

Whether, then, the account is not also true of what the name is true of, should be looked at on the basis of the topics related to the coincident; for there too the looking is always to see whether it is true or not true [of the thing].[280] For when we argue dialectically that a coincident belongs, we say that it is true, and when that it does not belong, that it is not true. If the opponent has not put the subject in its proper kind, however, or if the assigned account is not special to the subject, one must look at it on the basis of the topics related to the kind and the special affection.[281]

It remains to state how one must proceed to say whether the thing has either not been defined or not defined correctly. First, then, one must look to see whether it has not been defined correctly. For it is easier to do anything whatever than to do it correctly. It is clear, then, that error is more frequent where the latter is concerned, since it is more arduous work. So attack is easier where it is concerned than where the former is concerned.

Not defining correctly has two parts.[282] One consists in doing so by using an expression that is not perspicuous (for the definer must use the most perspicuous expression possible, since it is for the sake of making the thing known that the definition is being assigned). The second is if he has stated the account in a more extended version than is necessary; for any additional component in the definition is superfluous.[283] And each of the ones mentioned is again divided into several parts.

6.2

Non-perspicuously expressed definitions

One topic concerned with what is not perspicuously expressed is to look
to see whether what is said is homonymous with something—for example,

20   if someone says that coming to be is a leading into being, or that health is
a balance of hot things and cold things; for leading is homonymous, and
so is balance.[284] It is unclear, then, which of the things indicated by what is
said in several ways the opponent wishes to state. It is the same way too if
the thing defined is said in several ways and he has stated [the definition]
without distinguishing them; for then it is unclear of which of them he

25   proposes the definition, and it is also possible to make a trivial objection
to it on the grounds that the account does not fit everything he has given
the definition of.[285] It is especially possible to make one of this sort when
the homonymy is unnoticed. But it is also possible for someone to distinguish himself the various ways in which what is assigned in the definition

30   is stated, and produce a pertinent deduction; for if it is adequately stated
in none of the ways, it is clear that he would not have defined it properly.

Another topic is to look to see whether the definer has stated it metaphorically—for example, if he has defined scientific knowledge as "inflexible,"
or the earth as a "nurse," or temperance as a "harmony"; for everything

35   stated metaphorically lacks perspicuousness.[286] Also, it is possible to make
a trivial objection to what is stated metaphorically by supposing it to have
been stated literally; for then the definition stated will not fit—for example,
in the case of temperance; for all harmony consists of notes. Further, if
harmony is the kind of temperance, the same thing will be in two kinds,

140^{a}1   neither of which encompasses the other; for harmony does not encompass
virtue, nor virtue harmony.

Further, look to see whether he uses names that are not established, as
when Plato defines the eye as "brow-shaded," or the poisonous spider as
"bite-necrotic," or marrow as "bone-produced"; for everything that is not

5   customary is non-perspicuous.[287]

But there are some things that are stated neither homonymously nor
metaphorically—for example, that the law is a measure or likeness of what
is by nature just. Things of this sort are worse than metaphors. For a metaphor in a way makes known the thing it signifies, because of the similarity

10   involved (for all makers of metaphors make their metaphors in accord with
a certain similarity), while something of this sort does not make anything
known; for there is no similarity in accord with which the law is a measure
or likeness, nor is it customarily said to be such in the literal sense.[288] So,
if someone says that the law is literally a measure or a likeness, he speaks

falsely (for a likeness is something whose coming to be is through imitation, and this is not a feature that belongs to the law). If, on the other hand, it is not literally so, it is clear that he has said something non-perspicuously, and something worse than anything said metaphorically.

Further, look to see whether the account of the contrary is not clear on the basis of what is said; for correctly assigned definitions signify the accounts of the contraries as well. Or, look to see whether, when it is stated by itself, it is not evident what it is the definition of, but rather, like the figures in old-style painters: unless there was an inscription, one used not to recognize who each of them was.

6.3

Definitions involving superfluous material

If, then, the definition is not expressed perspicuously, look at it on the basis of topics such as the preceding ones.

If, on the other hand, the definer has stated the definition in too extended a form, first, look to see whether he has made use of anything that belongs to everything, either to the beings in general, or to those that fall under the same kind as the thing defined; for then it is necessarily stated in too extended a version. For the kind must separate the thing defined from the other things, and the difference must separate it from the ones in the same kind. Well, what belongs to everything separates it from simply nothing, while what belongs to everything that falls under the same kind does not separate it from those in the same kind, so that this sort of addition is pointless.

Or, again, look to see whether, though the addition is special [to the thing defined], yet, when it is subtracted, the remainder of the account is also special and indicates the substance. For example, in the account of human the addition of "receptive of scientific knowledge" is superfluous; for when it is subtracted the remainder of the account is special and indicates the substance. Simply speaking, anything is superfluous if, when it is subtracted, the remainder makes clear the thing defined. The definition of soul would be of this sort, if indeed it is "number that moves itself"; for in fact the soul, as Plato has defined it, "is what moves itself."[289] Alternatively, perhaps what is stated, though special, does not indicate the substance if "number" is subtracted. Which of these holds is difficult to determine perspicuously. But in all such cases one must have an eye to what is advantageous—for example, saying that the definition of phlegm is "the first fluid, produced from nourishment that is unconcocted."[290] For only one thing is

first, not many, so that unconcocted is superfluous; for in fact when it is
subtracted, the remainder is a special account; for it is not possible for both
phlegm and something else to be the first thing to come from the nourishment. Alternatively, perhaps phlegm is not unconditionally the first thing
to be produced from the nourishment, but only the first of the unconcocted ones, so that unconcocted must be added (for stated the other way
the account will not be true, if indeed phlegm is not the first of all).

Further, look to see whether something in the account does not belong
to all the things that fall under the same form; for an account of this sort
defines in a worse way than those that make use of something that belongs
to everything; for in the latter way, if the remainder of the account is special, all of it will be special; for it is unconditionally the case that if anything whatever that is true is added to what is special, the whole account
becomes special. But if something in the account does not belong to everything that falls under the same form, it is impossible for the whole account
to be special; for it will not be counterpredicated of the thing at issue.²⁹¹ For
example, "two-footed terrestrial animal six feet tall"; for such an account
is not counterpredicated of the thing at issue, because six feet tall does not
belong to everything that falls under the same form.

Again, look to see whether the definer has said the same thing several
times—for example, saying that appetite is a desire for something pleasant;
for all appetite is for something pleasant, so that what is the same as appetite will be for something pleasant. [The definition of appetite] becomes,
then, "the desire for something pleasant for something pleasant"; for there
is no difference between saying appetite and saying the desire for something pleasant, so that either will be for something pleasant.

Alternatively, perhaps this involves no absurdity; for human is also two-
footed animal, so that what is the same as human will also be two-footed,
but two-footed terrestrial animal is the same as human, so that two-footed
terrestrial animal is two-footed. But nothing absurd comes about because
of this; for two-footed is not predicated of terrestrial animal (for in this way
two-footed would be predicated twice of the same thing), rather, it is about
a two-footed terrestrial animal that two-footed is said, so that two-footed
is only predicated once. And the case of appetite is similar; for it is not of
desire that being for pleasure is predicated but of the whole thing, so that
here too the predication occurs only once.

Absurdity results, not when the same name is uttered twice, but when
the same thing is predicated of something several times, as happens when
Xenocrates says that wisdom is [a science that] defines, and gets a theoretical grasp on, the beings; for a science that defines something is the sort
of science that gets a theoretical grasp on it, so that he is saying the same
thing twice, when he again adds "and gets a theoretical grasp on."²⁹² It is

the same way too with those who say that coldness is a privation of heat
in accord with nature; for every privation is a privation of what belongs in   10
accord with nature, so that it is superfluous to add "in accord with nature,"
but was enough to say "a privation of heat," since the "privation" itself
makes it known that what is meant is the heat in accord with nature.[293]

Again, look to see whether, after a universal has been stated, the definer
has added a particular case as well— for example, if one has defined decency   15
as "taking less than one's share of the advantageous and the just"; for the
just is a sort of advantage.[294] For after stating the universal, he has added a
particular case. Also, if he has defined medicine as "scientific knowledge of
what is healthy for animal and human," or law as "a likeness of what is by
nature noble and just"; for the just is something noble, so that he is saying   20
the same thing several times.

6.4

Whether a definition defines an essence

Whether a definition is given correctly or incorrectly, then, should be
looked at by means of these and these sorts of topics. But whether the
opponent has defined the essence or not must be looked at on the basis of
the following ones.   25

First, look to see whether he has not produced the definition through
prior and better known things. For since a definition is assigned for the
sake of knowing the thing stated, and we know not on the basis of random
things, but rather on the basis of prior and better known ones, just as in
the case of demonstrations (for this holds of all teaching and learning), it   30
is evident that the person who has not defined it through such things has
not defined it at all.[295] Otherwise, there will be more than one definition of
the same thing; for it is clear that a person who has defined it through prior
and better known things has also defined it and done so better, so that both
would be definitions of the same thing. But they do not seem to be such; for
what is precisely the being for each of the beings is one thing. So, if there
are several definitions of the same thing, what is precisely the being for the   35
thing defined will be the same as each of the things indicated by the definitions. But these things are not the same, since their definitions are distinct.
It is clear, then, that a person who has not defined through prior and better   **141**^b**1**
known things has not defined at all.

The fact that the definition has not been stated through better known
things may be taken in two ways; for either it is produced from things that
are unconditionally less well known or less well known to us; for both ways

are possible. Unconditionally, what is prior is better known than what is posterior—for example, a point than a line, a line than a plane, and a plane than a solid, just as a unit is more so than a number; for it is prior to and a starting-point of every number. Similarly, a letter is more so than a syllable. To us, on the other hand, it sometimes happens that the reverse is the case; for the solid falls most under perception, the plane more than the line, the line more than the point. For ordinary people know things of the former sort earlier; for to learn them is a task for random thought, while to learn the others is a task for exact and extraordinary thought.²⁹⁶

Unconditionally, then, it is better to try to make what is posterior known through what is prior; for proceeding in this way is more scientific. Nonetheless, in relation to those who cannot know through things of the latter sort, it is presumably necessary to produce the account through things known to them. Among definitions of this sort are the following ones of the point, the line, and the plane; for all of them indicate prior things through posterior ones; for they say that the point is the limit of the line, the line of the plane, and the plane of the solid. One must not overlook, however, that it is not possible for those who define in this way to indicate the essence of the thing defined, unless it so happens that the same thing is better known both to us and also unconditionally better known, if indeed a correct definition must define through the kind and the differences, and these are among the things that are unconditionally better known than the form and prior to it.²⁹⁷ For the kind and the difference do away with the form, so that these are prior to the form.²⁹⁸ They are also better known; for if the form is known, it is necessary for both the kind and the difference to be also known (for a person who knows human knows both animal and terrestrial), while if the kind or the difference is known, it is not necessary for the form to be known, so that the form is less well known.²⁹⁹

Further, those who say that definitions of this sort—those produced from things known to a given person—are in accord with the truth will, as a result, have to say that there are many definitions of the same thing; for different things happen to be better known to different people, not the same things to all, so that a distinct definition would have to be given to each one, if indeed the definition must be produced from things that are better known to each.

Further, to the same people distinct things are better known at distinct times—initially perceptible things, then, as they become more exact [knowers], the reverse, so that neither must the same definition always be given to the same person by those who say that a definition must be given through the things that are better known to each one.

It is clear, then, that one must not define through these sorts of things, but rather through those that are unconditionally better known; for only in this way would one and the same definition always result. But presumably what is unconditionally known is also what is known not to everyone, but rather to those with good dispositions where their thought is concerned, just as what is unconditionally healthy is what is so to those in a good state where their body is concerned.

Each point of this sort, then, must be made exact, but made use of with an eye to what is advantageous in arguing dialectically. But it is most of all agreed to be possible to do away with a definition if the definer has produced his account neither from what is unconditionally better known nor from what is better known to us.

One way, then, of not defining by means of things that are better known is to indicate what is prior through what is posterior, as we said previously.[300] Another is if the definer has assigned his account to us of what is at rest and definite through what is indefinite and in movement; for what remains at rest and what is definite is prior to what is indefinite and in movement.[301]

There are three ways of not proceeding from things that are prior. The first is when an opposite has been defined through its opposite—for example, good through bad; for opposites are by nature simultaneous. To some people too it seems that the science of both is the same, so that the one is not better known than the other either. One must not fail to notice, however, that it is presumably impossible to define some things in any other way—for example, the double without the half, and whatever is said to be intrinsically relative to something. For the being for all such things is the same as having some sort of relation to something, so that it is impossible to know the one without the other. That is why it is necessary for the one to be included in the account of the other. We must, then, know all the things of this sort, and make use of them as seems to be advantageous.

Another way is when the definer has made use of the thing defined itself. This goes unnoticed when the name of the thing defined itself is not used—for example, if he has defined the sun as "star that shines by day"; for in using day, he makes use of the sun.[302] To uncover these sorts of things, one should substitute the account for the name—for example, that day is the spatial movement of the sun over the earth; for it is clear that a person who has spoken of the spatial movement of the sun over the earth has spoken of the sun, so that in using day, he has made use of the sun.

Again, look to see whether he has defined one coordinate member of a division by means of another coordinate member—for example, odd number as "one greater by a unit than an even number." For the coordinate

members of a division drawn from the same kind are by nature simultaneous; and odd and even are coordinate members, since both are differences
of number.

Similarly, look to see whether he has defined a higher one through a
lower one—for example, even number as "what is bipartitely divisible"; or
good as "a state of virtue"; for bipartitely is derived from two, which is an
even number, and virtue is a sort of good, so that the former are lower than
the latter. Further, in making use of what is lower than a thing, one will
necessarily make use of the thing itself as well. For a person who makes use
of virtue, makes use of good, since virtue is a sort of good, and, similarly, a
person who makes use of bipartitely makes use of even, since "bipartitely
divisible" signifies divisible by two, and two is an even number.

6.5

Kind

Speaking in universal terms, then, one topic is not producing the account
through things that are prior and better known, and its parts are the ones
mentioned.³⁰³ A second is to see whether, though the thing at issue is in a
kind, it is not proposed in the kind. This sort of error is found in all cases
in which the what-it-is is not proposed first in the account—for example,
in the definition of body as "what has three dimensions," or the definition
of human, if someone were to define it as "what scientifically knows how
to count." For it has not been stated what it is that has three dimensions,
or what it is that scientifically knows how to count. The kind, on the other
hand, is meant to signify the what-it-is, and, of the things mentioned in the
definition, is put first.

Further, look to see whether, though the thing defined is said in relation
to several things, the definer has not applied it in relation to all of them—
for example, if he has defined grammar as "the scientific knowledge of
writing from dictation"; for he should add that it is also that of reading. For
a person who assigns "the scientific knowledge of writing" as the definition
has no more defined it than one who assigns "the scientific knowledge of
reading." So neither of them has defined it, but only the one who has stated
both of these things, since there cannot be several definitions of the same
thing. In some cases, certainly, what has been said is in accord with the
truth, but in some cases it is not—for example, in those in which the definition is not said in relation to both things intrinsically, as when medicine
is defined as "what produces health and disease"; for it is said in relation
to the first intrinsically, but in relation to the second coincidentally; for,

unconditionally, it is foreign to medicine to produce disease. So a person who assigns it in relation to both has no more defined it than a person who assigns it in relation to one of the two. On the contrary, he has presumably done even a worse job, since any practitioner whatever of the remaining ones is capable of producing disease.

Further, look to see whether, though the thing defined is said in relation to several things, the definer has assigned it not in relation to the better but in relation to the worse; for every science and capacity seems to be of what is best.

Again, if what is mentioned is not proposed in its proper kind, look at it on the basis of the elements concerned with the kind, as was stated previously.[304]

Further, look to see whether the definer states the definition in a way that jumps over the kinds—for example, if he defines justice as "the state productive of equality or allocative of what is equal"; for a person who defines in this way jumps over virtue. Leaving out the kind of justice, then, he does not state the essence; for the substance of each thing involves its kind. This is the same as not putting the thing in the closest kind; for a person who puts it in the closest one has stated all the higher ones, since all the higher kinds are predicated of the lower ones. So, either it must be put in the closest kind, or else all the differences, through which the closest kind is defined, must be attached to the higher kind; for this way nothing would be omitted, but rather instead of the name, the account of the lower kind would be stated. But a person who states only the higher kind by itself does not state the lower kind as well; for the one who states "plant" does not state "tree."

6.6

Difference

Again, in the case of differences, one must in a similar way look to see whether the definer has mentioned the differences that are those of the kind. For if he has not defined the thing at issue by the differences special to it, or has mentioned a sort of thing that does not at all admit of being a difference of anything (for example, animal or substance), it is clear that he has not defined it; for the things mentioned are not differences of anything whatever. Also, see whether there is anything coordinate in a division with the difference mentioned. For if there is not, it is clear that the one mentioned would not be a difference of the kind; for every kind is determined by differences that are coordinate members of a division, just as animal is by terrestrial and winged. Or else, see whether, though there is a coordinate difference, it is not true of the kind. For it is clear that neither of them would be a difference of the kind; for all the coordinate differences are true of their proper kind. In a similar way, look to see too whether, though the coordinate difference is true of the kind, its being added to it does not make a form. For then it is clear that it would not be a difference of the kind; for every difference, together with the kind, makes a form. If, however, it is not a difference, what is mentioned as a difference would not be a difference either, since it is a coordinate of it in a division.

Further, look to see whether he divides the kind by a negation, as those do who define line as "length without breadth"; for this signifies nothing other than that it does not have breadth. The result, then, will be that the kind participates in the form; for every length either is without breadth or has breadth, since of everything either the affirmation or the negation is true, so that the kind of line, which is length, will also either be without breadth or have breadth.³⁰⁵ But length without breadth is the account of a form, as, likewise, is length having breadth. For without breadth and having breadth are differences, and the account of the form is composed of the difference and the kind, so that the kind would admit of the account of the form. Similarly, it would also admit of the account of the difference, since one or other of the differences just mentioned is of necessity predicated of the kind.

The topic just mentioned is useful against those who posit the existence of Forms. For if there is length-itself, in what way is it to be predicated of the kind having breadth or without breadth? For one or the other of these must be true of every length, if indeed it is going to be true of the kind. But this does not happen; for there are lengths without breadth and lengths having breadth. So this topic is useful only against those who say that every kind is one in number. This, though, is what those who posit the Forms do say; for they say that the kind is length-itself or animal-itself.³⁰⁶

But perhaps in some cases it is necessary for the definer to use a negation—for example, in the case of privations; for blind is not having sight when it is natural to have it. But there is no difference between dividing a kind by a negation and by means of the sort of affirmation that must necessarily have a negation as its coordinate in a division—for example, if he has defined something as "length having breadth"; for coordinate in the division with having breadth is not having breadth, and nothing else, so that again the kind is divided by a negation.

Again, look to see whether he has assigned the form as a difference, as do those who define insolence as "wanton aggression accompanied by satirizing"; for satirizing is a sort of wanton aggression, so that satirizing is not a difference but a form.³⁰⁷

Further, look to see whether he has stated the kind as a difference—for example, stating that virtue is a good or excellent state; for good is the kind

of virtue. Alternatively, perhaps good is not the kind but the difference, if
indeed it is true that the same thing does not admit of being in two kinds,
neither of which encompasses the other. For good does not encompass
state, nor state good; for not every state is good, nor is every good a state.
So they would not both be kinds. If, then, state is the kind of virtue, it is
clear that good is not its kind but rather a difference. Further, "state" signifies the what-it-is of virtue, while "good" signifies not what it is but a quality; and a difference seems to signify a quality.³⁰⁸

See too whether the assigned difference signifies not a quality but a this
something; for it seems that every difference indicates a certain quality.³⁰⁹

Look to see too whether the difference belongs coincidentally to the
thing defined. For no difference is among the things that belong coincidentally, just as no kind is either; for a difference does not admit of belonging to something and of not belonging to it.

Further, if the difference, the form, or any of the things under the form
is predicated of the kind, the thing would not have been defined; for none
of the things just mentioned admits of being predicated of the kind, since
the kind has the widest extension of all of them. Again, look to see whether
the kind is predicated of the difference; for the kind seems to be predicated
not of the difference but of the things the difference is predicated of—for
example, animal is predicated of human, ox, and other terrestrial animals,
not of the difference itself that is said of the form. For if "animal" is going to
be predicated of the differences one by one, many animals would be predicated of the form; for the differences are predicated of the form.³¹⁰ Further,
all differences will be either forms or individuals, if they are animals; for
each animal is either a form or an individual.

In a similar way, look to see too whether the form or any of the things
under the form is predicated of the difference; for this is impossible, since
the difference has a wider extension than the forms.³¹¹ Further, the result
will be that the difference is a form, if indeed any of the forms is predicated
of it; for if "human" is predicated, it is clear that the difference is [predica-
tively] human. Again, look to see whether the difference is prior or not
prior to the form; for the difference must be posterior to the kind but prior
to the form.³¹²

Look to see whether the stated difference also belongs to a distinct kind,
neither encompassed by nor encompassing the first; for the same difference does not seem to belong to two kinds neither of which encompasses
the other. Otherwise the result will be that the same form will also be in
two kinds neither of which encompasses the other. For each of the differences imports its own proper kind—for example, terrestrial and two-footed
import animal along with them. So, if what the difference is predicated of,
both of the kinds are also predicated of, it is clear that the form is in two

kinds neither of which encompasses the other. Alternatively, perhaps it is
20   not impossible for the same difference to belong to two kinds neither of
which encompasses the other. But "if they do not both fall under the same
[kind]" must be added. For "terrestrial" and "winged" are kinds neither
of which encompasses the other, and two-footed is a difference of both of
them, so that it must be added that they do not both fall under the same
25   [kind]; for they both fall under "animal." It is also clear that it is not necessary for a difference to import every proper kind along with it (since the
same difference admits of belonging to two kinds neither of which encompasses the other), but only that it import one or other of the two along
with it, as well as all of the higher kinds, just as two-footed imports either
30   winged or terrestrial along with it.

See also whether the definer has assigned being in something as a difference of substance; for it seems that one substance does not differ from
another by where it is. That is also why people criticize those who divide
animals by terrestrial and aquatic, on the supposition that "terrestrial" and
"aquatic" signify the where. Alternatively, perhaps they do not criticize in a
35   correct way; for "aquatic" does not signify "in something" or "where," but a
certain quality.[313] For even if the thing is on land, it is nonetheless aquatic.
Similarly, a land-animal, even if it is in water, will be a land-animal, not an
145^a1   aquatic-animal. Nonetheless, if the difference ever does signify being in
something, it is clear that the definer will have made an error.

Again, look to see whether he has assigned an affection as a difference;
for every affection, if it becomes more intensified, utterly alters the substance, but a difference is not like this; for it seems that a difference rather
5   preserves what it is a difference of, and that it is unconditionally impossible
for a given thing to be without its own proper difference; for if terrestrial
does not exist, human will not exist.[314] And, simply speaking, none of the
things with respect to whose possession something undergoes alteration is
a difference of it; for all things of this sort, if they become more intensified,
utterly change the substance. So, if the definer has assigned anything of this
10   sort as difference, he has made an error. For, unconditionally, we undergo
no alteration with respect to our differences.

Also, look to see whether he has not assigned the difference of a relative as relative to something else. For the differences of relatives are themselves relatives—for example, those of scientific knowledge. For it is said
15   to be theoretical, practical, and productive.[315] And each of these signifies a
relative. For it is theoretical scientific knowledge of something, productive
scientific knowledge of something, and practical scientific knowledge of
something.[316]

Look to see too whether the definer assigns each relative as relative to its
20   natural correlative. For in some cases it is possible to use the thing only in

relation to the natural one, and in relation to nothing else, while in others it is also possible to use it in relation to something else—for example, the eye can only be used for seeing, but a strigil can also be used as a sort of instrument for drawing off liquid.[317] Nonetheless, if someone had defined a strigil as "an instrument for drawing off liquid," he would have made an error; for that is not its natural correlative. And the definition of a natural correlative is "that for which a practically wise person, and the science proper to the given thing, would use it."

Or again, look to see whether he has not assigned it to the primary correlative, when the thing happens to be said in relation to several—for example, if he has defined practical wisdom as the virtue of a human or of a soul and not of the rationally calculative part; for practical wisdom is primarily "the virtue of the rationally calculative part"; for it is in accord with this that the soul and the human being are said to be practically wise.

Further, if what the thing defined has been stated to be an affection or disposition of is not receptive of it, he has made an error; for every disposition and every affection naturally comes to be in what it is a disposition or an affection of—for example, scientific knowledge in the soul, since it is a disposition of soul. But sometimes people make errors in cases of this sort—for example, those who say that sleep is an incapacity of perception, that puzzlement is equality of contrary rational calculations, or that pain is the splitting apart of naturally grown-together parts, involving force. For sleep does not belong to perception (though it should belong to it, if indeed it is incapacity of perception), and neither, likewise, does puzzlement belong to rational calculations, nor pain to naturally grown-together parts; for inanimate things will feel pain, if indeed pain will be present in them. The definition of health is also of this sort, if indeed it is "a balance of hot and cold things"; for then it is necessary for the hot and cold things to be healthy. For a balance of a given thing belongs in each of the things of which it is the balance, so that health would belong to them. Further, the result for those who define in this way is that what is produced is put in what is productive of it, or the reverse. For the splitting apart of naturally grown-together parts is not pain, but productive of pain, and incapacity of perception is not sleep either, but one is productive of the other; for either we go to sleep because of the incapacity, or we have the incapacity because of sleep. Similarly too equality of contrary rational calculations would seem to be productive of puzzlement; for when we are rationally calculating both ways [of doing something], and everything that comes about appears to be similar either way, we are puzzled about which of the two to do in action.

Further, look at all the periods of time to see whether there is a discordance somewhere—for example, if immortal has been defined as "animal *aphtharton* now"; for an animal now *aphtharton* will be [only] now immortal [but not at other times].[318] Alternatively, perhaps this does not follow in this case; for "now *aphtharton*" is ambiguous; for it either signifies that the thing has not passed away now or that it is not capable of passing away now, or that it is now of a sort never to have passed away. When, then, we say that an animal is *aphtharton* now, we mean this: that it is now an animal of a sort never to pass away. But this latter was the same as saying that it is immortal, so that it does not follow that it is now immortal [but not at other times]. Nonetheless, if it happens that what is assigned in accord with the account belongs now or earlier [but not at other times], but what is assigned in accord with the name does not belong [in that way], they would not be the same thing. The topic must, then, be used in the way stated.

6.7

The more and the less

Look to see too whether the thing defined is said more in accord with something else than in accord with the assigned account—for example, if justice is defined as "capacity allocative of what is equal." For a just person is more one who deliberately chooses to allocate equally than one capable of it, so that justice would not be capacity allocative of what is equal; for then a person who is capable of allocating equally would also be most just.

Further, when the thing at issue admits of the more, look to see whether the one in accord with the assigned account does not admit of it, or—the reverse—whether the one in accord with the assigned account does admit of it, while the thing at issue does not; for either both must admit of it or neither, if indeed what is assigned by the account is the same as the thing at issue. Further, look to see whether, though both admit of the more, they do not both get the increase simultaneously—for example, if love is defined as "appetite for sexual intercourse"; for a person who is more in love does not have more appetite for sexual intercourse, so that they do not both admit of the more simultaneously.[319] But they certainly would have to, if indeed they were the same thing.

Further, two things being proposed, look to see whether what the thing at issue is more said of, the account is less said of—for example, if fire is defined as "the most fine-grained body." For flame is fire more than light is, while flame is the most fine-grained body less than light is. But both should have belonged more to the same thing, if indeed they were the same. Again, look to see whether one belongs in a similar way to both of the things proposed, while the other does not belong in a similar way to both, but more to one of them.   20

Further, look to see whether he assigns the definition in relation to two things, taken severally—for example, if he defines beautiful as "pleasant to sight or pleasant to hearing," or being as "capable of being affected or capable of affecting"; for then the same thing will be both beautiful and not beautiful, and likewise, will both be and not be.[320] For pleasant to   25
hearing will be the same as beautiful, so that not pleasant to hearing will be the same as not beautiful; for the opposites of things that are the same are themselves the same, and not beautiful is the opposite of beautiful, and not pleasant to hearing the opposite of pleasant to hearing. It is clear, then, that not pleasant to hearing is the same as not beautiful. If, then, something is pleasant to sight but not to hearing, it will be both beautiful and not beautiful. And in a similar way we will prove that the same thing   30
both is and is not.

Further, of kinds, differences, and all the other things assigned in defin-itions, put accounts in place of names and look to see whether there is any discordance.   35

6.8

Definitions of relatives

If the thing defined is a relative, either intrinsically or with respect to its kind, look to see whether the definer has not stated in the definition what it is said relative to, either intrinsically or with respect to its kind—for example, if he has defined scientific knowledge as "supposition incapable   **146ᵇ1**
of being persuaded to change," or wish as "desire without pain"; for the sub-stance of everything relative is relative to something else, since the being for each relative is the same thing as it precisely having some relation to something.[321] He should, then, have said that scientific knowledge is sup-position about the scientifically knowable, and that wish is desire for the   5
good. It is the same way too if he has defined grammar as "scientific knowl-edge of letters"; for he should have assigned in the definition either what grammar itself is relative to or what the kind is relative to.[322] Or, again, look to see whether, although the relative has been stated, it is not assigned in relation to its end; and the end in a given case is the best thing or what the other things are for the sake of. The best one, then, must be stated, or the   10
ultimate one—for example, appetite must be defined not as "for what is pleasant," but "for pleasure"; for it is for the sake of pleasure that we also choose what is pleasant.

Look to see too whether what he has assigned the definition in relation to is a coming to be or an activity; for nothing of these sorts is an end; for having finished the activity or having finished the coming to be is more an end than the coming to be and the being active. Alternatively, perhaps this is not true in all cases; for pretty much everyone wishes to be pleased more than to have ceased to be pleased, so that the activity is more of an end than having finished it.[323]

Again, in certain cases, one must look to see whether he has not determined the quality, quantity, place, or other relevant differences of the thing—for example, with an honor-lover, the quality or quantity of honor he desires; for everyone desires honor. So it is not enough to say that an honor-lover is a person who desires honor, but one must add the differences just mentioned. Similarly, with a money-lover too, the quantity of money he desires, or with a person who lacks self-control, the quality of pleasure he is concerned with; for it is not a person controlled by any pleasure whatever who is said to lack self-control, but the one controlled by certain pleasures.[324] Or, again, when people define night as "a shadow over the earth," earthquake as "a movement of the earth," cloud as "a condensation of air," or wind as "movement of air"; for quality, quantity, and due to what must be added. And similarly in other cases of this sort; for when one leaves out any difference whatever, one does not state the essence. And one must always attack what is deficient; for not just any manner of movement of the earth whatever or any quantity of it whatever is an earthquake, nor similarly is any manner of movement whatever of any quantity of air whatever wind.

Further, in the case of desires, and in the case of any other things where it is fitting, look to see whether the definer has not added "apparent"—for example, in saying that wish is a desire for good, or appetite a desire for pleasant, instead of for apparent good or apparent pleasant. For often the thing that is good or pleasant escapes the notice of those who feel desire, so that [what they desire] is not necessarily good or pleasant but only apparently so. He should, then, have made the one he assigns in this way. On the other hand, if a person who posits the Forms does assign the addition just mentioned, he must be led to the Forms. For there is no Form of anything that is [merely] apparent, but a Form seems to be said in relation to a Form—for example, appetite-itself for pleasant-itself and wish-itself for good-itself.[325] They will not, then, be for the apparent good nor for the apparent pleasant. For it is absurd for there to be an apparent good-itself or pleasant-itself.

6.9

State and privation, relatives, and opposites

Further, if the definition is of the state [or having], look at what has it, or if of what has it, look at the state, and similarly in all cases of this sort—for example, if the pleasant is precisely the beneficial, the one who is pleased is benefited. Speaking in universal terms, in definitions of this sort, the definer in a way defines more than one thing. For a person who defines scientific knowledge in a way also defines ignorance, and likewise he also defines what has scientific knowledge and what lacks scientific knowledge, and knowing scientifically and being ignorant; for when the first has become clear, in a way the remaining ones also become clear. Look, then, in all cases of this sort, to see whether there is not some discordance, making use of the elements [or topics] based on contraries and coordinates.[326]

Further, in the case of relatives, look to see whether the form is assigned relative to what the kind is assigned relative to. For example, if supposition is relative to supposable, see whether this sort of supposition is relative to this sort of supposable, and if the multiple is relative to the fraction, whether this sort of multiple is relative to this sort of fraction; for if it has not been given in this way, it is clear that an error has been made.

See too whether the account of the opposite is the opposite account—for example, whether the opposite of the account of the double is the account of the half; for if the double is what exceeds the equal, half is what is exceeded by the equal. And in like manner in the case of contraries; for the contrary account will be that of a contrary, in accord with one or other of the combinations of the contraries. For example, if beneficial is what is productive of good, harmful is what is productive of bad or destructive of good; for one or other of these is necessarily contrary to what was stated initially. If, then, neither of them is the contrary of what was stated initially it is clear that neither of the accounts assigned later would be the account of the contrary, so that the one assigned initially would not be correctly assigned either.

Since some contraries are said of things as one being a privation of the other (for example, inequality seems to be a privation of equality, for unequal is said of things that are not equal), it is clear that a contrary that is said of things as a privation is necessarily defined through the other one, while the one remaining [to be defined] cannot then be defined through the one said in accord with a privation; for then the result would be that each would be known through the other. Be on the lookout, then, in the

15

20

25

30

35

147[b]1

5

case of contraries, for an error of this sort—for example, if someone were
to define equality as "the contrary of inequality"; for he is defining through
what is said of things in accord with a privation. Further, a person who
defines in this way necessarily makes use of the thing itself that is being
defined. And this becomes clear if the account is substituted for the name;
for saying inequality is no different from saying the privation of equality.
Equality, then, will be the contrary of the privation of equality, so that the
thing itself would be being used.

If neither of the contraries is said of things in accord with a privation,
but the account is assigned in a similar way, for example, good is the contrary of bad, it is clear that bad will then be the contrary of good; for the
account of things contrary in this way must be assigned in such a way. And
so the result again is that the definer makes use of the thing itself that is
being defined; for the good belongs in the account of the bad. And so if
good is the contrary of the bad, and bad is no different than the contrary of
the good, good will be the contrary of the contrary of good. It is clear, then,
that it itself has been used.

Further, look to see whether in assigning what is said in accord with
a privation, the definer has not assigned what it is a privation of—for
example, of the having of something, of the contrary, or of whatever it is
the privation of. Also, whether he has not added what it naturally comes to
be in, either unconditionally or what it naturally comes to be in primarily.
For example, if having said that ignorance is a privation, he has not said
that it is a privation of scientific knowledge, or has not added what it naturally comes to be in, or, though he has added this, has not assigned what
it naturally comes to be in primarily—for example, saying not that it is in
the rationally calculative part but in human or soul; for if there is any of
these things whatever that he has not done, he has made an error. It is the
same way too if he has not said that blindness is a privation of sight in the
eye; for in correctly assigning the what-it-is one must also assign what it is
a privation of and what it is that is deprived.

See too whether he has not defined by a privation what is not said
in accord with a privation—for example, in the case of ignorance, this
sort of error would seem to be committed by those who say what ignorance is in accord with negation.[327] For what has no scientific knowledge
seems not to be ignorant, but more so what is utterly deceived. That is
why we do not say that inanimate things or children are ignorant. So
ignorance is not said of things in accord with the privation of scientific
knowledge.

6.10

Inflections, Forms, homonyms, synonyms, things said in many ways

Further, look to see whether the inflections of the account fit with the cor-   10
responding inflections of the name—for example, if beneficial is what is
productive of health, whether beneficially is productively of health, and
what has brought a benefit is what has produced health.

Look to see too whether the definition stated fits the Form as well. For
in some cases this does not happen—for example, as Plato defines animals,   15
adding "mortal" in their definitions; for the Form (for example, human-
itself) is not mortal, so that the account will not fit the Form.[328] Unconditionally, in those cases where capable of affecting something or capable of
being affected by something is added, it is necessary for there to be discord
when the definition is applied to the Form; for Forms seem to be unaffect-
able and immovable to those who say there are Forms.[329] Against these   20
people even arguments of this sort are useful.

Further, look to see whether he has assigned one common account
to things said [to be what they are] homonymously; for things are synonymous when the account corresponding to their name is one. So the
assigned definition will fit none of the things falling under the name, if   25
indeed it fits all of the homonymous things equally. This is what happens in
fact to Dionysius' definition of life, if indeed it is "a congenital movement
inseparably connected to a kind of being capable of nourishment"; for this
belongs no more to animals than to plants.[330] Life, however, seems not to
be said of things in accord with one form, but one form seems to belong to
animals and a distinct one to plants.   30

It is also possible to deliberately choose to assign the definition as a synonym and to speak of all life in accord with one form. But there is also
nothing to prevent someone, even if he sees the homonymity and wishes
to assign the definition of one of the two homonyms, from unwittingly
assigning an account that is not special to it but common to both. None-   35
theless, if he has done either of these things, he has committed an error.
Since homonyms sometimes go unnoticed, when questioning, treat them
as synonyms (for the definition of the one will not fit the other, so that it   **148^{b}1**
will not seem to be [correctly] defined this way, since it must fit everything
that is synonymous), but, when answering oneself, distinguish them. Since
some answerers say, on the one hand, that what is synonymous is homonymous, when the assigned account does not fit all cases, and, on the other   5
hand, that what is homonymous is synonymous, when it fits both cases,
one must obtain an agreement beforehand on these matters or else pre-
deduce that the thing is a homonym or a synonym, whichever of the two

[is most useful]; for people concede something more readily when they do not foresee what the result will be.^{331}

10 If, however, when there has been no agreement, someone says that what is synonymous is homonymous because the account he has assigned does not also fit this case, look to see whether the account of the case in question fits the remaining cases as well, since then it is clear that it would be synonymous with the remaining ones.^{332} Otherwise, there will be several accounts 15 of the remaining cases. For the two accounts that are in accord with the name fit them: both the one assigned earlier and the one assigned later.

Again, if someone, defining something said of things in many ways, and finding that the account does not fit all the cases, were to say not that the thing is homonymous, but that the name does not apply to all of them, because the account does not apply to them either, one must say to such a 20 person that one must use the traditional and constantly attributed names, though in some cases one should not speak in the same way as ordinary people.^{333}

6.11

Complexes, composites, and substitution of names

If a definition has been proposed of something complex, subtract the account of one of the components of the complex, and look to see whether the remainder is an account of the remainder; for if it is not, it is clear that 25 neither is the whole an account of the whole. For example, if someone has defined limited straight line as "limit of a plane having limits whose mid-point blocks the view of the limit-points," and if the account of limited line is "limit of a plane having limits," that of straight must be the remain- 30 der: whose mid-point blocks the view of the limits.^{334} But an unlimited line, though straight, has neither a mid-point nor limit-points, so that the remainder is not the account of the remainder.

Further, when what is being defined is a composite, look to see whether the assigned account is isomerous to what is being defined. An account is 35 said to be isomerous when the component parts in the thing are as many as the nouns and verbs in its account. For it is necessary, in cases of this sort, for the substitution to be name for name, either in the case of some or of all, since no more names are uttered now than before, while a person giv- 149^{a}1 ing a definition must assign an account in place of the names, preferably in place of all, but if not, then of most.^{335} For in the former way, in the case of simple things too, a person who had changed the name would have given a definition—for example, substituting "cloak" for "cape."

Further, and a greater error, look to see whether he has made a substitution for names that are even less well known—for example, "glistening mortal" for "pale human"; for not only has it not been defined, but it is less perspicuous stated this way.[336]

Look to see too whether in the exchange of names it does not any more signify the same thing—for example, if theoretical scientific knowledge has been said to be theoretical supposition. For supposition and scientific knowledge are not the same; but they should be, if indeed the whole thing is going to be the same. For "theoretical" is common to both accounts, but the remainder is different.

Further, look to see whether in making a substitution of one or another of the names he has made a substitution not of the difference but of the kind, as in the example just stated. For theoretical is less well known than scientific knowledge; for the latter is a kind, the former a difference, and the kind is best known of all. So the substitution should have been made not of the kind but of the difference, since the latter is less well known. (Alternatively, perhaps this objection is ridiculous; for there is nothing to prevent the difference from being stated by the better known name, not the kind. In which case, it is clear that it is for the name of the kind, not of the difference, that the substitution must be made.[337]) But if he is substituting not a name for a name but an account for a name, it is clear that it is of the difference rather than of the kind that an account should be assigned, since the definition is given for the sake of making the thing known; for the difference is less well known than the kind.

6.12

Errors in definitions

If the definer has assigned the definition of the difference, look to see whether the assigned definition is common to something else as well. For example, if he has said that odd number is "number that has a middle." For number belongs in common to both accounts, but it is for odd that he has made the substitution. But a line and a body also have a middle, though they are not odd. So this would not be a definition of odd. On the other hand, if things are said to have a middle in many ways, in what way something has a middle must be defined. So that there will be a criticism to make, or a deduction that he has not given a definition.

Again, look to see whether he has assigned a definition of something that is of one of the beings, while what falls under the account is not one of the beings—for example, if he has defined white as "color mixed with fire";

149^b1   for it is impossible for what is bodiless to be mixed with body, so that there could not be color mixed with fire, but there is white.

Further, those who, in the case of relatives, do not determine what the thing is said in relation to, but, in stating it, include it among too many things, are either wholly or partly mistaken—for example, if someone said that medicine is the science of being. For if medicine is the science of none of the beings, it is clear he was wholly mistaken, while if it is the science of some, but not of others, partly mistaken; for it must be the science of all beings, if indeed it is said to be such intrinsically, and not coincidentally, as holds of all the other relatives; for everything scientifically knowable is said to be such relative to science. It is the same way too with the others, since all relatives are convertible.[338] Further, if indeed a person assigning not intrinsically, but coincidentally, is correctly producing what he assigns, each relative would be said not in relation to one thing, but in relation to several. For there is nothing to prevent the same thing from being a being, a white thing, and a good thing, so that one would be assigning correctly if one assigned in relation to any of these whatever, if indeed a person assigning coincidentally is assigning correctly. Further, it is impossible for an account of this sort to be special to what it is assigned as the account of; for not only medicine, but the majority of the other sciences as well, are said in relation to being, so that each of these will be a science of being.[339] It is clear, then, that a definition of this sort is not the definition of any science whatever; for the definition must be special and not common.

Sometimes people define not the thing at issue but the thing at issue in its good state or when complete. Of this sort are the definition of the orator and of the thief, if indeed an orator is defined as "a person who gets a theoretical grasp on what is persuasive on a given occasion and leaves nothing out," while a thief is defined as "a person who takes things by stealth"; for it is clear that if each is of that sort, one will be a good orator and the other a good thief. For it is not the one who takes by stealth, but rather the one who wishes to take by stealth, that is the thief.

Again, look to see whether he has assigned what is choiceworthy because of itself either as productive or practical or in some other way choiceworthy because of something else—for example, saying that justice is what is preservative of laws, or that wisdom is what is productive of happiness; for what is productive or preservative is one of the things choiceworthy because of something else.[340] Alternatively, perhaps there is nothing to prevent what is choiceworthy because of itself from also being choiceworthy because of something else, but nonetheless a person who has defined what is choiceworthy because of itself in this way has made an error; for what is best in a given thing is most of all in its substance, and what is choiceworthy because of itself [in that thing] is better than what is choiceworthy

[only] because of something else, so that it is the former that the definition should have signified more.

6.13

Compound definitions

Look to see whether the definer in assigning a definition of something has defined it as "these things here," or "what is composed of these," or as "this one plus that one."   **150ᵃ1**

For if he defines it as "these things here," the result will be that it belongs to both and neither—for example, if he has defined justice as "temperance and courage"; for if there are people each of whom has one of these, both will be just and neither will, since the two together will have justice, while   5 each individually will not. If what has been said is not yet utterly absurd, because this sort of thing does happen in other cases (for there is nothing to prevent two people together from having a mina, though neither individually has it), well, at any rate, that contraries should belong to these people would seem to be completely absurd.³⁴¹ This is what will happen if   10 one of them has temperance and cowardice, the other courage and intemperance; for both together will have justice and injustice; for if justice is temperance and courage, injustice will be cowardice and intemperance. In general too the ways of arguing dialectically that the parts and the whole   15 are not the same are all useful against what we are now discussing; for it seems that a person who defines in this way is saying that the parts are the same as the whole. These arguments are most of all proper to cases where the putting together of the parts is immediately clear, as in the case of a house or other things of that sort; for then it is clear that, though the parts exist, there is nothing to prevent the whole from not existing, so that the   20 parts are not the same as the whole.

If, however, he has said not that what is being defined is "these things," but rather "what is composed of them," first look to see whether it is not natural for one thing to come to be from the things mentioned; for some things stand in such relation to each other that no one thing can come to be composed of them—for example, a line and a number. Further, look to   25 see whether what is being defined naturally comes to be in one thing primarily, while the things he has said it is composed of do not come to be in one thing primarily, but each in a distinct thing. For then it is clear that it would not be composed of them; for the things the parts are in, the whole too necessarily belongs in, so that the whole is not in one thing primarily, but in several. If, though, both the parts and the whole are each in some   30 one thing primarily, look to see whether they are not in the same one, but rather the whole in one thing and the parts in another.

Again, look to see whether the parts pass away together with the whole; for the reverse must happen: if the parts pass away, the whole does, but if the whole passes away, it is not necessary for the parts to pass away too.

Or, again, look to see whether the whole is good or bad, but the parts neither, or the reverse, the parts good or bad, but the whole neither; for it is impossible for something either good or bad to be composed of things that are neither, or for one composed of bad or good things to be neither.

Or, again, look to see whether one thing has more good in it than the other has bad, yet what is composed of them is not more good than bad—for example, if shamelessness is composed of courage and false belief; for courage is more good than false belief is bad. What is composed of them, then, should have followed along with this more, and be either unconditionally good or more good than bad. Alternatively, perhaps this is not necessarily so, if each of the two things is not intrinsically good or bad; for many of the things that are productive [of something] are not intrinsically good, but only when mixed together, or the reverse, are each individually good, but when mixed together are bad or neither good nor bad. What we are now speaking of is most visible in the case of things conducive to health or to disease; for some drugs are such that each individually is good, but if both are administered mixed together, bad.

Again, look to see whether the whole, when composed of a better and a worse [part], is not worse than the better and better than the worse. Alternatively, perhaps this is not necessarily so either, unless things from which it is composed are not intrinsically good, otherwise there is nothing to prevent the whole from not being good, as in the examples just mentioned.

Further, look to see whether the whole is synonymous with one of its parts; for it must not be, any more than in the case of syllables; for the syllable is not synonymous with any of the letters of which it is composed.

Further, look to see whether the definer has not stated the mode of composition; for to state what the thing is composed of is not by itself sufficient to make it known. For the substance of a given composite is not what it is composed of but in what way it is composed of what it is composed of, as in the case of a house; for these things composed in any way whatever are not a house.

But if he assigns this one plus that one as his definition, the first thing one must say is that this plus that is the same either as these things here or as what is composed of them; for a person who speaks of honey plus water is speaking either of honey and of water or of what is composed of honey and water. So, if he agrees that this plus that is the same as either of the things mentioned, it will be fitting to say the very same things as were said before against each of them.

Further, distinguish in how many ways things are said to be one thing plus another, and look to see whether the thing in question is in no way a this plus that. For example, if "this plus that" is said as [two things] being in the same thing receptive of them (as justice and courage are in soul), or else, as being in the same place or in the same period of time, and if this is in no way true of the things in question, it is clear that the assigned definition would not be a definition of anything, since the thing in question is no way a "this plus that." If, however, of the ways distinguished, it is true that each of the two things belongs in the same period of time, look to see whether it is possible that it is not in relation to the same thing that each of them is said to be such. For example, if courage has been defined as "daring plus correct thinking"; for it is possible to have daring to steal and correct thinking about matters of health, but a person who has this plus that in the same period of time is in no way courageous. Further, look to see too whether both of them are said of things in relation to the same thing (for example, in relation to what is healthy); for there is nothing to prevent someone from having both daring and correct thinking in relation to medical matters. Nonetheless, a person who has "this plus that" in this way is not courageous either. For each of the two must be said of things neither in relation to distinct things nor in relation to the same random thing, but in relation to the end that is the end of courage—for example, in relation to the dangers of war, or of something else, if there is something else that is more its end than this.[342]

Some definitions that are assigned in this way do not at all fall under the division of ways just mentioned—for example, that of anger as pain plus a supposition of being treated with contempt. For that the pain comes about because of a supposition of this sort is what the definition wishes to indicate. But the "coming about because of this" is not the same as "this plus that" in any of the ways just mentioned.

6.14

Recapitulation and conclusion

Again, if the definer has stated that the whole is a composite of these things here (for example, that animal is a composite of a soul and a body), first look to see whether he has not stated what sort of composite, as, for example, if flesh or bone is defined as "a composite of fire, earth, and air." For it is not enough to speak of composition, but rather one must in addition determine what sort of composition; for it is not that once these things are composed in any way whatever the flesh comes to be, but composed in this way, flesh does, composed in that way, bone. It seems that neither of the things just mentioned is at all the same as a composite; for, for every composite, there is a contrary dissolution, while of the things that were mentioned nothing is a contrary. Further, if it is equally persuasive that everything that is composed is a composite, or else that none is, and, of the animals, each is composed but is not a composite, neither would any of the other things that are composed be a composite.

Again, if it is equally natural for a pair of contraries to belong to a certain thing, and if he has defined it through one of the two, it is clear that he has not defined it. Otherwise, the result will be that there are several definitions of the same thing; for in what way is the person who has stated it through this contrary giving more of a definition than the one who has stated it through the other, since both equally well occur naturally in it? The definition of soul, if we define it as "substance receptive of scientific knowledge," is of this sort; for it is also equally well receptive of ignorance.

Also, even if one cannot attack the definition as a whole, because the whole is not known, one must attack some part of it, if it is known and it is evident that it has not been correctly assigned; for if a part is done away with, the whole is also done away with. When, again, definitions are non-perspicuous, having corrected and at the same time reconfigured them so as to have something to attack, in this way proceed to examine them; for it is necessary for the answerer either to accept the assumption of the questioner or make perspicuous himself what exactly is indicated by the account. Further, just as in assemblies it is customary to introduce a law, and if what is introduced is better, to abrogate its predecessor, one should do the same in the case of definitions, and adduce another definition oneself; for if it is evident that it is better and more indicates what is being defined, it is clear that the definition that was proposed will have been done away with, since there are never several definitions of the same thing.

Against all definitions, not the least important element [or topic] is to take a good guess oneself at defining the thing proposed, or else adopt some correctly stated definition; for it is necessary, by looking at a paradigm as it were, to see clearly what is missing from the things that the definition must have and what is superfluously proposed in addition, so as to be better equipped with lines of attack.[343]

About definitions, then, let this much be said.

7.1

Sameness and distinctness

Whether things are the same or distinct, in the strictest of the ways that are mentioned concerning the same—and it was said that what is numerically one is what is in the strictest sense the same—must be looked at on the basis of their inflections, coordinates, and opposites.[344] For if justice is the same as courage, the just person is the same as the courageous one, and justly the same as courageously. And similarly in the case of their opposites; for if these things are the same, their opposites—in accord with whatever ways things are said to be opposites—are as well; for it makes no difference whether one takes this or that opposite, since they are the same. Again, look on the basis of the things that are productive or destructive of the things in question, the comings to be and passings away of them, and, in general, at the things that stand in a similar relation to each of them; for when things are unconditionally the same, their comings to be and passings away are the same, as are the things productive and destructive of them.

   Look to see too, when one of the two things is said to be most of all something or other, whether the other of the same two things is said to be most of all something or other in the same respect. For example, Xenocrates demonstrates that the happy life and the excellent one are the same, since of all lives the excellent one and the happy one are most choiceworthy; for only one thing is most choiceworthy and greatest.[345] It is the same way too in other cases of this sort. But each of the two things said to be greatest or most choiceworthy must be numerically one thing. Otherwise, it will not have been proved that they are the same. For it is not necessary, if the Peloponnesians and the Spartans are the most courageous of the Greeks, that the Peloponnesians are the same as the Spartans, since Peloponnesian is not numerically one thing, nor is Spartan, but rather what is necessary is that the one be encompassed by the other, as the Spartans are by the Peloponnesians. Otherwise, the result will be that each is better than the other, if one is not encompassed by the other. For it is necessary for the Peloponnesians to be better than the Spartans, if indeed one is not encompassed by the other; for they are better than all the rest. But similarly it is necessary for the Spartans also to be better than the Peloponnesians;

for they too are better than all the rest. So each is made to be better than
the other. It is clear, then, that what is said to be best and greatest must be
numerically one thing if it is going to be proved to be the same [as another
thing]. That also is why Xenocrates has not demonstrated it; for neither
the happy life nor the excellent life is numerically one thing, so that it is
not necessary for them to be the same due to the fact that both are most
choiceworthy, but only for one to fall under the other.

Again, look to see whether, when one of two things is the same as [a
third] something, the other is too; for if they are not the same as the same
[third] thing, it is clear that neither are they the same as each other.

Further, look at them on the basis of their coincidents or on the basis of
the things of which they are coincidents; for whatever is a coincident of one
must be a coincident of the other, and whatever one is a coincident of, the
other must also be a coincident of. But if there is any discordance among
any of these, it is clear that the things are not the same.

See too whether they are not both in one kind of predication, but rather
one indicates a quality, the other a quantity or a relation. Again, see whether
the kind of each is not the same, but rather one is good, the other bad, or
the one virtue and the other scientific knowledge. Or whether, though the
kind is the same, the differences predicated of either of them are not the
same ones, but rather that of one is theoretical scientific knowledge, that of
the other practical. It is the same in the other cases too.

Further, on the basis of the more, look to see whether one admits of the
more, while the other does not; or whether both admit of it, but not at the
same time, just as the one who loves more does not have more appetite for
sexual intercourse, so that love and appetite for sexual intercourse are not
the same thing.

Further, on the basis of addition, look to see whether each added to the
same thing does not make the same wholes; or whether subtracting the
same thing from each leaves a distinct remainder—for example, if someone has said that double of half and multiple of half are the same thing. For
then, if "of half" is subtracted from each, the remainders should indicate
the same thing, but they do not. For double and multiple do not indicate
the same thing.

And look to see not only whether something impossible follows right
away because of the thesis, but also whether it is possible for something
impossible to come about from a hypothesis to bring one about, as, for
example, happens to those who say that void and full of air are the same
thing; for it is clear that, if the air went out, it will not be less of a void
but more of one, though it will no longer be full of air.³⁴⁶ So, on a certain
hypothesis, whether false or true (it makes no difference which), one thing
is done away with, while the other is not. So they are not the same.

To speak in universal terms, look on the basis of every predicate whatever of each of the two things, and of everything of which they are predicated, to see whether there is any discordance anywhere; for whatever is
predicated of the one must be predicated of the other, and whatever the one
is predicated of, the other must also be predicated of.

Further, since things are said to be the same in many ways, look to see
whether the things in question are also the same in another way; for things
that are the same [only] in form or in kind cannot possibly be numerically
the same. But what we are looking at is whether it is in the latter way that
they are the same or not the same.

Further, look to see whether it is possible for one to be without the other;
for then they would not be the same thing.

7.2

Sameness and definition (1)

The topics related to sameness, then, are this many. And it is clear from what
has been said that all the topics capable of disestablishing sameness are also
useful against a definition, as was said previously; for if the name and the
account do not indicate the same thing, it is clear that the assigned account
would not be a definition.[347] On the other hand, none of the topics capable
of establishing sameness are useful in relation to a definition; for it is not
enough to have proved that what falls under the account is the same as what
falls under the name in order to have established that it is a definition, but
rather the definition must have all the other features we prescribed.[348]

7.3

Sameness and definition (2)

Always try, then, to do away with a definition in this way and through
these things. But if we wish to establish one, the first thing to know is that
none or few of those who argue dialectically deduce a definition, but all
take something of this sort as a starting-point—for example, those people
who are concerned with geometry and arithmetic as well as the other
such branches of learning.[349] The next thing to know is that it belongs to
another work to give an exact account of what a definition is and how one
must define things.[350] Now, though, to do so with an eye to present needs
is enough, so that it is necessary to say only this much: that it is possible
for there to be a deduction of a definition and of the essence of the thing

at issue. For if a definition is an account indicating the essence of the thing
at issue, and if the predicates in the definition must be the only ones predicated in the what-it-is of the thing at issue, and if the kinds and the differences are predicated in the what-it-is, it is evident that if one assumed that
only these are predicated in the what-it-is of the thing at issue, then the
account containing these would of necessity be a definition; for it is not
possible for anything else to be a definition, since nothing else is predicated
in the what-it-is of the thing at issue.

That there is room, then, for a deduction of a definition is evident. On
the basis of what things a definition must be established has been determined more exactly elsewhere, but for the proposed methodical inquiry
the same topics are useful.³⁵¹ For it is necessary to look into the contraries
and the other opposites, and to do so looking at the whole accounts and at
their parts; for if the opposite account is a definition of the opposite, the
stated one is necessarily the definition of the thing proposed. Since opposites combine in several ways, take from among the contraries the one,
whichever it is, whose contrary definition is most evident.

Look at the whole accounts, then, in the way just stated, but at their
parts as follows. First, see that the assigned kind is correctly assigned. For
if the contrary thing is in the contrary kind, and the thing proposed is
not in the same kind, it is clear that it would be in the contrary one, since
it is necessary for contraries to be in the same kind or in contrary kinds.
Also, we think that the differences that are predicated of contrary things
are contraries, like those of white and black; for the one is contracting and
the other dilating of sight.³⁵² So, if contrary differences are predicated of the
contrary thing, then the assigned ones would be predicated of the thing proposed, so that, since both the kind and the differences have been correctly
assigned, it is clear that the one assigned would be the definition. Alternatively, perhaps it is not necessary for contrary differences to be predicated
of contrary things unless the contrary things are in the same kind, while
for those whose kinds are contraries, there is nothing to prevent the same
difference from being said of both—for example, of justice and of injustice;
for the one is a virtue and the other a vice of soul, so that "of soul" is said
as a difference in both cases, since there is also vice and virtue of body. But
this is true, at any rate, that the differences of contraries are either contrary
or the same. If, then, the contrary difference is predicated of the contrary
thing, but not of the one in question, it is clear that the stated difference
would be predicated of it. To speak in universal terms, since a definition
is composed of kind and differences, if the definition of the contrary is
evident, the definition of the thing proposed will also be evident. For since
the contrary is either in the same kind or in the contrary one, and likewise
the differences predicated of contraries are either contrary or the same, it is

clear that either the same kind would be predicated of the thing proposed precisely as of its contrary too, while its differences are either all contrary or else some are contrary and the remaining ones the same; or, the reverse,   20
the differences are the same and the kinds contrary; or both the kinds and the differences are contrary. For it is not possible for them both to be the same; otherwise, the contraries would have the same definition.

Further, look on the basis of inflections and coordinates; for here it is necessary for kinds to follow along with kinds, and definitions with def-   25
initions. For example, if forgetfulness is the loss of scientific knowledge, to forget will be to lose scientific knowledge, and to have forgotten will be to have lost scientific knowledge. If, then, any one of these whatever is agreed to, it is necessary for the remaining ones to be agreed to as well. Similarly too, if destruction is dissolution of substance, to be destroyed is   30
to have one's substance dissolved, and destructively is dissolvingly. And if destructive is dissolvative of substance, again destruction is dissolution of substance. And similarly in the case of the others. So, if any of them is accepted, all of the remaining ones are agreed to as well.   35

Also, look on the basis of things that have similar relations to each other. For if what conduces to health is productive of health, what conduces to a good state will be productive of a good state, and beneficial will be produc-tive of good. For each of the things mentioned has a similar relation to its proper end, so that if the definition of one of them is "productive of the   154^a1
end," this would also be the definition of each of the remaining ones.

Further, look on the basis of the more and the equally in all the ways in which it is possible to establish something by comparing things two by two. For example, if this is more a definition of that than this other is of   5
that other, and the one that is less so is a definition, the one that is more so is as well. Also, if this is equally a definition of that as this other is of that other, and if one or other of the two is a definition of the other, so is the remaining one of the remaining one. But when one definition is compared to two things, or two definitions with one thing, looking at them on the basis of the more is not at all useful; for there cannot be one definition of two things, or two definitions of the same thing.   10

7.4

The handiest topics

Also, the handiest of the topics are those just mentioned and those based on coordinates and inflections. That is why indeed one must master these most of all and have them ready to hand; for they are most useful in

15 relation to the most cases. And of the others, the most common ones are the handiest (for these are the most effective of the remaining ones)—for example, looking at the particular cases and looking at the various forms to see whether the account fits them, since the form is synonymous.[353] This sort of procedure is useful against those who posit Forms, as was stated previously.[354] Further, look to see whether the opponent has used a name

20 metaphorically, or predicated it of itself as if it were something else.[355] Also, look to see whether there is any other of the topics that is common and effective.

7.5

Establishing versus disestablishing a definition

That it is more difficult to establish than to disestablish a definition is evident on the basis of the things that will be said next. For in fact to see for oneself and to get from those being questioned the relevant sort of prem-

25 ises is not easy—for example, that of the things in the assigned account, one is kind, the other difference, and that the kind and difference are predicated in the what-it-is. Without these it is impossible for a deduction of a definition to come about. For if some other things are also predicated in

30 the what-it-is of the thing at issue, it is unclear whether the one stated or another one is the definition of it, since a definition is an account signifying the essence.

This is also clear from the following considerations. It is indeed easier to draw one conclusion than many. When doing away with a definition, then, it is enough to argue dialectically against one point; for if we have disestablished any one point whatever, we will have disestablished the definition.

35 When establishing one, on the other hand, it is necessary to infer that all the things in the definition belong in it.

Further, when establishing, one must adduce a universal deduction; for it is necessary for the definition to be predicated of everything of which

154^b1 the name is predicated, and, further, to be convertible with them, if the assigned definition is going to be special. When disestablishing, on the other hand, it is no longer necessary to prove the universal; for it is enough to prove that the account is not true of any one of the things falling under

5 the name. Also, even if it is necessary to disestablish it universally, it is not necessary even then for it to be convertible before disestablishing it; for it is enough when disestablishing universally to prove that the account is predicated of none of the things of which the name is predicated. But it is not necessary to prove contrariwise that the name is predicated of things

of which the account is not predicated. Further, even if it belongs to everything that falls under the name, but not to them alone, the definition is
done away with.

It is similar too where special affection and kind are concerned; for in
both cases it is easier to disestablish than to establish. Where a special
affection is concerned, then, this is evident from what has been said; for a
special affection is for the most part assigned in combination, so that it is
possible to disestablish it by doing away with [only] one part, while when
establishing it is necessary to deduce all of them.³⁵⁶ And it is fitting to state
pretty much all of the remaining points about definition about a special
affection as well; for a person establishing a special affection must prove
that it belongs to all of the things that fall under the name, while when disestablishing it is enough to prove that it does not belong to one; and even
if it does belong to all, but not only to them, in that way too it is disestablished, as was said in the case of definition.

Where the kind is concerned, [it is clear] that there is necessarily only
one way to establish it, to prove that it belongs in every case, while it is
disestablished in two ways; for if in fact it has been proved to belong in
none and also if it has been proved not to belong in some, what was said
initially is done away with. Further, when establishing, it is not enough to
prove that it belongs, but rather one must also prove that it belongs as kind.
When disestablishing, on the other hand, it is enough to prove that it does
not belong either in some or in all cases. And it seems that, just as in other
areas it is easier to destroy than to produce, so, in these sorts of cases too,
disestablishing is easier than establishing.

In the case of a coincident, the universal is easier to disestablish than
to establish; for when establishing, one must prove that it belongs in every
case, while when disestablishing, it is enough to prove that it does not
belong in one. In the case of the particular, it is the reverse: it is easier to
establish than to disestablish; for when establishing, it is enough to prove
that it belongs in one case, while when disestablishing, one must prove that
it belongs in none.

It is evident too why a definition is the easiest of all to disestablish; for
since in it many things are assigned, many things are stated, and the more
things it is based on, the faster a deduction comes about; for error is likely
to occur more in many things than in few. Further, a definition also admits
of being attacked through the others; for if the account is not special, or if
what is assigned is not the kind, or if something in the account does not
belong, the definition is done away with. Against the others, by contrast,
neither the things derived from the definition nor all the rest can be used to
mount an attack; for only the ones against a coincident are common to all
those mentioned. For each of those mentioned must belong to the thing.

But if the kind does not belong as something special, the kind is not yet done away with. Similarly too it is not necessary for a special affection to belong as a kind, or for a coincident to belong as a kind or a special affection, but rather merely to belong. So it is impossible to attack one lot on the basis of the other, except in the case of definition. It is clear, then, that a definition is easiest of all to do away with but the most difficult to establish; for there one must deduce all these; for one must deduce that the things mentioned belong, that what is assigned is a kind, and that the account is special, and further, beyond this, that the account indicates the essence, and has done this correctly.

Among the others, the special affection is most like this; for it is easier to do away with because for the most part it is based on more things, and more difficult to establish, because one must infer more things, and in addition, prove that it belongs to and is counterpredicated of the thing at issue.

A coincident is the easiest of all to establish; for in the case of the others, one must prove not merely that it belongs, but also that it belongs in the requisite way, while in the case of a coincident it is enough to prove that it merely belongs. To disestablish it, on the other hand, is the most difficult, because the fewest things are assigned in it; for it is not additionally signified in the coincident in what way it belongs. So in the other cases there are two ways to do away with them, either by proving that they do not belong or that they do not belong in the requisite way, while in the case of a coincident there is no doing away with it except by proving that it does not belong.

The topics through which we will be well equipped to argue dialectically in relation to each of the problems have now been pretty much adequately enumerated.

8.1

How to ask dialectical questions (1)

After this we must speak about arrangement, that is, the way one should ask questions. A person who is going to frame questions must, first, find the topic from which to make his attack; second, frame the questions, and arrange them one by one for himself; it remains, third, to ask these, this time to someone else. Up to the point of finding the topic, then, the philosopher's investigation and the dialectician's are similar, but then arranging these things and framing questions is special to the dialectician; for everything of this sort is in relation to someone else. But the philosopher, who is investigating by himself, does not care whether, though the things through which his deduction proceeds are true and known, the answerer does not grant them (because they are close to what was initially at issue, and he foresees what is going to result), but rather the philosopher is presumably eager for his claims to be as known and as close to what is at issue as possible; for it is from things of this sort that scientific deductions proceed.

The things on the basis of which topics must be taken, then, were stated previously.[357] We must now discuss arrangement and the framing of questions, determining which premises, beyond the necessary ones, must be obtained. The ones said to be necessary are the ones through which a deduction proceeds. The ones to be obtained beyond these are of four sorts. They are either for the sake of an induction to assign the universal, to add bulk to the argument, for the concealment of the conclusion, or to make the argument more perspicuous. Beyond these there are no premises one must obtain, but rather it is through them that one must develop [their arrangement] and frame one's question. The ones for concealment are for the sake of competition.[358] But since every work of this sort is in relation to someone else, it is necessary to make use of these too.[359]

One must not propose the necessary premises through which a deduction directly proceeds, but rather one must stand off as far above them as possible. For example, do not expect to obtain that the science of contraries is the same, if that is what one wishes to obtain, but rather that it is of opposites; for if he grants this, it can be deduced that the science of contraries is the same too, since contraries are opposites, while, if he does not, one must obtain it by induction, by proposing premises about

35 particular contraries. For one must obtain the necessary premises either by
deduction or by induction, or else some by induction, others by deduction
(but if they are extremely evident beforehand, even they themselves may
be proposed); for both in standing off and in induction it is less clear what

156ª1 is going to result, and at the same time it is still open to one to propose the
useful premises themselves if one cannot obtain them in those ways.

Those beyond the ones mentioned must be obtained for the sake of these
[necessary ones], and each must be used in this way: when arguing induc-

5 tively, [argue] from particular to the universal, and from the known to the
unknown (for the known is what is in accord with perception, whether
unconditionally or to most people); but, when concealing, pre-deduce the
things through which the deduction of what was initially at issue comes
about, and obtain as many of these as possible. And this would come about
if one deduced not only the necessary premises, but also some of those use-

10 ful for obtaining them. Further, do not state the conclusions, but instead
state them as a body later on; for this way one would stand farthest off from
what was posited initially.³⁶⁰

To speak in universal terms, a person who is obtaining answers in a
concealed way must so ask questions that when the whole argument has
been framed as questions and he states his conclusion, the why is looked

15 for [by the answerer]. But this will most of all come about in the way just
stated; for if only the ultimate conclusion is stated, it will be unclear how
it follows, because the answerer does not foresee what it follows from, if
the prior deductions were not fully articulated. And the deduction of the

20 conclusion would be least fully articulated if we propose not the premises of that deduction, but rather those in virtue of which that deduction
comes about.³⁶¹

It is also useful not to obtain the claims from which the deductions proceed as a continuous series, but rather alternating the claims related to one
conclusion with those related to the other; for if the ones proper [to the

25 deduction bearing on the posit] are put next to each other, what results
from them will be more easily foreseen.³⁶²

Also, in those cases that admit of it, one should obtain the universal
premise by means of a definition that applies not to the things at issue
themselves, but rather to their coordinates. For people fallaciously deceive
themselves, when the definition of the coordinate has been obtained, that

30 they have not conceded the universal—for example, if what one must
obtain is that an angry person desires revenge, and it could be obtained
that anger is a desire for revenge because of apparent contempt; for it is
clear that once this has been obtained we would have the universal we
wanted. On the other hand, it often happens to those who propose [one
that applies to] the things at issue themselves that the answerer refuses

it because he is more ready with an objection to it—for example, that an   35
angry person does not desire revenge; for we get angry with our parents,
but do not desire revenge. Presumably, his objection is not sufficient; for in
the case of some people, merely paining them or making them regret is a
sufficient revenge. Nonetheless, as regards not seeming to be unreasonably
refusing what is proposed, he has something persuasive [to say]. But in the   156^b1
case of the definition of anger, it is not equally easy to find an objection.

Further, propose something as if not proposing it because of itself but
for the sake of some other proposals; for people are on the lookout for
things that are useful against the posit. And, to speak simply, make it as   5
unclear as possible whether one wishes to obtain what one proposes or its
opposite; for if it is unclear which one is useful to the argument, people will
more readily accept what seems to be so to them.

Further, obtain answers through similarity; for it is both persuasive and   10
better hides the universal. For example, arguing that since the science as
well as the ignorance of contraries is the same, so too the perception of
contraries is the same; or—the reverse—since the perception is the same,
the science is too. This is similar to induction, but certainly not the same;
for there one obtains the universal from the particulars, while in the case   15
of similar things what one obtains is not the universal under which all the
similar things fall.

Also, one must sometimes bring an objection against oneself; for
answerers have a minimally suspicious attitude toward those who seem to
be arguing dialectically in a just way.[363] It is also useful to add that such-
and-such is customary and a saying; for people hesitate to disturb what is   20
customary if they have no objection to offer, and at the same time, since
they make use of such things themselves, they guard against disturbing
them.

Further, do not be eager, even if the point is an altogether useful one; for
people are more likely to resist those who are eager. Also, proposing something as if in a comparison; for if something is proposed because of some-   25
thing else and not because it is useful because of itself, people more readily
accept it.[364] Further, do not propose the thing itself that is to be obtained,
but something from which it follows of necessity; for people more readily
concede it because it is not equally evident what is going to follow from
this, and once the latter has been obtained, the former has also.

Also, wait till almost the last moment to ask for what one most wishes   30
to obtain; for it is the first things that people most refuse, because most
questioners state first the things they are most eager about. Against some
people, these are the things to propose first; for hagglers most readily concede the first things, if it is not completely evident what will result, but   35
haggle toward the end.[365] It is the same way too with people who think

themselves incisive answerers; for after they have accepted most points, toward the end they become extremely subtle on the presumption that things do not follow from what has been proposed.[366] They accept things off-handedly, trusting in their talent and supposing that they will not suffer any loss.

157ᵃ1   Further, lengthen the argument and throw in things that are of no use to it, like those who draw false diagrams; for when there are many things, it is unclear in which one the falsehood lies.[367] That is also why questioners escape notice by putting forward in a hole-and-corner way things that would not be accepted if proposed by themselves.

5   For concealment, then, use the things mentioned, while for ornamentation, use induction and the division of things that are akin. Well, what sort of thing induction is, is clear. Division is this sort of thing—for example, one science is better than another either by being more exact or by being the science of better things; or, of the sciences, some are theoretical, some practical, and some productive.[368] For each of these sorts of things ornaments the argument, though they are things it is not necessary to state to obtain the conclusion.

For perspicuousness adduce paradigms and comparisons, and the paradigms must be relevant and drawn from things known ("as Homer says," not "as Choerilus says"); for in this way what is proposed would be more perspicuous.[369]

8.2

How to ask dialectical questions (2)

In arguing dialectically, use deduction with those skilled in dialectic more than with ordinary people; contrariwise, use induction more with ordinary people. This was also spoken about previously.[370]

In some cases, it is possible when doing an induction to frame the universal as a question. In others, however, this is not easy because a common name has not been established for all the similar cases, but rather, when the universal [premise] must be obtained, they say, "it is this way in all cases of this sort." But this is one of the most difficult things, to determine which of the cases proposed are of the relevant sort and which are not. Also, by means of this people often cheat each other in arguments, some saying that things are similar when they are really not, others disputing the similarity of things that are similar. That is why one must try to make a name oneself that will apply to all the things of the relevant sort, so that it will neither be open to the answerer to dispute, saying that what is being introduced is not

said of things in a similar way, nor to the questioner to quibble, saying that
it is said of things in a similar way, since many that are not said of things in
a similar way appear to be said of them in a similar way.[371]

When one does an induction from many cases and someone does not
grant the universal [premise], then it is just to demand an objection. But
when one has not said oneself in which cases it holds, it is not just to ask in   35
which cases it does not hold; for one must previously have done an induction to demand an objection in this way. Also, one must expect him to
bring objections not to the thing proposed alone, unless it is the one and
only thing of the relevant sort, as two is the only even number that is prime;
for the objector must either bring his objection against another case or say   157^b1
that this is the only case of the relevant sort.[372]

Against objectors to the universal [premise] who bring their objection
not against the thing itself but against some homonym of it, for example,
that someone could have a color, a foot, or a hand that was not his own (for
a painter could have a color and a cook a foot that was not his own)—in   5
cases of this sort, then, one must draw distinctions when framing questions; for if the homonymy remains concealed, the objector will seem to
have objected well to the premise.

If, on the other hand, the answerer blocks the question by objecting, not
to a homonym, but to the thing itself, subtract the point to which the objection is made, proposing the remainder and making it the universal, until   10
one obtains what is useful.[373] For example, in the case of forgetfulness, that
is, of having forgotten; for people do not want to grant that someone who
has lost scientific knowledge has forgotten it (because if the thing at issue
changes, he has lost scientific knowledge, but has not forgotten). Subtracting, then, what the objection applies to, one must state the remainder—for
example, if, when the thing at issue remains as it is, someone loses his sci-   15
entific knowledge, it is because he has forgotten it. It is the same way too
in the case of those who object to the statement that to a greater good a
greater bad is opposed; for they propose the fact that to health, which is
a lesser good than good condition, a greater bad is opposed; for disease is
a greater bad than bad condition. In this case too subtract what the objec-   20
tion applies to; for when it is subtracted, the answerer would more readily
accept the remainder, for example, that to a greater good a greater bad
is opposed unless one brings the other along with it, as good condition
does health.

Do this not only if the answerer has made an objection, but also if, without making an objection, he has refused [the universal premise], because
he foresees something of this sort. For when what his objection applies to   25
is subtracted, he will be compelled to accept it, because he does not foresee
in the remainder any case of which it does not hold; and, if he does not

accept the premise, when one demands an objection, he will not have any
to give. Premises of this sort are those that are false in some cases and true
in others; for it is in their case that it is possible to leave a true remainder
30   by subtracting.

But if, when one proposes a premise based on many cases, he brings no
objection, he is expected to accept it; for a premise is dialectical if it holds
in many cases and there is no objection to it.

When the same thing admits of being deduced both without [reduc-
tion to] the impossible and through [reduction to] the impossible, then,
35   although when demonstrating it makes no difference whether it is deduced
in one way or the other, when arguing dialectically with someone else, one
should not use the deduction through the impossible. For against someone
who has deduced without the impossible, it is not possible to dispute. On
the other hand, when he has deduced the impossible thing, unless it is
158^a1   extremely evident that it is false, people say that it is not impossible, so that
questioners do not get what they wish.

One must also propose whatever premises hold in many cases and to
which either there is no objection at all or none that is visible on the surface; for if people cannot see cases in which something does not hold, they
5   accept it as true.

But one should not make the conclusion into a question. Otherwise,
if the answerer shakes his head in refusal, it seems that no deduction will
come about. For often, even when one does not ask the conclusion, but
puts it forward as what follows, people refuse it, and by doing this they will
10   seem not to be refuted to those who are not able to see that it follows from
what has been accepted. When, then, one asks it without even saying that
it follows and the answerer refuses it, it seems as if no deduction has come
about at all.

It does not seem, however, that every universal question is a dialectical
premise—for example, What is a human being? or, In how many ways are
15   things said to be good? For a dialectical premise is one to which it is possible to answer yes or no. But to the ones just mentioned it is not possible.
That is why questions of this sort are not dialectical, unless one assigns
the definition oneself or goes through the ways it is said in stating them—
for example, Is it not the case that things are said to be good either in this
way or that? For to things of this sort it is easy to answer either by affirm-
20   ing or denying. That is why one must try to propose premises of this sort
in this way. At the same time, it is also presumably just to inquire from
the answerer in how many ways things are said to be good, when, though
one has oneself determined them and proposed them, he concedes none
of them.

Someone who spends a long time asking questions on a single line of
argument is getting answers in a bad way. For if the one being questioned   25
is answering, this is clear, because he is asking many questions or the same
ones repeatedly, so that he is either babbling or has no deduction (for
every deduction is composed of few things); on the other hand, if he is
not answering, it is again clear, because he does not criticize him or cut off
discussion.   30

8.3

Hypotheses difficult to attack

The hypotheses it is difficult to attack and those easy to maintain are the
same. And the things that are first by nature and the ones last are of this
sort. For the first ones require definition, while the last ones are inferred by
means of many steps by anyone wishing to take a continuous series from
the first ones (otherwise the attacks appear sophistical); for it is impossible   35
to demonstrate anything without starting from the proper starting-points
and making connections as far as the last ones. Answerers neither think it
requisite for things to be defined nor, if the questioner does define them, do
they take heed.[374] Yet if it has not been made evident what exactly the thing
proposed is, it is not easy to attack it. But this sort of thing happens most
of all concerning the starting-points; for other things are proved through   158ᵇ1
them, but they do not admit of being proved through other things, instead
it is necessary to know each thing of this sort by means of a definition.
    Also difficult to attack are things that lie extremely close to the starting-
point; for it is not possible to equip oneself with many arguments against   5
these, since there are few intermediate steps between it and the starting-
point, through which it is necessary for what comes after these to be proved.
    Among definitions, however, the most difficult of all to attack are those
in which names have been used of such a sort that it is, first, unclear
whether they are said of things simply or in many ways, and, second, it is   10
not known whether they have been used by the definer in their literal sense
or metaphorically. For because they lack perspicuousness, they do not have
points of attack; and because one is ignorant as to whether it is because of
their being said of things metaphorically that they are like this, they do not
have a point of criticism.   15
    In general, any problem, when difficult to attack, must be supposed
either to require definition, to contain things said in many ways or metaphorically, or to be not far from the starting-points, or because it is not evident to us in the first place in which of ways just mentioned our puzzlement

20   is produced; for when the mode is evident, it is clear that we must either define, distinguish, or be equipped with the intermediate premises; for it is through these that the last ones are proved.

And with many posits, if the definition is not correctly assigned, it is not
25   easier to argue dialectically and attack them—for example, whether one thing has one contrary or several. But when contraries have been defined in the appropriate way, it is easy to infer whether it is possible for there to be several contraries of the same thing or not. And it is the same way in the other cases too.

It seems that in mathematics too it is not easy for a diagram to be drawn
30   in proof of some things because of omission of a definition—for example, that the line cutting the plane parallel to a side divides both the line and the area similarly.[375] When the definition is stated, what is said is evident at once; for the areas and the lines have the same reciprocal subtraction, and this is
35   the definition of same ratio.[376] The first elements are easily proved when the definitions (for example, what a line is and what a circle is) are accepted, except that the arguments that can be used to attack each of these are not many, because there are not many intermediates.[377] But if the definitions of the starting-points are not accepted, this is difficult to do, perhaps wholly
159ᵃ1   impossible. Similar things hold in the case of [dialectical] arguments.

We should not overlook, then, when a posit is difficult to attack, that it is because it has one of the affections just mentioned. But when it takes greater work to argue dialectically for the claim (that is, the premise) than
5   for the posit, one might be puzzled as to whether such things must be accepted or not. For if he will not accept it, but will expect one to argue dialectically for it as well, he will be prescribing something greater in place of what was initially at issue, while if he will accept it, one will be persuading on the basis of what is less persuasive. If, then, the problem must not be made more difficult, he must accept it, while if the deduction must proceed
10   through better known things, he must not accept it. Or else: by someone who is learning, it must not be accepted if it is not better known, while by someone who is training, it must be accepted only if it appears true. So it is evident that one must not expect to grant acceptance to a questioner and to a teacher in the same way.

8.4

How to answer dialectical questions (1)

15   As for how one must frame questions and arrange them, what has been said is pretty much enough.

Where answering is concerned, one must first determine what the function of a good answerer is, as of a good questioner.[378] It belongs to a questioner to lead the argument in such a way as to make the answerer state the least acceptable of the beliefs that are necessary because of the posit, while it belongs to an answerer to make it appear that it is not because of him that   20
anything impossible or unacceptable appears to result, but because of the posit; for agreeing at first to what one must not agree to is a distinct error from not defending properly what has been agreed to.

8.5

How to answer dialectical questions (2)

But these things are indeterminate for those who produce arguments for   25
the sake of training and examination. For the aims of teachers and learners are not the same as those of competitors, nor those of the latter as those who spend time together for the sake of investigation; for a learner must always accept the things that seem true; for no one tries to teach a falsehood. Among competitors, a questioner must at all events appear to be   30
producing some effect, while the answerer must appear not to be affected at all. In the case of dialectical meetings, by contrast, for those who produce arguments for the sake, not of competition, but of examining and investigating, it has never been fully articulated what the answerer must aim at, or what sorts of things he must grant and what sorts he must not grant to correctly defend the posit. Since, then, nothing has been handed down by   35
others, we must try to say something ourselves.

It is necessary for the answerer to take up the argument by accepting a posit that is either acceptable, unacceptable, or neither, and one that is acceptable or unacceptable either unconditionally or in a definite way—for example, to a certain person, whether himself or someone else. It makes no   **159^b1**
difference, however, in whichever way the posit is acceptable or unacceptable; for the way of answering well, of conceding or not conceding what is asked, will be the same.

If the posit is unacceptable, the conclusion that results must necessarily be acceptable, and if it is acceptable, unacceptable; for the questioner   5
always tries to conclude the opposite of the posit. And if what is proposed is neither unacceptable nor acceptable, the conclusion will also be of this sort. And since a person who deduces correctly demonstrates the problem from more acceptable and better known things, it is evident that if what is proposed is unconditionally unacceptable, the answerer must grant neither what does not seem unconditionally to be the case nor what seems to be   10

the case but less so than the conclusion.^{379} For if the posit is unacceptable, the conclusion is acceptable, so that all the things obtained must be acceptable, and more acceptable than the thing proposed, if it is through things that are better known that less well known ones are going to be inferred. So, if one of the things asked is not of this sort, the answerer should not accept it.

15

   If the posit is unconditionally acceptable, it is clear that the conclusion is unconditionally unacceptable. The answerer must accept, then, both all the things that seem so and whatever things do not seem to be so, but are less acceptable than the conclusion; for then it would appear to be argued dialectically in a sufficient way.

20

   It is the same way if the posit is neither acceptable nor unacceptable; for in this case too, the answerer must grant both everything that appears so, and whatever things do not seem to be so, but are more acceptable than the conclusion; for in this way the resulting arguments will be more acceptable.

   If, on the other hand, what is proposed is unconditionally acceptable or unacceptable, it is with respect to things that seem so unconditionally that he must make the comparison.^{380} But if what is proposed is acceptable or unacceptable, not unconditionally, but to the answerer, it is with respect to what seems to be so to himself or does not seem to be so that he should judge what to accept or not accept.

25

   If the answerer is defending someone else's belief, it is clear that he must accept or refuse each thing by looking to that other person's thought. That is why those who introduce the beliefs of others—for example, that the same thing is good and bad, "as Heraclitus says"—do not grant that contraries cannot belong to the same thing at the same time, not because of believing this themselves, but because according to Heraclitus this is what one must say.^{381} This is also what those people do who take over posits from each other; for they aim at saying what those who posited it would say.

30

35

8.6

How to answer dialectical questions (3)

It is evident, then, what the answerer must aim at, whether what is proposed is acceptable unconditionally or to a certain person. But since everything asked must be either acceptable or unacceptable or neither, and what is asked must be either relevant to the argument or not relevant to the argument, if it seems to be so, and is not relevant to the argument, having said that it seems to be so, he must grant it, while if it does not seem to be so, and is not relevant to the argument, he must accept it, but indicating in addition that it does not seem to be so, as a precaution against [a charge of] simplemindedness.

160^{a}1

If it is relevant to the argument, and seems to be so, he must say that, though it seems to be so, it is too close to what was initially at issue, and that what is proposed is done away with if this is accepted.   5

If the claim is relevant to the argument but too unacceptable he should say that, though the conclusion results if it is accepted, what is proposed is too simpleminded.

If it is neither unacceptable nor acceptable, if it has no relevance to the argument, he must grant it without drawing distinctions, while if it is relevant to the argument, he must indicate in addition that what was posited   10 initially is done away with by it. For in this way the answerer will appear not to be affected at all because of what he himself does, if he accepts each thing with foresight, and the questioner will bring to pass his deduction, since everything more acceptable than the conclusion is granted to him.

Those, on the other hand, who try to deduce from things more unaccept- able than the conclusion, clearly do not deduce correctly, which is why one   15 must not accept what is posited [and grant it] to the questioners.

8.7

Answering questions that lack perspicuousness
or are said in many ways

One must also reply in the same way to questions that lack perspicuous- ness or that are said in many ways. For since it is granted to the answerer who does not understand to say, "I do not understand," and, if the question is said in many ways, not to have of necessity to agree or decline, it is clear,   20 first, that if what is said is not perspicuous, he must not hesitate to say that he does not comprehend it; for in many cases, as a result of conceding what is not asked perspicuously, he would confront something difficult. But if what is said is something known, and, though it is said in many ways, is true or false in all of them, he should accept or refuse it uncondi- tionally. On the other hand, if it is false in one case and true in another, he   25 should indicate in addition that it is said in many ways, and that it is false in the one and true in the other; for if he draws this distinction later on, it will be unclear whether he also saw the ambiguity initially. But if he did not see the ambiguity earlier, but accepted looking at one of the two ways it is said, he must say to a questioner leading him to the other one, "I did   30 not grant it looking to that one but to the other of them"; for if there are several things falling under the same name or account, disputation eas- ily arises. But if what is asked is perspicuous and simple, he must answer either yes or no.[382]

8.8

Answering particular versus universal questions; haggling

35   Since every deductive premise is among those the deduction is composed of or else is for the sake of one of them (and it is clear when someone is obtaining it for the sake of another one, because of his asking for several similar things; for it is either through induction or through similarity that people for the most part obtain the universal), the answerer must accept all the particular cases, insofar as they are true and acceptable but should

160^b1   try to bring an objection against the universal; for to prevent the argument without a real or seeming objection is haggling.[383] If, then, he does not grant the universal when it appears so in many cases, though not having an objection, it is evident that he is haggling. Further, if he has not even

5   got it in him to counter-argue that it is not true, he would seem all the more to be haggling. (And yet even this is not enough; for we have at our disposal many arguments against [acceptable] beliefs that are difficult to resolve—for example, Zeno's argument that it is not possible to move or to traverse the stadium, but one must not, because of this, refuse to accept their opposites.[384]) If, then, though neither having an objection nor being

10   able to counter-argue, he does not accept, it is clear that he is haggling; for haggling in arguments is answering in a way beyond the ways just mentioned, that is, in a way destructive of deduction.

8.9

Practicing on oneself; unacceptable hypotheses

To uphold a posit or a definition, one must try developing counter-arguments to it by oneself ahead of time; for it is clear that the things one

15   must oppose are the ones on the basis of which those obtaining answers do away with what was proposed.

One must beware of upholding an unacceptable hypothesis. And there are two ways it could be unacceptable; for it could be so by being one from which saying absurd things follows (for example, if someone were to say that everything or nothing is in movement) or by being what someone with a worse character would choose, or what is contrary to our wishes (for

20   example, that pleasure is the good, or that doing injustice is better than suffering injustice); for on the supposition that these are not things one says merely for the sake of argument but the things that seem so to you, people hate you.

8.10

Resolving arguments that deduce a falsehood

As for arguments that deduce a falsehood, resolve them by doing away with the thing through which the falsehood comes about; for it is not the person who does away with any thing whatever that resolves it, not even if what is done away with is false. For the argument might contain several falsehoods—for example, if someone obtained that the person seated is writing, and that Socrates is seated; for it follows from these that Socrates is writing. When "Socrates is seated" is done away with, the argument is no closer to being resolved, although the claim is false. But it is not by depending on it that the argument is false; for if someone happened to be seated but not writing, the same resolution will no longer fit such a case. So it is not this that must be done away with, but rather that the person seated is writing; for not every seated person is writing.[385] The person, then, who does away with what the falsehood depends on has entirely refuted the argument, and it is the person who knows that the argument depends on it who knows the resolution (as in the case of drawing false diagrams).[386] For it is not enough to object, not even if what is done away with is false, but one must also demonstrate why it is false; for this way it would be evident whether or not he makes his objection with foresight.

There are four ways to prevent an argument from reaching a conclusion: by doing away with what the falsehood depends on; by stating an objection to the questioner (for often he has not resolved anything, yet the one obtaining answers is not able to lead him any further); third, objecting to the questions asked (for it may happen that what the questioner wishes does not come about on the basis of the questions asked, because they have been framed incorrectly, though when something is added the conclusion does come about). If, then, the questioner cannot advance any further, the objection would be against the questioner, while, if he can, against his questions. The fourth and worst sort of objection is the one relating to the time (for some people raise an objection of this sort, that it would take longer to dialectically argue against than the present discussion allows).

Objections, then, as we said, come about in four ways. But only the first of those mentioned is a resolution, while the remaining ones are sorts of preventions and impediments to conclusions.

8.11

Criticism of arguments as such versus when framed as questions

Criticism of an argument intrinsically as an argument is not the same as criticism of it when it is framed as questions. For often the person questioned is responsible for the argument having not been dialectically argued correctly, because he does not concede the things from which it was possible to dialectically argue correctly against the thesis; for it is not up to one of two partners alone to ensure that their common work is correctly accomplished. Sometimes, then, it is necessary to attack the speaker not his posit: when the answerer is on the lookout for things that go contrary to the questioner and is abusive besides. By haggling, at all events, people make their discussions competitive not dialectical.

Further, since arguments of this sort are for the sake of training and examining, not of teaching, it is clear that not only true but also false conclusions must be deduced, and not always through truths but sometimes also through falsehoods; for often, when a truth has been posited, it is necessary for the dialectician to do away with it, so that he must use falsehoods as a premise. And sometimes, even when a falsehood has been posited, he must do away with it through falsehoods; for there is nothing to prevent things that are not so from seeming to be more so to someone than things that are true, so that if the argument comes about from things that seem to be so to him, he will be more persuaded than benefited.

Anyone who is going to change the course of an argument correctly, however, must change it in a dialectical way, not in a contentious way, just as the geometer must do so in a geometrical way, regardless of whether the conclusion is false or true. (What sort of deductions are dialectical was stated previously.[387])

Since it is a bad partner who impedes the common work, it is clear that it is so in argument as well. For there is also something common proposed in arguments, except in the case of competitive ones.[388] In these it is not possible for both to achieve the same end; for there cannot be more than one winner. It makes no difference whether one does this by answering or by questioning; for the person who questions in a contentious way argues dialectically in a bad way, and so does the answerer who will neither grant what is evident nor admit to understanding what the questioner can possibly wish to obtain with his question.

It is clear, then, from what has been said that an argument intrinsically as such must not be criticized in the same way as a questioner; for there is nothing to prevent the argument's being bad, though the questioner has argued dialectically as well as possible with the answerer. For, against

hagglers, one is perhaps simply not able to produce such deductions as one
wishes, but only such as one can.   10

Since it is indefinite when human beings assume contrary things and
when they assume what was initially at issue (for often when talking to
themselves they say contrary things, and, having refused something earlier,
grant it later on—which is why, when they are asked for contraries and
when they are asked for what was initially at issue, they often grant these),
bad arguments necessarily come about. The one responsible [in these   15
cases] is the answerer who at certain moments does not grant some things
but at other moments grants others of the same sort.

It is evident, then, that questioners and arguments must not be criticized
in the same way.

Of an argument as intrinsically such, there are five criticisms.³⁸⁹ First,
from the premises asked, neither what was proposed nor anything else at   20
all is concluded, since all or most of the premises in which the conclusion lies are either false or unacceptable, and the conclusion does not come
about either when some premises are subtracted or when some are added
or when some are subtracted and others added. Second, if it is not against
the posit that a deduction comes about (from the sorts of premises and in   25
the way mentioned just previously). Third, if a deduction comes about with
certain premises added, but these are worse than the ones asked for and
less acceptable than the conclusion. Again, if it comes about with certain
premises subtracted; for sometimes more premises are assumed than are
necessary, so that it is not through them that the deduction comes about.
Further, if it is from premises more unacceptable and less persuasive than   30
the conclusion; or if it is from premises that are true but require more work
to demonstrate than the problem does.

One must not require the deductions of all problems to be equally acceptable and persuasive; for simply by nature some objects of inquiry are easier   35
and others more difficult, so that if one has inferred from the most acceptable premises possible, one has argued dialectically in the correct way. It is
evident, then, that the same criticism also does not apply to an argument
in relation to the problem at issue and an argument intrinsically as such;
for there is nothing to prevent an argument from being intrinsically blameworthy but praiseworthy in relation to a problem; or, again, conversely,   40
intrinsically praiseworthy but blameworthy in relation to the problem: 162ᵃ1
when there are many premises both acceptable and true from which it is
easily concluded. It is possible too that an argument that reaches a conclusion may sometimes be worse than one that does not reach a conclusion:
when the first is concluded from simpleminded premises (the problem not   5
being of that sort), while the second needs additional premises, but of the
sort that are acceptable and true, and it is not in the additional ones [by

themselves] that the argument lies. As regards those that reach a conclusion through falsehoods, it is not just to criticize them; for a falsehood
must always be deduced through falsehoods, while it is sometimes possible
for a truth to be deduced even through falsehoods. This is evident from
the *Analytics*.[390]

When the argument stated is a demonstration of something, if there is
something else that is not related in any way to the conclusion, it will not be
a deduction of that. And if it were [made] to appear to be one, it would be a
sophism, not a demonstration. {A *philosophêma* is a demonstrative deduction; an *epicheirêma* is a dialectical deduction; a sophism is a contentious
deduction; and an *aporêma* is a dialectical deduction of a contradiction.[391]}

If something is proved from premises both of which seem so, but do not
seem equally so, there is nothing to prevent what is proved from seeming
more so than each singly.[392] But if one premise were to seem so and the other
to seem neither so nor not so, or if one were to seem so and the other not so,
then if these are equal, [the conclusion] would be equally so or not so, but
if one of the two is more, it will follow along with the one that is more so.[393]

There is also the following error regarding deductions: when someone proves something through a longer series of steps, though it could
be proved through fewer ones that actually belong in the argument. For
example, if to prove that one belief is more [a belief] than another, someone were to assume the following: a thing-itself is most of all [that thing],
there is a truly believable-itself, and so it will be more [that thing] than
the particular ones; but what is said in relation to the more is more [that
thing]; but again there is a true believable-itself, which will be more exactly
[that thing] than the particular ones.[394] He assumed the existence of a true
believable-itself and that each thing-itself is most of all [that thing], so [as
to prove] that this true belief is more exactly [a belief than another]. What,
though, is the defect? Or is it that what the argument depends on makes
hidden the cause?

8.12

Clear and false arguments

An argument is clear in one way, which is also the most commonly used
one, if it reaches a conclusion in such a way that no further questions are
needed; in another way, which is also the one most of all said to be such,
when the premises obtained are the ones it is necessary for the conclusion
to be deduced from, and it is concluded through conclusions; in a further
way, if anything missing is extremely acceptable.[395]

An argument is called "false" in four ways: one way is when it appears to reach a conclusion but does not reach a conclusion (this is called a "contentious deduction").[396] Another is when it reaches a conclusion, but not in relation to the thing proposed (which is just what happens most in those leading to impossibility).[397] Or it reaches a conclusion in relation to what is proposed, but not in accord with the methodical inquiry proper to it. And this is when it appears to be medical but is not medical, or geometrical but is not geometrical, or dialectical but is not dialectical, whether what results is true or false. Another way is if it reaches a conclusion through falsehoods. And its conclusion, though it will sometimes be false, will sometimes be true; for a falsehood is always inferred through falsehoods, but it is possible for a truth to be inferred even though not from truths, as was also stated previously.[398]

An argument's being false is an error of the arguer rather than of the argument (and it is not even always of the arguer, but only when he is not aware of it), since, as intrinsically such, we approve of it more than of many true ones, if from what seems most of all to be so it does away with some truth.[399] For an argument of this sort is a demonstration of other truths; for one of the things proposed must not be absolutely true, so that it will be a demonstration of this. But if a true conclusion were to be reached through false and very simpleminded premises, it would be worse than many that deduce a falsehood, and it might be of this sort even if reaching a false conclusion.

So it is clear that the first step in investigating an argument as intrinsically such is to see whether it reaches a conclusion; second, whether this is true or false; third, from what sorts of premises. For if it is from false but acceptable premises, it is a logico-linguistic argument; if from true but unacceptable ones, it is a bad one; if from false and extremely unacceptable ones, it is clear that it is a bad one, either unconditionally or in relation to the thing at issue.

8.13

Asking for what was initially at issue; asking for contraries

How a questioner asks for what was initially at issue and for contraries has been stated in accord with truth in the *Analytics*, and must now be stated in accord with belief.[400]

People appear to ask for what was initially at issue in five ways. The most evident and the first is if someone asks for the very thing that needs to be proved.[401] In the case of the very thing, this is not easy to conceal, but in the case of synonyms and in those cases in which a name and an account signify the same thing, it is easier. The second is when someone needing to demonstrate a particular asks for a universal—for example, trying to demonstrate that the science of contraries is one, he expects to obtain that the science of opposites in general is one; for he seems to be asking for what he needed to prove by itself, together with several other things. Third, if when it is proposed that a universal be proved, someone were to ask for a particular—for example, when it is proposed that the science of all contraries is one be proved, he expects to obtain this about these particular contraries; for this person too seems to be asking for what, together with other things, he needed to prove separately by itself. Again, if someone, dividing it up, asks for the problem—for example, if someone, needing to prove that medicine is the science of healthy and diseased, were to expect to obtain each of these separately. Or if someone were to expect to obtain one or other of the things that of necessity follow along with each other— for example, that the side is incommensurable with the diagonal, when he must demonstrate that the diagonal is incommensurable with the side.⁴⁰²

People ask for contraries in the same number of ways as they do for the starting thing. For the first is if someone were to ask for an opposed assertion and denial; second, for contraries by an antithesis—for example, [asking whether] the same thing is good and bad.⁴⁰³ The third is if someone who expected to obtain the universal were to ask for its contradictory in the case of particulars (for example, if having obtained that the science of contraries is one, he were to expect to obtain that there is science of healthy and a different science of diseased). Or if, having asked for the latter, he were to try to obtain the contradictory in the case of the universal. Again, if someone were to ask for the contrary of what results of necessity through the things proposed, and even if he were not to [try to] obtain the [pair of] contraries themselves, he were to ask for a pair such that from them there will be the opposing contradiction.⁴⁰⁴

Obtaining contraries differs from obtaining the starting thing, however, because the error in the second is in relation to the conclusion (for that is what we look to when we say that someone asks for the starting thing), while in the case of contraries it lies in the premises standing in a certain relation to each other.

8.14

Training and practice in dialectical arguments

For training and practice in arguments of this sort, first, it is necessary
to get into the habit of converting arguments; for this way we will be bet-   30
ter equipped in relation to what is said, and also we will know by heart
many arguments in knowing by heart a few. For converting is doing away
with one of the premises granted by taking the reverse of the conclusion
together with the remaining premises asked for; for it is necessary, if the
conclusion is not so, for some one of the premises to be done away with,
if indeed it was necessary, all of them being posited, for the conclusion to   35
be so.

  Also, in relation to every posit look both for a dialectical argument that
it is so and for one that it is not so, and, when it has been found, look
immediately for its resolution; for in this way the result will be that we will   163^b1
at the same time get training both in asking and in answering, and even if
we have no one else to argue with, we can argue with ourselves.

  Also, select the dialectical arguments concerned with the same posit and
set them alongside each other; for it makes one abundantly well-equipped   5
against being forced [to a conclusion], and also has much help to offer in
relation to refuting, when one is well equipped to argue both that it is so
and that it is not so (for the result is that one is put on one's guard against
contrary arguments).

  Also, in relation to knowledge and philosophical wisdom, being able to
get a comprehensive view, or to have gotten a comprehensive view, of the   10
consequences of either hypothesis is no small instrument; for it remains
[only] to choose one or the other of them correctly.[405] In relation to this sort
of thing, one must be naturally well-disposed. And this is what it is to be
naturally well-disposed as regards truth: to be able to correctly choose the
true and avoid the false. And this is just what the naturally well-endowed
are able to do; for it is by loving and hating in the correct way what is put   15
before them that they judge well what is best.[406]

  In relation to the problems that most often fall to one, one must learn
arguments by heart, especially about the first posits; for in the case of these,
answerers often give up in despair.[407] Further, one must be well equipped
with definitions and have both acceptable beliefs and primary [starting-   20
points] ready to hand; for it is through these that deductions come about.

  One must also try to get possession of the [headings] into the province
of which other arguments most often fall. For just as in geometry it furthers the work to be trained in the elements, and in arithmetic to have the
multiplication table up to ten at one's fingertips (it makes a great difference

25   to knowing the multiples of the other numbers too), so likewise in arguments does having things at hand about starting-points, and knowing the
premises by heart. For just as in mnemonics, the mere mention of their
places (*topoi*) immediately makes the things themselves be remembered,
30   so these [headings] will make one more capable at deducing, because one
sees these items defined and numbered.⁴⁰⁸ And it is a common premise,
rather than an argument, that should be committed to memory; for to be
well equipped with a starting-point—that is, a hypothesis—is [only] mod-
erately difficult.⁴⁰⁹

Further, get into the habit of making one argument into many, thus concealing [the conclusion] in the greatest possible unclarity.⁴¹⁰ And it would
35   be of this sort if one stands off as far as possible from things akin to those
the argument is about. Among arguments, it will be the most universal
ones to which this can be done—for example, that there is not one sci-
164ᵃ1   ence of several things; for this way it applies to relatives, contraries, and
coordinates.

The mnemonics of arguments should be made universal, even if the dialectical argument has to do with a particular case; for in this way too it will
be possible to make one argument into many.⁴¹¹ (It is the same way too in
5   rhetoric in the case of enthymemes.⁴¹²) For oneself [as answerer] one must
avoid as much as possible leading deductions toward the universal. And
one must always look at arguments to see whether they argue dialectically
on the basis of large number of cases; for all the ones that are particular
also do so universally, and the demonstration of the universal is present in
10   the particular one, because it is not possible to deduce anything without
universals.

Training in inductions must be assigned to a young person; training
in deductions to an experienced one. And try to get premises from those
skilled at deduction; comparisons from those skilled at induction; for it is
15   in this that each has been trained. In general, try to take away from training
in dialectic either a deduction about something, a resolution, an objection,
or whether someone asked something correctly or incorrectly (whether
oneself or someone else), and why it was so in either case. For it is on
164ᵇ1   these that the capacity is based, and training is for the sake of capacity—
especially where premises and objections are concerned; for, simply speaking, the person skilled at dialectic is the one skilled at proposing premises
and skilled at proposing objections. And proposing premises is making
many things into one (for what the argument aims at must, in general, be
5   taken as one thing), while objecting is making one thing into many (for
one either divides or does away with, grants or does not grant, the things
that are proposed).⁴¹³

One should not argue dialectically with everyone or train with a random person. For with certain people arguments necessarily become bad; for with someone who tries in every way to appear to escape, it is just to try in every way to produce a deduction, but it is not gracious. That is why one should not readily engage with random people. For the necessary result is worthless-argument; for even trained people are incapable of refraining from arguing dialectically in a contentious way.

One must also have readymade arguments related to the sorts of problems in which, though we are well equipped with very few, those we have will be useful in relation to the greatest number. These are the universal ones and the ones it is very difficult on the basis of things at hand to be well equipped against.⁴¹⁴

Sophistical Refutations

1

Apparent deductions and apparent refutations

164ᵃ20 Let us now discuss sophistical refutations, that is, arguments that appear to be refutations, but are really fallacies, not [genuine] refutations, beginning in accord with nature from what comes first.

That certain arguments are deductions, while others seem to be but are not, is evident. For just as in other cases this comes about because of a certain similarity, so it is likewise too in the case of arguments. For some people too are in good condition, while others [only] appear to be so, like tribesmen choristers puffing themselves up and bulking up, and some people are nobly beautiful because of their beauty, while other appear so, by using cosmetics.[415] And in the case of inanimate things it is likewise; for some of these are truly silver and other gold, while others are not, though they appear to be so to perception—for example, things made of litharge or of lead appear to be silver, and yellow-colored ones appear to be gold.[416] In the same way, one argument is a deduction or a refutation, while another is not, though it appears such due to lack of experience; for those who lack experience look at things from far away.

For a deduction is when certain things are posited, so that, on the basis of them, it is necessary to assert a thing distinct from the ones proposed, while a refutation is a deduction together with the contradiction of the conclusion.[417] Some of them, however, do not produce this effect, though—due to several causes—they seem to. Among these, one topic, which is most naturally well suited for this purpose and most commonly used, is the one through names. For since it is not possible to bring the things at issue themselves into dialectical arguments, but we use names as symbols instead of things, we think that what follows in the case of the names follows in the case of the things at issue as well, just as in the case of pebbles for those doing rational calculations.[418] But the two are not similar; for names are limited as is the number of statements, while things at issue are unlimited in number.[419] It is necessary, then, for the same statement or a single name to signify several things. Just as in the case of calculation those who are not clever at manipulating the pebbles are cheated by those with scientific knowledge, so in the same way in arguments too those inexperienced in the capacity of names argue fallaciously both when arguing themselves and when listening to others.[420]

Due to this cause, then, and others to be mentioned later, there exist both deductions and refutations that are apparent but not real. But since for some people it furthers their work to seem to be wise without being wise rather than to be it without seeming so (for sophistry is apparent wisdom, not real wisdom; and a sophist is someone who makes money from apparent but not real wisdom), it is clear that for them it is also necessary to seem to produce the work of a wise person rather than to produce it and not seem to.

To compare point by point: it is the work of the person who knows a given thing not to speak falsely himself about what he knows, and to be capable of exposing the one who does speak falsely. And of these, the first consists in being capable of giving an argument, the second in being capable of obtaining one. It is necessary, then, for those who wish to play the sophist to look for arguments of the kind just mentioned; for it furthers their work; for a capacity of this sort will make one appear to be wise, which is the end that, having the deliberate choice they have, they aim to achieve.[421]

It is clear, then, that there is a kind consisting of arguments of this sort, and it is this sort of capacity that those we call "sophists" aim at. Let us now speak about how many forms of sophistical arguments there are, how many in number the things are from which this capacity is composed, how many parts there are of a work on this subject, and about whatever other things contribute to this craft.

2

Didactic, dialectical, examinational, and contentious arguments

Of arguments in dialectical discussions, there are four kinds: didactic, dialectical, examinational, and contentious. Didactic ones are those that deduce from the starting-points proper to a given subject and not from the beliefs of the answerer (for the learner must take things on trust); dialectical ones are those that deduce from acceptable beliefs in way that reaches a contradiction; examinational ones are those that deduce from things that seem so to the answerer and that it is necessary for the one who pretends to possess the relevant science to know (in what way has been determined elsewhere); contentious ones are those that deduce or appear to deduce from what appear to be acceptable beliefs, but are not.[422]

Demonstrative arguments have been spoken about in the *Analytics*, and dialectical and examinational ones elsewhere.[423] About competitive and contentious arguments, let us speak now.

3

Aims of competitors and rivals

First, then, we must grasp the number of things that competitors and rivals in arguments aim at.[424] These are five in number: refutation, falsehood, disreputability, solecism, and, fifth, making the interlocutor babble (and this consists in being compelled to say the same thing repeatedly)—or else, not the real thing, but the appearance of each of them. For competitors and rivals most of all deliberately choose to appear to refute; second, to prove the opponent to be saying something false; third, to lead him into something unacceptable; fourth, to make him commit a solecism (and this is to have made the answerer utter a barbarism by means of the argument); and lastly, to make him say the same thing repeatedly.

4

Modes of refutation depending on speech

The modes of refutation are twofold; for one depends on speech, while the other occurs outside speech. The ways of producing an appearance of refutation depending on speech are six in number. They are homonymy, ambiguity, combination, division, accentuation, and style of speech. For this means of persuasion is through induction—when one assumes another argument to the effect that this is the number of ways in which we can fail to indicate the same thing by the same names or statements—as well as through deduction.

Depending on homonymy are arguments of the following sort:[425] That it is those possessing knowledge who learn (*manthanein*), for it is those who know their letters who understand (*manthanein*) what is dictated to them; for here *manthanein* is homonymous between "understanding by using scientific knowledge" and "acquiring scientific knowledge." Or, again, that evils are good; for what there needs must be is a good and evil is what there needs must be; for "what there needs must be" is equivocal: [it means] "what is necessary," which often applies to evils (for it is necessary for there to be some evil), and "needed," which we say good things are. Further, "the same person is seated and standing, sick and healthy." For it is the very one who stood up that is standing, and the very one who became healthy that is healthy. But it is the seated one who stood up and the sick one who became healthy. For "the sick person does or suffers such-and-such" does not signify one thing, but at one time "that the person who is now sick . . ." and at another "that the person who was previously sick . . ." But the person

who became healthy was both sick and the person who was sick, while the
one who is healthy is not sick, though he is the sick person, not sick now,
but the one who was so previously.   5

Depending on ambiguity are arguments of the following sort: "Wishing
that I myself the enemy may capture."[426] Also, "Surely if a person knows a
thing, knowing belongs there?" For it is possible to signify as the possessor
of knowledge in this statement both the knower and the thing known.
Also, "Surely, if a person sees something, seeing belongs there?" But he
sees a pillar, therefore seeing belongs to the pillar. Also, "Surely, if you insist   10
on something's being, it you insist on being?" But you insist on a stone's
being, therefore you insist on being a stone. Also, "Surely, it is possible for
speaking to pertain to the silent?"[427] For "speaking pertaining to the silent"
is equivocal between a speaker who is being silent and the things spoken
about being so.

There are three modes of arguing that depend on homonymy and ambiguity: One is when a statement or a name strictly speaking signifies several   15
things—for example, "eagle" and "dog."[428] Another is when we customarily
use them in that way.[429] A third is when the combination signifies several things, but the separate components signify only one. For example,
"scientifically-knowing letters"; for it may so happen that each of the two—
"knowing" and "letters"—signifies one thing, while the two together signify several, either that the letters themselves have scientific knowledge or   20
that something else has it of them. Ambiguity and homonymy, then, are
depended on in these ways.

Depending on combination are arguments of the following sort—for
example, "a person is capable of walking while sitting, or writing while not
writing"; for it does not signify the same thing if one is dividing and says,   25
capable of "walking-while-sitting," as it does if one is combining; and likewise in the other case, if combining one says, "writing-while-not-writing";
for it signifies that he has the capacity to write while he is not writing.
On the other hand, if one is not combining, it signifies that he has the
capacity, when he is not writing, to write. Also, "Now he can learn his letters, if indeed he has learned the things he scientifically knows."[430] Further,   30
"Someone who can carry only one thing can carry many."[431]

Depending on division: "Five is two and three, that is, even and odd," and
"The greater is equal to the less" (for it is so-and-so much and something
further besides). For the same statement divided and combined would not   35
always seem to signify the same thing—for example, "I made you a free
man slave," and "Of men one hundred fifty Godlike Achilles left alive."[432]

Depending on accentuation, in dialectical discussions that are not written down, it is not easy to produce an argument, but it is easier in writ-   **166ᵇ1**
ten exchanges and poetry. For example, some people rectify Homer in

response to those who refute as absurd his phrase, τὸ μὲν οὐ καταπύθεται ὄμβρῳ ("this is not rotted by the rain"); for they resolve it by a change of accent, saying the οὐ more sharply. Also, in the passage about Agamemnon's dream, they argue that Zeus did not himself say, δίδομεν δέ οἱ εὖχος ἀρέσθαι ("we grant him the fulfillment of his prayer") but ordered the dream to grant it.[433] Arguments of this sort, then, depend on accentuation.

Arguments depending on the style of speech come about when what is not the same is communicated in the same way—for example, a masculine by a feminine, a feminine by a masculine, or either of these by a neuter, or, again, a quality by a quantity, a quantity by a quality, a doing by a being affected, or a disposition by a doing, and so on for the others that were distinguished previously; for it is possible for something that is not among the doings to signify by its style of speech something that is among the doings.[434] For example, "being healthy (*hugianein*)" is, in its style of speech, said of things in a similar way to "cutting (*temnein*)" or "building (*oikodomein*)"; yet the former indicates a certain quality and a way of being disposed, the latter a certain doing.[435] And it is the same way in the case of the others.

Refutations depending on speech, then, are based on these topics.

Of fallacies occurring outside speech, on the other hand, there are seven forms: the first depends on the coincident; the second depends on what is said of things unconditionally or instead not unconditionally, but is so in some respect, place, time, or relation; the third depends on ignorance of what a refutation is; the fourth depends on [affirming] the consequent; the fifth depends on assuming what was initially at issue; the sixth depends on positing the non-cause as a cause; the seventh depends on making many questions into one.

5

Fallacies depending on the coincident

Fallacies depending on the coincident come about when it is claimed that any affection whatever belongs in the same way to the thing at issue and to its coincident. For since many coincidents belong to the same thing, it is not necessary for all these to belong to what is predicated of the thing as belong to the thing they are predicated of.[436] For example, "If Coriscus is other than a human, he is other than himself, for he is a human." Or, "If he is other than Socrates, and Socrates is a human," then, so they say, "the opponent has agreed that Coriscus is other than a human," because it happens coincidentally that the one he said that Coriscus was said to be other than is a human.[437]

Those depending on what is said of things unconditionally, or instead of things in some respect and not strictly, come about when what is said of things partially is taken as if it applied unconditionally—for example, "If what is not is believable, then what is not is"; for "to be something" and "to 167ᵃ1 be" unconditionally are not the same.[438] Or, again, "What is, is not" (if it is not one of the things that is—for example, a human being); for it is not the same thing not to be something and not to be unconditionally. But it appears to be so, because of closeness in speech: "to be something" differs little from "to be," and "to not be something" from "to not be." 5

Similarly, with the dependence on what is so in a certain respect and what is so unconditionally—for example, the Indian, being wholly black, is white in tooth, therefore he is white and not white. Or, if both affections belong in a certain respect, that contraries belong at the same time. In some cases this sort of fallacy is easily seen by everyone—for example, 10 if having obtained that the Ethiopian is black, the questioner were to ask, whether he was white in tooth; and then, if he obtained that he is white in that respect, he were to think that he had dialectically proved that he was black and not black, because he had reached the end of his questioning with a deduction. In other cases, however, the fallacy is often undetected: wherever, when something is said to be so in a certain respect, its being unconditionally so would also seem to follow, and in those where it is not 15 easy to see which of them is to be assigned in a strict way. This sort of thing occurs when opposites belong in a similar way; for then it seems that either both or neither must be granted to be predicated unconditionally— for example, if something is half white or half black, is it white or black?[439] 20

Fallacies depending on the non-determination of what a deduction is, or what a refutation is, instead depend on an omission from the account [of refutation].[440] For a refutation is a contradiction of one and the same thing, not of the name but of the thing at issue, and not of a synonymous name, but of the same one, following of necessity from the things granted (not counting what was initially at issue), in the same respect, in relation 25 to the same thing, in the same way, and at the same time.[441] (And it is the same way too in the case of stating a falsehood about something.) Some people appear to refute by omitting one of the stated conditions—for example, arguing that the same thing is the double and not the double; for two is the double of one, but not the double of three. Or, if the same thing 30 is the double and not the double of the same thing, but not so in the same respect; for it is double in length but not double in breadth. Or, if it is the double and not the double of the same thing and in the same respect and way, but not at the same time. That is why there is only an apparent refutation. (One might drag one of this sort into the class of those depending on the speech.) 35

The ones that depend on assuming what was initially at issue come about in the same way, and in the same number of ways, as those that demand what was initially at issue. They appear to refute because of the incapacity to take a comprehensive view of sameness and distinctness.

A refutation that depends on [affirming] the consequent is due to think-
167^b1 ing that the consequence is convertible; for when, if A is so, B is of necessity so, people also think that if B is so, A is also of necessity so. It is from this too that deceptions concerning belief based on perception come about;
5 for people often take bile for honey because honey is followed along by a yellow color. Also, since the ground becomes wet following rain, if it is wet, we assume that it has rained. But this is not necessarily so. In rhetori-cal arguments, demonstrations in accord with a sign are based on things that follow; for when speakers wish to prove that a person is an adulterer,
10 they take hold of the consequent—that he is well-dressed or that he is seen wandering about at night.⁴⁴² But these affections belong to many people of whom the predicate [adulterer] does not belong. It is likewise too in deduc-tive arguments—for example, the argument of Melissus that the universe is unlimited assumes that the universe cannot come to be (for nothing can come to be from what is not) and that everything that has come to be has
15 come from a starting-point; if, then, the universe has not come to be, it has no starting-point, and so is unlimited.⁴⁴³ But this does not necessarily fol-low; for even if what has come to be always has a starting-point, it does not also follow that what has a starting-point has come to be—any more than if
20 a feverish person is hot, it is necessary that a hot one has a fever.

A refutation depending on taking the non-cause as cause comes about when what is not a cause is added as if the refutation's coming about depended on it. This sort of thing happens in deductions leading to an impossibility; for in these it is necessary to do away with one of the things proposed. If, then, what is not a cause is counted among the questions that
25 are necessary for establishing the resulting impossibility, the coming about of the refutation will often seem to depend on it. For example, the follow-ing argument that soul and life are not the same: If coming to be is in fact contrary to passing away, to a certain sort of passing away a certain sort of coming to be is contrary; but death is a certain sort of passing away and is contrary to life; so life is a coming to be and to be alive is to be coming to
30 be; but this is impossible; therefore, soul and life are not the same. But the conclusion is not deduced at all; for the impossibility results even if one does not say that life and soul are the same, but only that life is contrary to death, which is a passing away, and that coming to be is contrary to passing away. Arguments of this sort are not unconditionally non-deductive, but
35 in relation to the thing proposed they are non-deductive. And this sort of thing often goes no less unnoticed by the questioners themselves.

Arguments depending on the consequent and the non-cause, then, are of this sort. Those depending on the making of two questions into one come about when the plurality is not noticed and one answer is given as if to one question.[444] In some cases it is easy to see that there are several questions involved and that one must not give one answer—for example, "Is the earth sea, or is the sky?" In other cases, however, it is less easy, and, on the supposition that it is really one, people either concede by not answering what is being asked or appear to be refuted. For example, "Is A a human and is B?"[445] So, were someone to strike this one and that one, he would strike *a* human and not human*s*.

168ᵃ1

5

Or, again, the things among which some are good and some bad, are they all good or not good? For whichever the answerer says would seem to produce either refutation or evident falsehood; for to say that something not good is good, or that something good is not good, is false. Sometimes, if certain premises are added, a genuine refutation might come about. For example, if one grants that one thing and several things are alike said to be white, naked, or blind. For if one thing's being blind is its not having sight when it is natural to have it, several things' being blind will also be their not having sight when it is natural to have it. When, then, one has sight while another does not have it, they will either both be able to see or both be blind—which is just impossible.

10

15

6

Fallacies based on ignorance of what a refutation is

We must either divide apparent deductions and refutations in this way, or drag all of them into the class of those ignorant of refutation, making this a starting-point; for it is possible to resolve all the ways mentioned into that of the definition of refutation.

20

First, see whether they are non-deductive; for the conclusion must follow from the things proposed, so that to state it is a matter of necessity, and does not merely appear to be so. Next, we must also see if they are in accord with the [other] parts of the definition. For of those lying in the speech, some depend on equivocation—for example, homonymy, [ambiguity in] the statement, uniform style of speech (for we habitually speak of everything as if it signified a this something); but composition, division, and accentuation are due to the statement not being the same or to the name being different. For the name too, like the thing at issue, must be the same, if there is going to be a refutation or a deduction—for example, if the thing at issue is a cape, do not deduce cloak, but cape. For though the latter is

25

30

also true, it is not deduced, but rather a further question must be asked, to satisfy the one looking for the why, as to whether "cloak" signifies the same thing.

Those depending on the coincident become evident when deduction is
35 defined. For the same definition must also apply to refutation, except for the addition of a contradiction; for a refutation is a deduction of a contradiction. If, then, there is no deduction of what is coincidental, no refutation comes about. For if, when A and B are, C must of necessity be, and C is [coincidentally] white, there is no necessity for it to be white because of
40 the deduction. Nor, if a triangle has angles equal to two right angles, and it
168^b1 is coincidentally a figure, primary thing, or starting-point, is it because it is a figure, starting-point, or primary thing that it has this affection; for it is not insofar as it is a figure or a primary thing that the demonstration comes about, but insofar as it is a triangle. And similarly in the other cases too.

So, if a refutation is a sort of deduction, one directed at a coincident
5 would not be a refutation. And yet both craftsmen and scientists generally are refuted by non-scientists on the basis of this; for the deductions they produce against those who know are directed at a coincident, while the latter, being incapable of drawing [the relevant] distinctions, either grant when questioned or, though they did not grant, are thought to have
10 granted.⁴⁴⁶

Fallacies depending on what is so in a respect and what is so unconditionally come about because the affirmation and the denial are not of the same thing. For not white in some respect is the denial of white in some respect, and not unconditionally white of unconditionally white. If, then, the questioner takes the concession that something is white in some respect as saying that it is unconditionally so, he does not produce a refuta-
15 tion, but appears to do so because of ignorance of what a refutation is.

The most evident fallacies (*paralogismos*) of all are those already mentioned as depending on the definition of refutation.⁴⁴⁷ That is why indeed they are so called; for it is by depending on (*para*) an omission from the account (*logos*) that the appearance [of refutation] comes about. And if we
20 divide fallacies in this way, we must posit as common to all these cases an omission from the account.

Also, those that depend on assuming what was initially at issue and positing the non-cause as cause are made clear by the definition.⁴⁴⁸ For the conclusion must result "because of these things being so," which is precisely what does not hold in the case of non-causes. And, again, the con-
25 clusion must follow "without counting what was initially at issue," which is precisely what does not hold of those that depend on demanding what was initially at issue.

Those depending on [affirming] the consequent are a part of those that depend on the coincident; for a consequent is a coincident, but differs from a coincident because a coincident can be obtained in the case of one thing only (for example, that the same thing is something yellow and honey, or white and a swan), while the consequent always involves several things; for we claim that things that are the same with respect to one and the same [third] thing are also the same as each other; which is why a refutation depending on [affirming] the consequent comes about.[449] But this claim is not entirely true—for example, where it is with respect to a coincident; for both snow and swan are the same with respect to white.[450]

Or, again, as in the argument of Melissus, the questioner assumes that having come to be and having a starting-point are the same thing, as are becoming equal and taking on the same magnitude.[451] For because what has come to be has a starting-point, he also claims that what has a starting-point has come to be, on the supposition that these two things, what has come to be and what has a limit, are the same thing as having a starting-point. Similarly too, in the case of things that have become equal, he assumes that if things taking on one and the same magnitude are becoming equal, then things that are becoming equal are also taking on one and the same magnitude. So he assumes the consequent. Since, then, the refutation depending on the coincident lies in the ignorance of refutation, it is evident that the one that depends on [affirming] the consequent does so too. But we must look at this issue from another point of view as well.[452]

Fallacies depending on making several questions into one are due to our failure to articulate the account of what a premise is. For a premise is one thing said of one thing; for the same definition applies to one single thing and unconditionally to the thing—for example, to a human and to one single human.[453] And it is the same way in the other cases too. If, then, one premise claims one thing of one thing, a question of this sort will be unconditionally a premise.[454] And since a deduction is based on premises, and a refutation is a deduction, a refutation is also based on premises. If, then, a premise is one thing said of one thing, it is evident that this fallacy too lies in ignorance of what a refutation is; for in it what appears to be a premise is not really a premise. If, then, a person has given an answer as though to one question, there will be a refutation, but if he has not given one, but only appears to have done so, there will be only an apparent refutation.

So all the modes [of refuting] fall into the province of ignorance of what a refutation is: those depending on speech because the contradiction—which is precisely what we saw to be special to refutation—is only apparent, and the others because they depend on the definition of a deduction.[455]

7

Sources of deception in fallacies

In fallacies depending on homonymy and [ambiguity in] the statement, the deception comes about due to being incapable of distinguishing the many ways in which they are said (for in some cases distinguishing them is not puzzle-free—for example, one, being, and same).[456] In those depending on combination and division, on the other hand, the deception is due to thinking that it makes no difference whether the statement is combined or divided, as in most cases. It is similar too in the case of those depending on accentuation; for a word or statement pronounced with a lower and with a higher pitch seldom if ever seems to signify something distinct.[457]

In those depending on the style, the deception is due to similarity in speech. For it is difficult to distinguish what sorts are said of things in one way, what sorts in another way (for the one capable of doing this is pretty much next door to seeing the truth, and it is he most of all who knows when to join in conceding them), because we take everything predicated of a thing to be a this something, and [so] we make our concession as if to one thing; for it is to what is one and a substance that this something and being seem most of all to pertain.[458] This is also why this mode [of refuting] must be put among those depending on speech: first, because the deception occurs more when we are investigating with others than by ourselves (for an investigation with another is through words, while one by oneself is no less through the thing at issue itself); next, because even by oneself one happens to be deceived when one makes one's investigation on the basis of words; still, the deception originates in similarity, and the similarity in speech.[459]

In fallacies depending on the coincident, the deception comes about because of not being able to judge same and distinct, one and many, and what sorts of predicates have all the same affections as the thing at issue. It is the same way too in those that depend on [affirming] the consequent; for the consequent is a particular case of the coincident. Further, in many instances it appears to be—and is claimed to be—the case that if this cannot be separated from that, then that cannot be separated from this either.

In fallacies depending on an omission from the account [of what a refutation is] and those depending on what is so in a respect and what is so unconditionally, the deception lies in depending on the smallness of the difference involved; for treating the particular case, the respect, the way, and the time as having no additional signification, we concede universally. It is the same way too in the case of those assuming what was initially at issue, those of the non-cause, and those making many questions into

one; for in all these the deception is due to depending on the smallness of
the difference involved; for we do not investigate in exact detail either the   15
definition of a premise or that of a deduction due to the cause just stated.[460]

8

Sophistical refutations

Since we have hold of the number of things apparent deductions depend
on, we also have hold of the number sophistical deductions and refutations
may depend on. And by a "sophistical refutation" and "sophistical deduc-   20
tion" I mean not only an apparent deduction and refutation that is not
really one, but also one that, though real, only appears to be proper to the
thing at issue. These are the ones that refute and prove people to be ignorant—which, as we saw, is precisely what it belongs to the examinational
craft to do—not in accord with the thing at issue.[461] The examinational
craft, though it is a part of dialectic, is capable of deducing a falsehood due   25
to the ignorance of the one conceding the argument. Sophistical refutations, by contrast, even if they deduce the contradictory [of what he pro-
poses], do not make clear whether he is ignorant; for people trip up even
those who do know with arguments of this sort.

That we get hold of them by the same methodical inquiry is clear; for   30
the things depending on which it appears to listeners that something has
been deduced as a result of questions are the same as those depending on
which the answerer would think so too, so that there will be false deductions through all or some of these; for what, without being questioned, one
thinks one has granted, one would also grant if questioned.[462] Except, of
course, in those cases in which it happens that as soon as the question on
the missing point is added, its falsehood becomes evident—for example,   35
in [fallacies] depending on speech and on solecisms. If, then, fallacious
deductions of the contradictory depend on apparent refutation, it is clear
that deductions of false conclusions must also depend on the same number
of things as an apparent refutation does.

An apparent refutation, however, depends on the parts of a true one; for   40
if a given part is omitted, there would be only an apparent refutation. For
example, the one depending on what does not follow because of the argu-   170ᵃ1
ment (the one leading to impossibility); also, the one making two questions
into one, depending on the premise; also, instead of the intrinsic, depending on the coincident, and—which is a part of this one—the one depending on [affirming] the consequent.[463] Further, the one that follows not in
the case of the thing at issue, but in that of the word; next, instead of the   5

contradictory being universal (and being so in the same respect, in relation to the same thing, and in the same way), depending on a particular case, or depending on one or other of these things; further, depending on not counting what was initially at issue, the one assuming what was initially at issue.[464] Thus we may have hold of how many things fallacies come about by depending on; for they could not depend on more things, but all will depend on the ones just mentioned.

A sophistical refutation is not unconditionally a refutation, but rather one in relation to someone, and the deduction is the same way. For, if the refutation that depends on a homonym does not obtain that it signifies one thing, and the one depending on a uniform style of speech does not obtain that it signifies a this [something] only, and the others in the same way, they will not be either a refutation or a deduction, either unconditionally or in relation to the answerer. But if they do obtain these things, while they will be a refutation or a deduction in relation to the answerer, they will not be so unconditionally; for they have obtained not that they do signify one thing but that they appear to, and from a particular person.

9

The nature of dialectic

Without having a scientific knowledge of all the beings, one must not try to get hold of how many things the refutations of those people who are refuted depend on. This, however, does not belong to any craft; for the sciences are perhaps unlimited in number, so that it is clear that their deductions are as well.[465] Plus there are also true refutations [as well as false or sophistical ones]; for wherever demonstration is possible, it is also possible to refute a person who posits the contradictory of the truth—for example, if someone posits the commensurability of the diagonal, one could refute him by demonstrating that it is incommensurable. So we would need to be scientific knowers of everything; for some refutations will depend on the starting-points in geometry and their conclusions, others on those in medicine, while others depend on those of the other sciences.

But then false refutations likewise also exist in unlimited numbers; for in accord with each craft there is a false deduction—for example, in accord with geometry a geometrical one, and in accord with medicine, a medical one.[466] And by "in accord with a craft" I mean in accord with its starting-points.

It is clear, then, that we must get hold of the topics, not of all refutations, but of those that depend on dialectic; for these are the ones that are common to every craft and every capacity. And as regards the refutation that is in accord with a particular science, it belongs to the corresponding scientist to get a theoretical grasp on whether it, not being a real one, only appears to be one, and if it is a real one, on why it is so. But to get one on a refutation based on what is common, and that falls under no craft, belongs to dialecticians. For if we have hold of what acceptable deductions about anything whatever are based on, we have hold of what refutations are based on; for a refutation is a deduction of a contradictory, so that [to have hold of] one or two deductions of a contradictory is [to have hold of] a refutation.

We have hold, therefore, of the number of things all refutations of this sort depend on. And if we have hold of this, we also have hold of their resolutions; for the objections to these are the resolutions. We also have hold, then, of the number of things that apparent refutations depend on—apparent, that is, not to anyone whatever, but rather to those of the sort mentioned; for if one were to investigate the number of things they depend on to appear so to random people, it would go on indefinitely.[467] So it is evident that to the dialectician it belongs to be capable of getting hold of the things that a refutation, or apparent refutation, that comes about through what is common depends on, that is, a dialectical one or an apparently dialectical or examinational one.[468]

10

Arguments against the name versus against the thought

The difference among arguments that some people state when they say that some arguments are directed against the name, others against the thought, does not exist; for it is absurd to suppose that some arguments are directed against the name, others against the thought, rather than the same ones.[469] For what is it not to be directed against the thought except what happens when the questioner does not use the name to apply to what the person being questioned was thinking of when he conceded? And this is the same as to be directed against the name; while it is directed against the thought when the name is used to apply to what the person being questioned was thinking of.

If, then, when a name signifies several things, some people—both the questioner and the one being questioned—were to think that it signifies one thing (for example, "being" and "one" presumably signify several things, but the answerer as well as the questioner in asking his questions are thinking they signify one thing, and the argument is that all things are

one), will it have been dialectically argued against the name or against the thought of the one questioned? But, if indeed someone thinks that it sig-
25   nifies several things, it is clear that it is not against the thought. For, first, [the distinction between] being directed against the name and against the thought concerns the sorts of arguments that signify several things, and, next, concerns any argument whatever; for its being directed against the thought does not lie in the argument, but rather in the answer's being
30   disposed in a certain way toward what has been granted. Next, it is possible for all arguments to be directed against the name; for, on the view under discussion, to be directed against the name is not to be directed against the thought. For if not all admit either of being directed against the name or against the thought, there will be another lot that is neither directed against the name nor against the thought. But these thinkers say all admit of it— that is, that all are divided either into those directed against the name or those directed against the thought, and there are no others.
35   But then again, among those deductions depending on what is [said in] many ways, [only] some depend on the name. For it is also absurd for them to say that "depending on the name" describes all arguments that depend on speech; on the contrary, there are some arguments that are fallacious not because of the answer's being disposed in a certain way toward them, but because the argument itself involves asking the sort of question that
40   signifies more than one thing.
171ᵃ1   Also, it is wholly absurd to discuss refutation without previously dis-cussing deduction; for a refutation is a deduction, so that we must also discuss deduction before false refutation; for a refutation of this sort is an apparent deduction of a contradiction. That is why, if there is an apparent
5   refutation, the cause [of its falsity] will lie either in the deduction or in the contradiction (for the contradiction must be added), but sometimes in both. In the case of "speaking pertaining to the silent," it lies in the con-tradiction, not in the deduction; in that of "giving away what one does not have," it lies in both; in that of "Homer's poetry being a figure because of
10   being a cycle," it lies in the deduction.⁴⁷⁰ An argument that errs in neither respect is a true deduction.
To return to the point from which the argument digressed: Are argu-ments in mathematics directed against the thought or not? If someone believes that "triangle" signifies many things, and has granted what he granted not on the supposition that this is the figure about which the ques-tioner has deduced the conclusion that it contains two right angles, has
15   the questioner argued dialectically against the answer's thought or not?⁴⁷¹
Further, if the name signifies several things, but the answer does not understand or think it to do so, how has the questioner not argued dialecti-cally against the thought? Or how else must the question be asked except

by conceding a distinction? Suppose then someone asks, "Is it or is it not possible for speaking to pertain to the silent, or is the answer in one way no and in another way yes?"[472] Then, if the answerer does not grant anything, and the questioner continues to argue dialectically, has he not argued dialectically against the thought? And yet the argument seems to be one of those depending on the name. Therefore, there is not any kind of argument directed against the thought.[473] But there are those directed against the name. Yet these do not include all refutations, not only not all real refutations but not even all apparent refutations. For there are also apparent refutations that do not depend on speech—for example, those depending on the coincident and others.

But if someone requires distinctions to be drawn, [for example,] that "By 'speaking pertaining to the silent' I mean sometimes one thing and sometimes another," the requirement is in the first place absurd; for sometimes the question does not seem to involve [something said in] many ways, and it is impossible to draw a distinction one does not think exists. Next, what else will teaching be but this? For it will make evident how things stand to one who has neither investigated nor knows nor supposes that the thing is said in another way; since what is to prevent this from also being done in cases that do not involve an equivocal signification?[474] "Are the units present in four equal to those present in two? But some twos are present in one way, others in another way."[475] Also, "Is the science of contraries one or not? But some contraries are known, others are not." So a person who makes this demand seems to be ignorant of the fact that teaching is distinct from arguing dialectically, and that a person who is teaching must not ask questions but himself make things clear, while the second must ask questions.

11

The examinational craft

Further, to require an answerer either to affirm or deny is the business not of the person who is proving something but of the one conducting an examination; for the examinational craft is a sort of dialectic and has in view not the person who knows, but the one who is ignorant and pretends to know.[476] The one who gets a theoretical grasp on what is common, as it applies to the thing at issue, is a dialectician, while the one who apparently does so is a sophist.[477] Also, there is a contentious and a sophistical deduction: in the first instance, this is [only] apparently deductive about the things that dialectic is examinational about, even if the conclusion is true (for it is deceptive about the why); and there are those fallacies that are not in accord with the methodical inquiry concerning each of the things, yet seem to be in accord with the craft.[478] For falsely drawn diagrams are not contentious arguments (for the fallacies are in accord with what falls under the craft), certainly not if what the falsely drawn figure concerns is true—for example, the one of Hippocrates, that is, the squaring of the circles by means of lunes; Bryson's way of squaring the circle, on the other hand, even if the circle is squared, is nonetheless sophistical, because it is not in accord with the thing at issue.[479] So, then, any apparent deduction concerning these things is a contentious argument, and any deduction that appears to be in accord with the thing at issue, even if it is a deduction, is a contentious argument; for it only appears to be in accord with the thing at issue, and so is deceptive and unjust.

For just as injustice in a competition is of a certain form and is a sort of unjust fighting, so in arguing against another, contentious argument is unjust fighting; for in the former case those who deliberately choose to win in any way use all the means, and, in the latter case so do contentious arguers. Those, then, who do this for the sake of victory itself seem to be contentious and disputatious human beings, while those who do it for the sake of reputation, with a view to making money, are sophists; for sophistry, as we said, is a sort of craft of making money from apparent wisdom.[480] That is why they seek apparent demonstration, and why, while the arguments of disputatious people and sophists are the same, they are not for the sake of the same things; and the same argument is both sophistical and contentious, though not in the same respect, but rather insofar as it is for apparent victory, it is contentious, while insofar as it is for apparent wisdom, it is sophistical; for in fact sophistry is a sort of appearance of wisdom without the reality.[481]

A contentious arguer stands in something of the same relation to a dialectician as a drawer of false diagrams does to a geometer; for it is on the basis of the same things as those used by dialectic that a drawer of false diagrams leads the geometer to fallacious reasoning.[482] But a drawer of false diagrams is not a contentious arguer, because he draws his false diagrams on the basis of the starting-points and conclusions that fall under the craft [of geometry]. It is clear that the one arguing about the others on the basis of those that fall under dialectic is a contentious arguer. For example, the squaring of the circle by means of lunes is not contentious, while Bryson's way is contentious; and while it is impossible to transfer the former to other subjects (on the contrary, it is directed against geometry only, because it is based on starting-points that are special to it), the former is directed against many people, namely, the ones who do not know what is possible and what is impossible in a given case; for the argument will apply [to many things].[483] Or there is the way Antiphon squared the circle.[484] Or,

164

again, if someone were to deny that it is better to take a walk after dinner because of Zeno's argument, it would not be doing medicine; for it is common.[485] If, then, a contentious arguer stood in every respect in the same relation to a dialectician as a drawer of false diagrams does to a geometer, a contentious argument concerning those things would never have existed.

As things stand, dialectical argument is not concerned with a definite kind, nor is it probative of anything, nor is it even of the same sort as the universal one.[486] For all the beings are not in one kind either, nor, if they were, would it be possible for them to fall under the same starting-points. So none of the crafts proving a certain nature is interrogative; for it is not possible to grant whichever of the two parts [one happens to choose]; for a deduction does not come about on the basis of both.[487] But dialectic is interrogative, while if it proved anything, it would not ask questions, if not about everything, at any rate, not about the primary things and the starting-points proper [to a given science]; for if an answerer does not grant these, one would not have anything further on the basis of which one will further argue dialectically against an objection.[488]

And the same craft is also examinational; for the examinational craft is not of the same sort as geometry either, but is rather one that someone could possess even without having knowledge. For even someone who does not know the thing at issue can undertake an examination of someone who also does not know it, if indeed the latter makes concessions based not on what he knows nor based on things special [to the subject matter of the relevant craft], but on their consequences—that is, on whichever things are of the sort that someone can know without knowing the craft in question, but which if he does not know, he is necessarily ignorant of the craft.

So it is evident that the examinational craft is not the scientific knowledge of anything definite. That is why it is also concerned with everything; for all the crafts also make use of certain common things. That is why everyone, even private individuals, makes a certain use of dialectic and the examinational craft; for everyone tries, up to a certain point, to test those who profess knowledge. And these are the common things; for they themselves know these no less [than the others do], even if they seem to speak from very far outside [the relevant sort of knowledge]. All, then, practice refutation; for they share in an un-craftlike way in what dialectic does in a craftlike one, and the one who by means of the craft of deduction is examinational is a dialectician.[489]

Since there are many of these [common things] and they apply with respect to everything, and are not such as to constitute a certain nature and kind, but instead are like negations, while others are not of this sort but special, it is possible, on the basis of them, to undertake an examination about anything, and for this to constitute a certain craft, though one that

172^b1   is not like the sorts that prove things.[490] That is precisely why a contentious
arguer does not in all respects stand in the same position as a drawer of
false diagrams; for a contentious arguer will not argue fallaciously on the
basis of the starting-points of a definite kind, but about every kind.

5   These, then, are the modes of sophistical refutation. And that it belongs
to the dialectician to get a theoretical grasp on them, and to be capable
where these are concerned, is not difficult to see; for the methodical
inquiry concerned with premises includes this entire branch of theoretical
knowledge.

12

False and unacceptable things

And so about apparent [or sophistical] refutations, we have now spoken.
As for proving the opponent to be saying something false and leading the
10   argument into something unacceptable (for this was second in the deliberate choice of the sophist), in the first place this most of all results from
getting answers in a certain way and through the questioning.[491] For asking
questions directed against no definite proposal is useful in hunting things
of this sort; for people are more likely to commit errors when they speak
at random, and they speak at random when they have nothing proposed
15   to them.[492] Also, asking several questions, even if what one is dialectically
arguing against is something definite, and demanding that the answerer
say what he believes, makes one well equipped to lead the answerer into
something unacceptable or false, and, if he affirms or denies one of these
when questioned, to lead him into things that one is well equipped to
attack.[493] Nowadays, though, questioners are less able to work mischief
20   by these means than they were previously; for people demand to know
what this has to do with what was initially at issue.[494] An element [or topic]
indeed for eliciting a falsehood or something unacceptable is not to ask for
any posit directly, but to say that one put questions wishing to learn; for
this way of investigating leaves room for an attack.[495]
          For proving the opponent to be saying something false, a topic spe-
25   cial to sophistry is to lead the answerer into the sorts of things one is well
equipped with arguments against. But it is possible to do this both correctly and incorrectly, as was said previously.[496]
          Again, for [getting people] to say unacceptable things, look to see what
group the one arguing dialectically belongs to, and then question him on
30   something this group says that to most people is unacceptable for in the
case of each school there is something of this sort. An element (or topic)

in these cases is having the theses of each group among the premises one has hold of. The fitting resolution to these too is to bring to light the fact that the unacceptable thing does not result because of the argument, which is what the opponent always really wishes.⁴⁹⁷

Further, [argue] on the basis of things wished for and on professed beliefs; for people do not wish for the same things they say they do, but say the words that make them look best, while they wish for the things that appear most profitable.⁴⁹⁸ For example, they say that one should die nobly rather than live pleasantly, and live in just poverty rather than in shameful wealth; but they wish for the contraries. A person, then, who speaks in accord with his wishes must be led to state his professed beliefs, while one who speaks in accord with those must be led to state his secret ones; for in either case it is necessary to speak in an unacceptable way; for they will speak contrary either to professed beliefs or to non-professed ones.

But to make people say unacceptable things, the most efficacious topic, as Callicles is represented as stating in the *Gorgias*, and which all the ancients thought conclusive, is the one that depends on what is in accord with nature and what is in accord with convention; for nature (they said) and convention are contraries, and justice is a noble thing according to convention, but according to nature it is not noble.⁴⁹⁹ Against a person who speaks in accord with nature, then, one must (they said) respond in accord with convention, while against one who does so in accord with convention one must lead [the argument] to nature; for in both ways it is possible to say unacceptable things.⁵⁰⁰ In the view of the ancients, what is in accord with nature was the truth, while what is in accord with convention was what seemed so to many. So it was clear that they too, like those nowadays, tried to refute the answerer, or make him say unacceptable things.

Some questions are such that the answer is unacceptable either way—for example, whether one should obey the wise or one's father, whether one should do what is advantageous or what is just, or whether it is more choiceworthy to suffer injustice or to do harm. One must lead the argument into what is contrary to the views of ordinary people or to the wise—if someone speaks like those who have to do with arguments, into those of ordinary people, if like ordinary people, into those involved in argument.⁵⁰¹ For the latter say that the happy person is of necessity just, while it is unacceptable to ordinary people that a king not be happy.⁵⁰² Leading an argument in this way into things that are unacceptable is the same as leading them into the contrariety between what is in accord with nature and what is in accord with convention; for convention is the belief of ordinary people, while the wise speak in accord with nature and truth.

13

Babbling

Unacceptable things, then, must be looked for on the basis of these topics.
As for making people babble, we have already said what we mean by "babbling."⁵⁰³ All arguments of the following sort wish to do this. If it makes no
difference whether one says a name or a statement, and double and double
35   of half are the same thing, then if double is double of half, it will be double
of half of half.⁵⁰⁴ And if "double of half" is again put in place of "double,"
the expression will be used three times, "double of half of half of half." Also,
is appetite for something pleasant?⁵⁰⁵ But appetite is desire for something
pleasant. Therefore, appetite is desire for something pleasant for something
40   pleasant.
173ᵇ1   All arguments of this sort lie in relatives, where not only the kinds but
also the things themselves are said in relation to something, and in relation
to one and the same thing (for example, desire is desire for something,
appetite is appetite for something, and double is double of something:
5   double of half); also where, though the things themselves are not relatives
at all, yet the substance, what they are states, affections, or the like of, is
indicated in their accounts, since they are predicated of these things.⁵⁰⁶ For
example, the odd is having-a-middle-number. But there is an odd number;
therefore, there is a having-a-middle-number number. And if the snub is
10   concavity in a nose, and there is a snub nose, then there is a concave nose
nose.⁵⁰⁷
Questioners sometimes appear to produce babbling, while not really
doing so, because they do not get a further answer as to whether "double," said by itself, signifies something or not, and, if it does signify something, whether it signifies the same thing or a distinct one, but instead state
15   the conclusion straightaway.⁵⁰⁸ But because the name is the same, it also
appears to signify the same thing.

14

Solecisms

What sort of thing a solecism is has already been stated.⁵⁰⁹ It is possible to
commit one, to appear to do so without doing so, and to commit one without seeming to, just as Protagoras used to say happened, if *mênis* ("anger")
and *pêlêx* ("helmet") are masculine.⁵¹⁰ For a person who says [*mênin*] *oulo-*
20   *menên* ["destroying anger": feminine] commits a solecism, according to
him, though he does not appear to others to do so, while one who says

[*mênin*] *oulomenon* [masculine] appears to do so, but does not.[511] It is clear, then, that someone could also produce this effect by craft. That is why many arguments appear to deduce a solecism, when they do not really do so, just as in the case of refutations.

Pretty much all apparent solecisms depend on *tode* ("this"), that is, when the inflection indicates neither a masculine nor a feminine but a neuter.[512] For *houtos* ("he") signifies a masculine, *hautê* ("she") a feminine, while *touto* ("it"), though supposed to signify a neuter, often signifies either a masculine or a feminine. For example, "What is it (*touto*)?" "Calliope" [feminine], "A log" [neuter], or "Coriscus" [masculine].

In the masculine and feminine the inflections are all different, while in the neuter some are and some are not. Often, then, when *tode* ("this") has been granted, people deduce as if *touton* ("him") had been said, and likewise substitute one inflection for another.[513] The fallacy comes about because *touto* is common to several inflections; for it signifies sometimes *houtos* ("he" [nominative masculine]) and sometimes *touton* ("him" [accusative masculine]). And it should signify them alternately: when combined with *esti* ("is") it should be *houtos*, while with *einai* ("be" [infinitive]), it should be *touton*—for example, *esti Koriskos* ("it is Coriscus" [nominative]) and *einai Koriskon* ("to be Coriscus" [accusative]). And in the case of feminine nouns it should be the same way, and in that of what are called "object words" that have masculine or feminine designations. For only those that end in *–on* have the [neuter] designation that belongs to objects—for example, *xulon* ("log"), *schoinion* ("rope"). Those that are not like that are masculine or feminine, and some of these we apply to objects—for example, *askos* ("wine-skin") is a masculine noun and *klinê* ("couch") a feminine one. That is why indeed in cases of this sort one with *esti* and one with *einai* will differ in parallel ways.

Also, solecism resembles in a certain way those refutations that are said to depend on similar names for dissimilar things. For just as there we meet solecism in the case of the things at issue, so here we meet it in the case of names; for human and white are both names and things.[514]

It is evident, then, that we must try to deduce a solecism on the basis of the inflections just mentioned.

These, then, are the forms of competitive arguments and the parts of their kinds, and the ways of employing them are the ones mentioned. But it makes no small difference whether the things having to do with the questioning are arranged in a certain way with a view to concealment, just as in the case of dialectical ones.[515] Next in order, then, after what has been said, first this must be discussed.

15

How to question effectively

With a view to refutation, one thing is length; for it is difficult to take a comprehensive view of many things at the same time. And to produce length the elements [or topics] that have been mentioned must be used.[516] One is speed; for when people are left behind, they see less far ahead. Fur-
20   ther, there is anger and rivalry; for when people are agitated, they are all less capable of being on their guard. Elements [or topics] having to do with anger are making it evident that one wishes to act unjustly, and to be altogether shameless. Further, putting one's questions alternately, whether one has several arguments related to the same point or arguments that some-
25   thing is so and that it is not so; for the result is that the answerer is made to be on his guard either against several or against contrary arguments at the same time.

In general, all the things useful for concealment that were mentioned before are also useful against competitive arguments; for concealment is for the sake of escaping detection, and escaping detection for the sake of deception.
30   Against those who refuse anything they think to be in favor of the argument, one must put the question negatively, as if wishing for the contrary of what one wishes, or, at any rate, putting the question impartially; for people haggle less when it is not clear what one wishes to obtain.

Also, in the case of particulars, when someone grants a particular one, often one must not, having done the induction, make the universal the subject of one's question, but rather use it as if it has been granted; for some-
35   times people themselves even think that they have granted it, and appear to their listeners to have done so, because they remember the induction, and suppose that the questions would not have been asked pointlessly.[517] And in those cases in which the universal is signified not by a name but by a similarity [between the particulars], one must use that to one's advantage; for a similarity often goes unnoticed.[518]
40   Also, to obtain a premise, one must get contrary answers side by side.
174^b1   For example, if one wishes to obtain that one should obey one's father in everything, one must ask, "Should one obey one's parents in everything, or disobey them in everything?" And ask, "Many times many, is it that one must concede many or few?"[519] For then, if he had to choose, he would
5   more believe it to be many: for the putting of contraries side by side makes them appear smaller or larger, worse or better, to people.

But often the most blatant of sophistical quibbles on the part of questioners produces an intense impression of refutation, when, not having deduced anything, they do not make the last thing a question, but state   10
it as a conclusion, as if they had deduced it: "Therefore, so-and-so is not the case."

It is also sophistical, when what is proposed is unacceptable, to demand to be answered with what appears to be so, having initially proposed what seems to be so, putting questions in some such way as this, "Does it seem to you to be so that . . . ?" For if the question is one of the things from which the deduction proceeds, either a refutation or something unaccept-   15
able must come about: if he grants it, it will be a refutation; if he does not grant it, and even denies that it seems to be so, it will be unacceptable and if he does not grant it, but agrees that it seems to be so, it will be refutation-like.

Further, as in rhetorical arguments, so in the same way in refutatory ones, one must look for things that are contrary either to the things the answerer says himself or to those that he agrees speak or act well, further,   20
to those that seem to be of this sort or to those similar to them, whether to most people or to all.⁵²⁰

Also, just as answerers, at any rate, when they are being refuted, produce an equivocation if their refutation is going to come about, so questioners too must sometimes make use of this against objectors: it works in this   25
way, but not in that—and the answerer has assumed it in the latter—as Cleophon does in the *Mandrobulus*.⁵²¹

Questioners who have been hindered in the argument must cut off the rest of their attacks, while an answerer, if he perceives this beforehand, must put in his objection before it happens and forestall it.⁵²²

And one must sometimes make one's attack against things other than   30
the stated one, having taken the latter in that sense, if one does not have an attack against the one proposed, just as Lycophron did when it was proposed that he deliver an encomium for a lyre.⁵²³

Against those who demand [an explanation of] what one is making one's attack against (since it seems one must assign the cause, yet some ways of stating it make the defense too easy), one should say (what is the universal result in refutations), "a contradiction" (that is, denying what one   35
has affirmed, and affirming what one has denied), and not that of contraries the science is the same or not the same.⁵²⁴

And one must not ask for one's conclusion as a premise, while some premises must not be asked at all, but treated as agreed to.⁵²⁵   40

16

How to answer effectively

175ᵃ1 What questions are based on and in what way they must be asked in competitive discussions have now been stated. Next we must speak about
answering, about how and what one must provide a resolution of, and for
what purpose arguments of this sort are beneficial.

5 They are useful for philosophy because of two things. For, in the first
place, as they depend for the most part on speech, they make us better
equipped with regard to how many ways a given thing is said of things, and
what sorts of things apply in the same way or in distinct ways both to the
things at issue and to their names. Second, they are useful for inquiries of
one's own; for a person who easily succumbs to fallacious reasoning due to
10 someone else, and who does not perceive it, will often succumb to it even
when it is due to himself.[526] Third, and last, there is a further one relating to
reputation: seeming to be trained in everything and not inexperienced in
anything; for if someone who is taking part in arguments finds fault with
arguments, without having anything determinate to say about their bad-
15 ness, it creates a suspicion that he seems to be making difficulties not due
to the truth of the matter but due to inexperience.[527]

How answerers should reply to arguments of this sort is evident, if
indeed we have correctly stated previously what fallacies are based on, and
those in which the getting of answers has more [of an upper hand] have
been adequately described.[528] But to take hold of an argument and see and
20 resolve the defect in it is not the same thing as being able to reply to it
quickly when one is asked a question; for what we know, we are often ignorant of in a changed context. Further, just as in other areas greater speed
or slowness comes about on the basis of training, so it is too in the case of
arguments. So, even if something may be clear to us, if we are untrained,
25 we come to it too late for the opportune moment.

And sometimes the same thing happens as with geometrical diagrams;
for there, even when we have analyzed, we sometimes cannot reconstruct;
so too in refutations we know what the connected thing is that the argu-
30 ment depends on, but are puzzled as to how to resolve the argument.[529]

17

Acceptable resolutions versus true ones

First, then, just as we say that we must sometimes deliberately choose to
deduce acceptably rather than truthfully, so too we must sometimes provide

a resolution acceptably rather than in accord with the truth. For, in general, we must fight against contentious arguers not as against refuters but as against apparent refuters; for we say that they are not really deducing, so that it is with a view to their not seeming to do so that one must correct them. For if a refutation is a non-homonymous contradiction based on certain things, there should be no need to draw distinctions against ambiguity and homonymy; for they do not produce a deduction. But there is nothing else for the sake of which one must draw a distinction ahead of time except that the conclusion appears refutation-like.

One must, then, beware not of being refuted, but of seeming to be, since the asking of ambiguous questions, ones depending on homonymy, and all other such ways of cheating, obscure even a true refutation and make it unclear who is refuted and who is not. For since it is possible at the end, when the conclusion is reached, to say that the questioner has not denied precisely what one has affirmed, but rather has done so homonymously, even if it mostly happened to refer to the same thing, it is unclear whether one has been refuted; for it is now unclear whether he is speaking the truth.[530] If, on the other hand, one had drawn a distinction and questioned about the homonymous or ambiguous expression, the refutation would not have been unclear. Also, the thing contentious arguers additionally seek, though less so nowadays and more so previously, that the person being questioned must answer either yes or no, would have come about. But nowadays, because those getting answers ask their questions incorrectly, the person being questioned is compelled to add something to his answer, by way of rectifying the defect in the premise; since if adequate distinctions are drawn, the answerer is compelled to say either yes or no.

If someone will suppose that an argument turning on homonymy is a refutation, it will not be possible for the answerer to avoid being refuted in a certain way; for in the case of visible things, it is necessary to deny about the name what one has affirmed, and affirm what one has denied.[531] For the way in which some people produce a rectification is of no benefit.[532] For they say not that Coriscus is musical and unmusical, but that *this* Coriscus is musical and that *this* Coriscus is unmusical. For the account [of] *this* musical (or unmusical) Coriscus will be the same as [of] Coriscus, [giving] precisely what one is affirming as well as denying at the same time. But perhaps it does not signify the same thing (for neither did the name there), so what is the difference?[533] But if in one case he is going to assign the simple expression "Coriscus," and in another he is going to add "a certain" or "this" to it, it is absurd; for the addition belongs no more in one than in another; for it makes no difference to whichever of the two he adds.

Nonetheless, since if one does not draw distinctions in a case of ambiguity it is unclear whether a person has been refuted or not, and since it

is allowed in arguments to draw distinctions in them, it is evident that
not to draw these distinctions, but to grant the question uncondition-
30   ally, is an error, so that even if the person himself does not seem to have
been refuted, at any rate, his argument is similar to a refuted one. It often
happens, however, that though people see the ambiguity, they hesitate to
draw the distinction, because of the great frequency with which people
propose things of this sort, in order not to seem to be making difficulties
35   in response to everything. Then, though they would never have thought
that the argument would depend on this, they are often confronted with
something unacceptable. So, since one is allowed to draw distinctions, one
must not hesitate to do so, as was said previously.[534]

If a person had not made two questions into one, a fallacy depending
40   on homonymy or ambiguity would not have come about either, but rather
a refutation or not a refutation. For what is the difference between ask-
176^a1 ing whether Callias and Themistocles are musical or whether two distinct
people with one name are? For if one name indicates more things than one,
one has asked more questions than one. If, then, it is not correct to demand
to obtain one simple answer to two questions, it is evident that it is not
fitting to give a simple answer to any homonymous question, even if it is
5   true of all the things [asked about], as some people claim it is. For it is no
different from asking whether Coriscus and Callias are at home or not at
home, when either they are both there or both not there; for in both cases
there are several premises involved; for it is not if the answer is true that
the question is one question. For it is also possible, when asked countless
10   distinct questions, for it to be true to say simply yes or no. Nonetheless, one
must not answer them with one answer; for this does away with dialectical
argument. And it is the same way if indeed distinct things have the same
name applied to them. If, then, one must not give one answer to two questions, it is evident that in the case of homonymous questions one must not
15   say either yes or no; for the speaker has not given an answer [if he does],
though he has spoken.[535] But among practitioners of dialectic this is what is
in a way demanded, because of neglecting to consider the result.[536]

As we said, then, since there are some seeming refutations that are not
20   really such, in the same way there are some seeming resolutions that are
not really resolutions. And these, we say, are the very ones we must sometimes propose rather than the true ones in competitive arguments and in
replying to equivocation. In the case of things that seem to be so, one must
answer, "let it be so"; for then in fact there is the least likelihood that any
refutation on a side issue would come about.[537] But if one is compelled
25   to say something unacceptable, in that case especially one must add "it
seems"; for in this way neither a refutation nor something unacceptable
would seem to have come about.[538]

Since it is clear how one asks for what was initially at issue, and people think that they must at all costs do away with things that lie close to [the conclusion], and that some things must not be conceded (on the supposition that the questioner is asking for what was initially at issue), so when someone demands something of such a sort as to necessarily follow from the posit, but is either false or unacceptable, we must say the same thing; for the necessary consequences seem to belong to the posit itself.[539]

Further, when the universal has not been obtained by a name but by a comparison, say that the questioner obtained it neither as granted nor as he proposed it; for a refutation often depends on this too.

If one is prevented from using these, one must go for the conclusion's not having been correctly proved, replying in accord with the division already stated.[540]

When names are used in their strict senses, one must answer either simply or by drawing a distinction. It is when we posit things by supplying the sense in thought—for example, when a question is not asked perspicuously but in a docked way—that a refutation comes about that depends on it.[541] For example: "Is whatever is of the Athenians a possession of the Athenians?" "Yes." "And it is the same way in other cases too?" ["Yes."] "Well then, is man of the animals?" "Yes." "Therefore, man is a possession of the animals." [But this is an error.] For we say that man is of the animals because he is an animal, just as we say that Lysander is of the Spartans because he is a Spartan.[542] It is clear, then, that where what is proposed is not perspicuous, one must not concede it in a simple way.

When it seems that of two things that are so, if one of the two is so, of necessity the second is so, while if the second is so, the first is not of necessity so, then, when one is asked which of the two is so, one must grant the weaker (for to produce a deduction based on more things is more difficult).[543] But if the questioner tries to prove that one thing has a contrary, while the other does not, if his argument is true, we must say each has a contrary, but that no name is established for the second one.[544]

About some of the things they say, ordinary people would maintain that anyone who did not concede them was speaking falsely, while about others they would not say it, for example, about those where they have no belief either way (for to ordinary people the question of whether the soul of living things can pass away or is immortal is not something that has been determined).[545] In those cases, then, in which it is unclear in which of two ways what is proposed is usually stated, whether in the way maxims are (for people call both true beliefs and general affirmations "maxims") or in the way "the diagonal is incommensurable" is, where there is no belief

20   either way about the truth, one would most of all go unnoticed in changing the names where these are concerned.[546] For because it is unclear on which side the truth lies, one will not seem to be playing the sophist, and because there being no belief either way, one will not seem to be stating a falsehood;
25   for the change will make the argument irrefutable.

     Further, whenever one foresees any question, one must formulate one's objection beforehand and state it ahead of time; for in this way one would most hinder the one putting the questions.

18

Correct resolutions

Since a correct resolution consists in bringing to light a false deduction,
30   showing what sort of question its falsity depends on, and since something is said to be a false deduction in two ways (for it is one either if a falsehood has been deduced or if what is not a deduction appears to be a deduction), there must be both the resolution mentioned just now and also the rectification of the apparent deduction, showing which of the questions its appearing so depends on.[547] So the result is that one resolves arguments
35   that are genuine deductions by doing away with something, while one resolves apparent ones by drawing distinctions.[548]

     Again, since some arguments that really deduce have a true conclusion, while others have a false one, it is possible to resolve those that are false with respect to their conclusion in two ways: either by doing away with one of the questions or by proving that the conclusion does not hold in the
40   relevant way. Those, on the other hand, that are false with respect to their
177^{a}1   premises can be resolved only by doing away with one of the questions; for the conclusion is true.

     So those who wish to resolve an argument must in the first place look to see whether it has proceeded deductively or is non-deductive, and next whether the conclusion is true or false, in order to resolve it either by drawing distinctions or by doing away with [one of the questions], that
5   is, doing away with it either in the one way or in the other, as previously stated.[549]

     There is the greatest possible difference between resolving an argument when one is being questioned and when not; for in the former case it is difficult to foresee it, while to see it when at one's leisure is easier.

19

Arguments depending on homonymy and ambiguity

Among the refutations that depend on homonymy and ambiguity, some involve a question that signifies several things, while others have a conclusion that is said in many ways—for example, in the case of "speaking pertaining to the silent," the conclusion is equivocal, and in the case of "not scientifically knowing what one scientifically knows," one of the questions involves an ambiguity.[550] Also, what is equivocal is sometimes so and sometimes not so—or rather, its being equivocal signifies that it is in one sense so and in another sense not so.[551]

When what is said in many ways appears at the end, no refutation comes about, unless the questioner also obtains the contradiction—as, for example, in the case of "seeing pertaining to the blind"; for without the contradiction there was no refutation.[552] When, on the other hand, what is said in many ways is in the questions, it is not necessary to deny the equivocal thing beforehand; for the argument is not directed at it but is due to it.

Initially, then, one must reply both to a name and to a statement that is equivocal in the following way, saying that in one way it is so and in another way it is not so—for example, that "speaking pertaining to the silent" is possible in one way, but in another not, and that "one needs must do the things that needs must be," is so of some things but not so of others; for things are said to "needs must be" in many ways.[553] But if one failed to notice the equivocation, one must rectify it at the end by adding to the questioning: "Is speaking pertaining to the silent possible?" "No, but speaking pertaining to this person when he is silent is." Similarly, when arguments have what is said in many ways in the premises: "Don't people scientifically know what they scientifically know?" "Yes, but not those who know scientifically in the relevant way." For that it is not possible to scientifically know what one scientifically knows, and that it is not for those who scientifically know in the relevant way, are not the same thing.[554] And, in general, even if the questioner deduces in a simple [or non-equivocal] way, one must contend that what he has denied is not the thing he affirmed but its name, so that there is no refutation.[555]

20

Arguments depending on combination and division

It is evident too how fallacies that depend on division and combination must be resolved; for if the statement signifies something distinct when it is divided and when it is combined, one must state the contrary of what

35   leads to the conclusion. And all arguments of the following sort depend on combination and division: "Was what you saw so-and-so being beaten with what he was beaten with?" and "Was what he was being beaten with what you saw him being beaten with?"⁵⁵⁶

177ᵇ1   This, then, also has something of ambiguous questions, but it depends on combination. For what depends on division is not equivocal (for the statement is not the same when divided), if indeed ὅρος and ὄρος, when pronounced in accord with the accentuation, did not signify a distinct thing.⁵⁵⁷ In writing, indeed, a name is the same when it is written in the

5   same letters and in like manner (and even there people now add distinguishing marks), but spoken names are not thereby the same. So that what depends on division is not equivocal. And it is evident too that not all refutations depend on equivocation, as some people say.⁵⁵⁸

10   It is for the answerer, then, to make the division; for I saw a man "being beaten with my eyes" is not the same as "I saw with my eyes" a man being beaten. Also, there is Euthydemus' argument, "Do you know now in Sicily that there are triremes in Piraeus?"⁵⁵⁹ And again, "Can a person who is good be a cobbler who is bad? Then there could be a bad cobbler who is

15   good. So he will be a good bad cobbler." Again, "Are things of which the sciences are excellent, excellent ones to learn? But the science of what is evil is excellent. Therefore, what is evil is an excellent thing to learn. But surely evil is both evil and a thing to learn, so that evil is an evil thing to learn. But the science of evil things is excellent." "Is it true to say now that you

20   were born? Therefore, you were born now." Or, does it signify something distinct when divided? For it is true to say now that you were born, but not that you were born now.

    "Can you do what you are capable of doing in the way you are capable of it? But when you are not playing the lyre, you are capable of playing it. Therefore, you can play the lyre while not playing it." But he does not have

25   the capacity for this, "to play the lyre while not playing it," but rather, when he is not doing it, to do it.

    But some people also resolve this in another way. For if the answerer has granted that a person can do it in the way he is capable of doing it, they say that it does not follow that he plays the lyre while not playing the lyre; for it has not been granted that he will do it in every way in which he is capable of doing it, and it is not the same thing to do something in some way in

30   which one is capable and in every way in which one is capable. But it is evident that they do not resolve it correctly; for the resolution of arguments that depend on the same thing is the same, while this resolution will not fit all cases asked for in every way, but is against the questioner, not against the argument.⁵⁶⁰

21

Arguments depending on accentuation

There are no arguments, either written or oral, that depend on accentua- 35
tion except for certain ones, few in number, that might be produced—for
example, the following argument: "A house is where (*hou*) you lodge isn't
it?" "Yes." "But isn't 'you do not (*ou*) lodge' the negation of 'you lodge'?"
"Yes." "But you said that where you lodge is a house. Therefore, a house is a 178ᵃ1
negation." How, then, this is to be resolved is clear. For *ou* does not signify
the same thing when pronounced with a more acute and with a more grave
accent.[561]

22

Arguments depending on things said in the same
way that are not the same

It is also clear how one should respond to arguments depending on things
said in the same way that are not the same, if indeed we possess the kinds
of predication.[562] For one person has granted, when asked, that something 5
signifying a what-it-is does not belong [to a subject], while another has
proved that something signifying a relation or a quality, but which seems to
signify a what-it-is because of speech, does belong [to a subject].[563]

For example, in the following argument: "Is it possible to be doing and
have done the same thing at the same time?" "No." "But it is surely possible to be seeing and to have seen the same thing at the same time and in 10
the same respect." [Or in this one:] "Is any being done to a doing?" "No."
"Aren't 'is cut (*temnetai*),' 'is burned (*kaietai*),' and 'is affected by a perceptual object (*aisthenetai*)' said of things in the same way, and don't they
signify a being done to? Again, 'saying (*legein*),' 'running (*trechein*),' and
'seeing (*horan*)' are said of things in a similar way to each other. But surely
seeing (*horan*) is being affected by a perceptual object (*aisthanesthai*), so
that it is both a being done to and a doing at the same time." 15

But if, in the first example, having granted that it is not possible to be
doing and have done the same thing, a person were to say that it is possible to be seeing a thing and to have seen it, he has not yet been refuted,
if he would not say that seeing is a sort of doing, but rather of being done
to; for this question is required in addition, though he is supposed by the
listener to have granted it when he granted that cutting (*temnein*) is a doing 20
and having cut (*tetmêkenai*) a having done, and so on with others that are
said of things in a similar way; for the listener himself adds the rest, on

179

the supposition that it [seeing] is said in a similar way. But it is not said of things in a similar way, though it appears to be, because of speech. And precisely the same thing happens as in cases of homonymy; for in cases of homonymy a person ignorant of arguments thinks that he has denied the thing he stated, not the name. But an additional question still needs to be asked, whether he said the homonym looking to that one thing; for if he has granted things in this way, there will be a refutation.

The following arguments too are similar to the preceding ones: "If what a person has, he later does not have, he has lost it. For a person who has lost only one die will not have ten dice." Or is it rather that although what a person does not have and had before, he has lost, it is not necessary for him to have lost as much or as many things as he does not have?[564] Having asked, then, about what he has, he draws [a conclusion] about how many he has; for ten is a how many. If, then, he had asked initially whether "someone not having as many things as he had before has lost that many," no one would have granted it, but would have said either "that many" or "some of them."[565]

Also, the argument that one could give what one does not have; for he does not have one die only. Rather, he has given, not what he has not got, but what he has not got in the way in which he has given it, as the [only] one he has. For "only" does not signify a this [something], a quality, or a quantity, but a certain relation to something else—for example, that it is not along with anything else. It is, then, as if he had asked "Could a person give what he does not have?" and, receiving the answer "No," were to ask whether a person could give something quickly that he does not have quickly, and, receiving the answer "Yes," were to deduce that he could give what he does not have.[566] And it is evident that it has not been deduced; for to give quickly is not to give a this [something] but to give in a certain way, and a person could give something in a way that he has not got it—for example, having got it with pleasure, he would give it with pain.

Similar too are all the arguments of the following sort: "Could a person strike a blow with a hand he does not have?" or "Could someone see with an eye he does not have?" (For he does not have only one.)[567] Some people resolve it by saying that a person who has more than one eye (or whatever it is) also has only one.[568] Others resolve it as they also resolve, "What a person has, he received"; for this person gave only one vote; and "That person," they say, "has only one vote, received from him."[569] Other people do away with the question immediately, saying that one can have what one has not been given—for example, one can have been given sweet wine but, because of its having been destroyed in the process of transfer, have sour wine.

But, as was also said previously, all these offer a resolution not against the argument but against the person [making it].⁵⁷⁰ For if this was a resolution, if anyone granted the opposite [of what he did], it would be impossible to achieve a resolution, just as happens in other cases. For example, if "it is so in one way, but in another it is not" is the resolution, and the answerer granted it as said unconditionally, the conclusion has been reached. But if   20
a conclusion is not reached, this could not be a resolution.⁵⁷¹ And in the cases mentioned, even if everything is granted, we say that no deduction comes about.

Further, the following also belong among arguments of this sort. "If something is written, did someone write it? But it is written now that you are sitting, which is a false statement, though it was true at the time   25
it was written. Therefore, a statement at once false and true was written." [No,] for the truth or falsity of a statement or belief signifies not a this [something], but a quality; for the same account also applies in the case of a belief. Also, "What does a learner learn? Is it what he learns? But someone learns what is slow fast." It is not what he learns that is meant,   30
therefore, but how he learns it. Also, "Does someone tread on what he takes a walk on? But he takes a walk on the whole day."⁵⁷² Rather, it is not what he takes a walk on that is meant but when he takes a walk; nor when he drinks a cup is the cup what he drinks but what he drinks from.⁵⁷³ Also, "Is it either by being taught or by discovering that a person knows what he knows? But if of two things he has been taught one and discovered the other, he has neither been taught nor discovered the two together." Rather, "what [he knows]" means "every individual thing" not   35
"everything collectively."⁵⁷⁴

Also, the argument that there is a third man beyond man-itself and the particular man; for "man" and everything common signifies not a this something but rather such-and-such a quality, quantity, relation, or something of this sort. It is the same way too in the case of Coriscus and musical Coriscus and whether they are the same or distinct. For the first   179ᵃ1
signifies a this something, the second a quality, so that it is impossible for the latter to have been set out.⁵⁷⁵ But it is not being set out that produces the *Third Man* but conceding that it is precisely a this something; for it is also not possible for precisely what is a man to be a this something, as Callias is.⁵⁷⁶ Nor will it make any difference if someone were to say that it   5
is not precisely what is a this something that is being set out but a quality; for there will still be a one over many, like man. It is evident, then, that it must not be granted that what is predicated as common to all is a this something, but that it signifies a quality, relation, quantity, or something else of this sort.   10

23

Arguments depending on speech

In general, in arguments depending on speech, the resolution will always be in accord with the opposite of what the argument depends on—for example, if the argument depends on combination, the resolution will be by division, if it depends on division, by combining. Again, if it depends on acute accentuation, grave accentuation will be the resolution, and if it depends on grave accentuation, acute accentuation. If it depends on homonymy, one can resolve it by saying the opposite name—for example, if [the argument] results in your saying that something is animate, having denied that it is so, make clear in what way it is animate, while if one has said that it is inanimate, but it has been deduced that it is animate, say in what way it is inanimate.[577] It is the same way too in the case of ambiguity. And if the argument depends on similarity of speech, the opposite will be the resolution. "Could one give what one does not have?" Surely not what one does not have, but rather in a way in which one does not have it—for example, one die only.[578] "Does someone scientifically know what he scientifically knows by being taught or by discovery?"[579] [Yes,] but not the things he scientifically knows. Also, whether a person treads on what he takes a walk on; [yes], but not the time.[580] It is the same way too in the case of the others.

24

Arguments depending on the coincident

As for arguments depending on the coincident, one and the same resolution works against all. For since it is indefinite at which time a predicate should be said of the thing at issue, when it belongs in the case of its coincident, and since on some occasions it seems and is said to belong, while on others it is said not necessarily to do so, one must, then, once the conclusion has been drawn, say against all of them alike that it does not necessarily belong. One must, however, have an example to put forward.

All arguments of the following sort depend on the coincident: "Do you know what I am going to ask you?" "Do you know the one who is approaching?" or "the one who has hidden his face?" "Is the statue a work of yours?" or "Is the dog your father?"[581] "Is the product of two small numbers a small number?" For it is evident in all these cases that it is not necessary for what is true of the coincident to be also true of the thing at issue; for it is only to things that are indistinguishable with respect to their substance and one, it seems, that all the same things belong; while

in the case of something good[, for example,] being good and being what
I am going to ask you about are not the same. Nor in the case of someone
approaching is being the one who is approaching (or the one who has hidden his face) the same as being Coriscus. So, if I know Coriscus but do not
know the person approaching, I know and do not know the same person.
Nor, again, if this is mine and also a work, is it a work of mine. Instead, it
may be my possession, or thing, or something else. And it is the same way   5
in the other cases too.

Some people resolve these by doing away with the question.[582] For they
say that it is possible to know and not to know the same thing, but not in
the same respect. When, then, they do not know the person approaching
but do know Coriscus, they say that they do know and do not know the
same thing, but not in the same respect. Yet, in the first place, as we have   10
already said, the rectification of arguments depending on the same thing
must be the same.[583] But this will not be so if one takes the same claim to
apply not to knowing but to being or being in a certain state—for example,
in "If this [dog] is a father and this [dog] is yours . . ."; for if this is true in
certain cases, that is, that it is possible to know and not to know the same   15
thing, even so, what has been said about it has nothing in common with
the latter case.[584]—

(There is nothing to prevent the same argument from having several
defects, but not every bringing to light of a defect constitutes a resolution; for it is possible for a person to prove that something false has been
deduced, but not to have proved what it depends on—for example, in the
case of Zeno's argument that movement is impossible. So even if he were to   20
try to infer an impossibility, in leading [the argument] to the impossible,
he is making an error, even if he has deduced it innumerable times.[585] For
this is not a resolution; for a resolution, as we just saw, is a bringing to light
of what the falsehood of a false deduction depends on.)

—If, then, it has not been deduced, or in addition he tries to infer a truth
or a falsehood, the making clear of that is a resolution.[586] Perhaps, indeed,   25
there is nothing to prevent this from happening in some cases, albeit in the
ones under consideration, at any rate, this would not seem to be so; for one
knows both of Coriscus that he is Coriscus and of the thing approaching that
it is approaching. But to know and not to know the same thing does seem
to be possible—for example, one can know the pale thing and not know the
musical one; for in this way one does know and does not know the same   30
thing, but not in the same respect. But, as for the thing approaching and
Coriscus, he knows both that it is approaching and that it is Coriscus.[587]

Those who resolve the argument that every number is small also err in
a similar way to those we have mentioned; for if, when the conclusion has
not been reached, they pass this over and say that the conclusion has been   35

reached and is true (for every number is both large and small), they make an error.

Some people also resolve the deductions by appeal to equivocation—for example, by saying that what is "yours" is a father, son, or slave. Yet it is evident that if the appearance of refutation depends on what is said of things in many ways, the name or the statement must be said literally of several things. No one says that B is literally A's child if A is the child's master; rather, the combination depends on what is coincidental. "Is B yours?" "Yes." "Is B a child?" "Yes." "Then B is your child" (because he is coincidentally both yours and a child). But he is not your child.⁵⁸⁸

There is also the argument that being something of evils is good. "For practical wisdom is scientific knowledge of evils." But being this of these is not said of things in many ways, but is said of a possession. If, however, it is said of things in many ways (for we say that man is of the animals, though not a possession of theirs, and if the relation of so-and-so to evils is said as its being of them, because of this it is a so-and-so of evils; but it is not one of the evils), it appears to depend on what is in a certain respect and unconditionally.⁵⁸⁹

Yet it is perhaps possible for something of evils to be equivocally good, although not in the case of this argument, but rather if one were to say a slave is good of the wretched.⁵⁹⁰ But perhaps it is not even this way here; for if something is good and of someone, it is not at the same time good of someone. Nor is the expression "man is of the animals" said in many ways; for if we sometimes signify something elliptically, this is said in many ways; for in fact by quoting the half-line, "Sing, goddess, the wrath," we signify "recite me the *Iliad*."⁵⁹¹

25

Arguments depending on strict and unconditional versus in some respect

Arguments that depend on what is said to be this in the strict sense, or else in some respect, place, way, or relation to something, and not unconditionally, must be resolved by looking at the conclusion in relation to its contradictory, to see whether it can possibly be qualified in any of these ways. For it is impossible for contraries and opposites, or an affirmative and a negative, to belong unconditionally to the same thing. However, there is nothing to prevent each from belonging in some respect, relation, or way, or one in some respect and the other unconditionally. So, if this one belongs unconditionally and this other one belongs in a certain respect, there is as yet no refutation; and this is something one must look at in the conclusion in relation to its contradictory.   30

All arguments of this sort involve the following: "Is it possible that what is not is? But surely it is, at any rate, something that is not." Similarly, what is will not be; for it will not be one of the beings. "Is it possible for the same person at the same time to be a keeper and a breaker of his oath?" "Is it possible for the same person at the same time to obey and disobey the same   35 order?" Or rather is it not that being something and being unconditionally are not the same (for it is not the case that if what is not is something, it also is unconditionally)?⁵⁹² Nor if a person keeps his oath on this or in this respect is he necessarily also [unconditionally] a keeper of oaths (and a person who swears that he will break his oath, has, in breaking it, kept this one only, but is not [unconditionally] a keeper of oaths).⁵⁹³ Nor does he who disobeys obey [unconditionally], but rather he obeys in this.⁵⁹⁴   **180ᵇ1**

The argument is similar too about whether it is possible for the same person to lie and at the same time be truthful. But because it is not easy to see whether one should assign the "unconditionally" to "be truthful" or to "lie," it appears difficult [to resolve].⁵⁹⁵ However, there is nothing to prevent the same person from being unconditionally a liar but truthful in a certain   5 respect or in relation to a certain thing, that is, truthful in some things, though not himself truthful.⁵⁹⁶

It is the same way too in cases of being in relation to some thing, place, or time; for all the arguments of this sort depend on the following: "Is health, or wealth, a good? But to a person without practical wisdom who uses it incorrectly, it is not good. Therefore, it is good and not good." "Is   10 being healthy, or having power in the city, good?⁵⁹⁷ But sometimes it is not better [than other things]. Therefore, the same thing is good and not good for the same person." Or is there nothing to prevent something from being unconditionally good but not good for a particular person, or good for a particular person, but not good now or not here? "What a practically wise person would not wish for, is it bad? But he does not wish to get rid of the good. Therefore, the good is bad." No, for it is not the same thing to   15 say that the good is bad and that to get rid of the good is bad. And it is the same way too with the argument about the thief; for it is not the case that if a thief is bad, taking is bad too. Therefore, he does not wish for the bad, but the good; for taking a good thing is good.⁵⁹⁸ Also, disease is bad, but   20 not to get rid of disease.

"Is what is just more choiceworthy than what is unjust and what is justly done than what is unjustly done? But it is more choiceworthy to be put to death unjustly." "Is it just for each to have his own? But whatever things someone has judged in accord with his own belief, even if false, have the controlling votes in the eyes of the law.⁵⁹⁹ Therefore, the same

25   thing is just and not just." Also, "Should judgment be in favor of those
who state just things or those who state unjust things? But surely it is just
for a person who suffers injustice to state fully the things he has suffered;
and these were unjust ones." [These are fallacies.] For if to suffer something unjustly is more choiceworthy, it does not follow that unjustly is
more choiceworthy than justly. On the contrary, unconditionally, justly
30   is more choiceworthy, although there is nothing to prevent unjustly from
being more so than justly in this case. Also, to have what is one's own is
just, while to have what is another's is not just, yet there is nothing to
prevent this judgment from being just—for example, when it is in accord
with the one who is doing the judging; for if it is just in this case or in
this way, it does not follow that it is also unconditionally just.[600] Similarly
35   too when things are unjust, there is nothing to prevent saying them, at
any rate, from being just; for if saying them is just, it does not necessarily follow that they are just, any more than if it is beneficial to say things,
they are beneficial. And it is the same way in the case of just ones too. So,
if the things said are unjust, it does not follow that the person who says
unjust things prevails; for he says things that are just to say, but that are
unconditionally unjust, that is, unjust to suffer.[601]

26

Arguments depending on the definition of a refutation

Arguments depending on the definition of a refutation must be replied
181ᵃ1   to, as suggested previously, by looking at the conclusion in relation to its
contradictory, and seeing in what way it will involve the same thing, in
the same respect, in relation to the same thing, in the same way, and at the
same time.[602] And if this additional question has been asked initially, one
5   must not agree that it is impossible for the same thing to be double and not
double, but state that it is possible, only not in such a way as was agreed to
be a refutation. All the following arguments depend on this sort of thing.
"Does a person who knows that a given thing is the given thing it is, know
the thing? And the same for a person who does not know it? But one who
10   knows that Coriscus is Coriscus might not know that he is musical, so that
he both scientifically knows and does not know the same thing." "Is what
is four cubits long greater than what is three cubits long? But what is three
cubits long might become four cubits long. But what is greater is greater
than the less. Therefore, the thing in question is greater and less than itself
in the same respect."

27

Arguments depending on asking for what was initially at issue

As for arguments that depend on asking for and obtaining what was
initially at issue, if this is clear, one must, when asked, not grant it, even if   15
it is acceptable, while stating the truth.[603] If, on the other hand, it is concealed, one must, because of the defectiveness of such arguments, turn the
charge of ignorance back on the questioner, saying that he is not arguing
dialectically; for a refutation must do without what was initially at issue.
Next, one must say that it was granted on the supposition that it would
not be used [as a premise], but used to produce a deduction against it, the   20
contrary way to that in the case of refutations on side issues.[604]

28

Arguments depending on affirming the consequent

Also, those arguments that infer by means of [affirming] the consequent
must be exposed in the course of the argument itself. For the logical
sequence of consequents is twofold; for it is either as the universal follows
[in a logical sequence of consequents] the particular, for example, as animal follows from human (for it is claimed that if this accompanies that,
that accompanies this), or else in accord with opposition (for [it is claimed   25
that] if this follows that, the opposite of the one follows the opposite of the
other).[605] It is on this too that the argument of Melissus depends; for [he
claims that] if what has come to be has a starting-point, what has not come
to be does not have one, so that if the heaven has not come to be, it is also
unlimited.[606] But this is not so; for the logical sequence is the reverse.   30

29

Arguments depending on an addition

One must look at any arguments where the deduction depends on an
addition to see whether, when it is subtracted, the impossibility follows
nonetheless.[607] And one must next bring this to light, and say that one had
granted it not as something one believed, but for the purposes of the argument, while the questioner has made no use of it for the purposes of the
argument.   35

30

Arguments depending on making many questions into one

Against arguments that make many questions into one, one must draw a distinction right at the start; for a question is one to which there is one answer, so that one must not affirm or deny several things of one thing or one thing of several things, but one thing of one thing. But just as in the case of homonyms, where a homonym sometimes belongs to both or to neither, so that, though the question is not simple, nothing results to affect those who give a simple answer, so it is too in these cases.[608] When, then, the several predicates belong to one thing, or the one predicate to several things, no contradiction results for those who have given a simple answer and made this error, but rather when something belongs to one and not to another thing, or several things are affirmed of several. And there is a way in which both belong to both, while in another way again they do not, so one must beware of this. For example, in these arguments: "If one thing is good and another is bad, it is true to say that these things are good and bad, and again that they are neither good nor bad (for each of the two is not each of the two), so that the same thing is both good and bad and neither good nor bad." Also, "If each thing is the same as itself and distinct from another thing, since these things are not the same as other things, but as themselves, and also distinct from themselves, the same things are both distinct from themselves and the same as themselves."[609] Further, "If the good becomes bad and the bad good, they would become both." Also, "Of two unequal things, each is equal to itself, so that they themselves are equal and unequal to themselves."[610]

These arguments also fall into the province of other resolutions; for "both" and "all" signify several things; therefore, it does not follow that one has affirmed and denied the same thing, except in name.[611] And this, as we saw, is not a refutation.[612] On the contrary, it is evident that if several things do not give rise to one question, but rather one predicate is affirmed or denied of one thing, there will not be [a deduction of] an impossibility.[613]

31

Arguments depending on babbling

Where arguments leading one to say the same thing several times are concerned, it is evident that one must not grant that predicates said as relatives signify something when in separation by themselves—for example, "double" without "double of half," just because it appears in it.[614] For "ten"

is also in "ten minus one," "do" in "not do," and, in general, the affirmation in the negation.[615] Nonetheless, if one says, "this is not white," one is   30
not saying that it is white. Perhaps "double" does not signify anything at
all, any more than in the case of half.[616] But even if "double" does signify
something, it is not the same thing as when it has been brought together
[with its correlate]. Nor does "scientific knowledge" in a form of it (for
example, if it is "medical scientific knowledge") signify precisely what the
common thing is, which, as we saw, is scientific knowledge of the scientifically knowable.[617]

   In the case of things that are predicated of the things through which   35
they are indicated, one must say that they are not the same separately as
in the account indicating them. For "concave" indicates the same common
thing in the case of the snub and the bandy, but when added, in the one
case to "nose" and in the other to "leg," there is nothing to prevent it from
signifying distinct ones; for in the first case it signifies snub and in the
second bandy, and it makes no difference whether one says "snub nose" or   182^{a}1
"concave nose."

   Further, one must not grant the expression in the nominative; for that
is false; for the snub is not snub nose [nominative] but something—for
example, an affection—characteristic of a nose [genitive], so that there is
nothing absurd in supposing that a snub nose is one having the concavity   5
characteristic of a nose.

32

Arguments depending on solecisms

Where solecisms are concerned, we said previously what their appearing
to follow depends on.[618] How they must be resolved will be evident from
the arguments themselves; for all of the following sort wish to establish a
solecism: "Is this ($ho_{n.\,nom.}$) truly what you truly state it ($touto_{n.\,acc.}$) to be? But   10
you say something is a stone ($lithon_{m.\,acc.}$). Therefore, something is a stone
(*lithon*) [nom. is required]." On the contrary, in speaking of a "stone," one
says not "he ($ho_{n.\,nom.}$)" but "him ($hon_{m.\,acc.}$)," and not "this ($touto_{n.\,nom.}$)" but
"this ($touton_{m.\,acc.}$)." If, then, one were to ask, "Is it this (*touton*) [$houtos_{m.\,nom.}$
is required] him ($hon_{m.\,acc.}$) you truly say?" one would not seem to be speaking correct Greek, any more than if one were to ask, "Is it he ($houtos_{m.\,nom.}$)
her ($hên_{f.\,acc.}$) [m. is required] one says he is?" But to say "wood ($xulon_{n.\,acc.}$)"
for "he," or whatever signifies neither something feminine nor something
masculine, makes no difference. That is why no solecism comes about if   15
you say, "Is this ($ho_{n.\,nom.}$) what you say it ($touto_{n.\,nom.}$) is? You say it is wood

(*xulon*~n. acc.~). Therefore, it is wood (*xulon*~n.~)." "Stone," on the other hand, and "he" (*houtos*) have masculine denomination.[619] If, then, one were to ask, "Can he (*houtos*) be a she (*hautê*)?" or, again, "Well, is he (*houtos*) not Coriscus?" and then were to say, "Therefore, he (*houtos*) is a she (*hautê*)," one has not derived a solecism, not even if "Coriscus" signifies precisely a she (*hautê*), because the answerer does not grant this. Instead, this point must be asked as an additional question. But if this is not the case and nor does the answerer grant it, then the solecism has not been deduced either in reality or in relation to the one who was questioned.

Similarly, then, in the first example too "he (*houtos*)" must signify the stone. If, however, this is neither so nor is granted, the conclusion must not be stated, although, by depending on the fact that the dissimilar case of the name appears to be similar, it appears to follow.[620]

"Is it true to say that this (*hautê*~f. nom.~) is just what you said this (*autên*~f. acc.~) is? You said it is a shield (*aspida*~f. acc.~); therefore, it is a shield (*aspida*) [nom. is required]." On the contrary, this is not necessary if "this (*hautê*~nom.~)" signifies not a shield (*aspida*~acc.~) but a shield (*aspis*~nom.~), while "this (*autên*~acc.~)" signifies a shield (*aspida*~acc.~).

Nor is it necessary, if he (*houtos*~m. nom.~) is who you say he (*touton*~m. acc.~) is, and you say he is Cleon (*Kleôna*~acc.~), is he (*houtos*~nom.~) therefore Cleon (*Kleôna*~acc.~); for he (*houtos*~nom.~) is not *Kleôna*~acc.~ [but rather *Kleôn*~nom.~]; for what was said was that he (*houtos*~nom.~], not him (*touton*~acc.~), is who you say he is; for it would not be correct Greek either if the question had been asked in the latter way ["Is him who you say he is?"].

"Do you scientifically know this (*touto*)? This (*touto*) is a stone (*lithos*~nom.~). Therefore, you scientifically know a stone (*lithos*~nom.~) [*lithon*~acc.~ is required]." On the contrary, "this (*touto*)" does not signify the same thing in "do you scientifically know this (*touto*)?" and in "this (*touto*) is a stone," but rather in the first it signifies this (*touton*~acc.~), and in the second this (*houtos*~nom.~).

"When you have scientific knowledge of something (*hou*~gen.~), do you scientifically know it (*touto*~acc.~)? But you have scientific knowledge of a stone (*lithou*~gen.~). Therefore, you scientifically know of a stone (*lithou*~gen.~)." On the contrary, "of something (*hou*~gen.~)" says "of a stone (*lithou*~gen.~)," and "it (*touton*~acc.~)" says a stone (*lithon*~acc.~). And it was granted that when you have scientific knowledge of something (*hou*~gen.~), you scientifically know not of it (*touto*~gen.~) but it (*touto*~acc.~), so that you scientifically know not of a stone (*lithou*~gen.~) but a stone (*lithon*~acc.~).

That arguments of this sort do not deduce a solecism, though they appear to do so, and why they appear to do so, and in what way one must reply to them, is evident from what has been said.

33

Simpleminded versus incisive arguments

We must also understand that, among all arguments, it is easier with some, more difficult with others, to see by depending on what, and at what point, they mislead the listener by arguing fallaciously—although the latter are sometimes the same arguments as the former; for one must call an argument "the same" that depends on the same thing.[621] But the same argument might seem to some people to depend on speech, to others on the coincident, and to others on something else, because, when [the words in it are] changed, each is not then equally clear.   10

Just as in the case of those that depend on homonymy, then, which seems to be the most simpleminded mode among the fallacies, some are clear even to random people. (For pretty much all ridiculous arguments depend on speech. For example, "A man was carried down from a ladder   15
by a chariot."[622] And "Where are you bound? To the yardarm." "Which of two cows will calve in front? Neither; but both will calve in the rear."[623] "Is Boreas pure? Certainly not; for he has killed the drunken beggar."[624] "Is he *Euarchos*? Certainly not. He is *Apollônidês*."[625] And it is the same way with   20
pretty much the vast majority of the rest.) Others, however, apparently escape the notice of even the most experienced. A sign of this is that people often fight about the names, for example, about whether "being" and "one" always signify the same thing, or something distinct; for to some people "being" and "one" seem to signify the same thing in all cases, while others   25
resolve the argument of Zeno and of Parmenides by saying that being and one are said of things in many ways.[626]

Similarly too where the coincident and each of the others is concerned, some of the arguments will be easier to see, others more difficult, and to grasp which kind they belong to, and whether one is a refutation or not a   30
refutation, is not equally easy for all of them.[627]

An incisive argument is one that makes one most puzzled; for it bites most deeply. A puzzle is twofold: one occurs in dialectical arguments that are deductive, when one is in doubt as to which of the questions asked one must do away with; the other occurs in contentious arguments, about how one is to state what has been proposed.[628] That is precisely why, among   35
deductive ones, the more incisive arguments make one inquire more.

A deductive argument is most incisive when from the things that seem most of all to be so it does away with the most acceptable belief; for though it is a single argument, it will, when the contradiction is converted, contain deductions that are all similar in character; for it will always, on the basis of acceptable beliefs, do away with one that is equally acceptable which is   183^{a}1 precisely why it is necessary to be puzzled.[629] This sort of argument, then, is most incisive, namely, one which puts the conclusion on an equal footing with the questions, while the one based on those that are on a similar footing is second; for this will produce similar puzzlement as to which of the questions must be done away with. But this is difficult; for one must do away with something, but what to do away with is unclear.

The most incisive of contentious arguments, on the other hand, is in the first place one where it is not immediately clear whether [the conclusion] has been deduced or not, that is, whether the resolution depends on a falsehood or on drawing a distinction; second among the others is where it is clear that it depends on drawing a distinction or doing away with something, but it is not evident which of the questions it is that, by doing away with it or drawing distinctions in it, one is to resolve it, but [only] whether it depends on the conclusion or on one of the questions.[630]

Sometimes, an argument that does not deduce is simpleminded, if the premises are too unacceptable or false; but sometimes it does not deserve to be despised.[631] For when one of the questions is omitted of the sort that the argument is about and which it is due to, the deduction that has both not obtained this in addition and not deduced [the conclusion] is simpleminded.[632] But when what is omitted is something extraneous, it is by no means to be lightly despised, rather the argument is decent, though the questioner has not asked his questions correctly.[633]

Also, just as it is sometimes possible to propose a resolution in relation to the argument, sometimes in relation to the questioner and his mode of questioning, and sometimes in relation to neither of these, so too it is possible to question and deduce in relation to the posit, in relation to the answerer, and in relation to the time (when the resolution needs more time than the present opportunity allows for dialectical argument leading to the resolution).[634]

34

Originality of the work

As for how many and what sorts of things the fallacies that come about among dialectical interlocutors are based on, and how we are to prove the opponent to be saying something false and how to make him say something unacceptable, further, on what basis a solecism comes about, how to ask questions, and what the arrangement of questions is, and, further, what all arguments of this sort are useful for, and about simply answering questions, both in general and as regards how to resolve arguments and solecisms, let the foregoing be what we have to say.[635] It remains to recollect our proposal at the start, say a few words about it, and bring our discussion to an end.

                                                     35

What we deliberately chose to do, then, was to discover a certain capacity to argue deductively about the thing put before us on the basis of the things that are taken to be the most acceptable ones; for this is the function of dialectic itself and of the examinational craft.[636] But since there is provided along with it, because of its proximity to sophistry, not only the capacity of examining dialectically, but also as if having knowledge, because of this, we proposed for our work not only the function we just mentioned of being capable of getting hold of the relevant argument, but also, when submitting to argument, of defending our posit in the same manner through the most acceptable beliefs.[637] And the cause of this we have stated, since this is also why Socrates used to ask questions and not answer them; for he used to acknowledge that he did not know.[638]

It has been made clear in the preceding discussion how many things this capacity will be related to and on how many it will be based, and from what sources we will become well equipped with these, further, how questions must be asked and questioning generally arranged, and about the answers and resolutions related to deductions.[639] And all the other issues have also been made clear that concern the same methodical inquiry about arguments. In addition, we have discussed fallacies in detail, as we have already stated previously.[640]

It is evident, then, that what was proposed has been adequately brought to an end. We must not overlook what has happened where this work is concerned. For in the case of all discoveries, those due to the previous labors of other people have been taken up and advanced bit by bit by those who took them up afterward, while original discoveries usually make progress that is small at first but is surely much more useful than what later develops from them; for perhaps the start is the most important thing of all, as the saying goes. That is why it is also the most difficult; for to the extent that it is greatest in capacity, it is smallest in magnitude and most difficult to see. But once it is discovered, it is easier to add to it and develop the rest in connection with it, which is precisely what has also in fact happened where rhetorical arguments are concerned, and also where pretty much all the other crafts are concerned. For those who discovered the starting-points advanced them in only a small way, while the ones who enjoy a good reputation nowadays are the heirs (so to speak) of a long series of predecessors who advanced it bit by bit, and in this way have developed it—Tisias coming after the first ones, Thrasymachus after Tisias, Theodorus after Thrasymachus, while numerous others have contributed numerous parts.[641] That is why it is no wonder that the craft has a certain magnitude.

Of this work of ours, by contrast, it is not the case that part of it had been
worked out before, while part had not. On the contrary, nothing existed
at all. For in fact the education given by the paid teachers of contentious
arguments were similar to the practice of Gorgias; for while the one lot
used to give [sets of] rhetorical arguments to learn by heart, the others gave
arguments based on questions, into which questioner and answerer each
thought that the arguments of both of them most often fell. That is precisely why the teaching they gave their students was rabid but un-craftlike;
for they supposed that they could educate by imparting not the craft but its
products, as if a person promising to impart a science dealing with having
no pain in the feet were then to teach not the craft of shoemaking, or even
from whom one will be able to be provided with such things, but were to
provide numerous kinds of shoes of every variety; for he has helped supply
one's need, but has not imparted a craft.[642]

Also, where rhetorical arguments are concerned there were many things
said long ago, while about deductive argument we had absolutely nothing
else earlier to speak of at all, but were for a long time laboring and inquiring by knack.[643]

If, then, having gotten a theoretical grasp on it, it appears to us, such
being the situation as it existed at the start, that our methodical inquiry
is adequate when compared with other works that have developed on the
basis of what has been handed down, there remains for all of us, or rather
for you, the ones who listen to it, the work of showing sympathetic consideration for the shortcomings of our methodical inquiry and much grati-
tude for our discoveries.[644]

Related Texts

11

20ᵇ22–30

22 If, then, a dialectical question is the request of an answer which is either
a premise or one member of a contradictory pair (and if the premise is a
member of one contradictory pair), there will be no one answer in these
25 cases (for the question is not one either), not even if it is true.[645] This is discussed in the *Topics*.[646] At the same time it is clear that the question "What
is it?" is not dialectical either. For the question must give one the choice
of asserting whichever member of the contradictory pair one wishes. The
30 questioner must specify in addition whether *human* is this or not this.

PRIOR ANALYTICS

1.1

24ª16–ᵇ15

A premise, then, is a sentence that affirms or denies something of something. This sentence may be universal, particular, or indeterminate. I call belonging "to every" or "to none" universal; belonging "to some," "not to some," or "not to every," particular. "Indeterminate" is belonging or not belonging without "universal" or "particular" (for example, "the science of contraries is the same"   20 or "pleasure is not (a) good." A demonstrative premise differs from a dialectical one in that the demonstrative premise is supposing one or the other part of a contradiction (for someone who demonstrates does not ask but instead supposes), whereas a dialectical premise is the asking of a contradiction. However, this will make no difference as to whether a deduction comes about   25 in either case; for both the one who demonstrates and the one who questions deduce by supposing something about something, either belonging or not belonging. Consequently, a deductive premise, unconditionally, will be either the affirmation or the denial of one thing about another in the way just said. It is demonstrative if it is true and has been obtained by means of the initial   30 assumptions, while a dialectical premise is, for someone getting answers, the posing of a contradiction as a question, but, for someone deducing, suppos-   24ᵇ1 ing something apparent and acceptable, for someone deducing, as was said in the *Topics*.[647] So then, what a premise is and how deductive, demonstrative, and dialectical premises differ will be stated more precisely in what follows, but let the definitions given now be sufficient for our present needs.   15

1.30

46ª3–30

The route is the same with respect to all things, then, whether concerning philosophy or concerning any sort of craft or learning whatsoever. For we must discern what belongs to each term and what it belongs to, and be   5 provided with as many of them as possible, and examine these through the three terms, refuting in this way and establishing in that; according to truth, from things that have been strictly proved to belong in accord with truth, but in dialectical deductions from premises in accord with belief.

10   The starting-points of deductions have been described universally,—
both what they are like and how we ought to hunt for them—in order
that we might not look to everything said of a subject, or inspect the same
things when establishing as when refuting, or the same things when establishing something to belong to all as to some, or when refuting a predicate
of all as of some, but rather that we should look to fewer and determinate
15   things, and that we should make a selection concerning each thing that is
(for example, concerning the good or science).

The majority of the starting-points of each science are special to it. That is
why it is the role of our experiences to deliver to us the starting-points concerning any given subject. I mean, for example, that it is astronomical experience that delivers the starting-points of astronomical science (for when the
20   appearances had been sufficiently grasped in this way, astronomical demonstrations were found), and similarly concerning any other craft or science
whatsoever. Consequently, once the facts concerning any subject have been
grasped, it is then already within our grasp to bring the demonstrations readily to light. For if nothing that truly belongs to the subjects has been left out
25   of our collection of facts, then concerning every fact, if a demonstration for it
exists, we will be able to find that demonstration and demonstrate it, while if it
does not naturally have a demonstration, we will be able to make that evident.

The way we ought to select premises has been sufficiently explained in
general, then. We have gone through this in exact detail, however, in our
30   treatise concerning dialectic.⁶⁴⁸

2.16

64ᵇ28–65ª25

Asking for or assuming the initial thing is, to put it in a kind, a matter of
not demonstrating what was proposed. But that happens in many ways:
30   if one entirely fails to deduce, or if one does deduce but through [prem-
ises] more unknowable [than what was proposed] or equally unknowable
[as it is], or if one deduces what is prior through what is posterior (for a
demonstration is through what is both more persuasive and prior). None
of these, then, is asking for the initial thing. However, given that some
things are of such a nature as to be known through themselves and some
are of such a nature as to be known through others—that is, the starting-
35   points are known through themselves and those below the starting-points
are known through other things—therefore, whenever someone tries to
prove through itself what is not knowable through itself, he is asking for
the initial thing.

This can be done in such a way as to claim directly what was proposed, but it is also possible to do it by transferring the argument over to other premises that are of such a nature as to be proved through the initial thing   40
and demonstrating the initial thing through them—for example, if A is proved through B and B through C but C is of such a nature as to be proved   65^{a}1
through A; for the result is that those who deduce in this way prove A through itself. This is precisely what those who think they construct proofs that there are parallels do; for they do not notice that they themselves sup-   5
pose premises that it is not possible to demonstrate if there are no parallels. Thus, it follows for those who deduce in this way that they are saying a given thing is so if it is so. But in that way everything would be knowable through itself, which is impossible.

So then, if someone should ask for the premise that A belongs to B   10
when it is not clear that A belongs to C and equally unclear that it belongs to B, although it is not yet clear whether he is asking for the initial thing, he is clearly not demonstrating (for what is equally unclear is not the beginning of a demonstration). However, if B is so related to C as to be the same, or if it is clear that they convert or one belongs to the other, he   15
is asking for the initial thing. For he could also prove that A belongs to B through those terms, if he converted it (this is what actually prevents him, not the way it is proved). But if he did this, he could do what was said and convert the three of them. And likewise, if he were to suppose that B belongs to C, though that was as unclear as that A did, he would not   20
yet be asking for the initial thing, but he is not demonstrating. However, if A is the same as B because A either converts with or follows it, then he is asking for the initial thing, due to the same cause. For it was said what "asking for the initial thing" means for us: it is proving through itself what is not clear through itself.   25

Therefore, if asking for the initial thing is proving through itself what is not clear through itself—which is to say, not proving—then if what is being proved and what someone is proving it through are equally unclear, either because the same things belong to the same thing or because the same thing belongs to the same things, it will be possible to ask for the initial thing both ways in the middle figure and in the third, and in a posi-   30
tive deduction in both the third figure and the first. When the conclusion is deduced negatively, it is possible when the same things are denied of the same, though not possible for both the premises similarly, because the terms do not convert with respect to negative deductions (and likewise in the middle figure). In demonstrations, it is asking for the initial thing   35
when the premises are so related in truth, but in dialectical arguments when they are so related in accord with belief.

2.23

68^{b}8–37

It is evident, then, how terms are related with respect to conversions and with respect to being more choiceworthy or more to be avoided. But now we must explain that not only do dialectical and demonstrative deductions come about through the figures previously mentioned, but so also do rhetorical ones and, in a word, any means of persuasion whatever, arising from whatever methodical inquiry.

We persuade about anything either through deduction or from induction. Induction, then—that is, a deduction from induction—is deducing one extreme to belong to the middle through the other extreme. For example, if B is the middle for AC, proving A to belong to B by means of C (for this is how we produce inductions). For example, let A be long-lived, B stand for not having bile, and C stand for the long-lived particular, such as a human, a horse, or a mule. Now, A belongs to the whole C (for everything bileless is long-lived); but B (not having bile) belongs to every C.[649] Then, if C converts with B and the middle term does not extend beyond the extreme, it is necessary for A to belong to B. For it was proved previously that if two terms belong to the same thing and the extreme converts with one of them, the other one of the predicates will also belong to the term that converts with it.[650] (But one must understand C as composed of every one of the particulars; for induction is through them all.)

This sort of deduction is of a first (that is, immediate) premise: for those premises of which there is a middle term, deduction is by means of that middle term, but for those of which there is no middle term it is through induction. And in a way, induction is the opposite of deduction. For deduction proves the first extreme to belong to the third term through the middle, whereas induction proves the first extreme to belong to the middle through the third. By nature, therefore, the deduction through the middle term is prior and better known, but the deduction through induction is more obvious to us.

POSTERIOR ANALYTICS

1.2

72ª8–11

A premise is one or other part of an assertion, one thing said of one thing. A dialectical premise is one that assumes either part indifferently, while a demonstrative premise is one that determinately posits one part, because it is true. 10

1.11

77ª26–35

All the sciences share with one another the common things (by "common things" I mean the ones people use as the basis on which demonstration proceeds, but not what they prove things about nor what they prove), and dialectic shares these with all of them, as would anything that tried to prove the common things in a universal way—for example, that everything is affirmed or denied, or that equals subtracted from equals leave equals, or 30 other things of this sort. But dialectic is not concerned in this way with any determinate sorts of things, or any one single kind. For if it were, it would not ask questions; for when one is demonstrating it is not possible to ask questions because the same thing cannot be proved from opposites. This was proved in the work on deduction.[651] 35

1.12

77ᵇ34–78ª13

One must not bring an objection to an argument if the premise is inductive. For just as there is no premise that does not apply to several things (for 35 otherwise it will not apply to all, and a deduction proceeds from universal premises), it is clear that there is no objection either. For premises and objections are the same; for what one brings as an objection may become a premise, either demonstrative or dialectical.

   ...

If it were impossible to prove truth from falsehood, to do analytics would be easy; for then there would of necessity be conversion. For let A be something that is the case; and if A is the case, then these things, which I know to be the case, are the case (call them B). Therefore, from these I will prove that A is the case. Conversion is more common in mathematics because mathematicians assume nothing coincidental—and in this respect too they differ from dialecticians—but [only] definitions.

1.19

81ᵇ18–23

For those who make deductions in accord with belief, that is, only dialectically, it is clear that the only thing that must be investigated is whether the deduction proceeds from the most acceptable premises possible, so that even if there is not in truth any middle term between A and B, but there is believed to be one, anyone who makes a deduction through it has deduced dialectically. But with a view to truth one must investigate by proceeding from what actually belongs.

2.13

97ᵇ37–39

If one must not argue dialectically by means of metaphors, it is clear too that one must neither define things by means of metaphors nor define what is said by means of metaphors; for then one will necessarily be arguing dialectically by means of metaphors.

PHYSICS

1.2

184^{b}25–185^{a}20

To investigate whether being is one and immovable is not to make an investigation concerning nature; for just as a geometer has no further argument against someone who does away with the starting-points of geometry— 185^{a}1 since this is a matter for another science or one that is common to all—so it is too where starting-points are concerned; for there will no longer be a starting-point if being is one thing only, and one in this way.[652] For a starting-point must be a starting-point of some thing or things.

To investigate, then, whether being is one in this way is like dialectically discussing any other thesis that is stated for the sake of argument, like that 5 of Heraclitus, or (if anyone were to state it) that being is one human being, or like refuting a contentious argument—which is precisely what the arguments of Melissus and Parmenides involve; for in fact they assume falsehoods and argue invalidly—or rather, the argument of Melissus is crude 10 and involves no puzzle. Grant him one absurdity and the others follow— nothing difficult in this.

As for ourselves, we must assume that the things that are by nature are in movement, either all of them or some of them. And this is clear from induction.[653] At the same time, we should not resolve every [contentious argument] at hand, but those that involve false demonstration from the starting-points, and not those that do not. For example, it belongs to the 15 geometer to refute a quadrature by means of segments, but not one like Antiphon's. Nonetheless, since Melissus and Parmenides happen to speak about nature, although the puzzles they state are not natural scientific ones, perhaps it would be good to discuss them briefly; for the investigation involves philosophy.[654] 20

De Caelo

1.7

275^{b}12–18

It is also possible to attack the issue in a more logico-linguistic way as follows.[655] For the unlimited, when uniform, cannot move in a circle; for there is no center of the unlimited, while what moves in a circle moves around the center.[656] But then neither can the unlimited spatially move in a straight line; for there would need to be another just as large (that is, unlimited) place that it will spatially move toward in accord with nature, and a distinct one, just as large, that it will move toward contrary to nature.[657]

ON COMING TO BE AND PASSING AWAY

1.2

316ª5–14

The cause of our being incapable of taking a comprehensive view of the agreed-upon facts is lack of experience. That is why those who are more at home among natural things are better able to posit the sort of starting-points that can string together a good many of these, while those who on the basis of their many [logico-linguistic] arguments do not get a theoretical grasp on the facts, but look at only a few, make their declarations too recklessly. One can see from this too how much difference there is between investigating in the way appropriate to natural science and in a logico-linguistic way; for concerning the existence of indivisible magnitudes, the latter lot say that the triangle-itself will [otherwise] be many, while Democritus would appear to have been convinced of this by arguments that are proper to and appropriate to natural science.

De Anima

1.1

402^{b}16–403^{b}16

It seems that not only is the knowledge of the what-it-is useful for getting a theoretical grasp on the causes of the coincidents connected to the
substances (as in mathematics knowing what the straight is and what the
curved is, or what a line is and what a plane is, is useful for seeing how
20   many right angles the angles of a triangle are equal to), but also, conversely,
knowing these coincidents contributes in great part to knowing the what-
it-is; for when we can give an account of all or most of these coincidents
that is in accord with what appears so, we will then be able to speak best
25   about the substance; for the starting-point of all demonstration is the
what-it-is, so that insofar as definitions [of it] do not lead us to know the
coincidents, or fail even to facilitate a likely conjecture about [how to dem-
403^{a}1   onstrate] them, it is clear that they have all been stated in a dialectical and
empty way.[658]

There is a puzzle too about the affections of the soul, as to whether
they are all also shared by what has the soul or whether there is also some
affection that is special to the soul itself; for it is necessary to get [a res-
5   olution of] this, but it is not easy. But it appears that in most cases the
soul is neither affected by nor does it act without the body—for example,
being angry, being confident, having an appetite for things, perceiving in
general—whereas understanding seems to be most of all special to the soul.
Yet if it too is a sort of imagination, or does not exist without imagination,
it would not be possible even for it to exist without a body.[659]

10   If, then, some function or affection of the soul is special to it, it will be
possible for it to be separated. But if there is nothing special to it, it will not
be separable, but will be like the straight, to which, insofar as it is straight,
many coincidents belong—for example, it will touch a bronze sphere at a
point, although, if separated, the straight will not touch it in this way; for it
15   is inseparable, if indeed it always involves some body.[660]

So too the affections of the soul—spiritedness, mild-manneredness,
fear, pity, confidence, and, further, joy, loving, and hating—would all seem
to involve the body; for at the same time as these, the body is affected in
a certain way. This is evidenced by the fact that sometimes, though strong
20   and vivid affections take place in us, we are not provoked or frightened,

206

whereas at other times we are moved by small and faint ones, as when the body is aroused (*orga[i]*) and its condition is like when someone is angry (*orgizêtai*). It is yet more evident that this is so; for sometimes, though nothing frightening is occurring, people come to have the affections of a frightened person.

If this is so, however, it is clear that the affections of the soul are enmattered accounts.[661] So their definitions will be of this sort, for example: "Being angry is a sort of movement of such-and-such a sort of body, or of a part or a capacity, as a result of this for the sake of that." And that is why it already belongs to the natural scientist to get a theoretical grasp on the soul, either all soul or this sort of soul.

But a natural scientist and a dialectician would define each of these differently—for example, what anger is.[662] For a dialectician it is "a desire for retaliation" or something like that, while for a natural scientist it is "a boiling of the blood and hot stuff around the heart." Of these, the natural scientist gives the matter, whereas the dialectician gives the form and the account. For this is the account of the thing, although it must be in matter of such-and-such a sort if it is to exist. And so of a house the account is this, that it is a shelter to prevent destruction by winds, rain, and heat. But one person will say that it is stones, bricks, and timbers, and another that it is the form in them for the sake of these other things.

Which of these people, then, is the natural scientist? Is it the one concerned with the matter but ignorant of the account, or the one concerned with the account alone? Or is it rather the one concerned with what is composed of both? Who, then, is each of the others? Or is there not someone who is concerned with the affections of the matter that are not separable and insofar as they are not separable? Or is the natural scientist rather the one who is concerned with everything that is a function or affection of this sort of body and this sort of matter? And isn't anything, insofar as it is not of this sort, the concern of someone else, in some cases a craftsman, if there happens to be one, such as a builder or a doctor? And aren't those things that are not separable, but are considered insofar as they are not affections of this sort of body and in abstraction from it, the concern of the mathematician? And insofar as they are separate, that of the primary philosopher?[663]

GENERATION OF ANIMALS

2.8

747ᵇ27–748ᵃ16

But perhaps a logico-linguistic demonstration might seem more persuasive than the ones just mentioned—I call it "logico-linguistic" because, in
being more universal, it is further away from the proper starting-points.
It is something like this: [P1] Suppose that from a male and a female of
the same form a male and a female naturally come to be that are of the
same form as their progenitors (for example, from a male and a female
dog a male and a female dog), [P2] while from a pair distinct in form,
one distinct from them in form comes to be (for example, if a dog is distinct in form from a lion, from a male dog and a female lion one distinct
from them in form comes to be, also from a male lion and a female dog).
So, since a male and a female mule come to be and are not different in
form from each other, and a mule comes to be from a horse and an ass,
and these are distinct in form from mules, it is impossible for anything to
come to be from mules; for something of a distinct kind cannot come to
be, because what comes to be from a male and female of the same form is
the same in form as they, and a mule cannot, because it comes to be from a
horse and an ass, which are distinct in form.

But in fact this argument is too universal and empty; for arguments not
from the proper starting-points are empty, but rather seem to be based on
the things at issue, but are not really.[664] For [arguments] from geometrical
starting-points are geometrical ones, and likewise in the other cases. But
what is empty, though it seems to be something, is nothing. And it is not
true; because many animals that come to be from ones not of the same
form are fertile, as was said previously.[665] One should not, then, inquire in
this way either concerning other things or concerning natural ones.

Rather it is from getting a theoretical grasp on what belongs to the horse
kind and the ass kind that one should get the cause.

METAPHYSICS

1.6

987^{b}29–988^{a}1

The fact that [Plato] made the one and the numbers be beyond the things, not treating them as the Pythagoreans did, and that he introduced the Forms, were due to his investigation of accounts (for the previous thinkers had no share of dialectic), and the fact that he made the other nature a dyad was because he thought that the numbers, except those that were prime, were naturally well disposed to being generated from this as from some plastic material.[666]

30

988^{a}1

3.1

995^{b}18–25

These, then, as we say, we must investigate, and also whether the theoretical knowledge [we are investigating] is concerned only with substances or also with the intrinsic coincidents of substances.[667] In addition, concerning same and other, like and unlike, and contrariety, and concerning prior and posterior, and all the other such things that dialecticians try to investigate, making their investigation on the basis of acceptable beliefs only—whose task is it to get a theoretical grasp on all these?

20

4.2

1004^{b}10–26

For just as of number, qua number, there are special affections (for example, oddness, evenness, commensurability, equality, excess, deficiency), and these belong to all numbers either intrinsically or in relation to each other (and similarly there are other special affections of what is solid, of what is immovable, of what is moving, of what is weightless, and of what has weight), so too there are certain special affections of being qua being and it is about these that it belongs to the philosopher to investigate the truth.

10

15

A sign of this is that dialecticians and sophists in fact cut the same figure as the philosopher; for sophistic is only apparently wisdom, and dialecti-
20   cians discuss all [these] things, and being is common to all [these], but clearly they discuss them because they properly belong to philosophy.⁶⁶⁸ So sophistic and dialectic are indeed concerned with the same kind as philosophy, but philosophy differs from dialectic in the way its capacity is employed, and from sophistic in the life it deliberately chooses; and dialec-
25   tic is examinational about the issues philosophy seeks to know about, while sophistic appears to be but is not.⁶⁶⁹

4.3

1005ᵇ5–25

5   So, it is clear that it belongs to the philosopher—that is, to the one who gets a theoretical grasp on the nature of all substance—also to investigate the starting-points of deductions. And it is fitting for the one who knows best about each kind to be able to state the most stable starting-points of his sub-
10   ject matter, and so when this is beings qua beings, the most stable starting-points of all things. And this person is the philosopher. But the most stable starting-point of all is the one it is impossible to be deceived about; for such a starting-point must be both the best known (for it is things that people do not know that they can all be fooled about) and unhypotheti-
cal.⁶⁷⁰ For a starting-point that must be possessed by anyone who is going
15   to apprehend any beings is no hypothesis. And what someone must know who knows anything at all, he must already possess. It is clear, then, that such a starting-point is the most stable of all.

What it is, however, we must next state. It is, that the same thing can-not at the same time belong and also not belong to the same thing and
20   in the same respect (and let us assume that we have also added as many other qualifications as might be needed to respond to logico-linguistic difficulties).⁶⁷¹ This, then, is the most stable of all starting-points; for it has the distinguishing feature that was mentioned. For it is impossible for anyone to take the same thing to be and not to be, as some people think
25   Heraclitus did.

7.4

1029^{b}1–1030^{b}13

Since at the start we determined in how many ways we define substance,   1029^{b}1
and of these one seemed to be the essence, we must get a theoretical grasp
on it.[672] And first let us say some things about it in a logico-linguistic way,
because the essence of each thing is what it is said to *be* intrinsically. For   13
the being for you is not the being for musical; for you are not intrinsically
musical.[673] [Your essence], therefore, is what you are [said to *be*] intrinsic-   15
ally. But not, certainly, all of this; for what is intrinsic in this way is not so
in the way that pale is to surface, because the being for a surface is not the
same as the being for pale. But neither is it the being that is composed of
both, the being for a pale surface. Why? Because surface itself is added.
Therefore, the account in which the thing itself is not present, but it itself is
said, this is the account of the essence for each thing.[674] And so if the being   20
for a pale surface is the being for a smooth surface, then the being for pale
and for smooth will be one and the same.

But since there are composites in accord with the other categories too
(for there is some underlying subject for each—for example, for the quality, the quantity, the time, the place, and the movement), whether there
is also an account of the essence for each of these must be investigated,   25
and whether the essence belongs to them as well—for example, to pale
human.[675] Let us, then, give this the name "cloak." What is the being for a
cloak? But then this is not one of the things said to *be* intrinsically either.
Or, are things said intrinsically *not to be* in two ways, one being from an
addition and the other not? For in one case what is being defined is said to   30
be by being added to another thing—for example, if someone defining the
being for pale were to state the account of pale human; in the other case,
what is being defined is said to *be* by another thing not being added to it—
for example, if cloak signified pale human, but someone were to define the
cloak as pale.[676] (The pale human is indeed something pale in that case, but
not, surely, what being for pale was.[677])   1030^{a}1

But [what about] the cloak? Is the being for it an essence at all? Or not?
For the essence is precisely what something is. But when one thing is said of
another, it is not precisely a this something—for example, the pale human
is not just a this something, if indeed the this belongs only to substances.[678]   5
And so there will be an essence only of those things whose account is a definition. We have a definition, however, not when a name and an account
signify the same thing (for then all the accounts would be definitions; for
there will be a name answering to any account whatever, so that even the
Iliad will be a definition), but when the account is of something primary;

10   and primary things are those that are said not by way of saying one thing
of another.⁶⁷⁹ Therefore, the essence will belong to things that are forms of
a kind and to nothing else (for these seem not to be said by way of participation and by way of being an affection, or in a coincidental way).⁶⁸⁰ But
there will be an account of each of the other things too and what it signi-
15   fies, [stating] if it is a name, that this belongs to this, or, instead of a simple account, a more exact one. There will not, however, be a definition or
an essence.

Or is something said to be the definition in many ways too, just like
the what-it-is? For in fact the what-it-is signifies in one way the substance
and the this something, and in another way it signifies each of the other
20   things that are predicated—quantity, quality, and the like. For just as *is* also
belongs to all of them, but not in the same way, but to one in a primary way
and to the others in a derivative one, so too the what-it-is belongs unconditionally to the substance and in a way to the others; for we can also ask
what quality is, and so quality too is something with a what-it-is—but not
unconditionally. Rather, just as in the case of what is not, some people say
25   in a logico-linguistic way that what is not is (not that it is unconditionally
but that it is what is not), so too with the quality.

We must, then, also investigate how we should speak about each of them,
but not more than how the thing in fact is. That is why now too, since what
is said is evident, it is also evident that the essence will belong in a similarly
primary and unconditional way to the substance, and derivatively to the
30   others, just as with the what-it-is—not the unconditional essence, but the
essence for a quality, or for a quantity. For it must either be homonymously
that we say that these things are beings, or by adding something or by subtracting something, just what is not scientifically known is scientifically
known, since what is correct, surely, is that they are said [to be] neither
homonymously nor in the same way, but as with medical, with reference
35   to one and the same thing—not saying one and the same thing, but not
1030^b1   speaking homonymously either; for a patient, a function, and an implement are said to be medical neither homonymously nor in accord with one
thing, but rather with reference to one thing.⁶⁸¹ But whichever of the two
ways we propose to say that these things [are beings] makes no difference.
This, however, is evident: that in the primary and unconditional way def-
5   inition and the essence belong to the substances. Not that they do not also
equally belong to the other things, except not in the primary way.

For it is not necessary, if we accept this view, for there to be a definition
of this sort whenever a name signifies the same thing as an account, but
rather the same thing as an account of a certain sort, and this occurs if it is
of something that is one—not by continuity, like the *Iliad*, and not in the

way in which things are one by being tied together, but one in the ways in   10
which things are said to be *one*.⁶⁸² But things are said to be *one* as they are
said to *be*, and being signifies, on the one hand, the this something and,
on the other hand, some quality or quantity. That is why there will be an
account of pale human and a definition, but in another way than there is of
pale and of substance.

7.17

1041ᵃ23–32

It is when something is [predicated] of something, then, that we inquire
about why it belongs to that thing (but that it does belong must be clear; for
if things are not that way, there is nothing to inquire about). For example,
"Why does it thunder?" is "Why is there noise in the clouds?" For this way   25
what we are inquiring about is one thing [predicated] of another. And why
are these—for example, brick and stones—a house? It is evident, accord-
ingly, that we are inquiring about the cause. This (one might almost say)
logico-linguistically is the essence. But in some cases it is what the thing is
for the sake of (for example, it is presumably this in the case of a house or
a bed), and in some it is what first initiated the movement; for this is also
a cause. But the latter is inquired about in cases of something's coming to   30
be and passing away, while the former is inquired about also in the case of
a thing's being.

11.3

1061ᵇ8–11

Dialectic and sophistry, on the other hand, although they are concerned
with the coincidents of things, are not concerned with them qua beings, or
with being itself, insofar as it is being. And so it remains that it is the philosopher who is capable of theorizing about the things mentioned, insofar   10
as they are being.

12.1

1069ᵃ25–30

The early philosophers also in effect testify to this; for it was substance that
they were inquiring about the principles, elements, and starting-points of.
Present-day thinkers, to be sure, posit the universals as substances to a
higher degree (for the kinds are universal, and these they say are starting-
points and substances to a higher degree, because they inquire in a logico-
linguistic way), while thinkers of olden days [posit] the particulars, such
as, fire and earth, as substances, but not what is common: body.

13.4

1078ᵇ17–30

Socrates, on the other hand, busied himself about the virtues of character,
and in connection with these was the first to inquire about universal definition (for among the physicists Democritus latched onto this only a little,
and defined, after a fashion, the hot and the cold, while the Pythagoreans
had previously done this for a few things, whose accounts they connected
to numbers—for example, what opportune is, or the just, or marriage).[683]
It was reasonable, though, that Socrates was inquiring about the what-it-is;
for he was inquiring in order to deduce, and the what-it-is is a starting-
point of deductions; for at that time there was not yet the strength in
dialectic that enables people, even separately from the what-it-is, to investigate contraries, and whether the same science is a science of contraries;
for there are two things that may be fairly ascribed to Socrates—inductive
arguments and universal definition, both of which are concerned with a
starting-point of scientific knowledge.[684]

13.5

1080ᵃ2–11

In the *Phaedo*, however, it is said in this way: the Forms are causes both
of the being and of the coming to be of things.[685] But even if the Forms do
exist, things would still not come to be unless there was a moving cause.
Also, many other things come to be—for example, a house or a ring—of
which they say there are no Forms. And so it is clear that it is also possible
for the things of which they say there are Forms both to be and to come to

be through the same causes as the things we mentioned just now, but not because of the Forms. But in the case of the Forms it is possible, both in this way and by more logico-linguistic and more exact arguments, to collect 10 many objections like those we considered.[686]

6.13

1144^b30–1145^a2

30 It is clear, then, from what we have said, that it is neither possible to be fully good without practical wisdom nor practically wise without virtue of character. Moreover, in this way we can also resolve the argument by which someone might contend dialectically that the virtues are separate from each other; for the same person is not naturally well disposed in the highest degree concerning all of them, so that he will at some point have
35 acquired one when he has not yet acquired another. In the case of the natural virtues, indeed, this is possible, but in the case of those in accord with which someone is called "unconditionally good," it is not possible; for at the
1145^a1 same time as the one, practical wisdom, is present, they will all be present.

7.1

1145^b2–7

We must, as in the other cases, set out the things that appear to be so and first go through the puzzles, and in that way prove preferably all the acceptable beliefs about these affections, or if not all of them, then most of them,
5 and the most authoritative ones; for if the objections are resolved and the acceptable beliefs are left standing, that would be an adequate proof.

7.2

1146^a21–27

Further, a certain sophistical argument constitutes a puzzle; for because [sophists] wish to refute people in unacceptable ways, in order to be clever when they engage in argumentative encounters, the resulting deduction turns into a puzzle; for thought is tied up when it does not wish to stand
25 still, because what has been concluded is not pleasing, but cannot move forward, because of its inability to resolve the argument.[687]

9.1

1164ª27–33

It makes perfect sense that those who get the money first and then do none of the things they said they would do, because of the extreme nature of their promises, are subject to complaint; for they do not deliver what they agreed to. This, however, is what the sophists are presumably compelled to do, because no one would pay them money for what they do scientifically know. So they take the wage, do not do what they said, and—as makes perfect sense—get involved in complaints.

30

EUDEMIAN ETHICS

1.8

$1217^b14-1218^b24$

So the good itself is the Form of the good; and it is indeed separable from
its participants, just as is also the case for the other Forms. To investigate
this belief fully, then, belongs to another sort of occasion, that is, to one
that of necessity is in many ways more logico-linguistic (for arguments that
are at once both destructive and common are in accord with no other science). But if one must speak succinctly about these issues, let us say, first,
that to speak of there being a Form not only of good but of anything else
whatever is to speak in a logico-linguistic and empty way.

. . .

Further, no one proves that health is good, unless he is not a doctor but a
sophist (for they are the ones who produce sophistries by using alien arguments), any more than he proves any other starting-point whatever.

2.3

1221^a38-^b9

A person is envious by being pained at more cases of others' doing well
than one should (for the envious are pained even by the doing well of
those who deserve to do well); the person who is the contrary is more
nameless, but is the one who is excessive by not being pained even at
those who are undeservedly doing well; he is tolerant, like a glutton
toward nourishment, while the other is intolerant in accord with his envy.
It is superfluous to define in each case that the relationship not be coincidental; for no other science, whether theoretical or productive, whether
in its arguments or its actions, adds this to its definitions. Instead it is
a response to the sophistries of the craftsmen of logico-linguistic arguments. Let us define them, then, simply in this way, but do so more exactly
when we speak about the opposite states.

15

20

40

1221ᵇ1

5

7.6

1240^b21–26

A good person does not reproach himself at once either, like the one who lacks control, nor does his later self reproach his earlier self, like the person who is full of regrets, nor his earlier self his later one, like the person who makes a false promise (in general, if one must draw the distinctions the sophists draw, it is like Coriscus and excellent Coriscus; for it is clear that their quantity of excellence is the same).

5.8

$1370^{b}30-40$

30   In well-mixed constitutions, then, just as care should above all be taken to ensure that no one breaks the law in other ways, small [violations] should be especially guarded against; for illegality creeps in unnoticed, in just the way that property gets used up by frequent small expenditures. The expense goes unnoticed because it does not occur all at once; for thought is

35   led to reason fallaciously by them, as in the sophistical argument, "if each is small, so too are all." In one way this is true; in another false; for the whole and the totality of parts is not small, but it is composed of small parts. One thing to guard against, then, is destruction that has a starting-point of this sort.

RHETORIC

1.1

1354ª1–1355ᵇ21

Rhetoric is the counterpart of dialectic; for both are concerned with such 1354ª1 common things as are, in a way, known to all and belong to no definite science.[688] That is why all, in a way, share in both; for to a certain extent all try both to examine and to uphold an argument as well as to defend someone 5 and accuse someone. Now among ordinary people, some do these things extemporaneously, others due to a state acquired by habit.[689] But since both ways are possible, it is clear that the same things could be done in a methodical way; for it is possible to get a theoretical grasp on the cause due to which some succeed because of habit and others because of chance; and getting such a grasp, all would immediately agree, is the function of 10 a craft.[690]

. . .

It is evident, however, that the methodical inquiry that is within the province of craft is concerned with the means of persuasion. And a means of persuasion is a sort of demonstration; for we are most persuaded when 5 we take something to have been demonstrated. And a rhetorical demonstration is an enthymeme; and this is (one might almost say) unconditionally the most controlling means of persuasion. And an enthymeme is a sort of deduction. And it belongs to dialectic, either as a whole or to one of its parts, to see about every sort of deduction. And since all that is so, it is clear that the person who is best able to get a theoretical grasp on the materials 10 on the basis of which, and the manner in which, a deduction comes about is also the one who is most competent in the use of enthymemes, when he also grasps what sorts of things an enthymeme is concerned with and what sorts of differences there are between it and logico-linguistic deductions; for it belongs to the same capacity to see the truth and what is like the truth, and at the same time human beings are naturally adequate as regards 15 the truth and in most cases hit upon it.[691] That is why the capacity to aim at and hit upon the acceptable beliefs belongs to the person who has a similar capacity with regard to the truth.

. . .

Further, not even the possession of the most exact scientific knowledge would make it easy for us in speaking to persuade some listeners on the

25 basis of it; for argument in accord with scientific knowledge is proper to
teaching, but teaching is impossible [in their case]. Instead, it is necessary
to produce our means of persuasion and arguments out of common things,
as we said in the *Topics* about encounters with ordinary people.[692]

Further, one should be capable of persuading people of contraries, just
30 as in the case of [dialectical] deductions, not so as to do both in action (for
one should not persuade people of base things), but in order that it not
escape our notice how things stand, and, if someone else uses arguments
in an unjust way, so as to be able to refute them for ourselves. None of the
other crafts deduces contraries; dialectic and rhetoric alone do this; for
35 both are alike concerned with contraries. To be sure the underlying things
at issue are not alike. On the contrary, true and better ones are always by
nature more easily deduced and unconditionally more persuasive.

. . .

It is evident, then, that rhetoric does not deal with a definite kind, but
is like dialectic, and that it is useful, and that its function is not to per-
10 suade but to see the persuasive factors belonging in each case, just as in
all the other crafts; for it is not the function of medicine to produce health
either, but rather to promote health as far as possible; for even to those
who are incapable of partaking in health it is nonetheless possible to give
good treatment.[693] In addition, it is evident that it is a function of the same
15 craft to see what is persuasive and what is apparently persuasive, just as in
the case of dialectic it is to see the deduction and the apparent deduction;
for sophistic is what it is in virtue not of its capacity but of the deliberate
choice.[694] Here, in the case of rhetoric, however, one person is an orator in
virtue of his scientific knowledge, another in virtue of his deliberate choice,
whereas there, in dialectic, a sophist is so called in virtue of his deliberate
20 choice, and a dialectician is so called not in virtue of his deliberate choice,
but in virtue of the capacity he has.[695]

1.2

1356ª25–1358ª35

25 Rhetoric is a sort of offshoot of dialectic and of work in ethics, which it is right
to call "politics."[696] That is why rhetoric cuts the same figure as politics, as do
those who pretend to a knowledge of it—some through lack of educatedness,
some through boastfulness, and some through other human causes.[697] For it
30 is a part of dialectic, and similar to it, as we also said at the start; for neither of
them is the science of how things stand with some definite [kind], but rather
both are capacities concerned with providing arguments.[698]

About their capacities themselves, then, and how they stand in relation to each other, pretty much enough has been said.

In cases of persuasion that operate through proving or appearing to prove something, just as in dialectical ones there is induction, deduction, and apparent deduction, so it is like that here as well; for a paradigm is an induction, and an enthymeme a deduction, and an apparent enthymeme an apparent deduction. I call a rhetorical deduction an "enthymeme," and a rhetorical induction a "paradigm." And everyone produces means of persuasion through proving something by means either of paradigms or of enthymemes, and of nothing beyond these. So, if indeed it is, in general, necessary to prove anything whatever either by deduction or by induction (and this is clear to us from the *Analytics*), it necessarily follows that enthymemes and paradigms are, respectively, the same as deductions and inductions.[699]

The difference between a paradigm and an enthymeme is evident from the *Topics* (for there deduction and induction were spoken about previously), namely, that to prove on the basis of many similar cases that things are a certain way is an induction in dialectic and a paradigm in rhetoric, whereas to prove that if some things are so, something beyond them follows by their being so, whether universally or for the most part, is called in dialectic a "deduction" and in rhetoric an "enthymeme."[700]

. . .

Since the persuasive is persuasive to someone (and is either immediately persuasive and convincing by itself or seems to be proved by such things), and since no craft investigates what is particular (for example, medicine does not investigate what is healthy for Socrates or Callias but for a person of such-and-such a sort or for persons of such-and-such a sort—for this is in the province of craft, whereas what is particular is unlimited and is not scientifically knowable), rhetoric does not get a theoretical grasp on a particular acceptable belief either (for example, one persuasive to Socrates or to Hippias) but on one persuasive to people of such-and-such a sort, just as in the case of dialectic.[701]

For even dialectic does not deduce from random things (for even to crazy people some things appear to be so) but from things [that appear to be so] to those in need of argument, as rhetoric does from things [that appear to be so] to those already accustomed to deliberate among themselves. But rhetoric's function is concerned with the sorts of things we deliberate about and have no crafts for, and in the presence of such listeners as are not capable of getting a comprehensive view of many or of rational calculation from a distant [starting-point].[702]

. . .

1358ᵃ1   There is a very great difference among enthymemes, however, that has
escaped the notice of pretty much everyone, even though the very same difference is also found in the dialectical methodical investigation of deductions; for some enthymemes are in accord with rhetoric, just as some are in
5   accord with the dialectical methodical investigation of deductions, while
others are in accord with the other crafts and capacities, whether those in
existence or those not yet acquired. That is why the difference escapes the
notice of the listeners, and the more they grasp in accord with a mode [of
inquiry], the more they stray beyond these [namely, rhetoric or dialectic].
This will be more perspicuous if stated in more detail.⁷⁰³

10   For I mean that dialectical and rhetorical deductions are those concerned with what we call "topics," which are common when they concern
what is just, what is natural, what is political, and many things that differ
in form—for example, the topic of the more and the less; for it is no less
15   possible to state a deduction or an enthymeme based on it about matters
of justice than it is about matters of natural science, or about anything else
whatever, even though these things differ in form.⁷⁰⁴ Special topics, on the
other hand, are the ones based on premises concerning a given form and
kind. For example, there are premises concerning natural things on which
neither an enthymeme nor a deduction can be based concerning ethical
things, and about the latter there are others on which none can be based
20   concerning natural ones. And the same holds in all cases. The common
topics will not make someone wise about any kind; for they are not concerned with any underlying subject.⁷⁰⁵ But as to the special ones, the better
someone is at selecting premises, [the more] he will—without noticing it—
produce a science that is distinct from dialectic and rhetoric; for if he hits
25   upon starting-points, it will no longer be dialectic or rhetoric, but instead
will be that science whose starting-points he possesses.⁷⁰⁶

And yet most enthymemes are based on these, the so-called forms, the
ones that are particular and special, fewer on the common topics. As in the
Topics, then, so also here a distinction must be made between the forms and
30   the topics, on the basis of which enthymemes are selected.⁷⁰⁷ By "forms" I
mean the premises special to a given kind, and by "topics" those equally
common to all.⁷⁰⁸ We may begin, then, with the form. But let us first take
up the kinds of rhetoric, so that having determined how many they are, we
35   may separately take up their elements and premises.

1.4

1359ᵇ2–16

Now to enumerate particular by particular in an exact way and divide into kinds the things that people are accustomed to deliberate about in public, or to define them, as far as is possible where they are concerned, in accord with the truth, is not an inquiry we should undertake at the present moment, because this is not a matter for the craft of rhetoric—to which many more things than the ones within its own proper theoretical grasp are at present assigned—but for a more thought-involving and more truth-focused one; for precisely what we said previously is true, namely, that rhetoric is composed of the science of analytics and the [part of] politics concerned with ethics, and is like dialectic, on the one hand, and sophistical arguments, on the other.[709] And to the extent that someone tries to establish dialectic or rhetoric not just as capacities but as sciences, to that extent he will—without noticing it—obscure their nature by the change, reestablishing them as sciences of certain underlying things, rather than only of arguments.

Notes

TOPICS, BOOK 1: DIALECTIC

Note 1

The proposed aim: Compare *SE* 183ª37–ᵇ1.

Methodical inquiry: (1) "In all methodical inquiries in which there is knowledge—
that is, scientific knowledge—of things that have starting-points, causes, or elements, it comes from knowledge of these" (*Ph.* 184ª1–3). (2) "Regarding every
sort of theoretical knowledge and every methodical inquiry, the more humble and
more estimable alike, there appear to be two ways for the state to be, one that
may be well described as scientific knowledge of the subject matter, the other a
certain sort of educatedness" (*PA* 639ª1–4). With exception of *Cael.*, all Aristotle's
treatises are self-described as methodical inquiries; see *APr.* 46ª32, *Top.* 100ª18,
SE 172ᵇ8, *Ph.* 200ᵇ13, *GC* 370ª30, *Mete.* 338ª25, *DA* 402ª16, *HA* 491ª12, *PA* 642ᵇ3,
GA 742ᵇ10, *Met.* 983ª23, *EE* 1214ª14, *NE* 1094ᵇ11, *Pol.* 1260ᵇ35, *Rh.* 1355ᵇ22,
1410ᵇ8, *Po.* 1447ª12.

Problem: Retaining προβλήματος. See 104ᵇ1–17.

Note 2

Demonstration: 101ª6n6.

Knowledge: Although there may be little difference between *gnôsis* (verb,
gignôskein), used here, and *epistêmê* (verb, *epistasthai*), *epistêmê* is usually applied
only to demonstrative sciences, crafts, or other bodies of systematic knowledge, so
that *epistêmê* is specifically *scientific* knowledge. *Gnôsis* is also used for perceptual
knowledge and knowledge by acquaintance—something familiar is *gnôrimos*.

Note 3

Starting-points: An *archê* ("starting-point," "first principle") is a primary cause:
"This is what it is for something to be a starting-point, that it is itself the cause of
many things, with nothing above it being a cause of it" (*GA* 788ª14–16).

Intrinsically: Something is intrinsically (*kath' hauto*) F or F "all by itself," in its
own right, or (Latin) *per se* if it is F unconditionally, or because of what F itself
essentially is. Thus Socrates is intrinsically rational, since being rational is part of
being human and Socrates is essentially human, but he is not intrinsically musical,
since being musical is not part of what it is to be human.

Note 4

What appear to be: *Phainomena* are things that appear (often to perception) to be so, but that may or may not be so. The corresponding verb *phainesthai* when used with a participle endorses what appears to be so and is translated "it is evident that," or "it is seen to be that," or the like, but when used with an infinitive it neither endorses nor rejects what appears to be so and is translated "appears." When it occurs without a participle or an infinitive, it may either endorse or reject.

Note 5

Contentious arguments: *SE* 171^{b}32–33.

Note 6

Fallacies . . . : *SE* 171^{b}11–22, 171^{b}34–172^{a}11.

Sciences: To understand what an Aristotelian science is, we must begin with the sorts of statements or propositions that figure as premises and conclusions within it.

(1) A *statement* (*logos apophantikos*) is the true (or false) predication of a single predicate term A of a single subject term B, either as an affirmation (*kataphasis*) (A belongs to B) or a denial (*apophasis*) (A does not belong to B) (*Int.* 5, 8). What makes a term a single subject term, however, is not that it is grammatically singular or serves as a grammatical subject but that it designates a substantial particular—a canonical example of which is a perceptible matter-form compound, such as Socrates. Similarly, what makes a term a predicate is that it designates a universal (man, pale)—something that can have many particular instances. When the role of predicate is restricted to universals, therefore, while that of subject is left open to both particulars and universals, it is more on ontological or metaphysical grounds than on what we would consider strictly logical ones. Subjects and predicates are thus ontological items, types of beings, rather than linguistic or conceptual ones, and logical principles, such as the principle of non-contradiction, are very general ontological principles, truths about all beings as such, or qua beings. Particular affirmations (Socrates is a man) and general affirmations (Men are mortal) have the same subject-predicate form, but when the subject is a universal, the affirmation may itself be either universal (All men are mortal) or particular (Some men are mortal)—that is to say, the predicate may be asserted (or denied) of the subject either universally (*katholou*) or in part (*kata meros*) or, if the quantifier is omitted (Men are mortal), indeterminately (*adihoristos*). Affirmations, as a result, are of four types: A belongs to all B (**a**AB), A belongs to no B (**e**AB), A belongs to some B (**i**AB), A does not belong to all B (**o**AB).

(2) A *science*, whether theoretical, practical, or productive, is a state of the soul that enables its possessor to give demonstrative explanations—where a *demonstration* (*apodeixis*) is a special sort of deduction (*sullogismos*) from scientific starting-points and a deduction is "an argument in which, certain things having been supposed, something different from those supposed things necessarily results because of their being so" (*APr.* 24^{b}18–20). The things supposed are the argument's premises; the necessitated result is its conclusion; each is an affirmation

of one of the four types we looked at. In Aristotle's view, such deductions are *syl-logisms* (*sullogismos*, again), which consist of a major premise, a minor premise, and a conclusion, where the premises have exactly one "middle" term in common, and the conclusion contains only the other two "extreme" terms. The conclusion's predicate term is the *major term*, contributed by the major premise; its subject is the *minor term*, contributed by the minor premise. The middle term must be either subject of both premises, predicate of both, or subject of one and predicate of the other. The resulting possible combinations of terms yield the so-called figures of the syllogism:

	First Figure		Second Figure		Third Figure	
	Predicate	Subject	Predicate	Subject	Predicate	Subject
Premise	A	B	A	B	A	C
Premise	B	C	A	C	B	C
Conclusion	A	C	B	C	A	B

Systematic investigation of the possible combinations of premises in each of these figures results in the identification of the *moods* or modes that constitute valid deductions. In the first figure, these are as follows:

Form	Mnemonic	Proof
aAB, aBC | aAC	Barbara	Perfect
eAB, aBC | eAC	Celarent	Perfect
aAB, iBC | iAC	Darii	Perfect
eAB, iBC | oAC	Ferio	Perfect

A mood is perfect when there is a proof of its validity that is *direct*, in that it does not rely on the validity of any other mood. Only first figure syllogisms have perfect moods.

(3) Besides their logical interest as admitting of direct proof, perfect syllogisms in Barbara are also of particular importance to science. First, because "of the [syllogistic] figures, the first is most scientific" (*APo.* 79^{a}17–18). Second, "only through this figure is it possible to hunt down scientific knowledge of the what-it-is" (79^{a}24–25): essences hold universally, only perfect syllogisms in Barbara have universal conclusions, and definitions of essences, which are scientific starting-points, must hold universally.

(4) Specifically *scientific starting-points* are of just three types (*APo.* 76^{a}37–^{b}22). Those *special* to a science are definitions of the real (as opposed to nominal) essences of the beings with which the science deals (90^{b}24, 93^{b}29–94^{a}19). Because these are definitions by kind and difference (96^{a}20–97^{b}39), a single science must deal with a single kind (75^{b}10–11, 84^{b}17–18, 87^{a}38–39). Other starting-points (so-called axioms) are common to all or many sciences (72^{a}14–24, 88^{a}36–^{b}3). A third sort of starting-point posits the existence of the kind with which the science deals, but this may often be left implicit if the existence of the kind is clear (76^{b}17–18).

The source of these starting-points, in turn, is perception and experience, which lead by induction, to a grasp of them by understanding (100ª3–9).

(5) To constitute a *demonstration* a deduction must be a valid syllogism in the mood Barbara, whose premises meet a number of conditions. First, they must be immediate or indemonstrable, and so must be reached through induction. Second, our confidence in them must be unsurpassed (*APo.* 72ª37–ᵇ4). Finally, they must be necessary (and so, of course, true) in a special sense: the predicates in them must belong to the subjects in every case, intrinsically, and universally (73ª24–27).

(5a) *In every case:* A predicate A belongs to every subject B if and only if there is no B to which it fails to belong and no time at which it fails to belong to a B: "for example, if animal belongs to every man, then if it is true to say that this thing is a man, it is also true to say that it is an animal, and if the former is the case now, the latter is also the case now" (73ª29–31).

(5b) *Intrinsically:* A predicate A belongs intrinsically to a subject B just in case it is related to B in one of four ways: (i) A is in the account or definition of what B is, or of B's substance, or essence (73ª34–37); (ii) B is a complex subject φB_1, where φ is an intrinsic coincident of B_1—for example, odd number or male or female animal—and A is in the definition of φB_1's essence; (iii) A just is B's essence; (iv) A is not a part of B's essence or identical to it but stems causally from it, so that being B is an intrinsic cause of being A (73ª34–ᵇ24).

(5c) *Universally:* A predicate A belongs to a subject B universally just in case "it belongs to it in every case and intrinsically, that is, insofar as the thing is itself" (73ᵇ26–27).

(6) Because intrinsic predicates stem in various ways from essences, the subjects to which they belong must have essences. In other words, they must be *intrinsic beings*, since—stemming as they do from essences—intrinsic predicates identify or make them clear: "The things said to *be* intrinsically are the very ones signified by the figures of predication" (*Met.* 1017ª22–23). These figures of predication are the so-called *categories* (*Top.* 103ᵇ7–25). For each of the intrinsic beings in these ten categories we can state its what-it-is (*Met.* 1030ª17–24), even if strictly speaking only substances have definitions and essences (1031ª7–24). Specifying these beings is one of the tasks of the *Categories*, where Aristotle explains how beings in categories other than that of substance are ontologically dependent on those in the category of substance.

(7) What all four types of intrinsic beings have in common, what makes them worth the attention of someone inquiring into ultimate starting-points and causes, is that they are the ontological correlates or truth-makers for scientific theorems—the beings responsible for the necessary truth of those theorems. Moreover, they would seem to be the only sorts of being that can play this role, since they constitute an exhaustive catalog of the necessary relations that can hold between a subject (A) and something (B) predicated of it: B is part of the essence of A; A is part of the essence of B; B is the essence of A; the essence of A (being A) is an intrinsic cause of (being) B.

Note 7
False diagrams: *SE* 171ᵇ12–16n479.

Note 8
Premises: 156ᵃ21n361.

Note 9
Forms: Aristotle uses the term *eidos* (always "form" in the translation) to refer to the forms of a *genos* (always "kind"), to form (as opposed to matter), and to a separate Platonic Form. But he also uses both it and *genos* in a more general sense in which there is little or no difference between them.

Note 10
Philosophical sciences: Introduction, pp. xxxiv–xxxviii.

Note 11
Argue dialectically: The verb *epicheirein* usually means "attack" in the *Topics*, but here, as elsewhere, it covers both attacking and defending, and is better translated as "argue dialectically."

Note 12
Ordinary people: Sometimes Aristotle uses *hoi polloi* (literally, "the many," "the multitude") to refer simply to a majority of people of whatever sort—to most people. But quite often, as here, he uses it somewhat pejoratively to refer to the vulgar masses (*NE* 1095ᵇ16) in contrast to cultivated, sophisticated, or wise people (1095ᵃ21). "Ordinary people" often seems to convey the correct sense.
Changing their minds: For a different sense of the verb *metabibazein*, see 161ᵃ33–36.

Note 13
Go through the puzzles: The process is described at *NE* 1145ᵇ2–7 (p. 216).

Note 14
Stand outside and examine: The adjective *exetastikos* occurs only here and at *Po.* 1455ᵃ34 (where it means "excitable") in Aristotle. The verb *exetazein*, which is used more frequently, often simply means to "examine" or "audit" political officials (for example, *Pol.* 1271ᵇ14). Deriving from that sense of the verb, the adjective *exetastikos* occurs at ††*Rh. Al.* 1421ᵇ10 applied to a sort of political speech. Here, however, context favors preserving something of the former sense, since dialectic provides a route toward the starting-points of all methodical inquiries precisely because it stands outside them, and so does not rely on their starting-points.

Note 15
Other capacities of this sort: Often, as here, crafts or sciences are lumped together with capacities as things that can be used to achieve opposite effects, as medicine can be used to cure but also to kill (*NE* 1129ᵃ13–14).

Note 16

He possesses the science adequately: "It is not the function of medicine to produce health . . . , but rather to promote health as far as possible" (*Rh.* 1355ᵇ12–13).

Note 17

Get a theoretical grasp on: The verb *theasthai*, with which *theôria* is cognate,
means "look at" or "gaze at." So *theôria* itself is sometimes what someone is doing in
looking closely at something, or observing, studying, or contemplating it. *Theôria*
can thus be an exercise of understanding (*nous*), which is the element responsible
for grasping scientific starting-points (*NE* 1141ᵃ7–8), such as (the definition of)
right angle in the case of geometry, or (the definition of) happiness in the case of
politics. Hence the cognate verb *theôrein* sometimes means "to be actively understanding" or "to be actively contemplating" something. "Get a theoretical grasp
on" often seems to convey the right sense.

Note 18

What we proposed: 101ᵇ5–6.

Note 19

Premises: A *protasis* is both a proposition and a premise in a deduction or argument. In the text, it is uniformly translated as "premise."

Note 20

Indicates: The verb *dêloun* means "make clear," "make known," "disclose," "reveal,"
and is used as an equivalent of *sêmainein* ("signify"). "Indicates" seems to capture
the intended meaning in *Top.* and *SE.*
Coincident: Aristotle standardly contrasts what has an affection B coincidentally
or contingently (*kata sumbebêkos* or *per accidens* in Latin) and what has B intrinsically or non-contingently (*kath' hauto* or *per se*). But he also recognizes a hybrid
class of *kath' hauta sumbebêkota*—intrinsic coincidents or *per se* accidents—that
belong to a subject intrinsically, and thus demonstrably, but are not part of its
ousia, or essence (*Apo.* 75ᵇ1, 83ᵇ19). These are contrasted with coincidents proper,
which belong to a subject contingently, and so non-demonstrably, which are
defined at *Top.* 102ᵇ4–26.

Note 21

Let us divide what is special . . . : To these we may add a *popular* sense of the term,
in which A is special to B if and only if A always accompanies B and belongs to B
alone (122ᵃ22–28, 131ᵇ8–9). A further, *temporal*, sense gives us now-special affections (131ᵇ5), where A is a now-special affection of B if and only if at the time that
is now, A is a popular special affection of B.
The essence: *To ti ên einai* is a phrase of Aristotle's coinage, literally meaning "the
what it was to be," of which "essence," from the Latin verb *esse* ("to be"), is the
standard translation.

Signifies: Aristotle uses the verb *sêmainein* and the cognate noun *sêmeion* to express (1) a relation between a linguistic element, such as a noun or name, and the thing it signifies, means, or denotes, but also, as here, (2) a relation between two non-linguistic elements. It is not always clear, therefore, whether quotation marks should or should not be supplied.

Definition: Definition is defined at *Top.* 101^{b}38 with important additions at 103^{b}15–16.

Note 22

Let no one suppose . . . : Because unlike a definition, a special affection, and the rest, "a premise, then, is a sentence that affirms or denies something of something" (*APr.* 24^{a}16–17; also *APo.* 72^{a}8–9).

Note 23

Said in this way . . . it is a premise: That is, a question generated by a premise in the questioner's background dialectical deduction.

Said in this way . . . it becomes a problem: That is, what the questioner and answerer are disagreeing about.

Note 24

Name: An *onoma* is not always what we call a "name," but a word more generally, or—when contrasted with a verb—a noun: "An *onoma* is a composite significant voiced sound, without a reference to time, the parts of which are not significant by themselves; for in double names we do not use any part as significant by itself—for example, in 'Theodorus,' 'dorus' is not significant. A verb is a composite significant voiced sound, involving a reference to time, the parts of which are not significant by themselves, just as in the case of names; for 'human being' or 'white' does not signify a time, while 'walks or 'walked' additionally signify, in the one case, the present time, in the other, the past" (*Po.* 1457^{a}10–18). A name signifies an account or (in some cases) a definition (*Met.* 1012^{a}22–24, 1045^{a}26) of the form (1035^{a}21) or essence (1029^{b}20) of the thing named.

Note 25

A special affection is one that . . . [1] belongs to that thing alone and [2] is counterpredicated (*antikatêgoreitai*) **of it:** [1] means A belongs to all B and only to B. It is omitted at 103^{b}11–12, 132^{a}4–9, 133^{a}5–11, but reappears at 155^{a}26–27. Notice, however, 102^{a}22–23: "no one would say that something is a special affection if it admits of belonging to something else." [2] B is counterpredicated of A if and only if A is predicated of B and B of A.

Note 26

Unconditionally: The adjective *haplous* means "simple" or "single-fold." The adverb *haplôs* thus points in two somewhat opposed directions. (1) To speak *haplôs* sometimes means, as here, to put things simply or in general terms, so that qualifications and conditions will need to be added later. (2) Sometimes to be F *haplôs* means to be F unconditionally, or in a way that allows for no ifs, ands, or buts (115^{b}29–35). In this sense, some things that are F *haplôs* are F in the strictest, most absolute, and most unqualified way (*Met.* 1015^{b}11–12), so that what is unconditionally F is what is intrinsically F (*NE* 1151^{b}2–3).

Note 27
A kind . . . : A definition signifies the essence of something, and so says what it is, by specifying its kind and difference, the latter of which divides the kind into forms.
The what-it-is: 103^{b}22n42.

Note 28
Animal is the kind of human: Noun phrases consisting of the definite article plus a noun ("The N") are ambiguous (homonymous) in English, as their corresponding ones are in Greek: they can be either singular terms referring to unique particulars ("The dog bit me") or generic terms ("The bat is a nocturnal creature"). Aristotle is aware of this: "Something is said to be the circle homonymously, [since the term is applied] both to the one said to be such unconditionally and to the particular one" (*Met.* 1035^{b}1–3). Here *tou anthrôpou* is clearly a generic noun phrase.

Note 29
To what is under definition: Reading τῷ ὑπὸ τὸν ὁρισμόν.

Note 30
The account given previously: 102^{a}9–10.

Note 31
Lacking in perspicuousness: 111^{a}8–9 offers "perspicuous" as an equivalent of "exact." It is this, it seems, that justifies the confident claim here: "It is characteristic of a well-educated person to look for the degree of exactness in each kind of investigation that the nature of the subject itself allows; for it is evident that accepting persuasive arguments from a mathematician is like demanding demonstrations from a rhetorician" (*NE* 1094^{b}23–27). Thus to seek a single methodical inquiry applicable to problems or premises (and so arguments) involving a special affection, a kind, a coincident, or a definition, would be to make an uneducated mistake about the level of exactness, and so of perspicuousness, appropriate in dialectic. On *akribeia* in science, see *Top.* 157^{a}9n368.

Note 32
Each of the kinds we have distinguished: That is, the four kinds of problems or premises, involving either a definition, a special affection, a kind, or a coincident, on which dialectical arguments are based. See 101^{b}13–19.

Note 33
The ones we mentioned . . . : That is, the things akin to definition (102^a5–10) that get assigned to the kind *definition*; the things special but not unconditionally so (102^a24–26) that get assigned to the kind *special affection*; and the comparisons that derive from coincidents (102^b15–16) that get assigned to the kind *coincident*. See also 103^a14–23.

Note 34
The number of ways in which things are said to be the same: Also 152^b30–33, *Met.* 1017^b26–1018^a15, 1054^a32–$^b3$.

Note 35
The strictest and primary way . . . : What numerical sameness is assigned to is cape or human. And what it is numerically the same as is in the one case given by the name assigned to it ("cloak"), so that cape is numerically the same as cloak, and in the other by the definition assigned to it ("two-footed terrestrial animal"), so that human is numerically the same as two-footed terrestrial animal. Note that human and cape are universals, not particulars: (1) "Definition is of the universal" (*Met.* 1036^a28–29). (2) "Particulars cannot be defined" (1040^a7).

Note 36
As was said: 103^a7–8.

Note 37
Means of persuasion: Ideally, a *pistis* is "a sort of demonstration" (*Rh.* 1355^a5), but actual *pisteis* need not be: "*pisteis* come about not only through demonstrative argument but also through argument expressive of character" (1366^a9–10). Indeed, only some *pisteis* "proceed through speech" (1356^a1) or "through proving" (1356^a35–36) at all. At a minimum, though, *pisteis* are persuasive items—items productive of conviction (another meaning of *pistis*).

Note 38
We saw: 102^a18–22.

Note 39
Underlying subject: In addition to being, as here, (1) a subject of predication, and (2) what underlies or persists through every change whether in affections or in the coming to be or passing away (*Ph.* 191^a13–$^b10$, *Met.* 1042^a32–$^b6$), a *hupokeimenon* can be (3) the subject matter of a science or body of knowledge (*NE* 1094^b12).

Note 40
A definition is composed . . . : "There is nothing else in the definition except the kind that is mentioned first and the differences" (*Met.* 1037^b29–30). Since the differences entail the kind, and each is the difference of a preceding difference,

"the ultimate difference will be the substance of the thing and its definition" (1038ª19–20).

Note 41
A coincident was said to be: 102ᵇ4–5.
What is neither a definition . . . : Differences are not explicitly mentioned, presumably because the one difference that is included in the definition, since it is an ultimate one, and entails the kind, has to be a special affection of the kind.

Note 42
What-it-is: When we ask, *Ti esti A*?, we are asking, What is A? The correct answer defines or indicates the what-it-is of A, or—a related notion—the being (*einai*) for A, or—another related notion—the essence of A (101ᵇ19n21), or—yet another related notion—the substance of A (103ᵇ28n43). Any intrinsic being, regardless of its category, has a what-it-is: "For in fact the what-it-is signifies in one way the substance and the this something, and in another way it signifies each of the other things that are predicated—quantity, quality, and the like. . . . ; for we can also ask what quality is, and so quality too is something with a what-it-is" (*Met.* 1030ª18–24).

Note 43
Substance: *Ousia* is a noun that is perhaps formed from the present participle *ousa* of the verb *einai* ("to be"). "Substance" is the traditional translation. (1) The substance of something (the sense relevant here) is its what-it-is or essence. (2) A substance, on the other hand, is a *tode ti* (a "this something")—an ultimate subject of predication, of which a particular human or a particular horse are examples.

Note 44
Dialectical premise: *APr.* 24ª22–28 (p. 197).

Note 45
Unacceptable: What is *paradoxos* is not what is paradoxical in our sense of the term but what is contrary to or goes against (*para*) beliefs (*doxa*), especially acceptable beliefs (*endoxa*). It is typically sophists who try to "refute people in unacceptable ways" (*NE* 1146ª21–24).

Note 46
Contraries: 1.14.
By way of contradiction: "Affirmation" and "denial" are *kataphasis* (or *phasis*) and *apophasis*. If X affirms that A is B and Y denies that A is B (by affirming A is not B), then what Y affirms is the contradictory (*antiphasis*) of what A affirms.
Established crafts: Here, as often, the term *technê* is being used as equivalent in meaning to *epistêmê* ("science"). But in the strict sense, a *technê* is in particular a productive science, as opposed to a practical (action-related) or theoretical (truth-focused) one. See *NE* 6.4.

Note 47
The science of contraries is the same: "All the capacities that involve reason [for example, crafts and sciences] are such that the very same one is a capacity for contraries, while the non-rational ones are such that one capacity is for one of them—for example, the hot is for heating only, but the craft of medicine is for both disease and health. The cause of this is that scientific knowledge is an account, and the same account makes clear both the positive thing and its privation, except not in the same way—that is, in a way it is of both, but in a way it is rather of the positive thing. And so it is also necessary that these sorts of sciences should be of contraries, but of one intrinsically and of the other non-intrinsically; for the account too is of one intrinsically and of the other in a way coincidentally; for it is by denial and removal that it makes the contrary clear. For the contrary is the primary privation, and this is the removal of the other [and positive] contrary" (*Met.* 1046^{b}4–15).

Note 48
Our discussion of contraries: 112^{b}27–113^{a}19.

Note 49
Speculation: A *theôrêma* is sometimes an object of contemplation (*NE* 1066^{a}26). But *theôrêmata* (plural) are theoretical views or speculations (*Somn.* 455^{a}25, *Mete.* 345^{b}2), such as the *mathêmatikôn theôrêmatôn* mentioned at *Met.* 1093^{b}15, and it is of this that *theôrêma* here is the singular.

Note 50
The why: "Experienced people know the that (*to ti*) but do not know the why (*to dia ti*), while craftsmen know the why, that is, the cause" (*Met.* 981^{a}28–30).

Note 51
Supposition: Supposition (*hupolêpsis*) is like belief but unlike scientific knowledge, in that it can be false as well as true (*NE* 1139^{b}15–18). But while (mature) belief must be based on rational calculation, supposition need not be: "supposition is that by which we play a double game with everything, as to whether it is so or not so" (†*MM* 1197^{a}30–31). The idea, then, is that supposition is what allows us to take something as true or to take it as false—for example, for the sake of argument.
Antisthenes: Antisthenes was an Athenian follower of Socrates, present at his death. He wrote widely, including on topics in what we would now consider the philosophy of language, and in many genres, including Socratic dialogs. The following text gives his argument: "A false account, insofar as it is false, is of things that are not, which is why every account is false of something other than what it is true of—for example, the account of a circle is false of a triangle. Each thing has in a way one account, that of its essence, and in a way many, since both it by itself and it with an affection are in a way the same (for example, Socrates and musical Socrates), while a false account is, unconditionally, not the account of anything. That is why Antisthenes was naive in thinking that nothing could be fairly put into words except by means of the account proper to it, one to one. From which

it follows that there is no such thing as contradicting, and almost that there is no such thing as speaking a falsehood either. But it *is* possible to put a given thing into words not only by means of the account of itself but also by means of the account of something else. This may be done altogether falsely indeed, but also in a way truly—for example, eight is a double number by the account of two" (*Met.* 1024^{b}26–1025^{a}1). A number m is a double number if and only if there is a number n such that m = 2 × n. Hence the account of 2 is part of the account of double number. Using that account, 8 can then be correctly put into words or symbols as 2 × (2 × 2), using the account of something other than itself. Similarly, 9 can be falsely put into words, using the account of something else, as it is when we define it as "a double number."

Heraclitus: DK 22 = TEGP pp. 135–200. The relevant thesis is presumably Heraclitus' supposed denial of PNC (*Met.* 1005^{b}23–25). The idea is that, because "all perceptibles are always flowing" (a view Aristotle attributes to Heraclitus at *Met.* 987^{a}33–34), they are all both F and not-F, and not stably or exclusively one or the other.

Melissus: DK 30 = TEGP pp. 462–485. Melissus' arguments are discussed in *Ph.* 1.2 and the key premise in them mentioned at *SE* 170^{b}21–24.

Note 52

As the sophists say: "Plato was in a way not wrong when he classified sophistry as being concerned with what is not. For the arguments of the sophists are (one might almost say) above all else concerned with the coincidental—for example, whether musical and grammatical, or musical Coriscus and Coriscus, are distinct or the same, or whether everything that is, but is not always, has come to be, so that if someone who was musical has come to be grammatical, he must also have been grammatical and come to be musical, and all the other arguments of this sort" (*Met.* 1026^{b}14–21). The argument referred to is apparently this: (1) Socrates was musical and became grammatical. (2) Therefore, Socrates, being musical, is grammatical. (3) Therefore, Socrates, being grammatical, is musical. (4) Socrates has not always, being grammatical, been musical. (5) Therefore, it must be that Socrates, being grammatical, has become musical. (6) Therefore, being musical, Socrates became musical and, being grammatical, he became grammatical. (7) Therefore, Socrates was musical before he became musical and grammatical before he became grammatical. (8) But Socrates was not always or eternally either musical or grammatical. On what a sophist is, see *SE* 165^{a}19–24.

Note 53

In need of arguments, not punishment: "Argument and teaching surely do not have strength in everyone but, rather, the soul of the listener must be prepared beforehand through habits to enjoy and hate in a noble way, like earth that is to nourish seed. For someone who lives in accord with his feelings will not listen to—or, what is more, comprehend—argument that encourages him to turn away. And in a state like that how is it possible to persuade him to change his ways? Moreover, feeling generally seems to yield not to argument but to force. Character, then, must in some way be there beforehand and properly suited for virtue, liking what is noble and repelled by what is shameful. . . . For ordinary people obey force rather than argument; and they obey penalties rather than what is noble" (*NE* 1179ᵇ24–1180ᵃ5; also *EE* 1215ᵃ2–3).

Or perception: "Even if things are truly in this state, as certain people say, and being is unlimited and immovable, at least it does not at all appear to be that way according to perception, but instead many beings appear to be in movement. . . . But to investigate this question at all, and to seek an argument when we are too well off to need an argument, is to be a bad judge of what is better and what is worse, and what is trustworthy and what is not trustworthy, and what is a starting-point and what is not a starting-point" (*Ph.* 254ᵃ24–33).

Note 54

Induction: Induction (*epagôgê*) begins with (1) perception of particulars, which leads to (2) retention of perceptual contents in memory, and, when many such contents have been retained, to (3) an experience, so that for the first time "there is a universal in the soul" (*APo.* 100ᵃ3–16). Finally, (4) from experience come craft knowledge and scientific knowledge, when "from many intelligible objects belonging to experience one universal supposition about similar objects is produced" (*Met.* 981ᵃ5–7). "To prove on the basis of many similar cases that things are a certain way is an induction" (*Rh.* 1356ᵇ14–15).

Note 55

Stated previously: 100ᵃ25–27.

Note 56

Those skilled in logico-linguistic disputation: If an argument is from false but acceptable premises, it is *logikos* (162ᵇ27), suggesting that *logikos* arguments overlap with, or are, dialectical ones, since both rely on acceptable beliefs. Similarly, when rhetoric is being distinguished from dialectic, rhetorical deductions, or enthymemes, are contrasted with "logico-linguistic deductions" (*Rh.* 1355ᵃ13–14). When we ask *logikôs* (adverb) why it is that these bricks and stones are a house, what we are asking for is a formal cause or an essence (*Met.* 1041ᵃ26–28), which is presumably why a deduction of the essence is a *logikos sullogismos* (*APo.* 93ᵃ15). Before we start defining essences, however, we should have intimate knowledge of the empirical data that they are supposed to explain: "The cause of our being incapable of taking a comprehensive view of the agreed-upon facts is lack of experience. That is why those who are at home among natural things are better able to posit the sort of starting-points that can string together a good many of these, while those who on the basis of their many [logico-linguistic] arguments do not get a theoretical grasp on the facts, but look at only a few, make their declarations too recklessly" (*GC* 316ᵃ5–10). Thus a frequent criticism of Plato and the Platonists is that in proceeding *logikôs* they leave the earth and the world of facts too far behind and proceed at too abstract and general a level (*Met.* 987ᵇ29–988ᵃ7, 1069ᵃ26–28). See also 105ᵇ23–24.

Note 57
As was stated previously: 1.4–11.

Note 58
Instruments: *Cat., Int., APr., APo., Top.,* and *SE* are collectively referred to as the *Organon.* "Instrument" is generally a better consistent translation of *organon* than "tool."

Note 59
As was stated previously: 104^{a}8–15.

Note 60
Seeming posit: Not a thesis in the technical sense, obviously, but a posit acceptable as an unargued starting-point by someone who does not see that it only apparently holds in all cases.
Empedocles . . . : His elements are earth, water, air, and fire (DK B17 = TEGP 41 F20).
Elements: A *stoicheion* was originally one of a row (*stoichos*) of things and later a letter of the alphabet or an element of any complex whole (Plato, *Tht.* 201e). Aristotle uses it in these ways and to refer to the five primary elemental bodies (earth, water, air, fire, and ether), from which all others are composed (*Cael.* 302^{a}15–19). At *Rh.* 1396^{b}20–22 a *stoicheion* is a topic.

Note 61
Logico-linguistic . . . : "Strength in dialectic . . . enables people . . . to investigate contraries, and whether the same science is a science of contraries" (*Met.* 1078^{b}25–27). Again implying that logico-linguistic premises and problems are—or are often—dialectical ones. See 105^{a}19n56.

Note 62
Paradigms: 157^{a}14n369.

Note 63
Opposites: "Things said to be opposites include contradictories, contraries, relatives, privation and having, and the extremes that comings to be and passings away are from and to. And all things that cannot be present at the same time in what is receptive of both are said to be opposed—either themselves or their components; for gray and white do not belong at the same time to the same thing, because their components are opposed" (*Met.* 1018^{a}20–25).
Contraries: "Said to be contraries are: Those things differing in kind that cannot belong to the same thing at the same time. The most different of the things in the same kind. The most different of the things in the same recipient. The most different of the things falling under the same capacity. The things whose difference is greatest either unconditionally or in kind or in form" (*Met.* 1018^{a}25–31; also 1055^{b}13–17).

Relatives: "We call 'relatives' all such things as are said to be precisely what they are, *of* or *than* other things, or in some other way in relation to something else—for example, what is larger is said to be *than* something else, since it is said to be larger than something, and what is double is said to be *of* something else, since it is said to be double of something. Similarly, with all other such cases" (*Cat.* 6ᵃ36–ᵇ2; also *Met.* 1020ᵇ26–32).

Note 64

Noble: The adjective *kalos* is often a term of vague or general commendation ("fine," "beautiful," "good"), with quite different connotations in different contexts. Similarly, the adverb *kalôs* often means something like "well" or "correct." Even in the general sense, however, *kalos* has a distinctive evaluative coloration suggestive of "order, proportion, and determinateness" (*Met.* 1078ᵃ36–ᵇ1), making a term with aesthetic connotation, such as "beauty," seem a good equivalent: to bear the stamp of happiness one must have *kallos* as opposed to being "very ugly (*panaischês*)" (*NE* 1099ᵇ3–4; also *Pol.* 1309ᵇ23–25). At the same time, it seems wrong to associate *kalon* with beauty in general, since to be *kalon* a thing has to be on a certain scale: "a *kalon* thing, whether a living being or any object composed of parts, must not only have these properly ordered, but also have a magnitude that is not random—for noble beauty consists in magnitude and order" (*Po.* 1450ᵃ34–37; also *Pol.* 1326ᵃ33–34). It is this requirement that makes "nobility" in its more aesthetic sense a closer equivalent than "beauty," although it is sometimes best translated as "noble beauty," when, for example, it is applied to bodies and the like (as at *Rh.* 1361ᵇ7–14).

Homonymous: "Things are said to be homonymous when they have only a name in common, but the account of the substance [essence] that corresponds to the name is distinct—for example, both a human and a picture are animals. These have only a name in common and the account of the essence corresponding to the name is distinct; for if we are to say what-it-is for each of them to be an animal, we will give a special account to each" (*Cat.*1ᵃ1–6).

Note 65

Voiced sound: Aristotle sometimes distinguishes *phonos* ("sound in general") from the *phônê* ("cry" or "voiced sound") of an animate being: "*Phônê* is a sort of sound, one belonging to something animate" (*DA* 420ᵇ5–6). Sometimes too he distinguishes *phônê* from *logos* ("speech") (*Pol.* 1253ᵃ10–15).

Note 66

To loving in thought . . . : The contrast is like that between our loving as a feeling or emotion and loving as making love. Since *philein* also means "kiss," this may be one of the bodily activities referred to.

Activity: The noun *energeia* is an Aristotelian coinage, which I have translated as "activity," or "activation," as appropriate, and the verbal forms *energeian* as "activate" and *energein* as "to be active." The etymology of the coinage is unclear, but Aristotle is explicit that it has been extended from movement to other things

(*Met.* 1046ᵃ1–2, 1047ᵃ30–32), and that it is related to another term with an *erg*-root, namely, *ergon*: "The *ergon* ('function,' 'work') is the *telos* ('end'), and the *energeia* is the *ergon*, and that is why the name *energeia* is said [of things] with reference to the *ergon* and extends to the *entelecheian* ('actuality')" (1050ᵃ21–23). Putting all this together: the activation or actualization of X is an activity, which is X active or actual, which is X achieving its end, which—since "the for-the-sake-of-which is the function" (996ᵇ7)—is X fulfilling its function, and being actively or actually X.

Note 67

Privation: To say what cold is we refer to the positive notion heat, of which cold is the privation, so that cold is what lacks heat: "The positive is prior to the privation" (*Cael.* 286ᵃ25–26). That is why "the same account makes clear both the positive thing and its privation, except not in the same way—that is, in a way it is of both, but in a way it is rather of the positive thing" (*Met.* 1046ᵇ8–9). Privation may be a matter of degree, so that what is colder lacks more of the hot than what is less cold. But while a privation can be of one of a pair of contraries, it can also be the lack of something—such as substance—that strictly speaking has no contrary (*Cat.* 3ᵇ24–27): "One of a pair of contraries is a privation no less [than a contrary], or a privation of substance, and a privation is the denial [of a predicate] to some definite kind" (*Met.* 1011ᵇ18–20). Privation of substance (or form) is evidenced in cases of existence changes, where a substance either comes to be or passes away. See also *Met.* 5.22, 1055ᵇ11–29.

Having: When contrasted with a privation, and sometimes in other contexts, a *hexis* is a "having"; when contrasted with disposition or capacity, it is a "state." See 111ᵃ22n96.

Note 68

One's own consideration: Athenian jurors swore an oath whose gist seems to have been something like this: "I will cast my vote according to the laws (*kata tous nomous*) and using my most just consideration (*gnômê[i] tê[i] dikaiotatê[i]*)." See Demosthenes, *Against Aristocrates* 96. "What is called 'consideration (*gnômê*),' due to which, people are said to be sympathetically considerate (*sungnômones*) and to have consideration, is the correct judgment of what is decent" (*NE* 1143ᵃ19–20).

Note 69

It is the rapid sound that is sharp: "The differences in things that have sounds are made clear in the sound when it is active; for just as without light colors are not seen, so too without sound the sharp and the dull are not heard. Sounds are said to be these, however, by transference from tangible objects; for the sharp moves the perceptual capacity a lot in a little time, while the dull moves it a little in a lot of time. Not, of course, that the sharp is rapid and the dull slow, but rather that in the one case, because of the rapidity, the movement comes to be of such a character, and in the other, because of the slowness. And it seems that there is some analogy with the sharp and dull in touch; for the sharp as it were stabs, while the dull as it were pushes, because the one causes movement in a short time, the other in a long one, so that it comes about that the one is rapid and the other slow" (*DA* 420ᵃ26–ᵇ3).

Those who do arithmetical harmonics: That is, "the Pythagoreans . . . who generate the harmonies by a putting-together of numbers" (Alex. *In. Top.* 106.24–26 = Van Ophuijsen, p. 114).

Note 70
Donkey: *Onos* means "ass," or "donkey," but also (by extension), "windlass," "millstone," "wine cup," and other things. Similarly, our word "donkey" refers both to the animal (*Equus asinus*) and to a sort of steam engine.

Note 71
Synonymous: "Things are said to be synonymous when they have a name in common and when the account of the essence that corresponds to the name is the same—for example, both a human and an ox are animals. Each of these is called by a common name 'animal,' and the account of the essence is also the same, since if we are to give the account of what-it-is for each of them to be an animal, we will give the same account" (*Cat.* 1ᵃ6–12).

Note 72
The differences of color . . . : "If white and black are contraries, and one is a dilating color and the other a contracting color, these differences—dilating and contracting—are prior" (*Met.* 1057ᵇ8–10). The reference there as here is to Plato's theory: "The parts that move from the other objects and impinge on the ray of sight are in some cases smaller than, in others larger than, and in others equal in size to, the parts of the ray of sight itself. The ones that are equal in size are imperceptible, and these we of course call 'transparent.' Those that are larger or smaller, by contrast, respectively contract and dilate the ray of sight, and so are quite similar to what is cold or hot in the case of the flesh [touch], and, in the case of the tongue [taste], to what is sour, or to all those things that generate heat and that we have therefore called 'pungent.' So black and white, it turns out, are really the same as these other affections, though of a different kind, which is why they present a different appearance. This, then, is how we should speak of them: white is what dilates the ray of sight, and black is what does the contrary" (*Ti.* 67d–e).

Note 73
All these are in the same kind: Because they are all virtues.

Note 74
Understanding: In the broadest sense of the term, someone with *nous* is someone with sound common sense, and the cognate verb *noein*, like *dianoeisthai*, means "to think" (*Ph.* 208ᵇ25, *Mete.* 340ᵇ14, *NE* 1110ᵃ11). *Nous*, in this sense, is what enables a soul to suppose, believe, deduce, calculate, reason, and believe, so that it is possible to *noein* something false (*DA* 427ᵇ9). In the narrow sense, *nous* is what makes possible a type of knowledge of universal scientific starting-points

that, unlike scientific knowledge proper, is not demonstrable from anything further: "*Nous* is of the terms or definitions (*horoi*) for which there is no reason" (*NE* 1142ª25–26).

Note 75
We usually separate . . . : (1) "The substance of each thing is special to it, in that it does not belong to anything else" (*Met.* 1038ᵇ9–10). (2) "For the purposes of knowing the special substance of each thing knowledge of differences is useful because the definition of each is composed of kind and differences. Hence if we know the differences proper to each thing, by which it differs from others, we can separate it from the others and know the substance of it" (Alex. *In. Top.* 122.2–6 = Van Ophuijsen, 131).

Note 76
What is predicated in the what-it-is would most likely be the kind: Since the difference—the other thing predicated in the what-it-is—is more likely to distinguish than to be something common.

Note 77
Point . . . unit: "What is indivisible in quantity, when it is indivisible in all dimensions and lacks position, is said to be a unit, and when it is indivisible in all dimensions and has position, a point" (*Met.* 1016ᵇ24–26). See also 141ᵇ8.

Note 78
Those who define things: Probably Platonists: "Socrates . . . was the first to fix his thought on definitions. Plato, accepting him [as a teacher], took it that this fixing is done concerning other things and not the perceptible ones, since it is impossible for there to be a common definition of any perceptibles, as *they* at any rate are always changing. He, then, called beings of this other sort 'Forms,' and the perceptible ones are beyond these and are all called after these" (*Met.* 987ᵇ1–9; also 987ᵇ29–33).
Accustomed to giving definitions in this way: "Those who say that the Forms are substances and separable, and at the same time make the Form be composed of the kind and the differences" (*Met.* 1039ª24–26).
The point is the starting-point of line: Plato himself seems not to have accepted this view: "Plato used even to contest this kind [= points] as being a geometrical dogma. Instead, he called it 'starting-point of line,' and often posited that it consisted of indivisible lines" (*Met.* 992ª20–22).

Note 79
Topics: Introduction, pp. xxxviii–xl.

BOOK 2: COINCIDENTS

Note 80
Among problems . . . : For apparent exceptions, see 120ᵃ6n156.

Note 81
When we have proved that F belongs to all: Literally: "when we have proved that it belongs to all." In cases of this sort, I have supplied a variable F, whose particular instances are the things said to belong. Alternatively, one could supply "predicable" or perhaps "affection" in place of F, since anything that belongs is predicated of a subject.

Note 82
The procedures for universally disestablishing: These (embodied in topics), with some identified as also useful for establishing, seem to remain in focus until 3.6, where the application to particulars is discussed.

Note 83
Convert: Here, and only here it seems, A and B convert if and only if (B *belongs* to A) ⊃ (A *is* B). More often, *antistrephein* is used to signify: (1) a logical relation between propositions, so that, for example, the universal negative converts, because if no B is A, then no A is B (*APr.* 25ᵃ5–6) and so on; (2) a logical relation between terms (51ᵃ4–5), equivalent to counterpredication (*Top.* 102ᵃ19n); (3) the substitution of one term for another, without logical convertibility (*APr.* 64ᵃ40); (4) the (valid) inference of (A admits of not being B) from (B admits of being A) (32ᵃ30); (5) the substitution of the opposite of a premise for a premise (59ᵇ4); (6) an argument in which from one premise in a deduction or syllogism, and the opposite of the conclusion, the opposite of the other premise is deduced (2.8–10, *Top.* 163ᵃ32–34).

Belonging in some way but not universally: "'This belongs to that' and 'this is true of that' should be taken in as many ways as the ways in which predications have been divided [into categories], and these either in some way or unconditionally and either simple or compound; and similarly also with not belonging" (*APr.* 49ᵃ6–9). Thus *katholou*, used here, is replaced by "unconditionally" at 109ᵃ20. The idea is that a predicate P can belong partially to (or to a part of) a subject S without belonging to it universally, or to all of it, so that to say that S is P will then be false. See *SE* 166ᵇ37–167ᵃ20.

Note 84
If it belongs to something to be . . . : That is, if two-footed terrestrial animal is the thing's definition.

Note 85
One topic: Reading τόπος. This is one of several places in Book 2 where some mss. read τόπος ("topic") and some τρόπος ("mode"). See 109ᵇ25, 111ᵃ24, 115ᵃ33, ᵇ7.

Note 86
Paronymously: "When things get their name from something, with a difference of inflection, they are said to be paronymous—for example, from grammar, the grammarian, and from courage, the courageous person" (*Cat.* 1ᵃ12–15). See *Top.* 106ᵇ30–107ᵃ2.

Note 87
The primary ones: That is, the ones that are the most universal. See 105ᵇ31–37.

Note 88
Objection: (1) "An objection (*enstasis*) is a premise contrary to a premise" (*APr.* 69ᵃ37). (2) "Premises from which it is possible to deduce the contrary conclusion are those on the basis of which we try to state objections" (69ᵇ28–29). (3) "Objections are brought . . . in four ways: based on itself, on what is similar, on what is contrary, or on what has been judged" (*Rh.* 1402ᵃ34–37). See also *Top.* 161ᵃ1–15.

Note 89
Decent person: "Decent (*epieikês*)" is sometimes used interchangeably with "good (*agathos*)" (*NE* 1137ᵃ34–ᵇ2), but, in a narrower sense (defined at 1137ᵇ34–1138ᵃ3), an *epieikês* person is characterized in particular by an attitude to legal justice that pays more attention to fairness than to the letter of the law. (*Epieikeia*, in this sense, is also discussed in *Rh.* 1374ᵃ26–ᵇ1.) When contrasted with the majority of ordinary people (*hoi polloi*), the decent people are the ones who are better off and more respectable (1167ᵃ35–ᵇ1).

Note 90
Attack: 162ᵃ16n391.

Note 91
The topic that one must look into cases . . . : 101ᵇ28–36.

Note 92
Said of things in many ways: When A and B are said to be C and the grounds on which they are said to be C differ in ways relevant to science, Aristotle says that C is said of A and B "in many ways" (*pollachôs*). These ways include (a) cases where C is homonymous (as both New York City and the Hudson are said to have *banks*); (b) cases in which C is not homonymous but a respect in which A and B are similar (*APo.* 99ᵃ11–12); (c) cases in which A and B are C by analogy; (d) cases in which A and B are C with reference to one thing (*pros hen*). When A and B are said to be C in many ways, "but with reference to one thing and one nature—that is,

not homonymously" (*Met.* 1003ᵃ33–34), the most illuminating contrast is with the case where A and B are said to be C by analogy. In that case, there is a single thing X present in both A and B, which is the ontological correlate of C, and which can be an object of genuine scientific knowledge (*Ph.* 191ᵃ8–9). When X is not present in A or B, however, but in something else D, to which A and B are related in robustly specifiable ways, then A and B are said to be C not by analogy but by relation to D. And as with being C by analogy, then, X once again provides a ground for scientific knowledge of C.

One cannot prove it in both: For simplicity, Aristotle is supposing that the many ways are actually just two.

Note 93

Claim: An *axiôma*, in the technical sense, is "an immediate deductive starting-point . . . which it is necessary for someone who is going to learn anything at all to grasp . . . ; for there are some things of this sort; for we are accustomed to use this name especially of such things" (*APo.* 72ᵃ14–18). Here, however—as at *Top.* 156ᵃ23—an *axiôma* is probably just a claim or supposition.

Note 94

Distinguish in how many ways it is said: 110ᵃ23n92 for a list of possibilities.

Note 95

It is coincidental to the equilateral . . . : There are two sorts of coincidental affections, coincidental affections proper, which belong contingently to their subjects, and intrinsic coincidents (*kath' hauta sumbebêkota*)—so-called *per se* accidents. The latter, which are the sort relevant here, are affections that belong to a subject intrinsically and thus demonstrably, but are not part of its substance or essence (*APo.* 75ᵇ1, 83ᵇ19, *Met.* 1025ᵃ30–32, 1078ᵃ5–9). The essence of the equilateral involves having three equal sides, but makes no reference to angles. Thus it is an intrinsic coincident of it (something demonstrable from its essence but not part of it) that it is a triangle.

Note 96

Disposition is the kind of scientific knowledge: A *diathesis* properly so called is "the arrangement of what has parts with respect either to place or capacity or form; for it must be some sort of position, as the name 'dis*position*' also makes clear" (*Met.* 1022ᵇ1–3). The kind to which scientific knowledge is more commonly assigned, however, is *hexis* ("state"): "The states in which the soul grasps the truth by way of affirmation and denial be five in number: craft knowledge, scientific knowledge, practical wisdom, theoretical wisdom, and understanding" (*NE* 1139ᵇ15–17). But a *hexis* is itself a sort of *diathesis*: "What is said to be a *hexis* in another way is a disposition in virtue of which what is disposed is either well or ill disposed, and either intrinsically or with reference to something else—for example, health is a *hexis*; for it is a disposition of this sort. Further, anything that is a part of such a disposition is said to be a *hexis*—which is why the virtue of [a thing's] parts is also a *hexis*" (*Met.* 1022ᵇ10–14).

Note 97
Paronymously: 109^{b}5n86.

Note 98
The forms of movement: "If the categories are distinguished as substance, quality, place, time, relation, quantity, and affecting or being affected, it necessarily follows that there are three sorts of movement—that of a quality [= alteration], that of a quantity [= increase and decrease or growth and withering], and that with respect to place [= spatial movement]" (*Ph.* 225^{b}5–9).

Note 99
For against defined things attack is easier: Retaining πρὸς γὰρ τοὺς ὁρισμοὺς ῥᾷον ἡ ἐπιχείρησις, which Brunschwig secludes on the grounds that what is under attack here is not a definition *per se*, but a thesis involving an undefined term, which the topic instructs us to replace with its definition. However, it is possible to understand τοὺς ὁρισμοὺς as referring not to definitions but metonymically to the things they define. Aristotle does think, though, that definitions are the easiest thing to attack. See 155^{a}3–22.

Note 100
If one wishes to establish it . . . : This topic seems to be a case of modus ponens. If you want to establish Q, look for a true P such that P ⊃ Q.

Note 101
If we prove . . . : This topic seems to be a case of modus tollens. If you want to disestablish P, look for a false Q (a true not-Q) such that P ⊃ Q.

Note 102
The sophistical topic: *SE* 172^{b}25–27, which refers back to this.

Note 103
Sometimes it will be a necessity . . . : Is the necessity in question (1) the *use* of the topic, specifying the conditions under which it must be used; (2) the argument, falling under the topic, that the questioner uses; or (3) a premise related to the answerer's thesis? 112^{a}7–9 strongly suggests that (3) is intended, since what is neither a necessity nor an apparent necessity is clearly something that, as not related to the thesis, is extraneous to it.

Note 104
It is a necessity when the answerer has refused to grant one of the things made use of (*ti chrêsimôn*) **in relation to the thesis** (*pros tên thesin*), **and the questioner makes his arguments against it** (*pros touto*), **and it happens to be of the sort against which he is well equipped with lines of attack:** The fact that *pros* occurs first with one of its meanings ("in relation to") and then with another ("against")

is one key to correct interpretation. The other lies in the account of *ti chrêsimôn*. It refers not to some premise that is merely useful (one meaning of *chrêsimos*) to the answerer in establishing his thesis T, or to the questioner in disestablishing T, since what is useful for doing something may not be necessary for doing it. Nor is it one of the things that the answerer has made use (another meaning of *chrêsimos*) of in establishing T, since he could hardly refuse that. Instead, it is some premise P that the answerer has made use of because he is defending T, and T commits him to P. Since the questioner is well equipped with lines of attack against P, he can attack T by attacking it.

Note 105
Abduction: *Apagôgê* literally means "a leading away," making it particularly appropriate to this topic. In *APr.* 2.25, indeed, it is defined as a process of leading an argument away from one problem to another that is more easily solved. It is usually applied, however, to indirect proof by deriving an impossibility or falsehood, as in reductio ad absurdum. The idea here is that the questioner abduces something from the thesis laid down that he is well equipped to attack. The questioner then tries to do away with the thesis by doing away with it. Both of the arguments in the topic make use of modus tollens, albeit against premises stemming from different sources: in the first the answerer himself supplies the target of attack; in the second the questioner must abduce it.

Note 106
The last mode of those stated: This is a place where all the mss. agree on τρόπον ("mode") but we expect τόπον ("topic"). But a single topic may have a number of different modes of application.

Foreign to the craft of dialectic: This is because it relies on chance or luck, which is antithetical to craft: (1) "'Experience made craft,' as Polus says, 'and lack of experience, luck'" (*Met.* 981ª3–5). (2) "Where there is most understanding and reason, there is least luck; and where there is most luck, there is least understanding" (†*MM* 1207ª4–6). (3) "[The sick] did not want to look on barefaced luck, so they entrusted themselves to craft instead" (Hippocrates, *Peri Technês* 4).

Note 107
Attacking by translating a name in accord with its [literal] account: This topic seems to be an outlier—indeed, an odd topic altogether—until we see it in association with, especially, the next one. Suppose, for example, the answerer is defending the thesis that what is *andreios* is not of necessity good. The questioner must first get him to agree, as in accord with established usage he will, that what is *andreios* is of necessity *eupsuchos*. He must then translate *eupsuchos* as literally "having good in one's soul," which is the contrary of the answerer's thesis. Thus the present topic relies on something like the necessity of what is analytic, and so fits in with the other theses in this chapter, all of which have to do with the modal status of theses.

Note 108

Xenocrates . . . : Xenocrates of Chalcedon was a follower of Plato and head of the Academy from 339 to 314 BC. Aristotle quotes F155 Isnardi.

The soul is each person's *daimôn***:** Compare Heraclitus of Ephesus DK B119 = TEGP 135 F90: "The character of a human is his *daimôn*."

*Daimôn***:** A *daimôn* is a god or the child of a god, who functions a bit like a guardian angel, in the way that Socrates' famous *daimôn* does (Plato, *Ap.* 27c–d, 40a–b). So when a person's *daimôn* does well (*eu*) by him or benefits him, he is *eudaimôn* ("happy"). Hence, "when your *daimôn* does well by you, what need of friends?" (Euripides, *Orestes* 667), which Aristotle quotes at *NE* 1169^{b}7–8.

Note 109

Posited something as a coincident of itself: Thereby treating what is so of necessity (for example, pleasure = enjoyment) as a contingent truth (or one that is as luck would have it). It is this that connects the present topic to its predecessor.

Prodicus: A 5th-cent teacher of rhetoric from the island of Ceos in Cyclades with an interest in fine distinctions of meaning (Plato, *Prt.* 337a–c, *La.* 197d) and the correctness of names (*Euthd.* 277e, *Crat.* 384a-c). Socrates is described as attending some of his lectures (*Chrm.*163d)—although not the deluxe fifty-drachma one (*Crat.* 384b–c; also mentioned at *Rh.* 1415^{b}15–17)—and as being educated by him (*Men.* 96d).

Note 110

Each of the contrary predicates . . . : Literally: "Each of the contraries will be combined with each of the contraries." The contraries in the examples are nominalized incomplete sentences ("to do good to friends," "to do evil to enemies") consisting of an infinitive ("to do good," "to do evil") and a noun ("friends," "enemies"), where both the infinitives and the nouns are themselves contraries. In a thesis, the incomplete sentences would be completed: "one must do (or it is choiceworthy to do) good to friends and evil to enemies." See 104^{a}22–26.

Note 111

True: Literally: "real (*ontos*)" (as at 111^{b}19).

Intelligible: An intelligible object or content (*noêma*) is a universal form. When encoded in an appearance, it can be grasped by the understanding when it contemplates that appearance: "To the understanding soul appearances are like perceptions. . . . The part that understands, then, understands the forms in the appearances" (*DA* 431^{a}14–^{b}2). It differs from an appearance, however, in being a propositional element—an element of something with a truth value: "imagination is distinct from affirmation and denial; for truth and falsity involve a combination of intelligible objects" (432^{a}8–12).

Note 112

Those who posit the Forms . . . : "[Plato,] having been from his youth familiar first with Cratylus and the Heraclitean beliefs that all perceptibles are always flowing, and that there is no scientific knowledge concerning them, these views he also held later . . . Socrates, on the other hand, was inquiring about what is universal and was the first to fix his thought on definitions. Plato, accepting him [as a teacher], took it that this fixing is done concerning other [intelligible] things and not the perceptible ones, since it is impossible for there to be a common definition of any perceptibles, as *they* at any rate are always changing. He, then, called beings of this other sort 'Forms'" (*Met.* 987ᵃ32–ᵇ8).

Note 113
The shape present in each thing: Aristotle often uses *morphê* and *eidos* ("form") interchangeably.

Note 114
It is the same thing that is receptive of contraries: (1) "Contraries both in other areas and in natural ones always occur, it is evident, in the same recipient and are affections of the same beings. I mean, for example, health and sickness, beauty and ugliness, strength and weakness, sight and blindness, hearing and deafness" (*Somn.* 453ᵇ27–31). (2) "Things in the same receptive subject that differ the most are contraries" (*Met.* 1055ᵃ29–30).

Note 115
The spirited part . . . is where anger is: Aristotle often uses *thumos* ("spirit") and *orgê* ("anger") interchangeably (*Rh.* 1369ᵃ7, ᵇ11) and very often uses *thumos* in contexts where its aggressive side is highlighted (*NE* 1116ᵇ15–1117ᵃ9). In other places (for example, here and at *Top.* 126ᵃ10) he says only that anger is "in (*en*)" the spirited part, alongside other feelings, such as fear and hatred (126ᵃ8–9). In one passage, indeed, he identifies spirit as the source not just of "negative" feelings but also of love and friendship: "spirit is what produces friendliness; for it is the capacity of the soul by which we love" (*Pol.* 1327ᵇ40–1328ᵃ1). This is in keeping with the claim here that if hatred is in the spirited part, then love, as its contrary, must be there too (113ᵃ33–ᵇ3). Presumably, then, we should think of spirit as passionate—as "hot and hasty" (*NE* 1149ᵃ30)—rather than as always aggressive.

Note 116
As was said: 113ᵃ18–19.

Note 117
Opposites are of four sorts: 105ᵇ33n63.
Obtaining it by induction: That is, obtaining the principle about reversing the sequence. See 113ᵇ22–26. The induction is intended to establish the principle for the answerer, and so is to be part of the dialectical argument, not something the questioner is to establish for himself beforehand. See 113ᵇ29–30.

Note 118
So far as is useful: Reading ἐφ᾽ ὅσον χρήσιμον.

Note 119
Cases of having and privation: Reading τῇ ἕξει καὶ τῇ στερήσει.

Note 120
Many people deny . . . : As Plato is thought to have done. See 113ᵃ27–28.

Note 121
Column . . . coordinates: At *Met.* 1054ᵇ35, 1058ᵃ13, a *sustoichia* is a "column of predication (*sustoichia tês katêgorias*)," which seems to be what is relevant here, where the adjective *sustoichos* applies to a column of coordinate predicates, some of which are inflections of the others.

Note 122
Stated previously: 113ᵇ27–114ᵃ6.

Note 123
The more and less: The more and less (*to mallon kai hêtton*) corresponds to our notion of degree, and so it is connected to the notion of increasing and decreasing—tightening and loosening (*epiteinein kai aniêsin*). Thus as musicians tighten or loosen their instrument's strings until a certain target note is struck (*Pol.* 1290ᵃ22–29), so too with vocal cords, sinews, and other string-like things (*GA* 787ᵇ10–24). Hence Aristotle employs the notion of tightening and loosening wherever a certain tripartite structure is thought to exist, consisting of a continuous underlying subject (*to mallon kai hêtton*), a pair of opposed affections that can vary in degree, and a target, typically a mean condition of some sort, that can be achieved by tightening or loosening the underlying subject to change the degree of the affections. As a result, he speaks of tightening and loosening in characterizing a wide range of phenomena, from the parts of animals to political constitutions (*Pol.* 1309ᵇ18–31, *Rh.* 1360ᵃ23–30). In the case of noses and other such parts, the continuous underlying subject is flesh and bone, the pair of opposite affections is hooked and snub, and the target—which lies somewhere in between the two, and so (as in political constitutions) in a mean of some sort—is being a straight nose, or at the very least a nose of some sort. In the case of colors, too, while many are constituted out of white and black in some definite ratio, others are constituted in "some incommensurable ratio of excess or deficiency," and so are apt for tightening and loosening (*Sens.* 439ᵇ30). Because *to mallon kai hêtton* is found in many different kinds, it cannot be the subject matter of any of the first-order sciences, since these are restricted to a single kind (*Rh.* 1358ᵃ10–17). The rhetorical equivalent of this topic is discussed at *Rh.* 1397ᵇ12–29.

Note 124
Of the more and less: Reading τοῦ μᾶλλον καὶ ἧττον.

Note 125
It is clear that it coincides with it: A coincident belongs to an underlying subject S if and only if a particular instance of it coincides with, or is present in, S. Thus S is white (*leukon*) if and only if *to ti leukon* (a particular instance of white) is present in S (*Cat.* 1ᵃ25–28, ᵇ8).

Note 126
Exceeding with respect to more: Where, as a result of an addition, the F thing becomes yet more excessively F than before the addition.

Note 127
And less: Reading καὶ ἧττον.

Note 128
Triballi: A savage Thracian tribe, living near the Danube.

Note 129
Since they are Triballi: Reading οὖσι Τριβαλλοῖς.

Book 3: Coincidents Again

Note 130
3.1–5: Many of the topics discussed in these chapters are also discussed in *Rh.* 1.7.

Note 131
Or those with scientific knowledge of a given kind: Retaining ἢ οἱ ἐν ἑκάστῳ γένει ἐπιστήμονες.
All things aim at the good: "Let good be whatever is choiceworthy for its own sake; or that for whose sake we choose something else; or what all things aim at, or all that have perception or understanding, or would aim at if they got understanding" (*Rh.* 1362ᵃ21–24).

Note 132
What is in accord with the better science: "The best kind of science is that of the theoretical sciences . . . ; for it is concerned with the most estimable of beings, and each science is said to be better or worse in accord with the scientifically knowable object that properly belongs to it" (*Met.* 1064ᵇ3–6).

Note 133
What is precisely a this something: "Terms that signify substance signify precisely (*hoper*): that thing of which they are predicated, or precisely that sort of thing. Those, on the other hand, that do not signify substance, but are said of some underlying subject that is neither precisely what that thing is nor precisely what sort of thing that thing is, are coincidents—for example, white is a coincident of a human. For the human is neither precisely white nor precisely a sort of white, but rather an animal, presumably; for a human is precisely an animal. But terms that do not signify substance must be predicated of some underlying subject, and there cannot be anything white that is not some other thing that is white" (*APo.* 83^{a}24–32). Thus to say that A is *hoper* B is to say that B is precisely what A is (in other words, that A is precisely B). Sometimes, as here, B is the kind of A (*Top.* 122^{b}18–20, *APr.* 49^{b}6–8), sometimes its essence (*Top.* 120^{b}21–26, *Met.* 1007^{a}33). **The kind of the good:** Reading τῷ ἀγαθῷ.

Note 134
Even if they may be in India: That is, too far away to affect us in any way. See *EE* 1226^{a}29.

Note 135
Intrinsic cause: "Just as being is either intrinsic or coincidental, in the same ways it is possible to be a cause—for example, the intrinsic cause of a house is the builder, but coincidentally it is the pale or the musical" (*Ph.* 196^{b}25–27). That is, the fact about the builder that scientifically explains the building of the house is not his being pale or musical but his knowing the craft of building.

Note 136
Luck . . . : "Luck is a coincidental cause in things that come about in accord with deliberate choice for the sake of an end" (*Met.* 1065^{a}30–31).

Note 137
More estimable: The core sense of *timios* ("estimable") is captured in the remark that ordinary people "commonly say of those they find especially estimable and especially love that they 'come first'" (*Cat.* 14^{b}5–7). Something is thus objectively *timios* when—like starting-points and causes—it "comes first by nature" (14^{b}3–5). To say that something is estimable is thus to ascribe a distinct sort of goodness or value to it: "By 'estimable' I mean things of the following sort: the divine, the better (for example, soul, understanding), the more ancient, the starting-point, and things of this sort" (†*MM* 1183^{b}21–23).

Note 138
The god: Aristotle recognizes the existence of a number of different divine beings or gods, among which he distinguishes a primary god, usually referred to as *ho theos* ("the god"), which he discusses in *Met.* 1.2, 12.8–10, and which is "the active understanding of active understanding" (1074^{b}34–35). In the *Topics*, however, as

is natural given its subject matter, he seems to rely on more generally accepted conceptions, so that *ho theos* here refers not to Aristotle's god in particular, or to his own recondite views about it, but (taking *ho* as generalizing) to whatever is a god (132^{b}10–11 may be an exception). Consider, for example, the use of *ho theos* at 126^{a}34–35: "For both *ho theos* and the excellent person are capable of doing base things." This is false of Aristotle's *ho theos*, who is incapable of doing anything except understanding himself, but is true of what is a god, as gods are popularly conceived.

Note 139
Health resides in . . . : According to *On Ancient Medicine*, for example, the human body contains a blend (*chrêsis*) of moist substances or humors (*chumoi*), each with a capacity (*dunamis*) to cause a specific effect: "These, when mixed and blended with one another are neither manifest nor cause the human being pain; but when one of them separates off and comes to be on its own, then it is both manifest and causes the human being pain" (14.4 Schiefsky). Plato adopts a somewhat similar view, with imbalances in the blood playing an important role in causing certain diseases (*Ti.* 81e–86a), as does Aristotle himself: "We say that all virtues are in [the category of] being related in a way to something. For those of the body, such as health and good condition, lie in a blending and proportion of hot and cold things, either of one in relation to another within the body or to what encompasses it" (*Ph.* 246^{b}3–6; also *Top.* 139^{b}20–21). He seems to criticize it, however, at 145^{b}7–11.

Note 140
The posterior consequence is better: That is, a better good, not better for dialectical purposes. If someone learns, it follows that he was ignorant before he learns (prior consequence) and scientifically knowledgeable after he learns (posterior consequence).

Note 141
A greater number of goods . . . : (1) "More is a greater good than one or fewer, provided that the one or the few are counted within it; for it exceeds and what is contained is exceeded" (*Rh.* 1363^{b}18–21). (2) "We think it [happiness = the greatest good] is the most choiceworthy of all things, when not counted among them. But if it is counted among them, it clearly would be more choiceworthy with the addition of the least of goods; for what is added would bring about a surplus of goods, and, of goods, the greater one is always more choiceworthy" (*NE* 1097^{b}15–20).

Note 142
Things that are not [all] good . . . : I have added "all" to make sense of the examples. Happiness plus something not good is an example of "things that are not good," but happiness is a good, indeed the best good. So things that are not good cannot mean things each of which is not good, but must mean things not all of which are good.

Note 143

Justice and temperance [are more useful] than courage: "Courage and resilience are for unleisure, philosophy for leisure, and temperance and justice are useful during both, and particularly when people remain at peace and are at leisure; for war compels people to be just and temperate, but the enjoyment of good luck and the leisure that accompanies peace make them wantonly aggressive instead. Much justice and temperance are needed, therefore, by those who seem to do best and who enjoy all the things regarded as blessings—people like those, if there are any, as the poets say there are, who live in the Isles of the Blessed; for these above all will need philosophy, temperance, and justice, to the extent that they are at leisure amidst an abundance of such goods" (*Pol.* 1334ª22–34).

Note 144

If all were just, courage would be of no use: "The person who is said to be 'courageous' in the full sense, then, is the one who is unanxious where noble death is concerned and the things that are an imminent threat of death. And the things that occur in war are most of all of this sort" (*NE* 1115ª32–35). The idea, then, is that if all were just, there would be no wars, and if there were no wars, courage—anyway in the full sense—would be useless. There would, of course, still be other sorts of danger that it would take courage of a sort to face.

Note 145

That of Odysseus to Nestor is strong: The wise Nestor is taken as an exemplar of the good.

Note 146

To do philosophy . . . : (1) "Philosophy seems to involve pleasures that are wondrous for their purity and stability" (*NE* 1177ª25–26). (2) "[Thales] collected a lot of money, proving that philosophers could easily become rich if they wished, but that this is not what they take seriously" (*Pol.* 1259ª16–18).

Note 147

Justice as compared to courage: Courageous bodyguards, for example, can play many of the roles of one's own courage, but justice is something one must have oneself.

Note 148

Capacity: The term *dunamis* (plural: *dunameis*) is used by Aristotle to capture two different but related things. (1) As in ordinary Greek, it signifies a power or capacity something has, especially one to cause movement in something else (productive *dunamis*) or to be caused to move by something else (passive *dunamis*). (2) It signifies a way of being F, being capable of being F (or being F in potentiality or being possibly F) as distinguished from being actively F (or F in actuality or actually). Here the reference is to power and ability, especially, no doubt, the sort exercised in politics.

Note 149
More controlling thing: In a key sense what is *kurios* is what has the sort of control that is fundamentally executive power or authority or the power to compel, so that a general has control over his army (*NE* 1116ª29–ᵇ2) and a politician has control over a city and its inhabitants. Since what has control in a sphere determines or partly determines what happens within it, it is one of the most estimable or important elements in the sphere, so that what is less estimable than something cannot or should not control it (1143ᵇ33–35, 1145ª6–7). The *kurios* definition of something, like the *kurios* use of a term, is its proper one (e.g., *Met.* 1020ª4, ᵇ14), or its definition in the strict sense, which thus exerts control over the extended uses of it (e.g., *DA* 408ª6). *Kuriôs* and *haplôs* ("unconditionally") are often used interchangeably (e.g., *Cat.* 14ᵇ24), as are *kuriôs* and *kath' hauta* ("intrinsically") (e.g., 5ᵇ8).

Note 150
Color that dilates sight: 107ᵇ29–31n72.

Note 151
The first universal topics mentioned: The reference could be to the topics in 2.2–3.5, all of which deal with universally quantified problems, even if the quantifier is not always made explicit. The use of *koinoi* ("common") at 119ª37, though, seems to further restrict the reference to topics that are not just universally quantified but also common, that is, usable in dealing with a problem regardless of its subject matter. This would limit the relevant topics to those in 2.2–11.

Note 152
Based on opposites, coordinates, and inflections: Discussed in 2.9.

Note 153
If some pleasure is good . . . : The opposites are contraries.

Note 154
If some perception . . . : The opposites are having and privation.

Note 155
If something supposable . . . : The opposites are relatives.

Note 156
The problem is indeterminate: A premise is indeterminate (*adioristos*) if it has no explicit quantifier (no "all" or "some") (*APr.* 24ª17–22). But that this cannot be its meaning here is shown by the examples of determinate problems at 120ª20–31. The indeterminate problem or premise is "some things are F," which is indeterminate in being refutable in only one way, by proving that all things are not-F (120ª6–10). *Level 1* of determination is some are F and some are not F (120ª20–24), which, as more determinate, is refutable in two ways (120ª21). *Level 2* is only one

single thing is F (120ª24–27), which, as more determinate still, is refutable in three ways (120ª25). *Level 3* is only this specific thing is F (120ª27–28), which, as yet more determinate, is refutable in four ways (120ª28).

Note 157
As was said previously: 109ᵇ15–16.

Note 158
Time is not moved . . . : *Ph.* 218ᵇ9–20.

Book 4: Kinds

Note 159
These are elements of the topics related to definitions: A special affection is not a *stoicheion*—in the sense of an element, or elementary constituent—of a definition (102ª18–30), so that the focus of these sentences cannot be definitions and their elements. An element, however, can itself be a topic (105ᵇ17n60), and that is probably how it should be understood here. What we are being told, then, is that the topics concerned with kind and special affection belong among the topics concerned with definitions.

Note 160
Just as in the case of a coincident: 109ᵇ13–29.

Note 161
It often is [a coincident] of the animal to walk or to be walking: Some animals (for example, human beings) have walking as their natural sort of spatial movement. For them to walk is not a coincident, though it is a coincident for them to be walking at any given moment. For other animals (for example, fish) walking is always a coincident, since though they might use their fins (as seals use their flippers) to get around on land, the sort of spatial movement natural to them is swimming, not walking.

Note 162
While the kind . . . : Reading τὸ δὲ γένος ἐν τῷ τί ἐστι κατηγορεῖται.

Note 163
It is possible for a thing to move itself: Reading κινεῖν τι αὐτὸ ἑαυτὸ.

Note 164
We said . . . : 102ᵇ6–7.

Note 165
Division: A division (*diairesis*) here, as at 121ᵃ6, is a category.

Note 166
Scientific knowledge is among the relatives: "Scientific knowledge, a kind, is said to be precisely what it is *of* another thing (it is said to be scientific knowledge of something), but none of the particular cases is said to be precisely what it is *of* another thing—for example, grammar is not said to be grammar of something or music music of something. If they too are said to be relative to something at all, it is with reference to the kind—for example, grammar is said to be scientific knowledge of something, not grammar of something, and music is said to be scientific knowledge of something, not music of something. So the particular cases are not relatives" (*Cat.* 11ᵃ24–32).

Note 167
The first division: Unlike at 120ᵇ36, a division here is a division of a kind into forms. Thus if the first division of the kind of animals were into mammals, birds, and fish, each of these would participate in the kind alone—that is, without participating in any of its forms.

Note 168
Movement is posited as the kind of pleasure: "When what is pleasant and what is painful arise in the soul, they are both a sort of motion, aren't they" (Plato, *Rep.* 583e); "But when things are restored to their own nature again, this restoration . . . is pleasure" (Plato, *Phlb.* 48d). Aristotle expresses an amalgamation of these views in *Rh.* 1.11, no doubt as suitable for rhetorical (dialectical) purposes: "Pleasure is a sort of movement of the soul, an intensive and perceptible settling down into its original natural state, and pain the contrary" (1369ᵇ33–35). In the *NE*, however, he shows that his own conception of pleasure is quite different (1152ᵇ33–1153ᵃ17, 1174ᵇ14–33).

Note 169
Have the same extension: Literally, "are said of an equal number of things (*ep' isôn legetai*)." But the implication is not that their extensions are equinumerous, but that they consist of the same things.

Note 170
Someone positing indivisible lines: 108ᵇ30–31.

Note 171
When one form falls under two kinds, one encompasses the other: Aristotle acknowledges that this simple rule of kind subordination may admit of exceptions in certain cases. But that does not mean that it cannot be used in dialectical argument, since the problem under discussion may not be one of those cases. The

fact that he continues to use the simple rule, therefore, as he does at 122^{b}1–6, is no cause for surprise or alarm. Advice on what to look for in establishing or disestablishing is just that. Look to see whether this—the simple rule—works. If it does, use it. If it does not, try the rule given a few lines later (121^{b}37–122^{a}2); for one of these rules must apply.

Note 172
They both fall under the same kind: A state is a sort of disposition (*Met.* 1022^{b}10–11). Hence the kind of states falls under the kind of dispositions. But not vice versa: "A state differs from a disposition in being more steadfast and longer lasting. And such are the sciences and virtues" (*Cat.* 8^{b}27–28).

Note 173
Look to see . . . : What this rule bids us to do is to see whether the assigned kind (scientific knowledge or virtue) is neither a state nor a disposition. For if it is neither, the assigned kind (practical wisdom in this case) cannot be the kind. But here this rule does not come into play, since one of the kinds (states) does fall under the other (dispositions).

Note 174
For all the higher kinds: Reading πάντα γὰρ τὰ ἐπάνω γένη.

Note 175
Odd is precisely number: 116^{a}23n133.

Note 176
Plato's definition: Plato, *Tht.* 181d, *Prm.* 138b–c.

Note 177
For pretty much . . . : Reading σχεδὸν γὰρ ἡ φορὰ ἐπὶ τῶν ἀκουσίως.

Note 178
Again, look to see whether the opponent has [1] put the difference into the form—for example, saying that [2] what is immortal is precisely god. For [3] it will follow that the form has the same extension or a wider one. But [4] the difference always has the same extension as the form, or a wider one: Begin with [1]. The difference (D) applies to the kind (G) and determines the form (S$_1$ and S$_2$). If D is put within S$_1$, the extension of D will be narrowed to S$_1$ and so will exclude S$_2$. (If two-footed applies to animal, and human and bird are given as the forms, put two-footed inside bird, and it will entail bird, and so exclude human from being two-footed.) Now turn to [2]: if what is immortal is precisely a god, the difference immortal (122^{b}12–13) is put inside the form god, with the result that god has [3a] an extension equal to that of immortal, or [3b] a wider extension than it. [4] explains why that is false, except in cases such as [3a], in which

the difference determines only a single form. On whether there are such cases, see 123ª30–32.

But the difference always: Reading ἀεὶ δ' ἡ διαφορά.

Note 179
Color is precisely contracting: 107ᵇ29–30n72.

Note 180
Prior in nature . . . : (1) "Things are said to be prior in nature and substance, when it is possible for them to be without other things, but not the others without them" (*Met.* 1019ª3–4). (2) "Things that are prior to others are not done away with together with them" (1040ª21–22). See also 141ᵇ28–29.

Note 181
The form is homonymous with regard to the kind . . . : Suppose the form is human and the kind animal. Look to see whether animal is said homonymously of human—that is, whether the name animal, but not its definition, is said of human. If so, the assigned kind is not the kind. Why? Because the kind is said synonymously of the forms—for example, both the name animal and its definition are said of human.

The elements [or topics] already stated: 106ª9–107ᵇ37.

Note 182
Metaphor: "A metaphor is the application to something of a name belonging to something else, either from kind to form, form to kind, form to form, or by analogy" (*Po.* 1457ᵇ6–9).

Notes: A *phthoggos* is any sound, but the word is used by technical writers on music to mean "note."

Note 183
The good: Aristotle has already argued that good is homonymous (107ª11–12), which precludes it from being a kind. So *tagathon* may refer here to the Platonic good-itself, which Aristotle did seem to think of as a kind (*NE* 1.6), or to the good (and the bad) as conceived by someone like Empedocles: "if we were to claim that Empedocles in a way says, and was the first to say, that the good and the bad are starting-points, we would perhaps be right—if indeed the cause of all good things is the good itself" (*Met.* 985ª7–10).

Note 184
[1] By way of negation . . . [2] as underlying subject: The middle term between justice and injustice is [1] by way of negation (123ᵇ21–23). In other words, it is the negation of "both just and unjust," which is "neither just nor unjust." In [2] the intermediate between the contraries is the underlying subject, which, as a result of undergoing changes, is first one and then the other, and so cannot be intrinsically or essentially one or the other.

Note 185
As virtue . . . : Reading καθάπερ ἀρετὴ κακίᾳ καὶ δικαιοσύνη ἀδικίᾳ.

Note 186
Ultimate kind: That is, the highest one.

Note 187
A certain sort of perception: Reading αἴσθησίς τις.

Note 188
As was stated in the case of the coincident: 113ᵇ15–26.

Note 189
Scientific knowledge is among the relatives . . . : 121ᵃ1n166.

Note 190
Are so *to* something: "Scientific knowledge is said to be of the scientifically know-able, and the scientifically knowable said to be scientifically knowable to scientific knowledge" (*Cat.* 6ᵇ34–35). Similarly, the supposable is supposable to supposition.

Note 191
[1] Others, by contrast, do not necessarily belong in those things relative to which they happen at any time to be said, although it is possible (for example, if [2] the soul (*hê psuchê*) is said to be scientifically knowable; for [3] there is nothing to prevent the soul from having scientific knowledge of itself, although it is not necessary; for [4] it is possible for this same scientific knowledge (*tên autên tautên*) to belong in something else): Since [2] is an example of [1], one of the things relative to which scientific knowledge is said must be the soul, and it must be possible for it not to belong in the soul, but not necessary. But scientific knowledge is a relative, so that the scientific knowledge that the soul has must be *of* something, X. [3] There is nothing to prevent X from being the soul itself, though, of course, it does not have to be, since there is scientific knowledge of many other things. But when X is the soul itself, the relevant scientific knowledge is both in the subject of the scientific knowledge and in its object, since these are the same. In other words, it is in the pair <the soul, the soul>. Now look at [4] and ask two questions: What does *tên autên tautên* refer to? What is the something else that it can belong in? Given its gender, and its need for an antecedent, it must refer either to [4a] scientific knowledge or [4b] scientific knowledge of soul. But whichever of these we choose, what it belongs in can only be the soul, since scientific knowledge of any sort cannot belong anywhere else. For as precisely a state of the soul, scien-tific knowledge, cannot exist except in the soul (*NE* 1139ᵇ15–16). It is at this point that [3] becomes crucial. For what it shows is that [4b] is the right answer, which is what the reflexive pronoun *autên* in any case strongly suggests. Why? Because the scientific knowledge that makes the soul scientifically knowledgeable only contin-gently belongs in <the soul, the soul>, it could equally well belong in <the soul,

mathematics> or <soul, grammar>. What it could not belong in is <the non-soul, X>. Notice that I have, for literalness and not to beg any questions, included the definite article *hê* before *psuchê* even though omitting it makes it clearer that it is not the individual soul, or the soul of a particular person, that is at issue: compare "all memory is in the soul" (125ᵇ9–10). For if the reference were to the individual soul, there would be no need for [3] to give the *outré* example it does, since scientific knowledge can, of course, exist in distinct individual souls, without being knowledge of the soul itself.

Note 192
Perception is a movement through the body: "Active perception is a movement through the body, when the perceptual capacity is affected in a certain way" (*Ph.* 244ᵇ11–12). The point is that the proposed definition does not acknowledge the existence of perception as a capacity. See 129ᵇ33–34.

Movement is an activity: "The name 'activity', which is connected to 'actuality', has been extended to other things from applying most of all to movements; for activity seems most of all to be movement" (*Met.* 1047ᵃ30–32).

Note 193
No memory is a state, but rather an activity: "Memory (*mnêmê*) is not perception or supposition, but a sort of state or affection connected with one of these, when time has elapsed" (*Mem.* 449ᵇ24–25). Our text is consistent with this, when *mnêmê* refers to the act or activity of remembering, as the pronoun *oudemia* ("no") implies. As with the proposed definition of perception, what is wrong with this one is that it fails to acknowledge the existence of occurrent memory.

Note 194
Someone who feels no [anger or fear that needs controlling]: A person can be *apathês* and yet be disgusted (*Rh.* 1378ᵃ4–5), so *apatheia* need not be freedom from all feelings, but simply—as in the cases of virtues, such as courage and mild-manneredness—from discordant ones that are either too much or too little, rather than being in a mean or being proportionate to their objects (*NE* 1102ᵇ25–28). Notice 125ᵇ27 ("not to feel *such* feelings at all").

Note 195
The being for courage . . . : The being for (*einai* + dative) A = what A is intrinsically = the essence of A (*Met.* 1029ᵇ13–1030ᵇ13). Hence when something considered in one way satisfies one account or definition and satisfies another account or definition when considered in a different way, the object considered in the first way differs in being from the same object considered in the second way.

Note 196
Anger is not pain unconditionally: 151ᵃ15–17.

Note 197

Shame is in the rationally calculative part: "Let shame be a sort of pain or disturbance concerned with the evils—whether present, past, or future—that appear to bring a person into disrepute, and shamelessness a sort of contempt and lack of feeling concerning these same things" (*Rh.* 1383ᵇ12–15). It is the reference to future evils in particular, apparently, that explains the location of shame, since the future is the focus of rational calculation, or deliberation: "Nobody deliberates about what happened in the past but they deliberate about what will happen in the future and what admits of being otherwise" (*NE* 1139ᵇ7–9). The definition of shame, however, makes its location there a little less intelligible: "Shame is not properly spoken about as a sort of virtue; for it is more like a feeling than a state. Shame is defined, at any rate, as a sort of fear of disrepute, and its effects are somewhat similar to those of the fear of frightening things; for people who are ashamed of themselves blush, and those who fear death turn pale. Both shame and fear appear, then, to be somehow bodily, which seems to be precisely what is characteristic of a feeling rather than a state" (*NE* 1128ᵇ10–15).

Note 198

All wish is in the rationally calculative part: "In the rationally calculative part there is wish" (*DA* 432ᵇ5; also *Rh.* 1369ᵃ2–4), so that "when something is moved in accord with rational calculation, it is moved in accord with wish" (*DA* 433ᵃ23–25). At *Pol.* 1334ᵇ22–25, however, as often elsewhere, Aristotle seems to deviate from the official view: "spirit and wish, and appetite besides, are present in children straight from birth, while rational calculation and understanding are made by nature to arise as they grow." But explanation for the deviation is probably this. When Aristotle discusses wish in the process of trying to explain deliberate choice, he writes: "[Deliberate choice] is not wish either, although it appears to be a close relative of it; for there is no deliberate choice of impossible things, and if someone were to say he was deliberately choosing them, he would seem silly" (*NE* 1111ᵇ19–22). And when wish is understood in this way, there is nothing especially rational about it, which makes it easy to see why children are said to have it. This suggests that "wish" is being used in two different ways, one technical, the other loose and popular. There is, however, a way to reconcile the two. And this lies in the very definition of wish itself as a desire that is "unconditionally and in truth . . . [for] the good" but in each individual for "the apparent good" (*NE* 1113ᵃ23–24). As a desire for the apparent good, wish *is* present in children straight from birth, but with proper habituation and training it can come to be for the real good, and so to be properly responsive to the deliberation that best furthers it, by having its "starting-point and cause" (*EE* 1226ᵇ19–20) in it.

Note 199

The coincident and what it is coincident with are in the same thing: For example, a color is in (on) a surface and both it and the surface it is coincident with are in (on) the substance whose surface it is. Similarly, for coincidents in other categories: they are in the matter distinctive of that category (the first recipient), which is itself in some substance: "We might say that there are three starting-points—the form and the privation and the matter. But each of these is distinct for each category (*genos*)—for example, in color they are white, black, and surface" (*Met.* 1070ᵇ18–21).

Note 200

Animal is said to be precisely what is perceptible or precisely what is visible: Reading (1) τὸ ζῷον ὅπερ αἰσθητὸν ἢ ὁρατὸν εἴρηται with Brunschwig and the mss. Compare αἰσθητὸν γάρ τι τὸ ζῷον at *Met.* 1036ᵇ28–29. Frede-Patzig plausibly argues for correcting αἰσθητὸν to αἰσθητ<ικ>ὸν ("capable of perception"). A similar correction may seem harder to justify here, given the rest of the argument. But because it is difficult to believe that anyone would offer (1) as a definition of animal, rather than (2) εἰ τὸ ζῷον ὅπερ αἰσθητ<ικ>ὸν ἢ ὁρατ<ικ>ὸν εἴρηται, it is worth pointing out that it is also in respect of its body, not its soul, that an animal is capable of perceiving and capable of seeing, since perception and sight require bodily perceptual organs (*DA* 413ᵃ3–5). See also *Top.* 138ᵃ23–25.

Note 201

A sophist, slanderer, or thief . . . : A thief steal's another person's property; a slanderer, another's reputation; a sophist, another person's beliefs or convictions: "those who have their beliefs stolen from them, I mean those who are over-persuaded, or those who forget; because argument, in the one case, and time, in the other, takes away their beliefs without their noticing" (Plato, *Rep.* 413b).

Note 202

The base . . . : "Deliberate choice . . . seems to be most proper to virtue and to be a better judge of people's characters than their actions" (*NE* 1111ᵇ5–6). For a base person may do a good action.

Deliberate choice: We wish for the end or target, we "deliberate about and deliberately choose what furthers it" (*NE* 1113ᵇ3–4). Deliberate choice (*prohairesis*) is thus a matter of choosing (*haireisthai*) one thing before or in preference to (*pro*) another (1112ᵃ16–17), and so of deliberating about what things should be done earlier than or in preference to others in order to further the desired end: "it seems characteristic of the person with understanding to choose the better of two things in every case" (*EE* 1237ᵇ37–38).

Note 203

Every capacity and everything productive . . . : "Every producer produces for the sake of something, and what is unconditionally an end (as opposed to in relation to something and for something else) is not what is producible but what is doable in action; for doing well in action is the end, and the desire is for it" (*NE* 1139ᵇ1–4).

Note 204

So that . . . difference: Reading ὥστε . . . διαφορά.

Note 205
What they are the intensity and excess of: Reading οὗ ἐστι σφοδρότης καὶ ὑπερβολή.

Note 206
Affection: What X *paschei* ("suffers" or "undergoes") is what happens to him, so that he is passive with respect to it, as opposed to what he *poiei* ("does as an agent," or "produces"). When Y does something to X, X is affected by it, so his *pathê* as a result are, in one sense, his affections or attributes and, in another, his passions or feelings. **Coincident:** As at *Ph.* 199ª1 and *Rh.* 1367ᵇ25, where *sumptôma* is equivalent to "by luck," "by coincidence."

Note 207
Empedocles speaks: DK B81 = TEGP 111 F66.

Note 208
In . . . said of: "Among the beings: Some are *said of* an underlying subject but are not *in* any underlying subject—for example, human is said of an underlying subject, the particular human, but is not in any underlying subject. Some are in an underlying subject but are not said of any underlying subject. I mean by 'in a subject' what is in something, not as a part, and cannot exist separately from what it is in—for example, this particular instance of grammar is in an underlying subject, the soul, but it is not said of any underlying subject; and this particular instance of white is in an underlying subject, the body, for all color is in body, but it is not said of any underlying subject" (*Cat.* 1ª20–29).

Note 209
If rest is better: "There is not only an activity of moving but also an activity of immobility, and pleasure is found more in rest than in movement" (*NE* 1154ᵇ26–31).

BOOK 5: SPECIAL AFFECTIONS

Note 210
Book 5: The authenticity and placing of this book have been doubted, but it seems to be referred to as coming after discussion of kinds in Book 4 at 120ᵇ11–12 and 139ᵇ4–5. Reinhardt argues (plausibly) for Aristotelian authorship with later additions.

Note 211
Assigned: The verb *apodidonai* ("give") often has a technical sense in the *Topics*, where it refers to the assignment of a predicate to a subject by an answerer in the form of a universal affirmation (see Reinhardt, pp. 63–67). In Book 5, as in Book 4 (where it involves what is assigned as a kind), this is its prevailing sense.

Note 212

A human is "by nature a tame animal": Humans are by nature tame animals in part, no doubt, because they by nature form couples and households (*Pol.* 1252ª24–ᵇ12). The comparable claim that "a human is by nature a political animal" (1253ª2–3) means, in part, that "an impulse toward this sort of community exists by nature in everyone" (1253ª29–30)—nature and impulse are again associated at *Met.* 1023ª9.

The one is suited for prescribing . . . : "A living being is composed of soul and body, and of these the first is by nature the ruler, the latter by nature the ruled" (*Pol.* 1254ª34–36).

Note 213

The special affection would be undermined: Compare 134ª7, 156ᵇ21.

Note 214

Virtue . . . : Virtue of character is in the rationally calculative and desiring part both (*NE* 1144ᵇ3–1145ª2); theoretical wisdom (*sophia*) in only the scientific part (1139ᵇ12–13, 1144ª1–9). And, of course, virtue more generally can be in things other than souls: artifacts can have virtues.

Note 215

"Composed of soul and body": This special affection is not mentioned in 1.5, since it seems not to separate its subject from everything else: Aristotle's primary god is a living thing (*Met.* 1072ᵇ26) but does not have a body (1071ᵇ21). Notice too that *to zô[i]on* must be "living thing" here, not "animal," since plants have souls and bodies, so that being composed of body and soul is not counterpredicated of animal as a special affection must be. Contrast 129ᵇ26, where *to zô[i]on* must mean "animal," since plants lack perception (*DA* 410ᵇ22–23).

Note 216

Human is always and in every case two-footed: Two-footed is a difference predicated of a form, not a coincidental affection (having two feet) predicated of particular members of the form. Hence cases of amputation or genetic abnormality are not counterexamples. See 134ª5–11.

Note 217

And the spirited part: Reading καὶ θυμικὸν here and at 129ª14.

Note 218

As we also said previously: 128ᵇ22–23.

Note 219

Looked out for: Reading παρατηρεῖν here, as at 129ª23. The verb is used again at 161ª23, where it has the sense of being on the lookout for an opportunity to attack.

Note 220

The one that is so at a time (*pote*) **we look at in relation to the now-said** (*to nun legomenon*) **time:** Suppose A says now that it is a special affection of B to be walking about in the gymnasium. The time he says it is the time of B's walking (the time that is now when he says it) and the time at which its truth value is to be determined. Thus it is at once the referent of *pote* and *to nun*.

Note 221

Things that are not better known . . . things that are better known: (1) "The natural route is from things that are better known and more perspicuous to us to things that are more perspicuous and better known by nature; for the same things are not known to us as are known unconditionally" (*Ph.* 184^{a}16–18). (2) "It advances the work to proceed toward what is better known. For learning comes about for all in this way—through things by nature less well known toward ones that are better known" (*Met.* 1029^{b}3–5; also *APo.* 93^{b}37–94^{a}14, *NE* 1095^{b}2–4, *EE* 1216^{b}32–39). And it is these primary causes and starting-points which, though hard for us to reach, are the most scientifically knowable by nature: "what is most scientifically knowable of all are the primary things and causes; for it is through these and proceeding from these that we know the other things, not these because of the ones that fall under them" (*Met.* 982^{b}1–4).

Note 222

It is for the sake of knowledge . . . : Also 130^{a}4–5, 131^{a}1, 12–13.

Note 223

In each of the two ways: Better known than its subject and better known to belong to it.

Note 224

Discordance: 111^{b}24, 114^{b}32.

Note 225

What was said previously: 129^{b}30–130^{a}14.

Note 226

One and simple: Because of the reference to definitions and babbling (*adole-schein*) in the next paragraph (130^{a}31, 34), it seems likely that the sort of simplicity requisite in the subject of a special affection is the sort required in the special affection itself. This suggests that it is the sort discussed in the following text: "There is a puzzle, though, . . . as to whether there will be a definition of any of the things that are not simple but coupled; for these must be made clear by an addition. . . . By 'addition' I mean the cases in which it turns out that the same thing is said twice" (*Met.* 1030^{b}14–1031^{a}6).

Note 227

Babble: Babbling is also associated with lack of perspicuousness at *Rh.* 1406ᵃ33–34, 1414ᵃ25, but there it does not seem to have the technical sense it has at *SE* 165ᵇ15–17, 173ᵃ31–ᵇ16, 181ᵇ25–182ᵃ6, and presumably here as well.

Note 228

"Supposition . . . since it is one": Reading ἓν ὄν. "One" is presumably to be understood as meaning "tightly unified." See *APo.* 72ᵃ37–ᵇ4: "Anyone who, on the other hand, is going to have scientific knowledge though demonstration must not only know the starting-points more and be more persuaded of them than of what is being proved, but also nothing else must be more persuasive or better known to him among the opposites of the starting-points from which there will be a deduction of the contrary error, if indeed someone who has unconditional scientific knowledge must be incapable of being persuaded out of it." See also 134ᵃ34–35.

Note 229
For the sake of learning: 129ᵇ7–8.

Note 230

The subject . . . : Suppose A is a special affection of B, and the opponent makes use of B in proposing A. Then A will not teach us about B, because we must already know B in order to understand A. Suppose that instead of using B itself in proposing A, the opponent uses X, which is a form of B. Then the definition of X will include B, and so A will again not teach us anything new about B.

Note 231
Simultaneous by nature: "Those things are said to be simultaneous by nature that reciprocate as to implication of being, provided that neither is in any way cause of the other's being—for example, double and half" (*Cat.* 14ᵇ27–30).

Note 232
The opposite of a thing . . . : A predicate F marks a distinction between its extension (all the things that are F) and its anti-extension (all the other things), so that these reciprocate as to implication of being.

Note 233
The sort of thing that may be absent: 131ᵇ19–36.

Note 234
The special affection: Reading τὸ ἴδιον.

Note 235
Every perceptible thing becomes unclear . . . : "Things that pass away are unclear to those who have scientific knowledge, when they have departed from perception, and, though accounts are preserved the same in their soul, there will still not be either definition or demonstration" (*Met.* 1040^{a}2–5; also *NE* 1139^{b}19–22).

Note 236
Must not indicate the essence: 102^{a}18–19.

Note 237
Not put [the subject] in its what-it-is: The Greek is unspecific as to what is not put in the what-it-is of what. The examples given make clear that the subject is meant.

Note 238
The first thing to be assigned must be the kind: In Greek the natural order in the definition of human is *zô[i]on pezon dipoun* (animal, terrestrial, two-footed), while in English the natural order is two-footed terrestrial animal, so that the kind comes last.

Note 239
A person who has stated . . . : He should, as 131^{a}4–5 makes clear, have stated as special affection "substance having a soul," where substance is the kind, which must be specified first in a special affection.

Note 240
When a false diagram is drawn: *SE* 171^{b}12–16n479.

Note 241
{This topic . . . }: Secluded as an abridged variant of the topic that follows.

Note 242
"Having a soul" would be a special affection of living thing: The special affection referred to could be (1) an affection that is special in the strict sense (one not signifying the essence); (2) one that is in other respects (in not signifying the essence) suited to be a special affection in the strict sense; or (3) a special affection in the popular sense, in which A is a special affection of B if and only if A belongs to B alone. The premises establish (3), and so somewhat favor it over (1), but they equally favor (2), making it the better interpretative choice. For up to this point in Book 5, Aristotle has clearly been focusing on special affections in the strict sense, so that making an unadvertised switch to affections special only in the popular sense would be hard to explain. On these different senses, see 101^{b}19–23n21.

Note 243

What is said to be in (*en*) **the underlying subject:** Here, unlike at 127^{b}1, *en* does not have its technical meaning, but simply means "predicated of." Notice *katêgoroumenou* at 132^{b}22.

Note 244

A person who proposes [1] "fire" as a special affection of [2] the body having the finest-grained particles . . . : [2] consists of [2a] a kind (body) and [2b] a special affection (composed of finest-grained particles). When [1] fire is proposed as a special affection of [2], therefore, it is being predicated of [2b] composed of finest-grained particles, which is in fact predicated of fire.

Note 245

What belongs by virtue of participation: "The definition of participate (*metechein*) is 'admit of the account of what is participated in'" (121^{a}11–12).
Contributes (*sumballetai*) **to the essence:** *Sumballein* seems to have the same meaning as *dêloun* ("indicate"), since it is replaced by the latter in the establishing part of this topic (133^{a}6). The definition of an essence is by kind and difference. So, if something contributes to an essence, it must do so either as kind or as difference. But a special affection, as counterpredicated of its subject, cannot contribute as kind (since the form is not predicated of the kind), and so must contribute, if it does, as difference.

Note 246

Since "walking through the marketplace" . . . : The human is human prior to walking in the marketplace and posterior to having walked in it.

Note 247

A tripartite soul: Plato, *Rep.* 435c–441c.

Note 248

Horse and human are the same in form: Because there is a form (sub-kind) of living thing—animal—to which they both belong.

Note 249

Pale human: In *Met.* 7.4 Aristotle raises the associated question of whether there is an essence and definition of pale human. He answers, yes, "but in another way than there is of pale and of substance" (1030^{b}13).

Note 250

Not *what* . . . but *who* . . . not *what* . . . but *which*: The scientific knower is masculine (*ho*); scientific knowledge, feminine (*hê*); what is incapable of being persuaded, neuter (*to*).

Note 251

His speech: What makes the issue one of speech (*lexis*) is this. If two-footed is correctly expressed as a special affection, the account of it must be (1) animal two-footed, so that the kind comes first ($132^a11–13$). Expressed without the kind, by contrast, "two-footed" means (2) having two feet. Since (2) is proposed as a special affection, however, but not as one in relation to something, or at a time, it must be one either (3) by nature or (4) always, since these are all the possibilities. But if it were (3) one by nature, it would have to separate human from everything (128^a35)— which it does not, since birds are also two-footed. So, if it is to be a special affection at all, it must be (4) one that is so always—which it is not, since some humans do not always have two feet. Notice that even these humans are "two-footed animals," in that they are animals that are by nature two-footed. The case is similar with "animal receptive of scientific knowledge"; this is true even of individuals not receptive of scientific knowledge, since they are by nature members of a form receptive of it.

Note 252

What the account is true of . . . : Both the name and the account of colored are true of surface: to be colored is to be a colored surface ($126^a14–15$n199), while the name but not the account applies to body. But if being colored is to be a special affection of surface, both the name and the account must be counterpredicated of surface, which they are not, since the name also applies to body. Similarly, if it is assigned as a special affection of body. See $134^b12–13$.

Note 253

Light: On Aristotle's own view "light is the activity . . . of the transparent insofar as it is transparent . . . a sort of color of the transparent, when it is made actually transparent by fire or something of that sort" (*DA* $418^b9–12$), and so is not (a form of) fire.

Note 254

A thing itself always indicates the being of it: For the same reason that the name that presents the thing signifies its essence or being. See 102^a1n24.

Note 255

The noble and the appropriate are the same thing: $102^a5–6$.

Note 256

Uniform things: Something is uniform in the strict sense if its parts, however small, are of the same sort as the whole—as parts of water, however small, are (or were thought to be) water too (*PA* $647^b17–20$).

Note 257

The greatest quantity of salt water: For other problems with superlatives as special affections, see $134^a31–32$, $134^b22–135^a9$, $139^a9–20$.

Note 258
Breathable: For other problems with dispositions or capacities as special affections, see 138^{b}27–37.

Note 259
[Appear to] be a special affection of human: The addition is made on the basis of a comparison with 136^{a}27–28.

Note 260
By **a human . . . :** The inflected forms are datives. See 124^{b}35–125^{a}13.

Note 261
As was said in the case of the earlier topics as well: Perhaps a reference to the topics on inflections at 114^{b}6–15, but more likely to those on opposites in 5.6, especially the ones on contraries (135^{b}7–16).

Note 262
"Best" . . . the good, "worst" . . . the bad: The lack of a morphological connection between *beltistos* ("best") and *agathos* ("good"), *cheiristos* ("worst") and *kakos* ("bad") shows—and is perhaps intended to show—that inflections are not to be thought of syntactically, but semantically, and also, presumably, ontologically.

Note 263
Productive of health: The reason it is a special affection of a doctor to be productive of health, but not to produce (*poiein*) it (136^{b}37), is this: "it is not the function of medicine to produce health either, but rather to promote health as far as possible; for even to those who are incapable of partaking in health it is nonetheless possible to give good treatment" (*Rh.* 1355^{b}12–14).

Note 264
See whether . . . : 137^{a}19–20 tells us that this topic involves "one thing [subject] brought into combination with several things [predicates]." So here (at least) three things are involved, a, b, c, and one relation R. The claim is (C$_1$) if aRb and aRc, and Rc is not a special affection of a, then Rb is not a special affection of a and (C$_2$) if Rc is a special affection of a, then Rb is not a special affection of a.

Note 265
For example, [1] since practical wisdom has the same relation to the noble and to the shameful (for it is the scientific knowledge of each of them), and [C$_1$] it is not a special affection of practical wisdom to be "the scientific knowledge of the noble," it would not be a special affection of practical wisdom to be "the scientific knowledge of the shameful." But [C$_2$] if it is a special affection of practical wisdom to be "the scientific knowledge of the noble," it would not be a special affection of it to be "the scientific knowledge of the shameful"; for

[P] it is impossible for the same thing be a special affection of several things: Brunschwig secludes all except [P] in this passage, discussing in detail the problems it presents and the solutions that have been proposed (pp. 185–190), none of which is entirely satisfactory. The most pressing of these problems is with [P] itself, which seems irrelevant to [C$_2$]: [C$_2$] involves one subject, practical wisdom (w), and several supposed special affections, scientific knowledge of the noble (Rn) and scientific knowledge of the shameful (Rs), while [P] involves several subjects and a single special affection (a similar principle with what seems to be the same import occurs at 138^{a}20). This may be where [1]—which is a special case of the principle that the scientific knowledge of contraries is the same (104^{a}16)—becomes relevant. It says that wRn and wRs. [C$_1$] draws on [1] and seems to understand Rn and Rs as meaning Rn-alone and Rs-alone. It says that if Rn-alone is not a special affection of w, then neither is Rs-alone. For what, given [1], could make one of them a special affection of w and not the other? [C$_2$] also draws on [1] and understands Rn and Rs in the same way as [C$_1$]. It says that if Rn-alone is a special affection of w, then Rs-alone is not a special affection of w. If Rn-alone is a special affection of w, however, it follows that [C$_3$] if there is a subject x of which Rs-alone *is* a special affection, then x ≠ w. For whatever makes Rn-*alone* a special affection of w cannot also make Rs-*alone* a special affection of it. (The same applies to Rs: if it is a special affection of x, then, if Rn is a special affection of some subject x, x ≠ w.) Since [C$_3$] explicitly involves two subjects, w and x, and one special affection Rn-alone, [P] applies to and justifies it, and—by implication—[C$_2$] as well. But because [C$_3$], though implied by [C$_2$], is not explicitly mentioned in the text, it is difficult to be confident that it is what Aristotle has in mind.

Note 266
Human-itself: That is, the Platonic Form of human.

Note 267
The more so . . . : In logical order: (1) what is least A is least B; (2) what is less A is less B; (3) what is unconditionally A is unconditionally B; (4) what is more A is more B; (5) what is most A is most B. This is the only place in Aristotle where five degrees of a predicate are recognized.

Note 268
Nor would "colored" be one of body at all: And so it would not be one of what is simply a body. See also 131^{b}33–36, 134^{a}22–25, 138^{a}15–20.

Note 269
More perceiving: (1) "Coarser-grained and hotter blood are more productive of strength, while finer-grained and colder blood is more conducive to perception and understanding" (*PA* 648^{a}2–4). (2) "Those animals with more-fine-grained and purer liquid have a perceptual capacity that is more easily moved" (650^{b}22–24).
More living: Though *zôntos* is a participle and not, like *zôon*, a substantive, only animals are perceptive, and Aristotle does think that some animals are more

animals—or more complete, or more perfect, animals—than others: "the more complete ones are hotter in nature and wetter and not earthen" (*GA* 732ᵇ31–32). Since human beings are the most complete or most perfect animals (737ᵇ26–27), they are also hottest and most estimable (*Juv.* 477ᵃ13–23).

Note 270
What is more fire: 146ᵃ13–18.

Note 271
[1] "Perceiving" is more a special affection . . . : It is not clear what makes B *more* or *less* a special affection of A than C is of D. But since specialness is a combination of (a) being counterpredicated and (b) not indicating the essence, degrees of it (or degrees of approximation to it) must be a matter of (a) or (b) or both. For convenience let us also consider here the next example: [2] "Since to be by nature 'tame' is less a special affection of human than 'living' is of animal, and it is a special affection of human to be 'tame by nature,' 'living' would be a special affection of animal" (138ᵃ10–12). Start with [1]. Animals when awake are always perceiving, but humans when awake are not always scientifically knowing (think of now-special affections). And if something is perceiving it must be an animal (since only animals perceive), while if something is scientifically knowing, it need not be human, since it might be a god (132ᵇ11). Next, [2]. Since "human" and "tame" are by nature counterpredicated and do not indicate the essence, yet "tame" by nature is *less* a special affection of animal than "living" is of animal, even though "living" and "animal" are not counterpredicated, it seems that (b) not (a) must be the relevant consideration. This suggests that what makes "tame" by nature less special is that it more indicates (or comes closer to indicating) the essence of human than "perceiving" does in the case of animal. Specialness, after all, involves something like distance from the essence, so that the closer to the essence, the less special. (But one could, it seems, go the other way: then "perceiving" would be more special because it is closer to indicating the essence.)

Note 272
Divisible: Some animals are divisible: "It is evident, too, that both plants and—among animals—some insects continue to live when divided, as having the same form of soul, even if not numerically the same one" (*DA* 411ᵇ19–21). But more are perceptible than are divisible. So perceptible is more a special affection of animal than is divisible.

Note 273
Perceiving is less a special affection . . . : Because animals are always living, but not always perceiving (a dead animal is only homonymously an animal).

Note 274
"Appetitive desiring" is not a special affection . . . : Because the appetitive part is not always appetitively desiring.

Note 275
The topic based on similarity relations . . . : $136^b33–137^a7$, $138^a30–^b22$.

Note 276
**When disestablishing, look to see whether, [1] in assigning the special affec-
tion as a capacity, [2] the opponent has not assigned the special affection also
as a capacity in relation to [3] what is not, [4] when the capacity does not admit
of belonging to what is not:** Look at the example: the opponent assigns breathable as a special affection of air. Start with [1]–[2]. Notice, first, that breathable
is only implicitly assigned in relation to anything at all. Thus the fact that it is so
assigned is presumably something that must be adduced by the questioner:
[5] Isn't something breathable if and only if it can be breathed? —Yes.— [6] And isn't
something such that it can be breathed if and only if there is something than can
breathe it? —Yes.— [7] And isn't something a thing that can breathe it if and only
if it is an animal? —Yes. Next look at [3]. Since the questioner has had to adduce
answers to [5]–[7], the answerer has obviously not violated the topic requiring
explicitness about whether what is being assigned is an intrinsically special, or a
now-special, affection ($131^b5–7$). Yet at this point it has become relevant: [8] Isn't
a quantity of air, A, breathable because there is some animal, B, that can breathe
it? —Yes.— [9] Can't B be (exist) at time t_1 and not be at time t_2? —Yes. [10] Is
A breathable at t_2? If the answer to [10] is no, the answerer is defeated, since at
t_2 being air and being breathable are not counterpredicated, since A is air but
is not breathable. That he does answer in this way is presupposed by [4]. What
has happened, in other words, is that the questioner has been able to unpack
the answerer's assigned special affection and exploit a concealed inadequacy or
unclarity in it. Notice that in this case "what is not" acquires a temporal operator:
what is not *at some time*. Suppose, though, that answerer had, in effect, answered
yes, only to [11] Isn't air breathable if and only if for any quantity of it there can
be an animal to breathe it? Then the questioner could attack it on the grounds
that breathable, so explained, cannot be a special affection of air, because it is
less well known than air ($129^b1–21$), or on the grounds that air's breathability is
simultaneous in nature with the existence of animals, and so once again has not
been made better known by the proposed special affection ($131^a12–15$). Notice
that in this case "what is not" acquires a modal operator: there *cannot* be. The
moral of the story, then, where [3] is concerned, is that it has no fixed interpretation, but instead acquires the relevant one in the course of the subsequent
dialectical argument.

Note 277
A person who assigns . . . : "I say, then, that a thing really is if it has any capacity
at all, either by nature to affect something else or else to be affected in even the
smallest way by even the most trivial thing, even if it only happens once. I'll posit
it as a definition that the things that are are nothing other than capacity" (Plato,
Sph. 247e).

Note 278

What the name is true of, the account is not true of: The supporting argument—which foreshadows discussions in the theory of reference by Gottlob Frege, Saul Kripke, and Hilary Putnam—is this: "fire" is a name; "the hottest body" is a definite description. In the actual situation, they refer to the same thing. But "fire" is a so-called rigid designator: even in a counterfactual situation, it refers to what it refers to in the actual situation. That is one reason why it is a necessary truth that fire burns. "The hottest body," by contrast, is a non-rigid designator. In the actual situation it refers to fire, but in a counterfactual situation it refers to whatever body in that situation happens to be hottest. That is one reason why it is not a necessary truth that the hottest body burns—for the hottest body need not be hot enough to burn anything.

BOOK 6: DEFINITIONS

Note 279

Definitions: Aristotle uses *horos, horismos* (both translated as "definition"), and *logos* ("account") more or less interchangeably: "a definition is an account that signifies the essence" (101^b38). He considers only topics that disestablish.
As was said previously: 101^b19–22.

Note 280

Topics related to the coincident: Coincidents are defined and discussed at 102^b4–26. See also 102^b29–35, 155^a28–36.

Note 281

Topics related to the kind and the special affection: Books 4 and 5 (respectively).

Note 282

Not defining correctly has two parts: "We should consider our definitions as adequate in each case if they neither lack perspicuousness nor are [too] exact" (*Rh.* 1369^b31–32).

Note 283

More extended version: 121^b1–14, 144^a31, $^b6$, *epi pleon* means "has a wider extension than," or "applies to more things." Here, however, it refers to the extension or length of the account (definition) itself, which is too extended when it contains superfluous things.

Note 284

A leading into being: Plato, *Sph.* 219b.

Note 285
Trivial objection: *Sukophantia* is often "quibbling," or "sophistry," as at *SE* 174^{b}9, *Rh.* 1402^{a}16, *Po.* 1456^{a}5. Here, however, the objection seems sound but easy, so that "trivial" seems to convey the right meaning.

Note 286
Inflexible: For the basis of the metaphor, see 130^{b}16n228.
Harmony: Plato, *Rep.* 430e: "[Temperance] is more like a sort of concord and harmony than the previous virtues."

Note 287
Plato: Probably not the philosopher, but the comic Athenian poet and contemporary of Aristophanes. See also *Rh.* 1376^{a}10.

Note 288
A metaphor . . . : (1) "Metaphor . . . most of all produces learning [in audiences]" (*Rh.* 1410^{b}13). (2) "To use metaphors well is to see likeness" (*Po.* 1459^{a}7–8). But in science, as in dialectic (139^{b}32–140^{a}2), metaphor is to be avoided: (3) "If one must not argue dialectically by means of metaphors, it is clear too that one must neither define things by means of metaphors nor define what is said by means of metaphors; for then one will necessarily be arguing dialectically by means of metaphors" (*APo.* 97^{b}37–39). (4) "Metaphor is a feature of poetry, but for the knowledge of nature it is not adequate" (*Mete.* 357^{a}27–28). See also *Top.* 123^{a}33–37, *Rh.* 3.2–6, 10–11, *Po.* 1457^{b}6–33.

Note 289
"Number that moves itself": "Some thinkers . . . declared the soul to be a self-moving number" (*DA* 404^{b}29–30). See Xenocrates, F85 Isnardi.
As Plato has defined it: "Since what is moved by itself has been proved to be immortal, it would not be shameful to say that this is the substance [or essence] and account of soul" (*Phdr.* 245e; also *Lg.* 895e–896a). Aristotle himself rejects such views: "It is not merely false that the substance of the soul is the sort of thing that it is said to be by those who say that the soul is what moves—or is capable of moving—itself, but rather for movement to belong to the soul is something impossible" (*DA* 405^{b}31–406^{a}2).

Note 290
Phlegm: (1) "Phlegm is a residue of the useful nourishment" (*GA* 725^{a}15–16). (2) "By 'residue (*perittôma*)' I mean a leftover of the nourishment" (724^{b}26–27).
Unconcocted: "Concoction is a completion due to the natural and proper heat and is [produced] from the opposing affectables, these being the matter proper to the given thing. For when it has been concocted, it is completed and has come to be. And the starting-point of the completion comes about due to the proper heat, even if certain of the external aids contributed to its accomplishment—for example, nourishment is helped in its concoctions even by baths and by other things of this

sort. But the starting-point, at any rate, is the heat within the body itself. And the end in some cases is the nature—but nature, we say, as form and substance. . . . Concoction, in fact, is what everything is affected by when its matter—that is, its liquid—is mastered. For this is what is determined by the heat in its nature" (*Mete.* 379^{b}18–35).

Note 291
Counterpredicated: 102^{a}19n25.

Note 292
Xenocrates says . . . : F3 Isnardi.

Note 293
Every privation . . . : 106^{b}21n67.

Note 294
If one has defined decency . . . : Plato, †*Def.* 412b gives this definition. Compare: "A decent person tends to take less than his share" (*NE* 1136^{b}20–21).
The just is a sort of advantage . . . : "Those constitutions that aim at the common advantage are—in accord with what is unconditionally just—correct" (*Pol.* 1279^{a}17–19).

Note 295
Prior and better known ones: 129^{b}3n221.
Teaching and learning: (1) "Teaching is argument based on scientific knowledge" (*Rh.* 1355^{a}26). (2) "It is from things already known, however, that all teaching proceeds; . . . for some is through induction and some by deduction" (*NE* 1139^{b}26–28).

Note 296
Exact and extraordinary thought: 157^{a}9n368.

Note 297
Unless it so happens that . . . : Compare: "the better someone is at selecting premises, [the more] he will—without noticing it—produce a science that is distinct from dialectic and rhetoric; for if he hits upon starting-points, it will no longer be dialectic or rhetoric, but instead will be that science whose starting-points he possesses" (*Rh.* 1358^{a}23–26).

Note 298
The kind and the difference do away with the form: That is, they do away with the form when done away with themselves. See 123^{a}14–15n180.

Note 299
They are also better known: "The prior is always better known than the posterior" (*Protr.* B33).

Note 300
As we said previously: 141ᵃ26–ᵇ34.

Note 301
What is at rest and definite . . . : This is probably one error ("what is at rest, that is, definite, through what is indefinite, that is, in movement") rather than two distinct errors, one of indefiniteness and the other of movement.

What remains at rest . . . : "If demonstration is of the necessary things and definition is a matter of scientific knowledge, and if, just as scientific knowledge cannot be scientific knowledge at one time and ignorance at another (but instead it is belief that is like that), so neither definition nor demonstration can be that way either (but instead it is belief that is of what admits of being otherwise), then it is clear that there will not be either definition or demonstration of such things [namely, movable and perceptible ones]. For things that pass away are unclear to those who have scientific knowledge, when they have departed from perception, and, though accounts are preserved the same in their soul, there will still not be either definition or demonstration. That is why, in issues relating to definition, when someone is defining one of the particular things, we must not be ignorant of the fact that it is always possible to do away with this definition, since particulars cannot be defined" (*Met.* 1039ᵇ31–1040ᵃ7). Definition, since it is of starting-points, is prior to demonstration.

Note 302
If he has defined the sun . . . : Plato, †*Def.* 411b.

Note 303
The ones mentioned: 141ᵃ26–142ᵇ19.

Note 304
As was stated previously: 139ᵇ3–5.

Note 305
The kind participates in the form: Which is impossible (121ᵃ13–14).

Note 306
They say . . . : Since something is in the kind F by participating in the F-itself.

Note 307
Wanton aggression: "Wanton aggression (*hubris*) consists in doing or saying things that involve shame for the one who suffers them, not in order that something or other [beneficial] may come about for the agent himself, or because something [bad] has happened to him, but in order to take pleasure in it" (*Rh.* 1378ᵇ23–25).

Note 308
A difference seems to signify a quality: 122ᵇ16–17, 128ᵃ26–27.

Note 309

This something: Brunschwig prints τόδε τι but translates only τόδε as the *lectio difficilior*. On either reading, the reference must be to a substance—that is, to a particular subject of predication (see *atoma* at 144^{b}2). For otherwise it would have to refer to the essence of something, and this topic would involve the same point as the one made at the close of the preceding one. For essence and what-it-is amount to the same thing in the *Topics*. *Tode ti*, for its part, involves a particularizing element and a generalizing element. I take the demonstrative pronoun *tode* as particularizing (as suggested by *Met.* 1030^{a}5–6) and the indefinite pronoun *ti* as generalizing, but since *tode* need not be particularizing (as it may not be at 1032^{b}6–21) and *ti* may be, it is possible to go the other way and translate it as "thing of a certain sort." Often *tode ti* appears in translations simply as "a this," and in at least one place Aristotle himself suggests that *tode* and *ti* are interchangeable (1069^{b}9, 11). (1) In very many cases, being a *tode ti* is a distinctive mark of *ousia* ("substance"), and so has some share in the ambiguity of the latter, as between (1a) an ultimate subject of predication and (2a) the substance or essence of something (103^{b}28n43). This is reflected in the fact that (1b) a particular man and a particular horse are primary substances (*Cat.* 2^{a}11–14), so that "it is indisputably true that each of them signifies a *tode ti*" (3^{b}10–12), while at the same time (2b) what is separable and a *tode ti* is "the shape or form of each thing" (*Met.* 1017^{b}24–26; also 1042^{a}27–29, 1049^{a}35, 1070^{a}11).

Note 310

Predicated of the differences one by one: The argument is apparently this: D_1, D_2, and D_3 are the differences of a form S, so that $S = D_1 + D_2 + D_3$. Animal is predicated of D_1, and of D_2, and of D_3 one by one. But because $D1 \neq D2 \neq D3$, the animal that is predicated of them in this way must be a distinct animal in each case, so that the A_1 predicted of $D_1 \neq$ the A_2 predicated of $D_2 \neq$ the A_3 predicated of D_3. (For otherwise D_1, D_2, and D_3 would be one and the same animal, and so would be numerically identical.) Since $S = D_1 + D_2 + D_3$, it follows that $S = A_1 + A_2 + A_3$, so that many distinct animals are predicated of S.

Note 311

The difference has a wider extension than the forms: The assumption, as in the previous topic, is that the form S is defined by a number of distinct differences, D_1, D_2, and D_3, each of which, taken one by one, has a wider extension than S.

Note 312

The difference must be posterior to the kind but prior to the form: The extension of the kind is wider than that of the difference, so that doing away with the kind does away with the difference, but not vice versa, making the kind prior (123^{a}14–15n180). Similarly, the extension of the difference is wider than the form, making it prior to the form (122^{b}35–123^{a}1). Two-footed is an example, since it is a difference of both terrestrial and winged animals. See 144^{b}22–24.

Note 313
A certain quality: That is, a difference. See 144[a]18–19.

Note 314
Every affection, if it becomes more intensified . . . : 114[b]37n123.

Note 315
Theoretical, practical, and productive: Reading καὶ πρακτικὴ. This tripartite division of the sciences is the common Aristotelian one: "all thought is either practical or productive or theoretical" (*Met.* 1025[b]25). See also 157[a]10–11.

Note 316
And practical . . . : Reading καὶ πρακτικὴ τινός.

Note 317
A strigil . . . : A strigil was an instrument with a curved spoon-like blade, used to scrape off sweat and dirt after exercising. In Aristophanes, *Thesmophoriazusae*, 556–557, the word is used to refer to a device for drawing off wine from a cask.

Note 318
Aphtharton: Verbals in Greek ending in *ton*—of which *aphtharton* is an example—sometimes have (1) the meaning of a perfect passive participle ("has not passed away") and sometimes express (2) possibility ("incapable of passing away").

Note 319
A person who is more in love . . . : The idea might be better conveyed the other way around: when the appetite is sated by actual intercourse, love is not simultaneously lessened. See also 152[b]7–9.

Note 320
He defines beautiful . . . : Plato, *Hp. Ma.* 298a, defines beauty as "pleasant both to hearing and to sight." Aristotle's definition is disjunctive.

Note 321
The being for each relative: 125[b]27n195.

Note 322
He should have assigned in the definition . . . : (1) Grammar = (2) the scientific knowledge of letters. In (2) we learn what the science is relative to, namely, letters, but not what grammar is relative to. If we think we have been told that (3) grammar is of letters, then substitution of (2) for grammar in (3) will show us our mistake, since it will result in (4) grammar is the scientific knowledge of letters of letters—which is babbling. See also 142[b]30–35.

Note 323
The activity is more of an end than having finished it: 106^{b}3n66.

Note 324
The one controlled by certain pleasures: That is, those of touching certain parts of the body (*NE* 1118^{b}1–8).

Note 325
Appetite-itself for pleasant-itself . . . : Aristotle is perhaps thinking of the following text: "But thirst-itself will never be for anything other than the very thing that it is in its nature to be an appetite for: namely, drink-itself; and, similarly, hunger is for food" (Plato, *Rep.* 437e).

Note 326
The elements [or topics] based on contraries and coordinates: 2.9.

Note 327
Those who say what ignorance is in accord with negation: "Ignorance, not of the sort that is so-called with respect to a negation, but with respect to a disposition, is error that comes about in a deduction" (*APo.* 79^{b}23–24).

Note 328
Plato defines animals . . . : No such definition occurs in Plato's extant writings.

Note 329
To those who say there are Forms: Reading τοῖς λέγουσιν ἰδέας εἶναι. See 154^{a}18–20, which refers back to the present text.

Note 330
Dionysius: Probably the little-known Dionysius the Sophist, mentioned at ††*Phgn.* 808^{a}16.

Note 331
Pre-deduce: 156^{a}7.

Note 332
Someone says that what is synonymous is homonymous . . . : The definer gives account A$_1$ as the account of name N, notes that it fits case C$_1$ to which N applies, but not the other case, C$_2$, and infers that N is homonymous. The questioner should respond by looking at the account A$_2$ of C$_2$, because if it also fits C$_1$, N is not homonymous after all, since a single account applies to all cases to which N applies. Consequently, A$_1$ cannot be the correct account (definition) of N.

Note 333
In some cases . . . : 110ª14–22.

Note 334
If someone has defined . . . : Plato, *Prm.* 137e: "Straight is that whose mid-point blocks the view of the two extremities."

Note 335
Name for name: *Onomata* now seems to cover both nouns and verbs, not just nouns (also *onomata*). The substitution mentioned is that of names for parts of the thing being defined.

Note 336
Not only has it not been defined: Because names have simply been substituted for names, rather than accounts for names, as definition requires.

Note 337
Alternatively . . . must be made: Reading ἢ τοῦτο . . . ποιητέον, which Brunschwig suspects on doctrinal, not textual grounds. It is true, to be sure, that Aristotle himself holds that the kind is unconditionally more knowable than the difference, since the latter is defined in terms of the former. But in a dialectical context the difference may be more knowable to us—more knowable to the participants. In which case, it would be ridiculous to insist on making a substitution for the kind, even though in a scientific context it is what must be done. See 141ᵇ3–22.

Note 338
All relatives are convertible: 125ª5–13 and, on conversion, 109ª10n83.

Note 339
Said in relation to being: Generally speaking, one of the starting-points of a science posits the existence of the kind with which the science deals (*APo.* 76ᵇ11–13). This kind, however, need not be a kind of substances, as the example of medicine makes clear, since health is not a substance. In implicitly referring to a minority of sciences that do not deal with being, therefore, Aristotle is not referring to sciences, such as mathematics, which, though they deal with beings, do not deal with separable substances (*Met.* 1077ᵇ31–34). Instead, as the following text shows, he is referring to the productive sciences, or crafts: "from experience, or from the entire universal having come to rest in the soul, the one beyond the many (this being whatever is present as one and the same in all of them), comes a starting-point of craft knowledge and scientific knowledge—of craft knowledge if it concerns production, of scientific knowledge if it concerns being" (*APo.* 100ª6–9).

Note 340

Wisdom: *Sophia*—usually theoretical wisdom for Aristotle himself, but here as elsewhere in *Top.* and *SE*, probably wisdom in general—is the virtue of the scientific sub-part of the part of the soul that has reason (*NE* 1144ª1–3) and the most exact form of scientific knowledge (1141ª9–ᵇ8).

Productive of happiness: "These states [practical wisdom and theoretical wisdom] must be intrinsically choiceworthy (for each is the virtue of one of the two parts that have reason) even if neither of them produces anything at all. Next, they do indeed produce something; not, however, as medicine produces health but as health does. *That* is also how theoretical wisdom produces happiness, since as a part of virtue as a whole, being possessed and actualized, it produces happiness" (*NE* 1144ª1–6).

Note 341

Mina: A drachma was a day's pay for someone engaged in public works; a mina was a hundred silver drachmas.

Note 342

The dangers of war . . . : "The person who is said to be courageous in the full sense is the one who is unanxious where noble death is concerned and the things that are an imminent threat of death. And the things that occur in war are most of all of this sort" (*NE* 1115ª32–35).

Note 343

Take a good guess . . . : The relevant sort of good guesswork (*eustochia*) is the sort that hits on "the middle term in an imperceptible amount of time" on seeing the extremes (*APo.* 89ᵇ10–15). For the middle term is what states the cause of the thing (89ᵇ37–90ª9), and the cause of the thing's being what it is, is what the real or scientific definition of it states (93ᵇ29–94ª10).

BOOK 7: SAMENESS AND DISTINCTNESS

Note 344
It was said . . . : 103ª23–24.

Note 345
Xenocrates demonstrates . . . : Fr. 158 Isnardi.

Note 346
Those who say that void and full of air are the same thing: "Those, then, who try to prove that a void does not exist in fact refute not what people mean by 'void,' but what they say in error about it, as Anaxagoras does and those who try

to refute it in this way. For they prove that air is something, by twisting wineskins and proving how strong the air is, and by trapping it in clepsydras. But what people mean by 'void' is an extended space in which there is no perceptible body. They, however, thinking that all being consists of bodies, say that what there is nothing at all in is void, because what is full of air is void. But it is not this that needs to be proved, that air is something, but that there is no extended space, either separable or actively existing, that is distinct from bodies, and that divides the totality of body so that it is not continuous (as Democritus, Leucippus, and many other of the physicists say), or is perhaps even outside the totality of body, which is continuous" (*Ph.* 213^{a}22–^{b}2).

Note 347
As was said previously: 102^{a}11–14.

Note 348
The other features we prescribed: 139^{a}25–35.

Note 349
None or few of those who argue dialectically deduce a definition: The inclusion of geometers and other scientists among those who argue dialectically is explained by the fact that definitions of essences are scientific starting-points and that dialectic provides "a route toward the starting-points of all methodical inquiries" (101^{b}2–4). See Introduction, pp. xl–xliii.

Note 350
It belongs to another work: *APo.* 2.3–13.

Note 351
Determined more exactly elsewhere: *APo.* 2.13.

Note 352
Dilating of sight: 107^{b}29–31n72.

Note 353
[1] Looking at the particular cases and [2] looking at the various forms . . . : If D is the definition proposed, what it is a definition of is some universal U, since there is no definition of particulars (*Met.* 1039^{b}27–29). [1] instructs us to look at particular instances of U to see whether D fits them (if it does not, it cannot be the definition of U). [2] tells us to look at the various sub-form of U, keeping in mind that D must not just fit them, but be synonymous with them.

Note 354
As was stated previously: 148^{a}14–22.

Note 355
Or predicated it of itself . . . : 112^{b}21–26.

Note 356
Assigned in combination: 132^{a}10–16.

BOOK 8: THE PRACTICE OF DIALECTIC

Note 357
Stated previously: Books 2–7.

Note 358
For the sake of competition: 159^{a}26–36, 161^{a}37–^{b}1, *SE* 165^{b}10–11.

Note 359
It is necessary to make use of these too: *SE* 183^{b}1–6.

Note 360
What was posited: Not a *thesis* in the technical sense, explained at 104^{b}19–28, but simply what is put forward for dialectical discussion. *Thesis* generally has this looser sense in Book 8.

Note 361
The premises (*lêmmata***) . . . those (***ekeina***) in virtue of which . . . :** A *lêmma* in the strict mathematical sense is a subsidiary theorem proven as a part of a larger overall theorem. Here too *lêmmata* have this status, since they are pre-deduced conclusions serving as premises in the primary dialectical deduction bearing on the posit at issue. But since *ekeina* refers back to these, but must also refer to the un-deduced premises of the pre-deductions themselves, "premise" is the best translation.

Note 362
Claims: 110^{a}38n93.

Note 363
A minimally suspicious attitude: *Anupoptôs* can mean wholly unsuspicious or minimally suspicious, as the alpha privative can convey either meaning: "something is said to be *un*-equal because it does not have the equality it is natural for it to have, and *in*-visible either because it has no color at all or because it has minimal color, and foot-*less* either because it has no feet or minimal feet" (*Met.* 1022^{b}32–36). Realism favors the weaker translation.

Note 364
As if in a comparison: A *parabolê* is an argument by analogy based on similarity: "Socratic arguments are cases of comparison. For example, if someone were to argue that officials should not be chosen by lot; for that would be like someone choosing athletes by lot—not those capable of competing, but those to whom the lot falls; or like choosing by lot one of the sailors to act as captain, on the grounds that it should be the one to whom the lot falls and not the one with scientific knowledge" (*Rh.* 1393^{b}4–8).

Note 365
Hagglers: "A deficient person (who is unpleasant in everything) will be a quarrelsome sort of person and disagreeable (*duskolos*)" (*NE* 1108^{a}29–30). In dialectic, however, the disagreeableness seems to be of a specific sort, and the verb *duskolainein* to have a narrower and somewhat technical sense, which "haggle" seems to capture. See 160^{b}1–13, 161^{a}21–^{b}10.

Note 366
Incisive answerers: The adjective *drimus*, which means "piercing," "pungent," "acrid," and, as applied to persons, "bitter" or "fierce," seems, like *duskolos*, to have acquired a somewhat technical sense in dialectic. See *SE* 182^{b}32–183^{a}13.

Note 367
Those who draw false diagrams: *SE* 171^{b}12–16n479.

Note 368
One science is better than another either by being more exact: In his focal discussion of exactness (*akribeia*), Aristotle makes clear that a science's degree of it is measured along three different dimensions: "One science is more exact than another, and prior to it, if it is both of the that and the why, and not of the that separately from the why; and if it does not have an underlying subject while the other does have an underlying subject (as, for example, arithmetic is more exact than harmonics); and if it makes fewer assumptions while the other makes some additional one (for example, arithmetic is more exact than geometry). By 'an additional assumption' I mean, for example, that a unit is a substance that does not have a position and a point is a substance that has a position—the latter depends on an additional assumption" (*APo.* 87^{a}31–37). The upshot is thus twofold. First, the most exact version or formulation of a science is the most explanatory one—the one consisting of demonstrations from starting-points. Second, of two sciences, formulated in the most exact way, one is more exact than the other if it demonstrates facts that the other deals with but does not demonstrate. Because a natural science has to posit sublunary matter in addition to such starting-points, the strictly theoretical sciences (theology, astronomy, and mathematics) are more exact than any natural science. Hence it is among these that the most exact one will be found. And it will be the one that explains what the others treat as a fact or undemonstrated posit. *Top.* 111^{a}8–9 offers *saphês* ("perspicuous") as an equivalent of *akribês*.

Or by being the science of better things: (1) "We suppose that knowing is a noble and an estimable thing, and that one sort is more so than another either in virtue of its exactness or by being about better and more wondrous things" (*DA* 402ª1–2). (2) "No science should be regarded as more estimable than this [theoretical wisdom, theology]. For the most divine science is also the most estimable. And a science would be most divine in only two ways: if the [primary] god most of all would have it, or if it were a science of divine things. And this science alone is divine in both these ways; for the [primary] god seems to be among the causes of all things and to be a sort of starting-point, and this is the sort of science that the [primary] god alone, or that he most of all, would have. All the sciences are more necessary than this one, then, but none is better" (*Met.* 983ª4–983ª11).

Some practical: Reading αί δὲ πρακτικαί. See also 145ª15–16.

Note 369

Paradigms: A *paradeigma* involves proving "on the basis of many similar cases that things are a certain way" (*Rh.* 1356ᵇ14–15).

Choerilus: Late 5th-cent BC epic poet from Samos, author of *Persica*, an epic on the Persian war.

Note 370

Spoken about previously: 105ª16–19.

Note 371

Quibble: 139ᵇ26n285.

Note 372

Bring his objection against another case . . . : (1) The only legitimate way to object to the conclusion of an induction is to object to something in the inductive base. (2) An exception to (1) is when the conclusion is itself the only case. To make it clear that one is not violating (1), one must claim that (2) applies.

Note 373

Subtract the point to which the objection is made . . . : The questioner asks, after giving an induction in support, "Aren't all A's B's?" The answerer objects that A_1 is not a B. The questioner asks, "Aren't all A's, with the exception of A_1, B's?" And so on, until the answerer gives the questioner something useful for his proposed dialectical deduction.

Note 374

Neither think it requisite . . . : The meaning is something like this: It is not in the interests of answerers for things to be defined, since definitions are easy to attack. So they should not require that they be given or, if questioners give them, they should simply accept them.

Note 375

A diagram . . . drawn in proof: *Graphesthai* is doing correctly what *pseudographein* (*SE* 171^{b}12–16n479) is doing falsely, namely, drawing a diagram as part of a proof. Things that are *graphetai* (literally, "drawn") are mathematical propositions at *Met.* 1077^{a}9.

Note 376

Reciprocal subtraction: If A is a larger magnitude than B, repeatedly subtract B from A until the remainder R_1 is less than B. Subtract R_1 from B until a remainder R_2 less than R_1 is reached. Continue in the same way. Stop if and when a fit is reached. If C is a larger magnitude than D, the pair <A, B> has the same reciprocal subtraction as the pair <C, D>, if the number of such subtractions is the same for each. If the procedure does not terminate, the magnitudes are incommensurable. Aristotle applies the procedure to parallelograms and their sides.

Note 377

Except that . . . are not many: Brunschwig brackets this as an insertion by a later corrector.

Note 378

Function: An *ergon* is (1) an activity that is the use or actualization of a state, capacity, or disposition; (2) a work or product that is the further result of such an activity (*NE* 1094^{a}5–6). It is intimately related to its possessor's end or final cause: "The function is the end, and the activity is the function" (*Met.* 1050^{a}21–22; also *Cael.* 286^{a}8–9).

Note 379

Demonstrates the problem: A problem is a proposition, and so is the sort of thing that can be demonstrated. See 104^{b}1–17.

Note 380

He must make the comparison: Namely, between the relative costs and benefits, measured in terms of things believed unconditionally, of accepting or refusing a premise.

Note 381

As Heraclitus says . . . : Aristotle discusses the Heraclitean denial of PNC at *Met.* 1005^{b}5–1009^{a}5.

Note 382

Simple: Here, as at 158^{b}10, the contrary of being said in many ways.

Note 383

Through induction or through similarity: On the difference, see 156^{b}14–17.

Note 384

Yet even this is not enough: That is, enough to avoid the charge of haggling. For an answerer could respond by means of an argument like Zeno's. But this too would be haggling.

Difficult to resolve: To resolve an argument is to untie (also, *luein*) the knot or puzzle that it produces when it conflicts with another argument: "For those who wish to be puzzle-free it advances the work to go through the puzzles well; for the subsequent puzzle-free condition is reached by untying the knots (*luein*) produced by the puzzles raised in advance, and it is not possible to untie a knot you are unaware of. But a puzzle in thought makes clear the existence of a knot in the thing at issue" (*Met.* 995^{a}27–31). See also *Top.* 160^{b}34–35.

Zeno's argument . . . : Zeno of Elea (DK 29 = TEGP pp. 245–270) was a follower and defender of Parmenides. Aristotle discusses the argument against movement at *Ph.* 233^{a}21–31 and its companions in 6.9.

Note 385

If someone obtained that [1] the person seated is writing, and that [2] Socrates is seated; for it follows from these that [3] Socrates is writing. [4] When "Socrates is seated" is done away with, the argument is no closer to being resolved, although the claim is false. But it is not by depending on it that the argument is false; for if someone happened to be seated but not writing, the same resolution will no longer fit such a case. So it is not this that must be done away with, but rather that the person seated is writing; for [5] not every seated person is writing: The argument from [1] and [2] to [3] is fallacious, since from true premises, and a sound deduction, it reaches a conclusion that is in fact false, since Socrates is not writing. The fallacy trades on an ambiguity in [1], which is revealed in [5]. The ambiguity is this. Noun phrases consisting of the definite article plus a noun ("the N") are ambiguous: they can be either singular terms referring to unique particulars or generic terms, roughly equivalent in meaning to a universally quantified term. If [1] = [1a] "All persons seated are writing," [3] follows from it and [2], and must be true, if they are. But if [1] = [1b] "The particular person seated over there is writing" [3] does not follow, since the person who makes it true may be Coriscus, not Socrates. Turn now to [4]. If we do away with or falsify [2], we do not resolve the argument, because we have not shown such arguments to be invalid (or "false," as Aristotle says), but only that this one is unsound.

Note 386

Drawing false diagrams: *SE* 171^{b}12–16n479.

Note 387

Stated previously: 100^{a}29–^{b}23, but also 159^{a}25–34.

Note 388

Proposed in arguments: Reading τὸ προκείμενόν.

Note 389

An argument as intrinsically such: A, the argument referred to, is the dialectical deduction guiding the strategy of questioning that questioner Q employs in his attempt to derive conclusion C. P is the set of A's premises. The possible defects in A are these: (1) There is no conclusion that P entails; (2) P does not entail C; (3) needed premises are omitted from P; (4) unneeded premises are included in P; (5) the needed premises in P are less acceptable than C; (6) the needed premises in P are more difficult to establish than C.

Note 390

This is evident from the *Analytics*: *APr.* 2.2, *APo.* 78^{a}6–13.

Note 391

{A *philosopheme* . . . contradiction}: Both Brunschwig and Smith seclude this passage; OCT retains. The grounds for seclusion are these: elsewhere a *philosophêma* seems to be a work of philosophy (*Cael.* 279^{a}30) or a puzzle that has become a standard philosophical one (294^{a}19), while an *aporêma* seems to be simply a puzzle (*APr.* 71^{a}29, *APo.* 92^{a}29, *Ph.* 211^{a}10, *GC* 327^{b}32, *Met.* 1004^{a}34, 1011^{a}6, 1077^{a}1). Moreover, a dialectical deduction is not a deduction of a contradiction *per se*, but rather of a proposition that contradicts one the answerer defends. It may be, though, that these terms—like others—have acquired other more technical meanings for use specifically in the context of dialectic. *Sophisma*, which Aristotle has just used (162^{a}14), and which clearly stands in need of an explanation, is like this, but so too is *epicheirêma*, which he uses at 110^{a}11 (where it is translated "attack"). *Philosophêma* and *aporêma* seem to be cut from the same cloth.

Note 392

If something is proved from premises both of which seem so, but do not seem equally so, there is nothing to prevent (*ouden kôluei*) **what is proved from seeming more so than each singly:** Argument A consists of premises P$_1$, P$_2$, and conclusion C. P$_1$ seems to be so to degree d$_1$, P$_2$ to degree d$_2$, where d$_1$ > d$_2$. To what degree d$_c$ can the conclusion C then seem to be so? Aristotle claims that d$_c$ > d$_1$ >d$_2$. But that seems wrong: a conclusion cannot rationally seem to be more so than each of its premises taken singly. Some mss. Read τοῦ ἑτέρου ("of one of the two") in place of ἑκατέρου ("than each singly"), which would solve the problem, but ἑκατέρου is better attested. What allows us to preserve both it and the logic of rational seeming is what Aristotle says about adding premises, since it suggests that A is something that can be modified, even if not all its premises can be replaced (162^{a}6–8). But any stronger version A* of A must have a premise P$_x$ that seems to be so to a degree d$_x$ > d$_1$. In keeping with the logic of rational seeming, suppose that d$_c$ is something like a mean between d$_1$ and d$_2$ = $\frac{d_1 + d_2}{2}$ (anyway it is greater than d$_2$ but not as great as d$_1$). Pick a P$_x$ such that $\frac{d_1 + d_2 + d_x}{2}$ > d$_1$ (there is nothing to prevent one from being available). Add P$_x$ to P$_1$ and P$_2$ to get A*. d$_c$ will now be greater than either d$_1$ or d$_2$. A piece of evidence in support of this interpretation is the locution *ouden kôluei*, which shows that Aristotle is not claiming that d$_c$ must be greater than either d_1 or d_2, but only that its being greater is consistent with P_1 and P_2 seeming so to the degrees they do. See next note.

Note 393
But [1] if one premise were to seem so and the other to seem neither so nor not so, or if one were to seem so and the other not so, then if these are equal, [the conclusion] would be equally so or not so, but [2] if one of the two is more, it will follow along with (*akolouthêsei*) **the one that is more so:** The shift from *ouden kôleuei* to *akolouthêsei* suggests that Aristotle is now talking about argument A (previous note) and the logical relations between P_1, P_2, and C. It is enough to notice, therefore, that in [1] $d_1 = d_2 = d_c$, while in [2] d_c follows along with whichever of d_1 and d_2 is greater (let it be d_1). This need not be to say that $d_c = d_1$, but only that $d_c > d_2$ (which follows from the fact that $\frac{d_1 + d_2}{2} > d_2$).

Note 394
If to prove that [C] one belief is more [a belief] than another, someone were to assume the following: [P1] a thing-itself is most of all [that thing], [P2] there is a truly believable-itself, and so [P3] it will be more [that thing] than the particular ones; but [P4] what is said in relation to the more is more [that thing]; but again [P5] there is a true believable-itself, which [P6] will be more exactly [that thing] than the particular ones: The error or defect here is that the argument (that is, the dialectical deduction guiding the questioner's questioning) has superfluous premises (for example, [P5] = [P2]), yet fails to make the crucial connection, required to establish [C], between being more a belief and the true or truly believable-itself. Yet [P3]–[P4] shows us how to construct what is missing, namely, [P7] a belief related to the true believable-itself is more a belief than one related to one of the particular believable things. [P1] is, of course, a Platonist premise.

Note 395
Concluded through conclusions: So that none of its premises is left unsupported. **Anything missing is extremely acceptable:** Reading τι. Since it can be readily supplied.

Note 396
A contentious deduction: A fuller definition is given at 100^b23–25.

Note 397
It reaches a conclusion, but not in relation to the thing proposed: By obtaining the premises of arguments like those of Zeno, a questioner can always derive a contradiction (or an apparent contradiction). But this will not constitute an attack on what is proposed, if these are not premises relevant to it. Aristotle discusses this in *APr.* 2.17. See also *Top.* 160^b6–10.

Note 398
Stated previously: 162^a9–11.

Note 399
If from what seems most of all to be so it does away with some truth: As happens, for example, in a reductio ad absurdum argument for a contradictory conclusion C from premises P$_1$ and P$_2$, both of which seem to be so, since it follows that at least one of P$_1$ or P$_2$ must, despite appearances, be false, and the argument demonstrates this.

Note 400
In the *Analytics*: *APr.* 2.15–16.

Note 401
Asks for the very thing that needs to be proved: That is, the thing expressed exactly as it is in the conclusion, as in so-called *petitio principii*, or begging the question.

Note 402
The diagonal is incommensurable with the side: As at 106^{a}38, the diagonal and side are those of a rectangle.

Note 403
Assertion (*phasin*) and denial: Usually, an affirmation (*kataphasis*) is something said of or predicated of something, but a phrase (*phasis*) is not: "A *logos* is a significant voiced sound some part of which is significant in separation—as a phrase (*phasis*), not as an affirmation (*kataphasis*). I mean, for example, that 'human' signifies something, though not that it is or is not (there will instead be an affirmation or negation if something is added), but not an individual syllable of 'human'" (*Int.* 16^{b}26–31). But sometimes, as here, Aristotle fails to keep the distinction in mind: "A *phasis*, however, is something [predicated] of something, as too is a denial, and each one is either true or false. But understanding is not like that in every case; on the contrary, that of the what-it-is in the sense of the essence is true, and is not something [predicated] of something" (*DA* 430^{b}26–29; also 432^{a}10–12).

Note 404
[1] If someone were to ask for the contrary of what results of necessity through the things proposed, [2] and even if he were not to [try to] obtain the [pair of] contraries themselves, he were to ask for a pair (*duo*) such that from them there will be the opposing contradiction: In [1] we have C$_1$, the contrary that of necessity results from the things proposed, and C$_2$, the contrary of C$_1$. In one version of this fifth way of asking for contraries, the questioner asks for C$_2$. In [2] we have a second version of the same way. But in this case the questioner tries to obtain not C$_2$, but rather two other things. I take these to be two other contraries from which a contradiction can be derived that is opposed to C$_1$.

Note 405

Philosophical wisdom: *Phronêsis* is not specifically practical wisdom here, but wisdom more generally.

Being able to get a comprehensive view . . . : "Rhetoric's function is concerned with the sorts of things we deliberate about and have no crafts for, and in the presence of such listeners as are not capable of getting a comprehensive view of many things or of rational calculation from a distant [starting-point]" (*Rh.* 1357ª1–4).

Note 406

By loving and hating in the correct way . . . : Introduction, pp. xxxvi–xxxviii.

Note 407

The first posits: These are presumably the ones that are especially difficult to argue for or against, because they are or seem to be starting-points (163ᵇ27). That would explain why those faced with the task of attacking or defending them often give up.

Note 409

Just as in mnemonics . . . : Some mnemonic devices associated the things to be remembered with places in, for example, a familiar room, so that by recalling the room, one was able to recall the things. The *topoi* from which the *Topics* takes its name, have a similar function in relation to dialectical arguments. Thus in the next sentence, we are encouraged to remember a "common premise" rather than an entire argument.

Note 409

Common premise: One common to all the arguments that fall under the same heading.

Note 410

Making one argument into many: 157ª1–5.

Note 411

Arguments . . . dialectical argument: The contrast is that between the argument intrinsically as such and when framed as questions. See 161ª16–17.

Note 412

Enthymemes: An enthymeme is the correlate in rhetoric of a demonstration in dialectic. See *Rh.* 1356ª35–ᵇ11.

Note 413

Putting forward premises is making many things into one: Compare: "In the case of understanding and making deductions about immovable objects . . . the end is a theoretical object, for when one understands the two premises, one understands and puts together the conclusion" (*MA* 701ª9–11).

Note 414
It is very difficult to be well equipped: Reading εὐπορίζεσθαι.

SOPHISTICAL REFUTATIONS

Note 415
Like tribesmen choristers . . . : The adverb *phuletikôs*, which appears nowhere else, making its precise meaning difficult to gauge, stems from the noun *phulê* ("tribe"). Tribes were the principal components or divisions of the citizen body. Among their other functions, they also provided choruses for choral competitions and other purposes, which were judged on the vocal power of the choristers, which, in turn, depended on their size and strength (Xenophon, *Memorabilia* 3.3.12–13, 4.5). This fits nicely with the participle *phusêsantes*, which also has to do with puffing and blowing, and so with lung capacity and spoken arguments. It also has a negative sense in which, as here, it means "puffing oneself up." *Episkeuazein*, which can mean "to pack onto" (Xenophon, *Cyropaedia* 7.3.1), might here have the sense of "stuffing themselves" with food, or "bulking themselves up." Strong voices required lung capacity and size, as with operatic tenors. Like *phusêsantes*, it can carry an implication of fakery.
By using cosmetics: In Plato, *Grg.* 463a–466a, *kommotikê* ("cosmetology") is associated with sophistry and is said to masquerade as physical training: the latter producing health and fitness, the former producing the appearance of it.

Note 416
Litharge: *Lithos* ("stone") + *arguros* ("silver"). Lead monoxide.

Note 417
Distinct from the ones proposed: Secluding διὰ τῶν κειμένων.
A refutation . . . : Compare: "A refutation is a deduction of a contradiction" (*APr.* 66^{b}11).

Note 418
We use names as symbols: Reading χρώμεθα συμβόλοις.
Those doing rational calculations: Rational calculation (*logismos*), of which deliberation (*bouleusis*) is a variety, is the function of the calculative or deliberative part (*logistikon, bouleutikon*) of the soul, of which practical wisdom is the virtue and action the primary focus (*NE* 1139^{a}11–17, 1140^{a}24–28). But sometimes, as here, calculation is a matter of measuring or counting, as when people use pebbles (or abacus beads) when calculating the produce tax on animals (†*Econ.* 1348^{a}23).

Note 419

Things at issue are unlimited in number: The claim is not that things in general are actually unlimited or infinite in number, since it is a central Aristotelian doctrine that things are only potentially unlimited (*Ph.* 204ᵃ20–31, *Met.* 1048ᵇ14–17, 1066ᵇ11–12). So this is probably another case in which the alpha privative in *apeira* is to be taken less than strictly (see 156ᵇ18n364). The idea, in any case, as the next sentence attests, is that there is a one-many relationship between names and statements, on the one hand, and the things they signify, on the other. Aristotle's argument requires no more.

Note 420

Just as in the case of calculation . . . : The argument is this: ignorance of the fact that there is not a one-to-one correspondence between names and things disposes one to think "same name, same thing" and "distinct name, distinct thing," both of which are false. This is like failing to grasp that the relationship of a pebble to the sheep it stands for need not be one-to-one.

Note 421

Having the deliberate choice they have: Introduction, pp. xxi–xxii.

Note 422

It is necessary for the one who pretends . . . : *SE* 172ᵃ21–36.
In what way has been determined elsewhere: For an argument that the reference is to *Top.* 8.5–11, see the Introduction, p. xxv.

Note 423

Dialectical and examinational ones elsewhere: Dialectical ones in the *Topics*; examinational ones perhaps in a lost work.

Note 424

Competitors and rivals: Compare *Top.* 159ᵃ30–32.

Note 425

Depending on homonymy: Reading παρὰ τὴν ὁμωνυμίαν.

Note 426

Wishing that I myself the enemy may capture: The ambiguity is syntactical, depending on whether "I myself" is the subject or object of the verb "capture": I wish that I may capture the enemy; I wish that the enemy may capture me.

Note 427

"Surely, it is possible for speaking to pertain to the silent": "'Am I to understand,' said Dionysodorus, 'that there can be speaking pertaining to the silent?'" (Plato, *Euthd.* 300b).

Note 428
"'Eagle' and 'dog'": *Aetos* is an eagle and a sort of fish (*HA* 540ᵇ18); *kuôn* is a dog, a sort of fish, and the Dog Star, Sirius.

Note 429
We customarily use them in that way: So that they are ambiguous in use, but not strictly, or semantically, so. Aristotle gives no examples.

Note 430
"Now he can learn his letters . . .": Reading μανθάνειν . . . ἐμάνθανεν. If the scope of "now" is both clauses (combination), the thought is that he is learning what he already knows, which is not learning. If the scope is the first clause, the times of learning and knowing can be different (dividing), so that the whole sentence can be true. Compare "Do those who learn learn what they scientifically know or what they do not scientifically know?" (Plato, *Euthd.* 277a).

Note 431
"Someone who can carry only one thing can carry many": Many at one time vs. many over many times.

Note 432
"I made you a free man slave": I made you a free slave (combination); I made you, a free [man], slave (division). Probably a quotation from an unknown comedy.
"Of men one hundred fifty Godlike Achilles left alive": Of men one hundred and fifty he left alive (combination); of men one hundred, fifty he left alive (division).

Note 433
Rectify Homer . . . : "Some problems must be resolved by appeal to accentuation, as Hippias of Thasos resolved, 'we grant (δίδομεν) him the fulfillment of his prayer' [by reading δίδόμεν ('let the dream grant his prayer')] and 'this is not (οὐ) rotted by the rain [by reading οὖ ('this part of it is rotted by the rain')]" (*Po.* 1461ᵃ22–23). The passage about wood and rain is *Iliad* 23.328, the one about Agamemnon's dream is *Iliad* 2.1–34, but the words quoted are spoken by Poseidon at 21.297. Hippias' identity is uncertain.

Note 434
Distinguished previously: *Top.* 1.9, where ten categories are listed.

Note 435
In its style of speech: Reading τῷ σχήματι τῆς λέξεως.

Note 436
These: Reading ταῦτα.

Note 437

It happens coincidentally that . . . : The claim is not that Coriscus is coincidentally a human: he is intrinsically and essentially a human. Rather the description, "the one he said that Coriscus was said to be other than," happens to pick out a human. If the one in question had been a lion, this would not be so.

Note 438

When what is said of things partially . . . : "I mean by 'partially' is the moon eclipsed? or is it waxing? For in such cases we are inquiring about whether it is or is not something. By 'unconditionally' I mean whether the moon or night exists or does not exist" (*APo.* 90ᵃ2–5).

Note 439

Predicated unconditionally: Retaining κατηγορεῖν.

Note 440

Instead depend . . . : Reading ἀλλὰ.

Note 441

A refutation is a contradiction of one and the same thing, [1] not of the name but of the thing at issue, and [2] not of a synonymous name, but of the same one: [3] Things cannot appear in dialectical arguments; only their names can do that (165ᵃ6–8). Nonetheless, a refutation must [1] target the thing at issue, not a mere name. It will do this, [2] tells us, if it is [2a] of a synonymous name that is also [2b] the same one as appears in the target of the refutation. [2a] alone is a strenuous requirement, since "things are said to be synonymous when they have a name in common and when the account of the essence that corresponds to the name is the same" (*Cat.* 1ᵃ6–7). Add [2b] and we have the closest thing possible to having the thing itself be present.
Not counting what was initially at issue: That is, not begging the question.

Note 442

Demonstrations in accord with a sign: "A sign, however, is intended to be a demonstrative premise, either necessary or acceptable. For whatever is such that if it is, some certain thing is, or if it happened earlier or later the thing in question would have happened, that is a sign of this thing's happening or being. (An enthymeme is a deduction from likelihoods or signs.) A sign is supposed in three ways, corresponding to the ways the middle term in the figures is supposed. That is, it is supposed either as in the first figure, or as in the middle, or as in the third. . . . If only one premise is stated, then, it is only a sign, but if the other premise is supposed in addition, it is a deduction" (*APr.* 70ᵃ6–25; also *Rh.* 1357ᵇ1–17).
He is well-dressed . . . : "When someone is well-dressed and wanders around at night, he is an adulterer; for adulterers are like this" (*Rh.* 1401ᵇ23–24).

Note 443
Melissus: *Top.* 104ᵇ22n51.
It has no starting-point: Reading ἀρχὴν οὐκ ἔχει.

Note 444
Those depending on the making of two questions into one: Dorion cites the following nice example from Aulus Gellius, *Attic Nights* 16.2: "Have you finished committing adultery, yes or no?"

Note 445
"Is A a human and is B?": If the answerer says yes, he is apparently refuted. Why? Because then it would follow that if someone strikes A and B he would strike one human, not two humans. Why? The questioner is asking, "Is A = a human being X and is B = a human being Y?" There is no presupposition that X = Y. A yes answer, however, since it presupposes that only one thing is being asked, does presuppose that X = Y, and so that A = B. But that is not what is being presupposed or asked.

Note 446
Being incapable of drawing [the relevant] distinctions: Since these are not special to their crafts or sciences.

Note 447
Those already mentioned: 167ª21–35.

Note 448
Also . . . : Reading τε.

Note 449
The consequent . . . : Reading παρεπόμενον.

Note 450
Snow and swan are the same with respect to white: The questioner has obtained that white (W) and swan (S) are the same, by obtaining that they are the same color (C), and (fallaciously) applying the principle of the transitivity of identity: W = C, S = C, therefore W = S. But this principle is false, Aristotle shows, when the identity is not unconditional, but only in a certain coincidental respect. For if it were true, snow and swan would be one and the same, which is clearly false.

Note 451
The argument of Melissus: 167ᵇ12–20 and *Top.* 104ᵇ22n51.

Note 452
From another point of view as well: A reference, perhaps, to Chapters 24 and 28.

Note 453
A premise is one thing said of one thing: *APr.* 24ª16–17; also *APo.* 72ª8–9.
The same definition . . . : "One human and a human who is and a human are the same thing, and no other thing is made clear by an expression that uses two of them, he is a human and a human who is" (*Met.* 1003ᵇ26–29).

Note 454
Unconditionally a premise: *Top.* 101ᵇ28–33.

Note 455
All the modes [of refuting]: Reading τρόποι.

Note 456
One, being, and same: *Met.* 5.6, 7, and 9.

Note 457
A word or statement pronounced . . . : When accentuation does make a difference, however, it is important to notice it, just as when a phrase signifies one thing when combined and another when divided. See 166ª23–38, 166ᵇ1–9, 177ᵇ3–4 for examples.

Note 458
Because we take everything predicated of a thing to be a this something: "Of things predicated, and the things they get predicated of, those that are said coincidentally of things, either of the same thing or of each other, will not be one thing. For example, a human is pale and musical, but the pale and the musical are not one thing; for they are both coincident with the same thing. And even if it is true to say that the pale is musical, the musical pale [thing] will still not be one thing" (*Int.* 21ª7–14).
Substance . . . this something: *Top.* 103ᵇ28n43, 144ª20n309.

Note 459
Through words . . . through the thing at issue itself: "Voiced sounds are symbols of affections in the soul. And just as written marks are not the same for everyone, voiced sounds are not the same either. But the primary things that these signify (namely, affections in the soul) are the same for everyone. And what these affections are likenesses of (namely, things) are also the same for everyone" (*Int.* 16ª3–8).

Note 460
The cause just stated: 169ᵇ10–12.

Note 461
As we saw: 165ᵇ4–6.

Note 462
The same as those: Reading ταῦτα.

Note 463
What does not follow because of the argument: 167ᵇ21–36.
Making two questions into one: 169ᵃ6–16.
[Affirming] the consequent: 168ᵇ27–35.

Note 464
The one that follows not in the case of the thing at issue . . . : 167ᵃ21–35.
Instead of the contradictory being universal: 167ᵃ7–20.
Not counting what was initially at issue: 167ᵃ36–39.

Note 465
Does not belong to any craft: Reading οὐδεμίας.
The sciences are perhaps (*isôs*) **unlimited** (*apeiroi*) **in number:** As at *Top.* 156ᵇ18, this is another place where it is important to bear in mind the message of *Met.* 1022ᵇ32–36: "something is said to be *un*-equal because it does not have the equality it is natural for it to have, and *in*-visible either because it has no color at all or because it has minimal color, and foot-*less* either because it has no feet or minimal feet." Add *isôs* (which in applying to the sciences applies to their deductions too) into the mix and the thought here is probably just that there are a large number of sciences, or that the sciences are many and various. This applies equally well, indeed, to other occurrences of *apeiros* in our treatises. See *Top.* 109ᵇ14, 148ᵇ31, and *SE* 165ᵃ12.

Note 466
Likewise also exist in unlimited numbers: Reading ὁμοίως ἐν ἀπείροις.

Note 467
Those of the sort mentioned: That is, dialectically competent ones.
Appear so to random people: Compare: "Likewise, there is no need to investigate the beliefs of ordinary people (for they speak at random about pretty much everything, and especially about happiness); for it would be absurd to present an argument to those who need not arguments, but rather to suffer" (*EE* 1214ᵇ28–1215ᵃ2).

Note 468
[1] A dialectical one or [2a] an apparently dialectical or [2b] examinational one: The contrast between [1] and [2a]–[2b], and the grouping of [2a] with [2b] is explained at 169ᵇ25–27.

Note 469
The difference among arguments that some people state . . . : Tarán prints 170ᵇ12–171ᵇ2 together with 177ᵇ7–9 as Speusippus F69a–b (commentary pp. 414–418).

Note 470

It lies in the contradiction: "Can speaking pertain to the silent?" "No." "Can speaking pertain to a stone?" "Yes." (Implicit) "Is a stone silent?" "Yes." "Then, speaking can pertain to the silent." This deduction is unproblematic, since there is a univocal interpretation of its premises and conclusion under which it is sound. But there is a problem with the conclusion, since it is ambiguous between a speaker who is being silent and the thing spoken about being so.

It lies in both: "Can someone give what he does not have?" "No." "Can someone give with pleasure what he does not have with pleasure?" "Yes." "Then, someone can give what he does not have." Here the problem is in the deduction and in the contradiction because the initial question is ambiguous between having unconditionally and having in a way, and no univocal interpretation makes the deduction valid.

It lies in the deduction: Reading κύκλου. "Is a cycle (circle) a figure?" "Yes." "Is Homer's poetry a cycle?" "Yes." "Then, Homer's poetry is a figure." The problem is in the deduction because it treats the "is" of predication as being the "is" of identity.

Note 471

If someone believes that "triangle" signifies many things . . . : The view Aristotle has now returned to discussing is that arguments are directed either against the name or against the thought. The new puzzle he raises for it seems to be this. The answerer grants (1) that triangle$_x$ has three interior angles. The questioner soundly deduces the conclusion that (2) the angles of a triangle equal two right angles. The answerer objects (3) that when he granted (1) he took it to be about triangle$_x$ not about triangle. However, the answerer's view that "triangle" signifies many things is false, since "triangle" is in fact univocal. So mathematically speaking, questioner has established (2): "In mathematics, fallacious argument is not possible in the same way, because the middle term is always twofold; for something is said of all of it, and, again, it is said of all of something else (but all is not said of what is predicated). But while it is possible to see as it were these things by the understanding, in [external] arguments, they escape notice. Is every *kuklos* a figure? (If one draws one, [the question] is clear.) Well then, are epic poems a *kuklos*? (It is evident that they are not.)" (*APo.* 77^{b}28–33). The question is, has he established it dialectically? The answer is not so clear. And therein lies the puzzle for the view under discussion.

Note 472

Suppose then . . . : Reading εἶτα.

Note 473

Therefore, there is not any kind of argument directed against the thought: The argument seems to be this. Suppose N is a name said of things in ways W$_1$ and W$_2$. Is such-and-such N or not? is an ambiguous question. But it can be transformed into a non-ambiguous one by addition: Is such-and-such N or not, or is it N in W$_1$

and not N in W₂ or vice versa? If it is not now directed against the thought, then no argument will be. Why? Because the basis for thinking it was directed against the name has been removed. We will be left then, contrary to the view under discussion, only with arguments directed against the name.

Note 474
In cases that do not involve: Reading ἐν τοῖς μὴ. The OCT omission of μὴ is an editorial slip.

Note 475
Some twos: Reading δυάδες.

Note 476
Has in view: *Theôrein* means "has in view" here, but seems better captured by "gets a theoretical grasp on" in the next sentence. See *Top.* 101^{b}11n17.

Note 477
What is common: 170^{a}35–36.

Note 478
The things that dialectic is examinational about: Namely, the things that are "common to every craft and every capacity" (170^{a}33–36).
There are those fallacies . . . : These concern things that merely seem to be in accord with the starting-points of a specific craft or science.
Each of the things: Reading ἑκάστων.

Note 479
Falsely drawn diagrams: These are falsely drawn in the following sense: they include irrelevant elements on which the deduction actually depends (*Top.* 167^{a}1–3), so that it is the person who knows that it depends on these who knows how to resolve them (165^{b}35–36). But while these elements themselves are neither true nor primary starting-points of geometry (101^{a}9–10), the *apparent* deduction embodied in the falsely drawn diagram *is* based on the starting-points and conclusions of geometry (*SE* 172^{a}1–2, *Ph.* 185^{a}15); that is why it can deceive even a geometer (*Top.* 132^{a}32–33), but the actual deduction, which includes the irrelevant elements, is of broader application, because those elements are (*SE* 172^{a}5–6).
The one of Hippocrates . . . : The reference is to the arguments of the great mathematician Hippocrates of Chios, who flourished c. 450–430 BC, for squaring the circle by means of lunes (the figure bounded by two arcs of a circle). It is a geometrical paralogism, in Aristotle's view, because it proceeds from starting-points proper to geometry and cannot be adapted to any subject matter except that of geometry, but involves an error (*SE* 172^{a}3–7). However, it concerns something true, because the circle can be squared in this way. See Heath, pp. 33–36, 183–201; Dorion, pp. 282–287.

Bryson: An early 4th-cent sophist from Heraclea Pontica on the coast of Bithynia in Asia Minor. He is also mentioned at *Rh.* 1405ᵇ9–10. Different accounts of his way of squaring the circle are given by the ancient commentators, but the basic idea of all of them is that of a two-sided convergent series of polygons with more and more sides, one lot with apexes touching the circumference from inside the circle, the other with sides touching it from outside. In just what way it is not in accord with the starting-points of geometry is unclear. See Heath, pp. 48–49; Dorion, pp. 285–287. See also 172ᵃ2–7.

Note 480
As we said: 165ᵃ21–23.

Note 481
The arguments . . . : Secluding οἵ² and reading εἴσιν.
It is for apparent victory: Rejecting the addition of ἕνεκα.

Note 482
By dialectic: Reading τῇ διαλεκτικῇ.
A geometer: Reading τὸν γεωμέτρην.

Note 483
For the argument will apply [to many things]: Namely, "to numbers, times, places, and other common things" (Ps. Alex. *in SE* 90, 18–19).

Note 484
The way Antiphon squared the circle: "Antiphon himself also tried to square the circle, but he did not adhere to the starting-points of geometry. He tried as follows: 'If,' he says, 'I draw a circle and I inscribe a square inside it. I bisect the segments of the circle cut off by the square. Then I draw a straight line from the intersection in both directions to the end points of the segment. Thus I produce the figure of an octagon. If we again bisect the segments enclosing the angles of this figure and again draw a straight line in both directions from the intersection to the end points of the segments, we produce a polygonal figure. If we then repeat this procedure, a figure with very many sides results that has very small angles, so that the straight lines enclosing them will coincide with the circle because of the smallness of the angles. Given that any rectilinear figure can be squared, if I square this polygon, since it coincides with the circle, I will have squared the circle too.' So he does away with geometrical starting-points. For it is a starting-point of geometry that a straight line never coincides with a curve, but he allows that, because of its smallness, a certain straight line coincides with a certain curve. . . . So Antiphon, by doing away with geometrical starting-points, namely, that a straight line never coincides with a curve, carried out his proof" (TEGP 22 F13b = Philoponus, *Physics* 31.9–32.3). That is why "[natural scientists] should not resolve every [contentious argument] at hand, but those that involve false demonstration

Notes 485–491

from the starting-points, and not those that do not. For example, it belongs to the geometer to refute a quadrature by means of segments, but not one like Antiphon's" (*Ph.* 185ᵃ14–17). Antiphon's argument is discussed in Heath, pp. 221–223.

Note 485
Zeno's argument: *Top.* 160ᵇ8–10n384.

Note 486
Dialectical: In the previous paragraph, *dialektikos* referred to the dialectician, but now its reference has shifted.

Note 487
None of the crafts proving a certain nature: 172ᵃ37–38.

Note 488
One will further argue dialectically against an objection: The "one" referred to is the scientist who is being imagined to proceed by asking questions. If the answerer refuses to grant a starting-point, he has nowhere further to go. The use of "argue dialectically (*dialexetai*)" is internal to the thought experiment. The scientist, as such, lacks the resources that dialectic possesses to respond to an objection against starting-points themselves.

Note 489
They share in an un-craftlike way . . . : Compare *Rh.* 1354ᵃ1–11 (p. 221).

Note 490
There are many of these [common things] and they apply with respect to everything: Reading (1) ἔστι πολλὰ μὲν ταῦτα καὶ for OCT (2) ἐστὶ πολλὰ μὲν ταὐτὰ ("many of these identical things"). On (2) the things referred to are axioms (*axiômata*), starting-points common to all or many sciences (*APo* 72ᵃ15–17, 76ᵇ14–15). The laws of logic, such as the principle of non-contradiction, which hold at least analogically of all beings, are examples, as are other somewhat less general laws, such as the axioms of equality, which are not universally applicable, but are also not proper to a single science or single kind of beings (*APo* 76ᵃ38–ᵇ2). On (1) the reference is more general (see 170ᵃ35–36), making it preferable. For axioms, as common to many sciences, cannot by themselves entail a proposition contrary to a conclusion proper to a specific science. Hence it is impossible to construct examinational refutations using axioms alone. Yet that is precisely what such refutations use "common things (*koina*)" to do.

Note 491
Second in the deliberate choice of the sophist: 165ᵇ14.

306

Note 492
Directed against: Reading πρὸς.
Useful in hunting things of this sort: That is, in achieving the second (and third) aim of sophists.

Note 493
Demanding that the answerer say what he believes: This so-called sincerity condition is one Socrates routinely imposes. See Plato, *Cri.* 49c–d, *Grg.* 500b–c, *Prt.* 331c–d.
To lead him: Reading ἄγειν.

Note 494
Nowadays . . . : Aristotle says that thinkers prior to Plato "had no share of dialectic" (*Met.* 987^{b}32–33), and remarks that at the time of Socrates "there was not yet the strength in dialectic that enables people, even separately from the what-it-is, to investigate contraries, and whether the same science is a science of contraries" (1078^{b}25–27). See also 175^{b}8–14.

Note 495
Say that one put questions wishing to learn: As Socrates, by disavowing knowledge, also often does. See 183^{b}6–8n638.
Leaves room for an attack: Reading ἐγχειρήματος.

Note 496
As was said previously: The reference, though not entirely clear, seems to be to *Top.* 2.5.

Note 497
To bring to light: Reading τὸ ἐμφανίζειν.

Note 498
[Argue] on the basis of things wished for and on professed beliefs: Compare: "Another [topic]—since people do not praise the same things openly as they do non-openly, but openly praise the just and the noble most of all, while in private they wish more for what is advantageous—is on the basis of these to try to draw on each; for among the ones that are unacceptable this topic is the most controlling one" (*Rh.* 1399^{a}30–34).

Note 499
As Callicles . . . : "I do not approve of Polus: he agreed with you that doing what's unjust is more shameful than suffering it. As a result of this admission he was bound and gagged by you in the arguments, too ashamed to say what he thought. Although you claim to be pursuing the truth, you are in fact leading the discussion around to the sort of crowd-pleasing vulgarities that are noble only by law and not

by nature. And these, nature and law, are mostly contrary to each other, so that if a person is ashamed and does not dare to say what he thinks, he is compelled to contradict himself. This is the sophism you have thought of, with which you work mischief in arguments" (Plato, *Grg.* 482e–483a).

Nature . . . (they said): Reading φασι φύσιν.

Note 500
It is possible to say: Reading εἶναι λέγειν.

Note 501
Or to the wise: Rejecting the addition of τὰ.

Those who have to do with arguments: Reading τοῖς ἐν λόγῳ.

Note 502
It is unacceptable to ordinary people that a king not be happy: "[*Polus*] It is clear, then, that you will not even say that the Great King [of Persia] is happy. [*Socrates*] Yes, and I will say that it is true; for I do not know how he is off for education and justice. [*P.*] What? Is the whole of happiness in that? [*S.*] Yes, so I say, Polus; for I say that the noble and good man or woman is happy, and the unjust and wicked one wretched" (Plato, *Grg.* 470e).

Note 503
We have already said: 165^{b}15–17.

Note 504
And double and double of half . . . : Reading διπλάσιον δὲ . . . εἰ ἄρα ἐστὶ ἡμίσεος διπλάσιον.

Note 505
Is appetite for something pleasant?: On this argument, see *Top.* 140^{b}27–141^{a}14.

Note 506
Yet the substance . . . predicated: Removing the obeli on ὅσων ἡ οὐσία . . . κατηγορουμένων with Hecquet.

Note 507
If the snub is concavity in a nose . . . : An implicit premise is that a nose that has concavity in it is a concave one. The following is the longer version: "If snub nose is the same as concave nose, then the snub and the concave will be the same. But if they are not the same, because it is impossible to say the snub without saying the thing of which it is an intrinsic affection (for the snub is concavity in a nose), then it must either be impossible to say the snub nose, or the same thing will be said twice, namely, concave nose nose (for the snub nose will be the concave nose nose). That is why it is absurd that the essence should belong to things like this. If

it does, it will go on without limit; for in snub nose nose there will be yet another one" (*Met.* 1030^{b}28–1031^{a}1).

Note 508
They do not get a further answer . . . : 181^{b}25–182^{a}6.

Note 509
Has already been stated: 165^{b}20–21.

Note 510
Protagoras: Protagoras was a famous sophist from Abdera (c. 490–c. 420 BC), who was perhaps the first to describe himself as such and to charge fees for his teaching (Plato, *Prt.* 317b, 349a). His best-known view is "that 'Man is the measure of all things, of those that are that they are and of those that are not that they are not'" (Plato, *Tht.* 152a2–4), which Aristotle discusses in *Met.* 1009^{a}6–16. His "division of the kinds of names into masculine, feminine, and neuter" is referred to at *Rh.* 1407^{b}6 (= DK A27 = TEGP 35).
Used to say happened . . . : The issue may be one of fitting the gender of nouns to the supposed gender of things: anger and rage are masculine things and so should have masculine nouns as their names. Or it may be one of morphology, claiming that nouns with certain endings should or do have certain genders: "Masculine names are those that end in *nu*, *rho*, or *sigma*, and in those letters composed with *sigma* (there are two of those: *ps* [*psi*] and *ks* [= *xi*]). Feminine names are those that end in the vowels that are always long, that is, in *êta* or *ômega*, or, of those that can be lengthened, in *alpha*" (*Po.* 1458^{a}8–12). The reason *oulomenon* appears to be a solecism is because *mênis* and *pêlêx* are both in fact feminine nouns.

Note 511
A person who says [*mênin*] *oulomenên*: As Homer does in *Iliad* 1.1.

Note 512
Tode ("this"), that is . . . : Reading τὸ τόδε and rejecting the seclusion of καὶ.

Note 513
When *tode* ("this") . . . : Reading τόδε.

Note 514
Solecism in the case of the things at issue: That is, where similar names designate dissimilar things. See 166^{b}16–18.

Note 515
Just as in the case of dialectical ones: *Top.* 155^{b}26–28.

Note 516
That have been mentioned: *Top.* 155^{b}26–157^{a}5.

Note 517

Having done the induction: Reading ἐπαγαγόντα. The idea, as the next clause shows, is this. If a questioner does not ask explicitly for the universal conclusion of his induction, the answerer himself and the audience may think he has granted it. But if it is asked for explicitly, remembering the induction, and supposing the question to have a point, he may refuse it.

People themselves even think: Reading οἴονται καὶ αὐτοὶ.

Note 518

In those cases in which . . . : 157ᵃ21–33.

Note 519

Many times many . . . ?: Many and few are the contraries that are put side by side, making answerers more likely to answer "few." If m and n are each many units (large numbers), then answerer will concede that (m × n) is many units (a large number) not few (a small number). But he will also concede that in comparison to (m × n)^n, (m × n) is only a few units (a small number). So he will have conceded that (m × n) is both many and few.

Note 520

As in rhetorical arguments . . . : "Another is based on a judgment about the same, a similar, or a contrary case, especially when all always [judge in that way]—but if not, at any rate, when most do, or the wise (either all or most of them), or the good, or if these judges themselves do, or those these judges approve, or those one cannot judge contrary to (for example, those with the controlling vote), or those it would not be noble to judge contrary to" (*Rh.* 1398ᵇ21–25).

Note 521

At any rate: Reading γε.

As Cleophon does in the *Mandrobulus*: Perhaps not, as long believed, a reference to the Athenian tragic poet, mentioned at *Po.* 1448ᵃ12, where his characters are said to be on the same level as ordinary people, and at 1458ᵃ20, where his style is criticized as being "low (*tapeinên*)," but rather to a character of the same name in the *Mandrobulus* of Xenocrates (T1 Tarán = DL 4.5.71).

Note 522

Questioners who have been hindered in the argument (*aphistamenous tou logou*) **must cut off the rest of their attacks:** The perfect (also present) passive participle *aphistamenous* is often translated so as to give the sense "break off the argument" or "withdraw from the argument," but this makes it difficult to explain "cut off the rest of their attacks." The idea seems rather to be that questioners whose argument is being thwarted by the answerer should give up whatever remains of it before its failure becomes apparent. The answerer, on the other hand, wants to prevent this, since he is winning.

Note 523

Having taken (*eklabontas*) **the latter in that sense:** Another ambiguous (in this case aorist active) participle, sometimes understood to give the sense "excluding it," but almost certainly better understood as translated.

Just as Lycophron did . . . : Lycophron is known only from Aristotle. The expressions attributed to him at *Rh.* 1405ᵇ35–36 and 1406ᵃ7–9 suggest that he was a follower or imitator of Gorgias. According to Ps. Alex. *in SE* 118.30–119.3, when he ran out of things to say about an actual lyre, he included the Lyre constellation in his remit. Compare: "if someone composing an encomium for a dog were to include the Dog Star or Pan in their account" (*Rh.* 1401ᵃ15–16).

Note 524

Denying . . . : Reading ἀποφῆσαι . . . φῆσαι.

Note 525

One must not ask . . . : Compare *Top.* 158ᵃ7–13.

Note 526

Who does not perceive it: Reading μὴ αἰσθανόμενος.

Note 527

Third, and last, there is a further one relating to reputation: Aristotle advertises two reasons, but seems to give three. Perhaps he nodded, or added the third later. However, the third has to do with reputation, not, like the other two, with actually being a good philosopher. So perhaps, especially considering the way Aristotle writes, we should understand things this way: "There are two reasons why these are useful to philosophy. . . . There is also a third one, not related to that, but related to reputation. . . ."

Note 528

Stated previously: Chapters 4–12.

Those in which . . . : Chapters 12–15.

Note 529

As with geometrical diagrams: "[Deliberators] take the end for granted and investigate in what way and through which things it will come about. And if it appears that it can come about through several, they investigate through which ones it will most easily and best come about. But if it is brought to completion through only one, they investigate in what way it will come about through this and through which things it, in turn, will come about, until they arrive at the first cause, which is the last thing in the process of discovery. For a deliberator seems to inquire and analyze in the way we said just as though he were dealing with a diagram—but while it is evident that not all inquiry is deliberation (for example, mathematical inquiry), all deliberation is inquiry. And the last thing found in the analysis seems to come first in bringing about the result" (*NE* 1112^{b}15–24). Faced with a developing dialectical argument, an answerer's position is the reverse of the deliberator's and the geometer's. They are analyzing in order to construct an argument or figure; the answerer has the parts of the argument (the questions being asked) but does not see the argument that is being constructed from them, and so does not know what to do in order to avoid being refuted by it.

Note 530
But rather has done so homonymously: Rejecting the addition of ἤ.
It is now unclear: *Top.* 160^{a}23–32.

Note 531
An argument turning on homonymy is a refutation: Rejecting the addition of ἔλεγχον.

Note 532
The way in which some people produce a rectification is of no benefit: The proposed rectification, as at 175^{b}12, is in a premise (conclusion), stating that [1] Coriscus is musical and unmusical. It operates by making the name "Coriscus" homonymous, by adding the demonstrative pronoun "this" (*touto*) to it, and then dividing [1] into [2] "*This* Coriscus is musical" and [3] "*This* Coriscus is unmusical." The idea is that "Coriscus" in [2] and "Coriscus" in [3], have different significations, so that [1] is not a contradiction. But this explanation will not work. For a name signifies an account of an essence (*Top.* 102^{a}1n24), and the account of Coriscus in [1] and the account of this musical (or unmusical) Coriscus in [2] and [3] are the same, so that the signification of "Coriscus" must be the same in [2] and [3] as in [1].

Note 533
But perhaps it does not signify the same thing . . . : A possible objection to Aristotle's argument, to which he responds that one cannot change the signification of a (not already homonymous) name by adding a demonstrative pronoun to it.

Note 534
As was said previously: *Top.* 160^{a}17–34.

Note 535
The speaker has not given an answer [if he does]: Since it is unclear which of the two (or more) questions being asked he has answered.

Note 536
Among practitioners of dialectic . . . : Dialectical questions must be answered yes or no. But homonymous questions are in fact two (or more) questions masquerading as one. Hence when an answerer thinks such a question worthy of a yes-or-no

answer, and so gives one, he does so because he does not see that the result is to do away with dialectical argument.

Note 537
Refutation on a side issue: *Top.* 112ª8.

Note 538
One must add "it seems": 174ᵇ12–18.

Note 539
It is clear how one asks for what was initially at issue: *Top.* 162ᵇ34–163ª13.
But is either false . . . : Reading ἤ.

Note 540
The division already stated: Most likely a reference to 168ª17–169ª21.

Note 541
In a docked way: The adjective *kolobos* means "docked" (as in docking a puppy's tail, or docking someone's salary), "curtailed," "stunted," "truncated"—the central idea is that of cutting off a projecting part, typically a non-essential one. Here the idea is that an ambiguous term ("belongs to") has been docked of a clarifying or disambiguating clause. Compare: "a short syllable, because of its incompleteness, produces something docked" (*Rh.* 1409ª18–19).

Note 542
Lysander: The great political leader and commander of the Spartan fleet who defeated the Athenians at Aegospotami in 405 BC, thereby effectively winning the Peloponnesian War.

Note 543
When it seems that of two things . . . : When A entails B, but B does not entail A, grant B, because A gives the questioner both A and B, while B gives him B alone. Hence, the questioner needs to obtain additional premises in order to produce his deduction. The more premises he has to obtain, however, the more difficult it is for him to produce it.

Note 544
No name is established for the second one: The questioner will then be forced to show that there is no similarity to unify the nameless class, which is difficult to do. Compare *Top.* 157ª21–33.

Note 545
No belief either way: The adjective *amphidoxos* means "doubtful," "ambiguous," "ambivalent." At *Rh.* 1356ª8 *to amphidoxein* is contrasted with *to akribes* ("exactness").

Note 546

Maxims: "A maxim is an affirmation, not though about particulars (for example, about what sort of person Iphicrates is), but about universals, and not about all of them (for example, that the straight is contrary to the crooked), but about the objects of actions, and with things that are to be chosen or avoided with a view to doing an action" (*Rh.* 1394ª21–25).

One would most of all go unnoticed . . . : That is, taking something proposed as a maxim, in the sense of a true belief, and so immediately acceptable, and calling it a maxim only in the sense of a general affirmation about which it is reasonable not to have beliefs either way (or vice versa, of course, if one were doing the questioning).

Note 547

Its appearing so depends on: Reading παρὰ τι. The contrast is between the sort of resolution that is provided acceptably rather than in accord with the truth, which is discussed in Chapter 17 (see 175ª32–33), and the sort of correct resolution under discussion here.

Note 548

One resolves arguments that are genuine deductions . . . : *Top.* 162ᵇ3–30.

Note 549

As previously stated: 176ᵇ36–177ª2.

Note 550

"Speaking pertaining to the silent": 166ª12–14.

"Not scientifically knowing (*sunepistasthai*) what one scientifically knows": The precise meaning of the rare verb *sunepistasthai* is difficult to gauge. See 177ª26–30.

Note 551

Or rather (*alla*) . . . : I take this clause as corrective. What is equivocal is not sometimes unequivocally so and sometimes not; instead, it is in one sense true and in another sense false.

Note 552

Without the contradiction there was no refutation: "Is there seeing pertaining to the blind?" "No." "Wasn't Homer blind?" "Yes." "But people could see him, couldn't they?" "Yes." "So there is seeing pertaining to the blind." The conclusion is not a refutation because it is open to the answerer to say that it was not in that sense that he took the first question when he answered, "No." To get a refutation the questioner must also get an answer to question in its second sense, in which it means "Do blind people see?" The contradictory of an ambiguous statement, in other words, is the contradictory of each of its disambiguated versions.

Note 553
That is equivocal: Omitting πρὸς.
That "speaking pertaining to the silent": Reading τὸ.

Note 554
Those who scientifically know in the relevant way: "For scientific knowledge, like knowing scientifically, is twofold, one potential, the other active" (*Met.* 1087ª15–16). That is the equivocation in the premise. We cannot, when asleep, have *active* scientific knowledge of the things we have *potential* scientific knowledge of, but we can have it when awake.

Note 555
One must contend . . . : 167ª23–27, 168ª28–31.

Note 556
"Was what you saw so-and-so being beaten with . . . ?": Composition: The answer is, for example, "Yes. I saw him being beaten with a stick." Division: The answer is "No. I saw him with my eyes being beaten with a stick."

Note 557
If indeed ὄρος . . . : Rejecting the addition of ὡς and seclusion of καὶ. Before the introduction of breathing marks the word pronounced ὄρος (*oros*: smooth breathing) was a homograph of the word ὅρος (*horos*: rough breathing). Nonetheless, it did not signify a distinct thing, since in speech it is divided, with *oros* meaning "mountain" and *horos* meaning "defining mark" or "boundary marker," and neither of these is equivocal. See 169ª27–29.

Note 558
Not all refutations . . . : Tarán prints this together with 170ᵇ12–171ᵇ2 as Speusippus F69a–b (commentary pp. 414–418).

Note 559
"Do you know now in Sicily that there are triremes in Piraeus?": "Another [topic] is for the speaker to combine what is divided or to divide what is combined; for since what is not the same often seems to be the same, whichever is more useful should be done. This is Euthydemus' [sort of] argument—for example, claiming to know that there is a trireme in the Piraeus; for he knew each of the [three] things involved. And claiming of the one knowing the letters that he knows the word; for the word is the same as these. Also, saying that since two doses of something cause illness, one dose is not healthy either: for it would be absurd if two goods equaled one evil. Put this way it is for refutation, but it is for proving in the following one: for two goods do not equal one evil. But the whole topic is fallacious" (*Rh.* 1401ª25–34). If the things involved in the Piraeus example are a trireme, in, and the Piraeus, the fallacy consists in arguing from knowing the parts to knowing

their combination. What this omits—as in the case of knowing the word because of knowing the letters—is the order of the parts. If a person is in the Piraeus, what he knows he knows in the Piraeus. He knows that there is a trireme (somewhere). But we cannot infer that he knows that there is a trireme (located) in the Piraeus, only that he (located) in the Piraeus knows that there is a trireme (somewhere). In our text the argument is: You are in Sicily now, so that what you know you know there now. One thing you know is that triremes are in Piraeus (sometimes). Those are illegitimately combined to yield the false conclusion.

Note 560

All cases asked for in every way: Reading ἐρωτωμένους.

Not against the argument: Since the argument could be rephrased so as to avoid this resolution of it. See also 178^{b}16–23, 179^{b}11–16.

Note 561

Ou **does not signify . . . :** 166^{b}3–6.

Note 562

The kinds of predication: That is, the categories. See *Top.* 103^{b}20–27.

Note 563

For one person has granted . . . does belong [to a subject]: Because it is not clear how this sentence bears on the examples given, Hecquet transposes it to follow the opening sentence of the next paragraph (178^{a}30), on the grounds that the example that follows is a better fit. Instead, I take Aristotle to be reminding us of what he said at 169^{a}30–35: "In those depending on the style, the deception is due to similarity in speech. For it is difficult to distinguish what sorts are said of things in one way, what sorts in another way (for the one capable of doing this is pretty much next door to seeing the truth, and it is he most of all who knows when to join in conceding them), because we take everything predicated of a thing to be a this something, and [so] we make our concession as if to one thing." The examples that follow are then all apropos, since in each a name is treated as a thing, with the result that a concession is made as if to one question. Notice the analogy with the case of homonymy (178^{a}24–28).

Note 564

As much or as many things as he does not have: Reading ὅσον δὲ μὴ ἔχει ἢ ὅσα.

Note 565

If, then, . . . : Rejecting the seclusion of εἰ.

Note 566

It is, then, as if . . . : Reading ὥσπερ οὖν.

Note 567

For (*gar*) he does not have only one: The argument is not spelled out, but the *gar* clause, which I treat as parenthetical, clues us in to the fact that it trades on the word "only," like the one discussed at 178ᵇ36–ᵃ7, but perhaps in a slightly different way: (1) "Could a person see with an eye he does not have?" "No." (2) "Suppose he saw with both eyes. Then is it true that he did not see with the left one only?" "Yes." "And isn't it also true that he did not see with the right one only?" "Yes." (3) "Then, he must have seen with an eye he does not have, since the left and the right are the only eyes he has."

Note 568

A person who has more than one eye . . . also has only one: That is, they treat "only" not as a way of having or possessing something but as a thing had, so that each thing had, regardless of how many there are, is an "only one." So, if a person saw with both eyes, he did see with the left only and also with the right only. See 179ᵃ21–22.

Note 569

Others resolve it as they also resolve, "What a person has, he received": I take this to be offering a second resolution of the initial argument, as follows: "Could a person strike a blow with a hand he does not have, or see with an eye he does not have?" "Yes, because what he has, he has received, and he has not received either his hands or his eyes." Here, then, *echein* is understood as meaning "having as a result of getting or receiving." But it can also simply mean "having without getting," so that this resolution is not a genuine one, as Aristotle goes on to point out (178ᵇ16–17).

Note 570

As was also said previously: 177ᵇ31–34.

Note 571

A resolution: Rejecting the addition of ἤ.

Note 572

Does someone tread on . . . : Also 179ᵃ24.

Note 573

Nor when: Reading οὐδ᾽ ὅταν.

Note 574

What [he knows] . . . : Also 179ᵃ23–24.

Note 575

It is impossible for the latter to have been set out: The verb *ektithenai* means "expose," "exhibit," or "set out." In Aristotle's logic *ekthesis* is a way of confirming the truth of a third figure syllogism (P belongs to all S, R belongs to all S, P belongs to some R) by exhibiting or setting out a particular S (call it, N). For N will be R and N will be P (*APr.* 28ª10–30). In our text, however, the term refers to the Platonic method, embodied in the "one over many" argument, of exhibiting or setting out a single Form for each many: "[*Socrates*] Do you want us to begin our investigation with the following point, then, in accord with our usual method? I mean, as you know, we usually posit some one particular Form in connection with each of the manys to which we apply the same name. Or don't you understand? [*Glaucon*] I do. [*S.*] Then, in the present case, too, let us take any of the manys you like. For example, there are surely many couches and tables. [*G.*] Of course. [*S.*] But the Forms connected to these manufactured items are surely just two, one of a couch and one of a table" (Plato, *Rep.* 596a–b). See *Met.* 1031^{b}18–22, 1086^{b}7–10, 1090^{a}16–20.

Note 576

The *Third Man*: "[*Parmenides*] I suppose you think that each Form is one on the basis of the following consideration: whenever some many seems to you to be large, there presumably seems to be one Form, the same one as you look at all of them, from which you conclude that the large is one. [*Socrates*] That's true. [*P.*] What about the large-itself and the other large things? If you look at all of them in the same way with the soul, won't some one large again appear by which all these appear large?" [*S.*] It seems so. [*P.*] So another Form of largeness will make its appearance, which has emerged beyond largeness-itself and the things that participate in it, and, in turn, another over all of these, by which all of them will be large. Each of your Forms will no longer be one, then, but unlimited in number" (Plato, *Prm.* 132a–b). It seems to be to this argument, or one of this sort, that Aristotle refers, with "man" substituted for "large," although he nowhere recognizes that Plato was himself the source of the argument. It is discussed in greater detail at *Met.* 1031^{b}28–1032^{a}4, and the problem with it succinctly characterized at 1038^{b}34–1039^{a}3: "it is evident that nothing that belongs universally to things is a substance, and that none of the things that are predicated in common signifies a this something but a such-and-such sort. If not, many other difficulties result, and especially the *Third Man*."

Note 577

The opposite name: Not the name of the opposite (a homonymous name does not have just one opposite), but the opposite sense of the one homonymous name. Hence *hôs* ("in what way") in the example.
Saying that something is animate: Reading ἔμψυχον.

Note 578

For example, one die only: 178^{b}8–10.

Note 579
Does someone scientifically know . . . : 178^{b}34–36.

Note 580
A person treads on . . . : 178^{b}31–33.

Note 581
"Is the dog your father?": "[*Dionysodorus*] Well now, the dog is yours? [*Ctesippus*] Yes. [*D*] He is a father and he is yours—so he turns out to be your father" (Plato, *Euthd.* 298e).

Note 582
Doing away with the question: Reading ἀναιροῦντες.

Note 583
As we have already said: What has already been said—at 177^{b}31–32—is that the resolution of such arguments must be the same, implying that a resolution and a rectification are pretty much the same thing.

Note 584
If this is true in certain cases . . . : The resolution or rectification of the argument, (1) "This dog is a father. This dog is yours. Therefore, this dog is your father" ought to be the same as that of (2) "Do you know the one who is approaching?" since they exploit the same thing. But the suggested resolution of (2), that one can know and not know the same thing, but not in the same respect, does not apply to (1). So it is not a genuine resolution of (2).

Note 585
Even if he were to try . . . : Reading ἐπιχειροίη συνάγειν ὡς ἀδύνατόν συνάγων εἰς ἀδύνατον, ἁμαρτάνει. The reference is to someone providing a putative resolution of an argument by producing a reductio ad absurdum argument against its conclusion, thereby proving the deduction false (next note). But even if he succeeds, he will not have brought to light what the false deduction is false through, and so will not have provided a resolution of it, and so will have made an error.

Note 586
[1] If, then, it has not been deduced, or [2] in addition he tries to infer a truth or a falsehood, [3] the making clear of that (*ekeinou*) **is a resolution:** Removing the obeli on ἢ καὶ ἀληθὲς ἢ ψεῦδος. For a deduction can be false in only two ways: if (a) it appears to be a deduction but is not one or (b) it deduces a falsehood (176^{b}31–33). The putative resolution of the knowledge argument about Coriscus accepts that the conclusion is true: it is possible to know and not to know the same thing (179^{b}7–8). This is what [2] refers to. Nonetheless, [1] the conclusion is not deduced. In [3] *ekeinou* refers to [1] and tells us again what a genuine resolution must do.

Note 587
For [1] one knows both that Coriscus is Coriscus and [2] that the thing approach-ing is approaching. But to know and not to know the same thing does seem to be possible—for example, [3] one can know the pale thing and not know the musical one; for in this way one does know and does not know the same thing, but not in the same respect. But [4] as for the thing approaching and Coriscus, he knows both that it is approaching and that it is Coriscus: Rejecting the addi-tion of ὄν in [4]. The principle underlying this initially opaque argument is this: "it is only to things that are indistinguishable with respect to their substance and one, it seems, that all the same things belong" (179ᵃ37–39). So in [1] all the same things belong to Coriscus and to Coriscus, since he is indistinguishable from himself in substance or essence. In [2] "the thing approaching" is not a classically understood definite description but is functioning in the context as an indexical: *that* thing approaching. So that whatever is true of *it* is true of whatever is indistinguishable from it with respect to its substance or essence. But it is—one and the same thing as—Coriscus, so everything true of it is true of Coriscus and vice versa. But it is true of the thing approaching that one knows it is approaching, so it is true of Coriscus that one knows that he is approaching. This is what underlies [4]. Contrast this with [3]. Pale and musical are coincidents, so the pale thing and the musical thing do not have essences, and so are not the same with respect to their substance or essence (see *Met.* 1029ᵇ25–27). So not everything true of one is true of the other.

Note 588
"Then B is your child" . . . : Reading ὅτι συμβέβηκεν εἶναι καὶ σὸν καὶ τέκνον. ἀλλ᾽ οὐ σὸν τέκνον.

Note 589
We say that man is of the animals: 176ᵇ1–5.
What is in a certain respect and unconditionally: 166ᵇ23.

Note 590
A slave is good of the wretched: As in, "the best of a bad lot."

Note 591
"Sing, goddess, the wrath": The opening words of the *Iliad*.

Note 592
If what is not is something, it also is unconditionally: (1) "In the case of what is not (*to mê on*), some people say in a logico-linguistic way that what is not is (not that it is unconditionally but that it is what is not)" (*Met.* 1030ᵃ25–26). (2) "In con-tentious arguments, by taking the unconditionally so and the not unconditionally so, but so in a certain respect, an apparent deduction results—for example, in the dialectical arguments that what is not is (for what is not *is* what is not) and that the unknowable is scientifically knowable (for it is scientifically knowable that it *is* unknowable)" (*Rh.* 1402ᵃ3–7). See also *Top.* 121ᵃ20–26, 121ᵇ1–3, *SE* 167ᵃ1–2.

Note 593
And a person who swears: Reading ὁ δ'.

Note 594
Nor does he who disobeys obey [unconditionally] . . . : "Is it possible for the same person at the same time to obey and disobey the same order?" "No." "But the order was to disobey the order."

Note 595
It is not easy to see whether: Reading ποτέρως.

Note 596
The same person: Reading τὸν αὐτὸν.

Note 597
Is . . . good: Reading ἀγαθόν.

Note 598
For taking a good thing is good: Reading τὸ γὰρ λαβεῖν ἀγαθὸν ἀγαθόν. The argument, since it must be similar to the previous one, is something like this: A thief is bad. Therefore, what he does (namely, taking) is bad. No, because what he wishes for, in taking, is something good, and taking a good thing is good.

Note 599
Have the controlling votes in the eyes of the law: *Top.* 106ᵇ31–33n68.

Note 600
To have what is one's own is just . . . : "Justice is the virtue due to which each has his own, and as law prescribes, while injustice is that due to which he has what is another's, and not as law prescribes" (*Rh.* 1366ᵇ9–11).
Just in this case: Reading τοδὶ.

Note 601
Prevails: Reading νικᾷ.

Note 602
As suggested previously: 167ᵃ21–27 mentions arguments depending on the definition of a refutation; 180ᵃ24–25 mentions looking at the conclusion in relation to its contradictory.

Note 603
While stating the truth: Reading λέγοντα. That is, that it begs the question. See 176ᵃ27–31.

Note 604
Used to produce a deduction against it: As in reductio ad absurdum.
The contrary way . . . : 176ᵃ23–27.

Note 605
A logical sequence (*akolouthêsis*) **of consequents:** *Int.* 19ᵇ19–22, *Top.* 115ᵇ15–26.

Note 606
The argument of Melissus: 167ᵇ13–20.
The heaven: *Cael.* 278ᵇ11–21. Here *ouranos* refers to the universe. Notice *to pan* at 167ᵇ16.

Note 607
The impossibility follows nonetheless: 167ᵇ21–36.

Note 608
Just as in the case of homonyms: *Top.* 148ᵇ4–9.

Note 609
Since these things . . . : Reading ἐπεὶ δ'.

Note 610
Also, . . . : Reading τε.

Note 611
"Both" and "all" signify several things: "But then even if this is best for a community, to be as far as possible one, this does not seem to have been proved by the argument that all at the same time say 'mine' and 'not mine' (for Socrates takes this as a sign that his city is completely one). For 'all' is ambiguous. If it means 'each individually,' perhaps what Socrates wants will more come about; for each will call the same person his 'son,' the same woman, of course, his 'wife,' the same things his 'property,' and so on, then, for each of the things that fall to him. As things stand, however, this is not how those who treat women and children as common will speak. Instead, though all [will say 'mine' and 'not mine'], they will not do so each individually, and similarly for property too—all, but not each individually. Therefore, it is evident that a sort of fallacy is involved in 'all say'; for 'all,' 'both,' 'odd,' and 'even' are ambiguous, and produce contentious deductions even in arguments. That is why in one way it would be noble if all said the same, although this is not possible, while in another way it is not at all productive of harmony" (*Pol.* 1261ᵇ16–32).

Note 612
As we saw: 167ᵃ23–25, 168ᵃ28–33, 177ᵃ30–32.

Note 613
Give rise to one question: Reading γινομένων.

Note 614
"Double" without . . . : Reading ἄνευ.

Note 615
"Ten" is in . . . : Reading τὰ.

Note 616
In the case of half: Reading τὸ ἐν τῷ ἡμίσει.

Note 617
As we saw: *Top.* 104ᵇ4–12, also 108ᵃ9.

Note 618
We said previously: 173ᵇ17–174ᵃ10. In what follows, genders and cases are indicated by suffixes with the usual abbreviations: m. (masculine), f. (feminine), n. (neuter), nom. (nominative), acc. (accusative), gen. (genitive).

Note 619
Masculine denomination: Reading κλῆσιν.

Note 620
It appears to follow: The reference is to the initial argument about a stone.

Note 621
Sometimes the same arguments: *Top.* 8.11, *SE* 175ᵃ20–30.

Note 622
"A man was carried down from a ladder (*kata klimakos*) **by a chariot:** A *klimax* (*klimakos* is the genitive) is, among other things, a ladder and a part of a chariot, and *kata* + genitive has several meanings. So perhaps the literal meaning was something like "A man was carried on the chariot steps." The actual double meaning of the sentence is obscure.

Note 623
Which of two cows will calve in front?: "In front" temporal vs. "in front" spatial.

Note 624
"Is Boreas pure?": Pure of guilt vs. pure in the sense of unadulterated or clean. Boreas, the North Wind, was thought to be a "clean" wind.

Note 625
"Is he *Euarchos*? Certainly not. He is *Apollônidês*.": *Euarchos* means "rules (*archein*) well (*eu*)," while *Apollônidês* seems to derive from *apollunai*, which means "to destroy utterly," "kill." Compare Plato, *Crat.* 404d–e: "The same thing

has happened to Apollo. Many people are afraid of his name because they think it indicates something terrifying."

Note 626
Others resolve: These include Aristotle himself: "things are said to be one and said to *be* in many ways" (*Met.* 1018ᵃ35–36).
Parmenides: DK 28 = TEGP pp. 203–244.

Note 627
Similarly too where the coincident and each of the others is concerned: Reading καὶ περὶ τὸ συμβεβηκὸς καὶ περὶ τῶν ἄλλων.

Note 628
Contentious arguments: Chapter 17.

Note 629
When the contradiction is converted: "To convert is to make a deduction either that the [first] extreme does not belong to the middle term, or that the middle term does not belong to the last extreme, by reversing the conclusion. For if the conclusion is converted and one premise remains, it is necessary for the remaining premise to be done away with" (*APr.* 59ᵇ1–5).
Will contain . . . deductions that are similar in character: Pacius, pp. 529–530, gives the following example. Start with (A): (1) All mothers love their children (very acceptable belief); (2) Medea was a mother (fact or very acceptable belief); therefore, (3) Medea loved her children (false). Then, taking the contradiction of (3), (3*) Medea did not love her children, construct two other deductions in which it is used in a changed position with each of (1) and (2) to subvert the other, as follows: (B) All mothers love their children; (3*) Medea did not love her children; therefore, Medea was not a mother. (C) (3*) Medea did not love her children; Medea was a mother; therefore, some mothers do not love their children. (A), (B), and (C) are similar in character, in that each subverts an acceptable belief by means of a conclusion based on acceptable beliefs. This produces a maximum of puzzlement because each of (1), (2), and (3) has had its contradiction shown to be also acceptable.

Note 630
But [only] whether: Reading ἀλλὰ πότερον.

Note 631
Premises: *Top.* 156ᵃ21n361.

Note 632
When one of the questions . . . : Reading περὶ οὗ ὁ λόγος καὶ δι' ὅ, καὶ μὴ προσλαβὼν τοῦτο.

Note 633
The questioner has not asked his questions correctly: Reading ἠρώτησεν.

Note 634
Also, . . . resolution: Reading τε, ἤ, and τὸ.

Note 635
A solecism comes about: Reading σολοικισμός.
Arguments and solecisms: Reading σολοικισμούς.

Note 636
What we deliberately chose to do: *Top.* 100ᵃ18–21.

Note 637
Since there is provided along with it . . . examining dialectically: Reading προκατασκευάζεται . . . ὥς οὐ μόνον πεῖραν δύναται.
As if having knowledge: The examinational craft targets the pretender to knowledge (171ᵇ5–6). To unmask him, to refute the sophist, we must understand his arguments from both the questioner's and the answerer's sides, as with dialectic itself.
Not only the function we just mentioned: I take the reference to be to the capacity, described at 183ᵃ37–38, "to argue deductively about the thing put before us on the basis of the things that are taken to be the most acceptable ones."

Note 638
The cause of this we have stated: Claiming not to know, and asking one's questions as one who wishes to learn, "leaves room for an attack" (172ᵇ21–24).
Socrates . . . used to acknowledge that he did not know: For example, Plato, *Euthphr.* 5a, *Hp. Mi.* 369d–e, *Rep.* 337e–338a.

Note 639
How many things . . . : The reference, as at 183ᵃ38, is to the categories of predicates, and the premises or propositions constructible from them, discussed in *Top.* 1.4–9. Notice: "If, then, we could grasp how many (*pros poson*) and what sorts of things (*poia*) arguments are related to, and on what they are based (*ek tinôn*), and how to become well equipped with these, we have an adequate grasp on what we proposed" (101ᵇ11–13).

Note 640
As we have already stated previously: 183ᵃ27–28.

Note 641
Tisias: A student of Corax, a 5th-cent teacher of rhetoric from Syracuse, and credited, along with him, with founding the craft.

Theodorus: Of Byzantium (c. 400 BC), a teacher of rhetoric and author of handbooks on the subject. He is mentioned by Plato at *Phdr.* 266e. Some of his views are discussed at *Rh.* 1400ᵇ15–16, 1412ᵃ26–29.

Thrasymachus: Sophist and rhetorician (fl. c. 400–430 BC) from Chalcedon in Asia Minor, who makes a memorable appearance in Book 1 of Plato's *Republic*. Aristotle refers to him on four other occasions: *Rh.* 1400ᵇ21, 1404ᵃ14, 1409ᵃ2, 11 1313ᵃ8.

Note 642
Such things: That is, shoes that reliably do not cause pain in the feet precisely because they are the products of the craft of shoemaking, whose producer *could* impart his science.

Note 643
About deductive argument we had absolutely nothing else earlier to speak of at all, but were for a long time laboring and inquiring by knack (*tribê*): Reading πρότερον ἄλλο λέγειν ἀλλ᾽ ἤ. The noun *tribê*, which appears only here in Aristotle, goes with "un-craftlike (*atechnos*)" at 184ᵃ1, as we see from Plato, *Phdr.* 260e, which refers to an "un-craftlike knack," and *Grg.* 463b, where a craft is contrasted with an "experience-based knack."

Note 644
It appears to us: Reading ἡμῖν.
Or rather for you: Reading ἡμῶν ἤ.

De Interpretatione

Note 645
Dialectical question: *Top.* 1.10–11.
Not even if it is true: Even if a question that lumps together several questions can be truly answered by a cumulative yes (or a cumulative no), it is still not a single answer.

Note 646
In the *Topics*: *SE* is here referred to as part of the *Topics*. See 169ᵃ7–18, 175ᵇ39–176ᵃ18, 181ᵃ36–ᵇ24.

Prior Analytics

Note 647
As was said in the *Topics*: 100ᵃ29–30.

Note 648
In our treatise concerning dialectic: The reference is probably to *Top.* 1.14.

Note 649
Bileless: Reading ἄχολον.

Note 650
It was proved previously: 68ª16–25.

POSTERIOR ANALYTICS

Note 651
This was proved . . . : *APr.* 57ª36–ᵇ17.

PHYSICS

Note 652
A matter for another science: In general a science does not prove or demonstrate its own starting-points, that is, the real definitions of the essences—or what-it-ises—of the beings in the kind with which it deals: "There are starting-points and elements and causes of the objects of mathematics, and in general every science that proceeds by thinking or that has some share in thinking is concerned with causes and starting-points, whether more exactly or more simply considered. All these sciences, however, mark off a certain being, a certain kind . . . [but do not] produce any account of the what-it-is. Instead, starting from the what-it-is—some making it clear by means of the perceptual capacities, some getting hold of it as a hypothesis—they in this way proceed to demonstrate the things that belong intrinsically to the kind with which they are concerned, either in a more necessary or in a weaker way. Which is why it is evident from such an induction that there is no demonstration of substance nor of the what-it-is, but some other way of making it clear" (*Met.* 1025ᵇ4–16). However, if a science S₂ is subordinate to a science S₁, as optics is to geometry, then S₁ can demonstrate the starting-points of S₂: "With regard to the same science, then, and with regard to the position of the middle term, these are the differences between a deduction of the that and one of the why. But when each of them is theoretically grasped by a different science, the why and the that differ in another way. These are the cases that are related to each other in such a way that one falls under the other—for example, as optics is related to geometry, mechanics to solid geometry, harmonics to arithmetic, and stargazing to astronomy. . . . For in these cases it is for the perceptual scientists to know the that, and for the mathematical ones to know the why; for the latter possess the demonstrations of the causes" (*APo.* 78ᵇ34–79ª4).

One [science] that is common to all: The science in question is probably dialectic, since it has a "route" to all scientific starting-points (*Top.* 101ᵃ34–ᵇ4). Also in favor of this is the phrase "against someone who does away with the starting-points of geometry" (*Ph.* 185ᵃ1–2), since scientific demonstrations are not directed against anyone, although demonstrations by refutation are (*Met.* 1006ᵃ11–18).

Note 653
Induction: Top. 105ᵃ11n54.

Note 654
Melissus and Parmenides . . . : Reading μὲν οὖ for OCT μὲν, οὖ ("although they [Melissus and Parmenides] do not speak about nature, they nonetheless happen to state natural-scientific puzzles"). The puzzles are not natural scientific ones because they involve the denial of a starting-point of any natural science, namely, that there are things that are by nature in movement.

DE CAELO

Note 655
A more logico-linguistic way: *Top.* 105ᵃ18n56.

Note 656
The unlimited, when uniform, cannot move in a circle: "'When uniform' is added not because the non-uniform and composite ones that revolve do not move around a center (for everything that moves in a circle moves around a center), but because the argument is now concerned with simple bodies. 'When uniform' is added in place of 'simple,' since he produces the demonstration in this case, because in the case of composite ones too natural movement comes about in accord with whichever of the simple bodies is the mastering one in it" (Simp. 239.3–8 = Hankinson, pp. 59–60).

Note 657
There would need to be another just as large (that is, unlimited) place . . . : "But it is impossible for there to be two unlimited places . . . if indeed the unlimited is everywhere" (Simp. 239.14–15 = Hankinson, p. 60).

DE ANIMA

Note 658
The coincidents connected to the substances: That is, the intrinsic coincidental affections entailed by the substances or essences of the relevant things.

Note 659

A sort of imagination: *Phantasia* often refers in particular to the imagination, though sometimes it refers to a perception-based content of some sort: "the sun appears to be a foot in diameter, though often something else contradicts the appearance (*phantasian*)" (*Insomn.* 460^{b}18–20). At *DA* 433^{a}10 imagination is characterized as a sort of understanding and at 432^{a}12–13, the objects of the two are related but distinguished.

Note 660

Like the straight: "For just as the universal propositions of mathematics are not about separate objects that exist beyond the magnitudes and the numbers, but with magnitudes and numbers, not however insofar as they are such as to have magnitudes or to be divisible, it is clearly possible that there should also be statements and demonstrations concerning perceptible magnitudes, not however insofar as they are perceptible but, rather, insofar as they are of such-and-such a sort. . . . So since it is true to say unconditionally not only that separable things exist but also that inseparable ones do (for example, that movable things exist), it is also true to say unconditionally that the objects of mathematics exist, and that they are such as they are said to be. . . . Many coincidents, though, belong intrinsically to things insofar as they are, each of them, of a certain sort—for example, insofar as the animal is female and also insofar as it is male, there are affections special to it (yet there is no male or female separate from the animals). So there are also such attributes of things only insofar as they are lengths or insofar as they are planes" (*Met.* 1077^{b}17–1078^{a}9).

It will touch a bronze sphere at a point . . . : The straight insofar as it is straight is the straight considered as an abstract mathematical object that is perfectly straight, like a geometrical straight line. If we consider the straight edge of a ruler in this abstract way, it will touch a bronze sphere, whose surface is being considered in an analogous way, at a point. But if we consider it as separated from the ruler, and so as simply an abstract object, it will obviously not touch the bronze sphere at all, since abstract objects cannot touch material ones. Similarly, if the soul were like the straight, we could establish many scientific truths about it, simply as such, considered in abstraction from the body. But it would not be able to affect any bodies, including the one whose soul it is, except insofar as it itself involved something bodily.

Note 661

Enmattered accounts: Aristotle is not always careful to distinguish linguistic items, such as accounts, definitions, or even phrases or sentences, from their ontological correlates. For example, he speaks of Socrates as not separating "the definitions" from perceptible objects, when it is the forms or essences that are the ontological correlates of the definitions to which he is referring (*Met.* 1078^{b}30–31). The present phrase may be a case in point, so that what is being said is that the affections of the soul are *forms* in matter, as 403^{b}2–3 suggests. Or, which might simply be another way of saying the same thing, they may be *ratios* in matter (*logos* can also mean "ratio") in the way that perceptual capacities are said to be (*DA* 426ª27–ᵇ7). It is just possible, however, that the problem lies rather with "enmattered (*enulos*)," which is not found elsewhere in Aristotle (indeed, some mss. read *en hulê(i)* in its place). For *Met.* 1033ª4–5 tells us that "the brazen circle does have the matter in its account (*en tô[i] logô[i] tên hulên*)," where the meaning clearly is that the brazen circle has a reference to the matter (the bronze) in its account. If *enulos* has a parallel significance, then *logos enulos* means simply "accounts that include a reference to matter."

Note 662

A dialectician . . . : The dialectician bases his definitions on acceptable beliefs, and so his definitions are like the nominal essence or meaning of the relevant word, since this is something that most users of it would accept. Thus rhetoric too, which also bases its arguments on *endoxa*, defines anger as "desire, involving pain, for apparent revenge, because of apparent contempt on the part of someone unfitted to treat the person himself, or one of those close to him, with contempt" (*Rh.* 1378ª30–32).

Note 663

The primary philosopher: "The primary science is concerned with things that are both separable and immovable" (*Met.* 1026ª10–21; also 1064ᵇ1–3).

GENERATION OF ANIMALS

Note 664

Arguments not from the proper starting-points . . . : "In each methodical inquiry, arguments stated in a philosophical way differ from those not stated in a philosophical way. That is why even politicians should not regard as wasted work the sort of theoretical knowledge that makes evident not only the that but also the why. For such is the philosophical way in each methodical inquiry. Yet much caution is needed here. For there are those who, because it seems to be characteristic of the philosopher never to speak at random but rather in accord with argument, often escape notice when they state arguments that are foreign to the thing at issue and empty (sometimes they do this through ignorance, sometimes through boastfulness). Under the influence of these sorts of arguments even people of experience and clever at doing things end up getting taken in by those who neither have nor are capable of architectonic or practical thought. And they suffer this fate due to lack of educatedness; for lack of educatedness regarding each thing is being incapable of judging arguments proper to that thing from those alien to it" (*EE* 1216ᵇ35–1217ª10).

Note 665

As was said previously: *GA* 746ª29–ᵇ11, 747ª31–33.

METAPHYSICS

Note 666
The fact that [Plato] made . . . : Throughout this paragraph the numbers referred to are the Form numbers (= Forms), which are composed of the one (as substance) and the large and the small (as matter). Here the one (as Form) generates the Form of a table (say), of which there can be only one (987b18), from the great and the small (as matter). Aristotle's objection is that if we look at actual cases of generation (of form being imposed on matter), such as in the manufacture of tables, we have a one-many relation between form and matter (the carpenter imposes the form of a table on different bits of wood to make many particular tables each with the same one form) and an efficient cause (the carpenter) that is different from the formal one. Yet these actual cases are supposed to be what they are by "imitating"—that is, "participating in" (Aristotle takes it that one name is as good or bad as the other)—the associated Form.

Note 667
Intrinsic coincidents: *Top.* 101^{b}18n20.

Note 668
Because they properly belong to philosophy: Since sophistry wishes to appear to be wisdom.

Note 669
Sophistic and dialectic: *SE* 171^{b}25–34.
The same kind as philosophy: "Rhetoric does not deal with a definite kind, but is like dialectic" (*Rh.* 1355^{b}8–9). So a kind here is not a first-order kind.
Examinational: Defined at *SE* 165^{b}4–6; discussed in *Top.* 8.5–11.

Note 670
Impossible to be deceived about: 1061b34–36.
Unhypothetical: As Aristotle understands it, "demonstration is not related to external argument, but to the one in the soul, since neither is deduction; for it is always possible to object to external argument, but not always to internal argument" (*Apo.* 76^{b}24–25; also *Met.* 1009^{a}16–22). There is no obstacle, therefore, to treating PNC as a hypothesis in an external argument. But there is an obstacle to so treating it in an internal one, since one cannot treat as a hypothesis in an internal argument what one cannot be deceived or fooled about. Anyone who denies PNC, then, must in fact believe it, even if in words he disavows doing so. A defense of PNC against him can at most get him to recognize his commitment. It cannot—except in cases of confusion—constitute his reason for believing it in the first place, since no reason is more basic than it.

Note 671
Logico-linguistic difficulties: *Top.* 105^{a}19n56.

Note 672
At the start we determined . . . : *Met.* 1028^{b}33–1029^{a}2.

Note 673
The being for you: *Top.* 125^{b}27n195.

Note 674
[1] The account in which the thing itself (*auto*) **is not present, but [2] it itself is said** (*legonti auto*), **this is the account of the essence for each thing:** A is an account of O. [1] tells us that O cannot then be present in A. Since very few objects are the sorts of things that could be present in an account in the first place, [1] is perhaps best understood as ruling out circular accounts. What cannot be in the account is the very thing the account is of, since its presence would make the account circular. In [2] it is less *legein* than *autos* that is doing the work. A is an account of O's essence when O itself—and not O plus something else—is said or expressed in it.

Note 675
There are composites . . . : *Met.* 1070^{b}16–21, 1089^{b}27–28.

Note 676
[1] By being added to another thing . . . [2] by another thing not being added to it: In the first case, a simple definiendum (pale) is defined by a complex definiens (pale + human); in the second an apparently simple but actually complex definiendum (cloak = pale + human) is defined by a simple definiens (pale). In [1] what is added to is the definiens; in [2] it is the definiendum. [1] is described as not telling us what pale intrinsically is "from an addition," because the definiens, which does the non-telling, contains an addition. [2] is described as not telling us what pale intrinsically is "by another thing not being added to it," because in this case nothing is added in the definiens. At 1030^{a}33, [2] is characterized in terms of subtraction, because in the definiens something is subtracted from the definiendum.

Note 677
The pale human . . . : (1) Cloak signifies pale human. (2) Cloak is defined as pale. (3) Therefore, pale human is defined as pale. (4) Therefore, the being for the pale human = the being for pale. (5) But (4) is false.

Note 678
If indeed the this belongs only to substances: A substance is a this something (*Top.* 144^{a}20n309). The "something" (*ti*), or generalizing component, belongs to things other than substances: pale is something, as is noon. But the "this" (*tode*), or particularizing component, belongs only to substances.

Note 679

Primary things: The primary things (*prôta*) in the wholly unconditional sense are the primary substances (*Met.* 1059^{a}33–34), and of these, the most primary is the one that is simple and an activity (1072^{a}31–32). Consequently, it has no matter (or no reference to matter) in its essence (1071^{b}19–21, 1074^{a}35–36). Unlike the essences of matter-form compounds, therefore, which have a structure like that of the compounds themselves (1037^{a}9–10), its essence is not a compound of this form in this matter, both taken universally (1030^{b}14–20). Equivalently, in its essence the activation or form is not predicated or said of anything else, in the way that it is predicated or said of the matter in matter-form compounds (1043^{a}5–6), and so in their similarly structured essences. That is why it is said or expressed "*not* by way of saying one thing of another" (1030^{a}10–11; see also 1051^{b}17–1052^{a}4). It is for this reason, too, that the primary things are what the most exact science—theoretical wisdom—is concerned with. For as the starting-points of unconditional demonstrations (1015^{b}8–9), they are the primary starting-points and causes (982^{b}1–4)—the "eternal and primary things" (*GC* 335^{a}29). So "if they were not, nothing would be" (*Met.* 1050^{b}19).

Note 680

By way of participation: Aristotle sometimes uses the verb *metechein* in a somewhat technical sense in which T_1 participates in T_2 just in case T_1 admits of the account of T_2 (*Top.* 121^{a}11–12). Here, however, *kata metochên* seems to be used in a looser sense, illustrated at 1037^{b}14–21, in which T_1 participates in T_2 just in case T_2 is truly predicable of T_1, and so may be an affection, even a coincidental affection, of it.

Note 681

What is not scientifically known is scientifically known: By subtracting "not." **With reference to one and the same thing:** *Top.* 110^{a}23n92.

Note 682

A definition of this sort . . . : There is a definition of the referent X of a name N that corresponds to an account A of X if and only if X is *one* in one of the ways in which a substance is one (explicit at 1037^{b}24–26). But what those ways are is something still to be worked out (1045^{a}14–15). A different though related point is that a sequence of words, such as the sentences constituting the *Iliad*, cannot themselves acquire the unity requisite in a definition simply by being conjoined by "and" (1030^{a}8–9): "An account is one in two ways: either by conjunction as the *Iliad* [might be], or by indicating one thing said not coincidentally of one thing" (*APo.* 93^{b}35–37; also *Met.* 1045^{a}12–14).

Note 683

Democritus latched onto this: "This" is "the form or the essence" (*Ph.* 194^{a}20–21) = the what-it-is and its universal definition.

The Pythagoreans . . . : DK 14 (Pythagoras), 44 (Philolaus) = TEGP pp. 486–515, 47 (Archytas of Tarentum). Aristotle seems to draw primarily on Philolaus, although his monograph *On the Pythagoreans* suggests that he also relied on other sources.

Note 684

Socrates was inquiring about the what-it-is: "Socrates the elder thought the knowledge of virtue to be [the] end, and used to inquire what justice is, and courage, and each of the parts of virtue. Indeed, he did this quite reasonably. For he thought all of the virtues to be sorts of scientific knowledge, so that both knowing justice and being just would occur at the same time; for at the same time as we have learned geometry and housebuilding, we are actually housebuilders and geometers. That is why he used to inquire about what virtue is, but not how it comes about or from what sources. And this is what happens in the case of the theoretical sciences; for nothing else is the end of astronomy, natural science, or geometry than knowing and having a theoretical grasp on the nature of the things that are the underlying subjects of those sciences—nonetheless, nothing prevents them from being coincidentally useful to us for many of the necessities of life" (*EE* 1216^{b}2–16).

Investigate contraries: Though the remark is clearly of broader application, the relevant contraries are presumably the virtues and vices.

Note 685

In the *Phaedo* . . . : (1) "Nothing makes something a beauty other than the presence—or community, or whatever the mode of means of accrual may be—of that beauty [namely, intrinsic beauty itself (100b)]" (Plato, *Phd.* 100d). (2) "You have no cause of coming to be two other than participating in twoness" (101c). It is probably these passages that Aristotle has in mind. It is unlikely, however, that they attribute *efficient* causal efficacy to Forms—something Aristotle acknowledges that Platonists do not do (*Met.* 988b1–4).

Note 686
More exact arguments: *Top.* 157^{a}11n368.

NICOMACHEAN ETHICS

Note 687
Argumentative encounters: Reading ἐντύχωσιν. See *Top.* 101^{a}26–34.

Rhetoric

Note 688
[1] Rhetoric is the counterpart of dialectic: *Rh.* 1356ᵃ30–31 [1] is glossed as follows: "[2] Rhetoric is a part of dialectic and similar to it, as we also said at the
start." A few lines previously the relationship is characterized in yet a third way:
[3] "Rhetoric is a sort of offshoot of dialectic and of work in ethics, which it is
right to call politics" (1356ᵃ25–26). The relationships in [1–3] are, on the face of
it, quite different, but this may be due to the fact that they have in mind different
aspects of dialectic. Thus [1] is followed by a description of the sorts of things that
rhetoric and dialectic are concerned with. Since [2] is presented as a restatement of
[1], it presumably has the same idea in mind, with the additional one that rhetoric
is concerned with only some of these. Not all dialectical topics are suitable for
rhetorical purposes. On the other hand, [3], with its reference to politics, suggests
that rhetoric draws on a sort of knowledge, provided by politics, that dialectic itself
does not draw on. See 1366ᵃ2–14. To a first approximation, rhetoric is the theory
and a speech the product. A *rhêtôr* is someone who knows the theory, knows how
to use it, and puts it to use. Insofar as he does so by writing speeches to be read,
or for others to deliver, he is a "rhetorician"—or, in the standard translation, an
"orator." But the one who actually delivers the speech, considered as such, is a
"speaker."
Definite science: That is, a first-order or special science dealing with a definite
kind. See 1355ᵇ8–9, 1355ᵇ33–34.

Note 689
Some do these things extemporaneously: As Socrates claimed to be doing at his
trial (Plato, *Ap.* 17c).
Others due to a state acquired by habit: Habituation (*ethismos*) is a process,
typically involving pleasure (reward) and pain (punishment), by which we
acquire a habit that is at once cognitive (as in the case of induction) and cona-
tive, because what we experience as pleasurable we tend to desire and pursue and
what we experience as painful we tend to be averse to and avoid (*DA* 431ᵃ8–ᵇ10,
NE 1114ᵃ31–ᵇ3, 1119ᵃ25–27, *Pol.* 1340ᵃ23–28). The forthcoming contrast between
rhetorical competence based on habit and one based on method and craft is cognate with the following distinction between experience-based knowledge and
craft: "We regard knowledge and comprehension as characteristic of craft rather
than of experience, and take it that craftsmen are wiser than experienced people,
on the supposition that in every case wisdom follows along rather with knowledge
than with experience. This is because craftsmen know the cause (*aitian*), whereas
experienced people do not. For experienced people know the that but do not know
the why, whereas craftsmen know the why, that is, the cause" (*Met.* 981ᵃ24–30).
Notice *aitian* at *Rh.* 1354ᵃ10.

Note 690
Craft: *Top.* 104ᵃ15n46.

Note 691
Logico-linguistic deductions: *Top.* 105ᵃ19n56.

Note 692
As we said in the *Topics*: 101ᵃ26–36.

Note 693
Its function is not to persuade . . . : 1355ᵇ25–31.

Note 694
Sophistic: *SE* 164ᵇ21–22.
Deliberate choice: *Top.* 126ᵃ35n202. The deliberate choice in question is to use dialectic (the capacity) in a dishonest way.

Note 695
In dialectic, a sophist is so called . . . : *SE* 165ᵇ3–8, 171ᵇ27–33.

Note 696
"Politics": *Politikê* is the practical science—notice *politikê[i] epistêmê[i]* at 1359ᵇ17—used in ruling a city (*NE* 1099ᵇ29–32, 1102ᵃ18–25, 1103ᵇ3–6, 1141ᵇ23–33, 1152ᵇ1–3, 1180ᵇ23–1181ᵇ23).

Note 697
Cuts the same figure: Compare: "Dialecticians and sophists in fact cut the same figure as the philosopher; for sophistic is only apparently wisdom" (*Met.* 1004ᵇ17–19).
Lack of educatedness: See Introduction, pp. xxxvii–xxxviii.

Note 698
We also said at the start: 1354ᵃ1.

Note 699
From the *Analytics*: "All teaching and all learning that involves thought proceed from already existing knowledge. This is evident if we look at all cases; for the mathematical sciences arise in this way and so do each of the other crafts as well. The same holds too where arguments are concerned, both those through deduction and those through induction; for it is through things previously known that they both do their teaching—the former getting hold of them as if from people who comprehend them, the latter proving the universal through the particular's being clear. Rhetorical arguments also persuade in the same ways; for they are either through paradigms, which is induction, or through enthymemes, which is precisely deduction" (*APo.* 71ᵃ1–11). See also *APr.* 2.23, *NE* 1139ᵇ26–28.

Note 700
From the *Topics*: 100ª25–30, 105ª10–19.

Note 701
What is particular . . . : (1) "It is impossible to have knowledge until we come to indivisibles . . . we cannot understand without making a stop" (*Met.* 994ᵇ21–24). (2) "How is it possible to get scientific knowledge of unlimited many things? For it is insofar as they are one and the same thing, and insofar as something universal belongs to them, that we know all things" (999ª26–29). This is because the starting-points of knowledge must have finite definitions (1043ᵇ34–36) and demonstrations (deductions) from them—like the chains of causes they describe—must be of finite length.

Note 702
The sorts of things we deliberate about . . . : *NE* 1112ª30–1113ª2.

Note 703
More perspicuous: *Top.* 102ᵇ37n31.

Note 704
Which are common: Reading κοινοί.
The topic of the more and less: Discussed in *Top.* 5.8.

Note 705
Any underlying subject: That is, any kind, for "the kind is the underlying subject of the differentiae" (*Met.* 1016ª26).

Note 706
The better someone is at selecting premises: *Top.* 141ᵇ15–28.
It will no longer be dialectic or rhetoric . . . : Compare 1359ᵇ12–18.
That science whose starting-points he possesses: He possesses these, but without realizing that they are scientific starting-points. That is why the fact that he is producing a science distinct from rhetoric and dialectic is unnoticed by him.

Note 707
As in the *Topics*: No such distinction is made in the extant *Topics*.

Note 708
By "forms" I mean . . . : This is perhaps best understood as drawing a distinction between two sorts of topics, specific ones (called *eidê*), which are special to a given kind, and common ones that apply in all kinds. Thus the topics referred to, for example, at 1376ª32, seem to be specific topics.

Note 709
We said previously: 1356ª25–27.
The [part of] politics: Reading πολιτικῆς.

Further Reading

Detailed and regularly updated bibliographies of works on Aristotle's logic and dialectic and on his philosophy generally are available online at:
https://plato.stanford.edu/entries/aristotle-logic/
http://plato.stanford.edu/entries/aristotle/

Thesaurus Linguae Graecae (http://www.tlg.uci.edu) has excellent searchable Greek texts and English translations of Aristotle's writings, with linked dictionaries and grammars.

The following are works I have found most useful.

Editions and Translations of the Topics *and* Sophistical Refutations

Fait, P. *Aristotele: Le confutazioni sofistiche* (Bari, 2007).
Forster, E. *Aristotle on Sophistical Refutations* (Cambridge, MA, 1955).
———. *Aristotle Topica* (Cambridge, MA, 1960).
Hasper, P. "Aristotle's *Sophistical Refutations*: A Translation," *Logical Analysis and History of Philosophy / Philosophiegeschichte und logische Analyse*, Vol. 15 (2013): pp. 13–54.
Pickard-Cambridge, W. *Topica and De Sophisticis Elenchis*, in D. Ross (ed.), *The Works of Aristotle*, Vol. I (Oxford, 1928).

Books and Collections of Papers

Allen, J. *Inference from Signs: Ancient Debates about the Nature of Evidence* (Oxford, 2001).
Bolton, R. *Science, dialectique et ethique chez Aristote* (Louvain-la-Neuve, 2010).
Fink, J., ed. *The Development of Dialectic from Plato to Aristotle* (Cambridge, 2012).
Owen, G. *Logic, Science, and Dialectic* (Ithaca, 1986).

———, ed., *Aristotle on Dialectic: Proceedings of the Third Symposium Aristotelicum* (Oxford, 1968).

Slomkowski, P. *Aristotle's* Topics (Leiden, 1997).

Wians, W., ed. *Aristotle and the Uses of Dialectic* (Leiden, 2024).

Relevant Works of Mine

Substantial Knowledge: Aristotle's Metaphysics (Indianapolis, 2000).

Aristotle: Rhetoric. Translation with Introduction and Notes (Indianapolis, 2018).

"The Role of Dialectic in an Aristotelian Science: *Politikê* in the *Nicomachean Ethics*." In W. Wians, ed., *Aristotle and the Uses of Dialectic* (Leiden, 2024).

Index

Note: In page reference to *Topics* and *Sophistical Refutations* the abbreviated titles and initial 1 are omitted—for example, *Top.* 101ᵃ = 01ᵃ. Line numbers are to the Greek text and are approximate in the translation. References are typically to key doctrines or discussions in the text and associated notes.

Index

Sophistical (*sophismatôdês*)
attacks that appear, 58ᵃ35
Sophistical (*sophistikos*)
saying about being and coming to be, 04ᵇ26
topic, 11ᵇ32
Sophistical argument(s) (*sophistikos logos*)
for the sake of apparent wisdom, 71ᵇ34
kind and form of, 65ᵃ31
Sophistical deductions, 69ᵃ19, 71ᵇ8
deceptive about the why, 71ᵇ10
Sophistical refutation(s), 64ᵃ20
depending on accentuation, 66ᵇ1, 69ᵃ27
depending on affirming the consequent, 67ᵇ1, 69ᵃ28, ᵇ6, 81ᵃ22
depending on ambiguity in a phrase, 66ᵃ6, 69ᵃ26
depending on assuming the thing initially proposed, 67ᵃ36, 68ᵇ22, 69ᵇ13, 81ᵃ15
depending on babbling, 81ᵇ25
depending on coincident, 66ᵇ28, 68ᵇ34, 69ᵇ3
depending on combination and division, 66ᵃ23
depending on combination of two questions into one, 67ᵇ38, 69ᵃ6, 81ᵃ36
depending on form of expression, 66ᵇ10, 69ᵃ29
depending on homonymy, 65ᵇ30, 69ᵃ22, 70ᵃ14; are most simpleminded, 82ᵇ14
depending on ignorance of what refutation is, 68ᵃ20
depending on mode of expression, 65ᵇ25, 69ᵃ36, ᵇ36; are mostly ridiculous, 82ᵇ16; ≠ those depending on a name, 70ᵇ38
depending on name vs. depending on thought, 70ᵇ13
depending on non-cause as cause, 67ᵇ21, 68ᵇ23, 69ᵇ13
depending on non-determination or definition of what a refutation is, 67ᵃ21, 69ᵃ21, 81ᵃ1
depending on omission of the account, 67ᵃ22, 68ᵇ19, 69ᵇ10

depending on questioner vs. depending on argument, 77ᵇ33
depending on side issue, 67ᵇ24, 81ᵃ31
depending on solecisms, 82ᵃ7
depending on uniformity of expression, 68ᵃ25, 70ᵃ15
depending on what is said in a respect and unconditionally, 66ᵇ37, 68ᵇ11, 69ᵇ10
non-deductive, 68ᵃ21
not unconditionally a refutation, but rather in relation to someone, 70ᵃ12
of craftsmen and scientists by non-scientists, 68ᵇ6
= fallacies, 64ᵃ21
= not only an apparent deduction and refutation that is not a real one, but also one that, though real, only appears to properly belong to the thing at issue, 69ᵇ20
Sophistry (*sophistikê*)
= a sort of appearance of wisdom without the reality, 71ᵇ34
Soul (*psuchê*)
= a number, 20ᵇ3
= number that moves itself, 40ᵇ2
= substance receptive of scientific knowledge?, 51ᵇ1
= what moves itself (Plato), 40ᵇ3
Special, special affection (*idion*)
and participation, 32ᵇ3
and the more and the less, 5.8, 38ᵃ5
belongs by nature vs. always, 34ᵃ5
cannot belong to several things, 38ᵃ20
counterpredicated of the thing at issue, 55ᵃ26
definition, 02ᵃ18, 28ᵇ16
establishing and disestablishing, 54ᵇ15, 55ᵃ23
for the most part assigned in combination, 54ᵇ16
in an extended sense, vs. in a strict sense vs. in a popular sense vs. in a temporal sense, 101ᵇ19–23